People's War

Far from being an anachronism, much less a kit-bag of techniques, people's war raises what has always been present in military history, irregular warfare, and fuses it symbiotically with what has likewise always been present politically, rebellion and the effort to seize power. The result is a strategic approach for waging revolutionary warfare, the effort "to make a revolution." Voluntarism is wedded to the exploitation of structural contradiction through the building of a new world to challenge the existing world, through formation of a counter-state within the state in order ultimately to destroy and supplant the latter. This is a process of far greater moment than implied by the label "guerrilla warfare" so often applied to what Mao and others were about. This volume deals with the continuing importance of Maoist and post-Maoist concepts of people's war. Drawing on a range of examples that include Peru, Colombia, Bolivia, the Caucasus, and Afghanistan, the collection shows that the study of people's war is not just an historical curiosity but vital to the understanding of contemporary insurgent and terrorist movements.

The chapters in this book were originally published as a special issue of *Small Wars & Insurgencies*.

Thomas A. Marks is Distinguished Professor and MG Edward Lansdale Chair of Irregular Warfighting Strategy, College of International Security Affairs (CISA) of the National Defense University (NDU) in Washington, DC, USA. He has authored hundreds of publications, to include the benchmark *Maoist Insurgency Since Vietnam*, and served as the Oppenheimer Chair of Warfighting Strategy at the Marine Corps University (Quantico), as well as longtime adjunct professor at AFSOS (Hurlburt Field) and the Sherman Kent School (Washington, DC). A former army and US government officer, he has worked as an independent contractor, including for Control Risks of London.

Paul B. Rich is editor of the journal *Small Wars & Insurgencies* and author/editor of over ten books including *The Routledge Handbook of Insurgency and Counterinsurgency*, *State Power and Black Politics in South Africa*, *Crisis in the Caucasus: Russia, Georgia and the West*, *The Counter Insurgent State*, and *Warlords in International Relations*. He holds a BA from the University of Sussex in International Relations and International History, an MA from the University of York in Politics, and a PhD from the University of Warwick. His research interests are in insurgency, counterinsurgency and hybrid warfare with particular reference to the Middle East and post-Soviet politics.

People's War
Variants and Responses

Edited by
**Thomas A. Marks and
Paul B. Rich**

LONDON AND NEW YORK

First published 2018
by Routledge
2 Park Square, Milton Park, Abingdon, Oxon, OX14 4RN, UK

and by Routledge
711 Third Avenue, New York, NY 10017, USA

Routledge is an imprint of the Taylor & Francis Group, an informa business

© 2018 Taylor & Francis

All rights reserved. No part of this book may be reprinted or reproduced or utilised in any form or by any electronic, mechanical, or other means, now known or hereafter invented, including photocopying and recording, or in any information storage or retrieval system, without permission in writing from the publishers.

Trademark notice: Product or corporate names may be trademarks or registered trademarks, and are used only for identification and explanation without intent to infringe.

British Library Cataloguing in Publication Data
A catalogue record for this book is available from the British Library

ISBN 13: 978-1-138-48484-9

Typeset in Myriad Pro
by RefineCatch Limited, Bungay, Suffolk

Publisher's Note
The publisher accepts responsibility for any inconsistencies that may have arisen during the conversion of this book from journal articles to book chapters, namely the possible inclusion of journal terminology.

Disclaimer
Every effort has been made to contact copyright holders for their permission to reprint material in this book. The publishers would be grateful to hear from any copyright holder who is not here acknowledged and will undertake to rectify any errors or omissions in future editions of this book.

Contents

Citation Information vii
Notes on Contributors ix

Introduction: Back to the future – people's war in the 21st century 1
Thomas A. Marks and Paul B. Rich

1. Revolutionary leadership as necessary element in people's war: Shining Path of Peru 18
David Scott Palmer

2. People's war antithesis: Che Guevara and the mythology of *Focismo* 43
Paul B. Rich

3. FARC, 1982–2002: criminal foundation for insurgent defeat 80
Thomas A. Marks

4. Was FARC militarily defeated? 116
Carlos Alberto Ospina Ovalle

5. Critical ingredient: US aid to counterinsurgency in Colombia 138
Carlos G. Berrios

6. A double-edged sword: the people's uprising in Ghazni, Afghanistan 168
Matthew P. Dearing

7. The North Caucasus: from mass mobilization to international terrorism 201
Elena Pokalova

8. Bolivia, a new model insurgency for the 21st century: from Mao back to Lenin 221
David E. Spencer and Hugo Acha Melgar

Index 253

Citation Information

The chapters in this book were originally published in *Small Wars & Insurgencies*, volume 28, issue 3 (June 2017). When citing this material, please use the original page numbering for each article, as follows:

Introduction
Back to the future – people's war in the 21st century
Thomas A. Marks and Paul B. Rich
Small Wars & Insurgencies, volume 28, issue 3 (June 2017), pp. 409–425

Chapter 1
Revolutionary leadership as necessary element in people's war: Shining Path of Peru
David Scott Palmer
Small Wars & Insurgencies, volume 28, issue 3 (June 2017), pp. 426–450

Chapter 2
People's war antithesis: Che Guevara and the mythology of Focismo
Paul B. Rich
Small Wars & Insurgencies, volume 28, issue 3 (June 2017), pp. 451–487

Chapter 3
FARC, 1982–2002: criminal foundation for insurgent defeat
Thomas A. Marks
Small Wars & Insurgencies, volume 28, issue 3 (June 2017), pp. 488–523

Chapter 4
Was FARC militarily defeated?
Carlos Alberto Ospina Ovalle
Small Wars & Insurgencies, volume 28, issue 3 (June 2017), pp. 524–545

Chapter 5
Critical ingredient: US aid to counterinsurgency in Colombia
Carlos G. Berrios
Small Wars & Insurgencies, volume 28, issue 3 (June 2017), pp. 546–575

CITATION INFORMATION

Chapter 6
A double-edged sword: the people's uprising in Ghazni, Afghanistan
Matthew P. Dearing
Small Wars & Insurgencies, volume 28, issue 3 (June 2017), pp. 576–608

Chapter 7
The North Caucasus: from mass mobilization to international terrorism
Elena Pokalova
Small Wars & Insurgencies, volume 28, issue 3 (June 2017), pp. 609–628

Chapter 8
Bolivia, a new model insurgency for the 21st century: from Mao back to Lenin
David E. Spencer and Hugo Acha Melgar
Small Wars & Insurgencies, volume 28, issue 3 (June 2017), pp. 629–660

For any permission-related enquiries please visit:
http://www.tandfonline.com/page/help/permissions

Notes on Contributors

Hugo Acha Melgar is a Defense and Security Consultant based in Miami, Florida, USA.

Carlos G. Berrios is currently Subject Matter Expert for Building Partner Capacity, Defense Security Cooperation Agency (DSCA), Washington, DC, USA. Formerly, he was Security Cooperation/Security Assistance Officer, US Military Group (MILGRP)–Colombia (June 2003–June 2005), Executive Officer, US Military Group (MILGRP)–Colombia (June 2005–June 2006), and former Chief, US Military Advisory and Assistance Group (USMAAG)–Peru (June 2011–June 2014).

Matthew P. Dearing is Assistant Professor and Director of the South and Central Asia Security Studies Program (SCAP), College of International Security Affairs (CISA) at the National Defense University (NDU), Washington, DC, USA.

Thomas A. Marks is Distinguished Professor and MG Edward Lansdale Chair of Irregular Warfighting Strategy, College of International Security Affairs (CISA) at the National Defense University (NDU), Washington, DC, USA.

Carlos Alberto Ospina Ovalle is Distinguished Professor of Practice, College of International Security Affairs (CISA) at the National Defense University (NDU), Washington, DC, USA. He is the former commander of both the Colombian Army and Colombia's joint command, commanded at every level in combat, and ended his career as one of the most highly decorated combat officers in the Colombian forces.

David Scott Palmer is Professor Emeritus of International Relations and Political Science at the Pardee School of Global Studies of Boston University, Boston, Massachusetts, USA. He was both the Founding Director of the Latin American Studies and former Head of Latin American Studies program at the university.

Elena Pokalova is Associate Professor, International Security Studies Department (ISS), College of International Security Affairs (CISA) at the National Defense University (NDU), Washington, DC, USA.

NOTES ON CONTRIBUTORS

Paul B. Rich is editor of the journal *Small Wars & Insurgencies*. He has taught at the universities of Bristol, Warwick, and Melbourne, and is the author of several studies on warlordism, guerrilla insurgencies, and terrorism. He has recently completed a book titled *Cinema and Unconventional Warfare in the Twentieth Century: Insurgency, Terrorism and Special Operations*.

David E. Spencer is Professor of Counterterrorism and Counterinsurgency, William J. Perry Center for Hemispheric Defense Studies at the National Defense University (NDU), Washington, DC, USA.

INTRODUCTION

Back to the future – people's war in the 21st century

Thomas A. Marks and Paul B. Rich

This issue of *Small Wars and Insurgencies* focuses on the continuing importance of Maoist and post-Maoist concepts of people's war. It has assembled a collection of papers that addresses various examples from around the world, with an emphasis on South America, where the premier illustration, that of Colombia's FARC, was Marxist-Leninist but not Maoist, yet embraced the form and strategy of people's war in a bid which at one point had the state in a critical situation. The collection comes in the wake of previous papers published in this journal on politically Maoist insurgent movements in South Asia, notably Mika Kerttuenen's study of Maoist insurgents in Nepal and Prem Mahadevan's survey of Maoist insurgencies in India and their links to organized crime (Kerttunen, "A Transformed Insurgency," 78–118; Mahadevan, "The Maoist Insurgency in India," 203–20). The papers confirm that people's war remains an important analytical framework in the study of small wars and insurgencies, for some even a 'model' through which to understand distinct types of insurgent movements and their strategies.

People's war as strategy for power

There is a key point on display in relation to the question of people's war. Far from being an anachronism, much less a kit-bag of techniques, people's war raises what has always been present in military history, guerrilla warfare, and fuses it symbiotically with what has likewise always been present politically, rebellion and the effort to seize power. The result is a strategic approach for waging revolutionary warfare, the effort 'to make a revolution'. Voluntarism is wedded to the exploitation of structural contradiction through the building of a new world to challenge the existing world, and through formation of a counter-state within the state in order ultimately to destroy and supplant the latter. This is a process of far greater moment than implied by the label 'guerrilla warfare' so often applied to what Mao and others were about. In fact, it misleads as much as it illuminates.

Building a counter-state involves the same sort of military means as existing states use in times of war. Guerrilla warfare may, at one point in time, play an important role in carving out the political space necessary for the emergence of the alternative polity, but it looms large only when necessary as a weapon of asymmetry. Mao was quite explicit that 'regularization' was necessary if a determined foe and his military were to be vanquished. Ultimately, then, the counter-state vs. state dynamic must be assessed in the same manner as is in any inter-state conflict. What is unique is that one of the contestants must create himself from scratch, but having become a contender, the new counter-state utilizes all means available to it in its strategic quest for victory.

Victory ensures the attainment of power necessary so that the targeted populace can be brought under a new political order. Such an objective frees the strategic approach from its original Marxist-Leninist roots and makes it available to any ideology. That Marxism was integral to the emergence of people's war stemmed from its bringing to rebellion and resistance (the traditional term applied to rebellion against a foreigner occupier) an awareness that absent structural reordering, agency would soon encounter a revitalized foe, albeit in a different time and place. That Marx's key structural determinant was economic was demonstrated as inadequate by Max Weber, who added to that system of social stratification the political and status – again, opening the way for greater not lesser utility of what ultimately was made a systematic approach for the seizure of power by Lenin.

Lenin, it hardly needs to be emphasized, emerged in his own time and place. Mao absorbed the Bolshevik success and very much more, to include the key works of military theorists in translation, notably Clausewitz. His emphasis upon the peasantry rather than the urban working class was a logical product of the challenge that confronts any state at war: the need through mobilization to gain manpower and resources. Mao's own trajectory, unfolding as it did even as Ho Chi Minh – once the COMINTERN representative to the pre-Mao Chinese Communist Party (CCP) – developed his own variant. For both, being Marxists first but also Leninists, mobilization was possible through exploitation of the contradictions of the old order which was to give way to the new order. Their insight was that changes in *local* correlations of forces would allow new worlds to emerge from the bottom, from which position these 'liberated' areas could gradually be joined to form a challenge sufficient to overthrowing *ancien régime*. With power newly gained went the opportunity to reformulate structure.

Violence was necessary for creation of local political domination, but it was only one tool among an array of possible weapons. Further, violence as with nonviolence could take different forms as appropriate to the situation. Though Mao stated the obvious – strategy for seizing power would proceed from the defensive to stalemate to offensive – the Vietnamese raised to the level of doctrine the reality that local circumstances dictated whether offense or defense dominated tactically and which form of action played the leading role. What the Chinese termed 'political warfare', the use of nonviolence to make violence more effective, if used properly, could make violence itself secondary. In this, the impact of Sun Tzu was evident in a manner that extended far beyond the penchant of Western analysts for displaying menus of hackneyed maxims. The same might be said for the parameters under which guerrilla war was to be executed as just one form of violence.

The objective of violence in people's war, therefore, was twofold: to carry out the normal functions of military warfighting, neutralization of the armed capacity of the enemy; but, more fundamentally, to carve out the space necessary for the political activities of (alternative) state-building achieved through mobilization and construction of capacity. The most efficacious methodology for mobilization was to minimize the local fights picked within the existing matrix of power by bringing all under a united front dedicated to facing common foes and issues. The all but unassailable issue in both the Chinese and Vietnamese cases was resistance against foreign occupation (respectively, the Japanese and the French, then the Americans). In identifying this foe, a certain 'near enemy, far enemy' mode of assessment was at work, because Marxist–Leninism demanded that analysis be conducted at tactical, operational, and strategic levels. Hence, regardless of the local opponent, a larger, more powerful foe invariably loomed, whether this was an actual nation-state (e.g. the US) or a reified societal form ('capitalism' or 'imperialism').

It is easy to see how such analysis could be transferred to the assessment of national space. 'Occupation', for Marxist–Leninists, rather than being but a matter of foreigners, was a matter of ideology. Thus 'capitalists' (by a variety of names due to the plethora of forms in which capital could manifest itself) existed in a state of occupation vis-à-vis their fellow citizens. Indeed, within such analysis, the oppressed were not citizens at all but subjects, who, as is well known from Marx's exhortation, had nothing to lose in revolting save their chains. To proceed, both in terms of framing an alternative to existing oppression through narrative construction and in terms of constructing the strategy for seizing the power that would allow societal reordering, was the most fundamental task of revolutionary leadership. Their knowledge placed them in the vanguard of the effort to mobilize liberated subjects by appealing to whatever local and individual concerns galvanized action. Made overly complicated today by the 'greed versus grievance' discussion, this is the very essence of political action, and Mao made the 'mass line' central to his approach. That is, it was the central task of leaders to discern the contradictions at work, which were primary and secondary, and to come up not only with course of action but message that inspired the masses to move from passive to active participation in the political project at hand.

This volume thus begins with treatment of a premier recent case of such a project at work, *Sendero Luminoso* or Shining Path, but with a focus upon the role of leadership – of agency – within structural unfolding. David Scott Palmer, long a premier *Senderologist*, examines how a tightly knit group of Peruvian intellectuals penetrated the local world to produce a national nightmare. The Shining Path project developed the violent facets of its strategy so aggressively that ultimately the Peruvian state was also able to mobilize in developing an effective response.

Considerable irony attends the fact that a similar end befell Che Guevara, whose *foco* theory was in most senses the very opposite of Shining Path's people's war. Not only did Che tout the mobilization power of guerrilla action, but he explicitly enjoined against terrorism, for the obvious reason that it would turn the masses against the political project. As Paul Rich demonstrates, the romance of the revolutionary terrorist swallowed this commonsense advice, leaving Che dead in an obscure corner of Bolivia in 1967. More than the man, the approach died with him, for it was in fact a false representation of what had unfolded in the Cuban Revolution, as much a product of revolutionary hubris – Che joined to the French philosopher and revolutionary tourist, Regis Debray – as a coherent strategy for seizing power.

Something very similar is discussed in the three contributions that delve into the people's war approach adopted by the Revolutionary Armed Forces of Colombia or FARC. Though an explicit embrace of the Vietnamese approach demanded that popular mobilization undergird all FARC did, Thomas A. Marks highlights that, coterminous with the promulgation of the *Strategic Plan* in 1982, went a formal embrace of criminality (especially via the drug trade) to generate the necessary means. This proved disastrous, as Carlos Ospina, former commander of the effort during the bulk of the first Uribe administration (2002–2006), discusses, because it destroyed the necessary legitimacy required for popular mobilization and galvanized decisive democratic mobilization by the state. Fittingly, state response unfolded in a plan termed *Democratic Security*. In an approach that turned insurgent reality on its head, it was the military, through its *Plan Patriota*, that served as the shield for democratic empowerment of the citizenry. In the process, US assistance was of considerable importance, as detailed by Carlos Berrios, in a chapter which for the first time places in the public record just what and in what amounts the US did to assist the Colombian military.

Such counterinsurgency success against a would-be mass mobilization movement caused many official actors for a time to look to Colombia for possible 'lessons learned' or 'best practices' that could be brought to the struggle in Afghanistan. This proved largely stillborn, because at heart the Afghan challenge was that which earlier had vexed the US in South Vietnam: how and where to apply external assistance in such manner as to strengthen state-building built upon fostering legitimacy. Matt Dearing looks at popular uprising in Ghanzi to examine the often very different threads that make up any popular impulse for empowerment and security. It can be argued from our vantage point that the Peruvian and Colombian cases mobilized the power of such local phenomena – both states, after all, however imperfect, were functioning democracies with federal institutions and market economies. By contrast, in Afghanistan state-building continues as an imperfect project parallel with Taliban counter-state-building. The tragic result is little of the foundation and institutional glue that proved essential for the Peruvian and Colombian successes.

Elena Pokalova, in dealing with the North Caucasus, takes such discussion to its logical end. If people's war is rooted in popular mobilization, democratic counter builds upon legitimacy to produce decisive effects within the polity. Empowerment serves as self-defence for democracy. In contrast, in the case of Russia, authoritarian assessment views insurgent challenge not as impetus for reform but as spark for repression. All armed action of any sort features at some level sealing off the battle-space. In certain cases of irregular war – notably Chechnya in the case at hand, but also, say, Tibet or Xinjiang in China – this is possible, hence reducing the contest to one of raw military power.

One need not agree with the framing and narrative that propel forward an insurgent political project to recognize that negative mass mobilization within a democracy demands reform in the political opportunity structure to the extent necessary to empower the counterinsurgency. The calculation is very different in authoritarian states, where challenge identifies not systemic imperfection but the challengers themselves as those demanding 'reform' in the sense of elimination. In the extreme, this takes genocidal forms. Even if mass mobilization intent remains, then, an insurgency invariably will be forced back into embrace of ever more limited options. Pokalova highlights how in her case, this steady deterioration of action based in the masses to terrorism conducted by actors divorced structurally from those they claimed to represent. There is again irony that the Peruvian and Colombian insurgent cases feature similar descent into structural isolation and thus arguably terrorism as logic rather than as method.

Globalization has thrown up possibilities on both sides of this equation. On the one hand, we have now grown weary of the 'ungoverned spaces' trope as an explanation for the emergence of certain violent actors. What is labelled ungoverned is normally but alternatively governed. The sheer level of resources that can be leveraged through the global mechanisms of linkage, as illustrated well by FARC's exploitation of the drug trade, regularly facilitate accumulation of means by counter-states that in an earlier era would not be viable. This allows them to challenge states, which themselves both benefit and lose from the same processes. Assuming, though, that a state plays its cards well, it has in the present global context access to power and assistance from abroad which can be decisive.

Dave Spencer and Hugo Acha Melgar conclude this volume by demonstrating the extent to which certain groups, aware of the need for mass mobilization but also the pitfalls of clinging dogmatically to the known parameters of people's wars as they have unfolded historically, have produced a new synthesis. In the Bolivian example it proved decisive, and the insurgents now rule. This is especially significant, since the challenge achieved salience through the very narcotics industry which, in the Colombian case, served as the foundation for FARC's defeat even as it allowed the accumulation of unparalleled resources for realization of the Marxist-Leninist revolutionary project. As demonstrated in the Bolivian case but also prominently in others in Latin America, such as Venezuela or El Salvador, subsuming Marxist analysis in a larger frame of populism serves to exploit the present global context to a far greater degree than clinging openly to the labels of the past. It is the inability of democracies to treat seriously continuing challenges to both their legitimacy and their existence that makes such an approach such a danger.

Maoist foundations

Modern analysts tend to emphasize the political context in which movements embracing people's war operate in the contemporary global order, in contrast to the previous tendency of some civilian strategists, stretching back to the 1960s, of focusing on the techniques and tactics of Maoist-type guerrillas largely divorced from wider politics.[1] Historically, Maoist-inspired movements committed to various forms of people's war have emerged in the remote regions of weak states where there are still distinct peasantries or landless rural populations. They have not always been linked in this way. War involving the mass mobilization of the 'people' broadly emerged in the aftermath of the French Revolution at the end of the eighteenth century, while as late as the Second World War, many people in Britain considered they were fighting a 'people's war for a people's peace'.[2] Only in the post-1945 period has 'people's war' been specifically linked to revolutionary forms of warfare in states such as China and Vietnam and become a form of war emulated by radically inclined insurgent and terrorist movements across the globe.

One of the chief figures associated with this form of war has been Mao Tse-tung (or Mao Zedong in *pinyin*). Though the leader of the communist revolution in China in 1949, Mao has, until recently at least, been relegated to the history books in modern China, even if his portrait continues to gaze across Tiananmen Square in Beijing. He was ignored at the 2008 Beijing Olympic Games, and his reputation remains tarnished by the disastrous legacy of the Great Leap Forward and the Cultural Revolution (with a collective death toll variously estimated at anything between 40–70 million people). Officially the Chinese regime has declared that he was 70 per cent right and 30 per cent wrong, but he has remained sufficiently controversial for Chinese film producers to steer clear of him, preferring other, safer historical figures, such Chou En-lai. Yet there is a growing resurgence of interest in Mao among many Chinese, confronted with catastrophic environmental pollution, endemic corruption, huge income disparities and declining job opportunities.[3] Even so, the modern Chinese government avoids any debate on Maoist ideas of people's war, given that there is, as mentioned above, a growing domestic insurgency among the Uighurs and other minority groups.

Elsewhere, people's war continues to inspire various insurgent and terrorist formations, living on from generation to generation and constantly reinventing itself as it does so (witness Spencer and Acha Melgar's analysis of Bolivia). Maoism as a political approach also remains extant, notably in South Asia. It is one of the major ideological constructs to survive from the Twentieth Century alongside fascism, Nazism, and Marxism-Leninism, though this has often been poorly recognized by scholars of political ideology. Maoism – as much about perceived equality as objective reality – is, for many, a romantic form of peasant revolutionary warfare, though it has emerged in situations of rapid social breakdown or transition, in which peasantries see their way of life being under threat or their control of land and livestock under attack by capitalist forms of agriculture.

It is important, first, to establish the general political context in which Maoism emerged following the communist revolution in China in 1949. As a doctrine, Maoism was poorly understood in the West until the 1960s, when work on peasant upheaval by scholars such James C. Scott and Eric Wolf facilitated a more sophisticated understanding of the Chinese peasant revolution, with a stress on its roots in earlier millenarian movements as well as a strong base in popular nationalism.[4] This view of Maoism and people's war was largely hidden in the West during the late 1930s and 1940s, due mainly to the domination of information flow by the drama of emerging nationalism and resistance to Japanese fascism. It could also be argued that the China lobby (of which missionaries were an important component) was salient, together with the U.S. the war-time alliance with the KMT against the Japanese and the refusal of Hollywood film producers to release a film about Mao and the Chinese communist guerrilla movement, an important reason, arguably, why the eventual revolution of 1949 came as such as shock, especially to the U.S Republican right, angered over what they claimed was the 'loss' of China. The one group of military intellectuals who did have a clear insight into Maoist-type guerrilla warfare were the French exponents of *guerre revolutionnaire*, especially military intellectuals such as David Galula and Roger Trinquier, who had fought the Viet Minh in Indochina and, in some cases, been taken prisoner. Outside France, the group was not taken especially seriously, particularly when they conflated the Indochina and North African cases, and they became dispersed after Algerian independence in 1962.[5]

In its early years, the Chinese regime under Mao only partly conformed to the 'Maoist' label that would eventually be attached to it. The revolutionary government already had considerable experience in running whole areas of the country before 1949 in north and east China, encompassing a population estimated at some 100 million people. It proved to be relatively pragmatic during the early 1950s and conformed broadly to a Soviet style top-down model of bureaucratic management, for all its dependence upon the mass line on the way to the seizure of power.[6] Likewise, its diplomacy proved to be quite conciliatory, supporting the partition of Vietnam at Geneva in 1954 and promoting the Maoist 'model' in only muted form in arenas such as the 1955 Bandung conference of non-aligned states. While proceeding domestically with a social revolution, it was willing for most of the 1950s to play second fiddle to the Soviet Union, confirming for many Cold War zealots in the West that they were confronted with a monolithic communist bloc.

Nevertheless, this was a very different model of revolutionary change when compared to that of the Soviets. Maoist people's war had been based on at least six key conditions: peasant support, protracted war, a national appeal, strong leadership, strong organization, and a breakdown of the opposing regime.[7] These conditions could lead to a variety of political outcomes, especially in terms of foreign relations. They could have implied an isolationist 'China first' strategy, on lines similar, very possibly, to those that emerged in North Korea, leading to a completely totalitarian state. Another possibility might have been to orient policy towards promoting revolution wherever possible abroad, as seemed to be the case for much of the 1960s under the influence of defence minister Lin Biao, Mao's early heir apparent until his contrived death in a plane crash in September 1971. Finally, the Maoist model might have led from an early stage to an opening up towards the West, as would eventually occur in the 1970s following the visit of Richard Nixon in 1971 and the subsequent emergence of Deng Xiaoping in a post-Maoist regime in Beijing after 1979.

The Maoist model and ideas of revolutionary protracted war thus emerged in a changing set of political circumstances in the early 1960s, following the disastrous Great Leap Forward and the humiliation of Nehru's India in the 1962 Border War. The Sino-Soviet split provided Mao's regime with a growing incentive to go onto the ideological offensive in a context of rapid decolonization by European empires in Asia and Africa, two continuing wars of 'national liberation' in Indochina and Algeria, as well as prospects that other states too would undergo revolutionary transformation, such as Indonesia before the 1965 military coup. Maoism at this time became increasingly identified as a distinctive 'model' of political and military mobilization capable of being applied throughout the Third World, especially where dispossessed or radicalized peasantries seemed ready to embark on a revolutionary overthrow of regimes that were the all too obvious creations of Western colonialism and its legacy efforts. Mao himself emerged from the relative obscurity of the collective leadership of the 1950s to become the dominating charismatic revolutionary persona exerting a considerable force in radical circles around the world, aided by the *Little Red Book*, published in 1964 under the auspices of Lin Biao. Mao's global revolutionary charisma never quite reached that of Che Guevara, which, as Rich suggests in this issue, best embodied the metaphor of pure revolution for many in the Western New Left in the 1960s. But the American pop artist Andy Warhol produced a huge range of prints of Mao during the 1970s, emphasizing the multiple ways that it is possible to interpret Mao's persona, even glamming him up in one large portrait with rouged lips and blue shaded eyes and his mole transformed into a beauty spot, like a French courtesan.[8]

Guevara's heresy was by no means the only one on the Maoist world of the 1960s and 1970s, an arena that has so far escaped much serious attention by students of International Relations. One far more serious heresy was that of the Khmer Rouge in Cambodia, who were also exponents of people's war even if their championing of an extreme variant of the Cultural Revolution led them eventually to engage in a war against the Cambodian people in the regime led by Pol Pot in the late 1970s before its eventual overthrow in 1979 by Vietnam. This is, perhaps, an extreme version of Maoism, though one that needs to be seen alongside Mao's own war in China a few years previously. It remains all the more noteworthy for the vigor with which contemporary Maoists, such as those in Nepal, deny that the 'autogenocide' ever even occurred, so damning are its implications for those who fervently embrace Maoist tenets.

Mao and Maoism are thus capable of multiple interpretations in postmodern global cyberspace, though it remains difficult, perhaps, for a younger generation fully to grasp the degree to which Mao attracted some figures on the Western radical left in the 1960s. Richard M. Pfeffer, for instance, in 1971, welcomed Mao's attack on the Chinese Communist Party in the Cultural Revolution, seeing it as nothing less than the 'radical in power, perhaps the first radical in history who substantially retained his radical purity after being in power for over a generation'.[9] Unlike Guevara, Mao was a figure who was in command of a state ruling over a huge Asian population. It appeared as if, briefly, the Cultural Revolution might breathe life into Marxism-Leninism and give it a populist turn on Rousseau-like lines, driving forward a new purified model of revolution that could be applied throughout the post-colonial world. In the event, it proved but another bloody diversion from the realities of governance.

This was to detach 'revolution' from people's war, which had been the way that Mao had come to power in the first place. It supplied a narrative that overlooked the realities of power, which is another way of looking at Mao Tse-tung's career. The 2005 biography of Mao by Jung Chang and Jon Holliday stirred debate among China specialists by suggesting a far more Machiavellian and power-obsessed interpretation of Mao, whom they saw as a figure centrally concerned with the accumulation of power and willing to make massive tactical retreats in pursuit of this objective, though some suggest the biography remains compromised by its extensive use of unobtainable sources. Chang and Halliday posit, nevertheless, that Mao was effectively allowed to retreat in 1935 by the Kuomintang at a time when his son was being held captive by Stalin in Moscow and he had a mere 10,000 men.[10] This implies that a Mao myth was being constructed even before the outbreak of the Second World War by sympathetic outside observers such as Edgar Snow in his influential book *Red Star Over China* (1937), at a time when Mao was little more than a relatively minor regional warlord. Porch is probably correct when he observes, 'Mao may only have become a footnote in history had not Japanese intervention into China prevented Chiang from finishing off the Chinese communist movement when it was weakened after the Long March in 1935'.[11]

Mao's eventual success was due to the victories of the Chinese People's Liberation Army (PLA) in the latter stages of the civil war in the late 1940s. The theory of protracted war was premised on the virtues of guerrilla war in the early stages of conflict, but the inevitable need for escalation to the conventional level if power was to be seized.[12] The three-stage theory of protracted war was one that most guerrillas would recognize, though the actual pace and escalation could obviously vary, based on the wider political and military context in which the war was being fought. The theory was both a rationalization of present weakness and the application of a Marxist teleological outlook promising inevitable military victory. It was a strategic framework of a kind but failed to identify exactly how military victory could be achieved or the precise circumstances in which the conflict needed to be escalated from the guerrilla to the conventional level.

Mao is usually seen as dominating discussion about people's war in the post-war period, even though the Chinese military was undergoing a transformation in the 1950s and 1960s into a more conventional military formation. One of the major factors behind this was the war of the Viet Minh in Indochina against French rule in the years before Dienbienphu in 1954. This first phase of the war is inextricably linked to the Vietnamese general Vo Nguyen Giap, (who died in 2013), whom Lawrence Freedman has described as Mao's 'most assiduous follower'.[13] Giap certainly borrowed some of Mao's concepts of people's war, in the sense of mobilizing where possible the huge labor power of a peasant population to overcome shortcomings in weaponry. But he did not start publishing his own approaches until the late 1940s, alongside those of his fellow military strategist Truong Chinh. O'Dowd has observed quite correctly (and as noted above) that Vietnamese military doctrine started to emerge much earlier under the major influence being Ho Chi Minh. In fact, as early as 1938, Ho visited Yenan before later making Hengyang his base. It was here that Ye Jiangying (Wade Giles, Yeh Chien-ying), later Chief of Staff of the 8th Route Army, formed a guerrilla warfare school, mainly to train troops of the Kuomintang. Ho joined the faculty of the school for several months, and it is fair to assume this experience was crucial in his own text on guerrilla warfare, which has been published in this journal.[14]

That essay itself displays considerable familiarity with Chinese guerrilla tactics and could very broadly be considered 'Maoist' in orientation. That it is concerned principally with tactics rather than strategy, though, suggests that guerrilla units which remain constantly on the defensive will very likely end in failure.[15] Generally-speaking, there was little in Ho's text that would not have been understood by any mobile military formation engaged in sudden hit and run attacks, whether these be Caesar's legions or the wartime SAS and U.S Army Rangers. The text compares well with *The Art of Guerrilla Warfare* by Major Colin Gubbins of the British wartime SOE, though Gubbins at least stressed the need to distinguish between 'friendly', 'hostile', and 'neutral' populations.[16] Ho stresses the importance of good intelligence, coherent planning, and appraisal of the 'enemy situation'. He has little to say about 'people's war' as such, beyond a few brief remarks on the need for 'close ties' between guerrillas and people, 'because the guerrillas fight the French and Japanese troops to protect the people'.[17]

In the late 1940s and early 1950s, Giap applied to fighting the French in Vietnam his own variant of the Maoist three-phased approach. He saw the war starting, first, with the retreat, retraining, and reformation of the Viet Minh; followed, second, by an offensive against the French posts in Tonkin (with Chinese assistance); and then, finally, the destruction of the French army.[18] The strategy was broadly Clausewitzean, in the sense that the Viet Minh was fighting, first and foremost, an anti-colonial war aimed at defeating the French military, rather than Mao's more complex dual struggle against the Japanese and the Kuomintang in China. The Viet Minh lacked the huge terrain of China to retreat into, while there was also a pressing sense that time was not necessarily on their side in the 1950s, with fears that undue delay might prompt the US into direct intervention in support of the French.

Giap proved willing, at points, to discard Maoist principles in favor of a 'blitzkrieg' strategy aimed at forcing the French into fighting a longer war than they would have otherwise have wished and one that they lacked the political and psychological means to fight over an indefinite stretch of time.[19] Given his Napoleonic aversion to protracted war and eagerness for escalating conflict where possible to conventional levels, it is hard to see Giap providing much of a guide to Maoist people's war. As Douglas Pike warned in the 1960s, it is important for military analysts to avoid a 'Mao Giap' cult developing that clouds serious analysis of actual military and strategic achievements.[20] Giap was an impatient strategist, prone to taking risks by escalating the conflict to near conventional levels. He placed a rather greater emphasis than Mao on the psychology of the enemy he was confronting, the French in the first instance followed later by the Americans. He appears to have recognized that domestic opinion in both these counties would eventually ensure that the war could not be prolonged indefinitely, a strategy that eventually bore fruition with the Tet Offensive in 1968 and the decision to embark on 'Vietnamization' by the incoming Nixon administration.

Conversely, another figure incorrectly associated with people's war, Che Guevara, had few such psychological insights, though he lives on in popular memory and has re-emerged as a revolutionary icon fifty years after his ignominious death in Bolivia (again, see Rich in this volume). Unlike Mao, Che remains a figure who embodies the idea of pure revolutionary commitment, though this is disconnected from his military strategy of the guerrilla *foco*, which became increasingly promoted in the mid-1960s as an alternative to the dilatoriness of Soviet-dominated communist parties and the demographic demands of the Chinese and Vietnamese people's war models, based on huge pools of peasant labor simply unavailable in most parts of Central and South America. Guevara, too, was a quixotic adventurer, seeing the *foco* as a kind of quick do-it-yourself version of Maoist people's war. Guevara abandoned protracted warfare in favor of a select group of *focoist* armed missionaries, who would galvanize the peasantries of South America into revolutionary struggle in a manner different from their suspicious Asian counterparts. In the event, Guevara failed to use proper intelligence to check beforehand the situation at the local level, an omission made all the worse by his group being unable to speak the local language or understand the transformative impact of the Bolivian government's policy of land reform.

It is thus Mao Tse-tung who is inextricably at the centre of the study of people's war, along with post-Maoist types of insurgency and terrorism. People's war has emerged from Twentieth Century history as a mix of political propaganda, guerrilla tactics that can be taught at staff colleges, and a strategic 'model' debated and categorized by academic analysts since the 1960s. Taking propaganda first, Maoist agitprop is now a rarity in the West, though only a few months ago, a Labour Shadow Chancellor (to widespread laughter) quoted from Mao's *Little Red Book* in the House of Commons.[21] Some long-standing Maoists can still be found among far left political groupings in the West, invariably engaged, any search of the internet will reveal, in elaborate doctrinal debate not with rival Trotskyites and Stalinists but with other, ever proliferating, Maoist splinters. The antique quality to this sort of Maoism should not distract from serious engagement with the ideology in various part of the developing world such as South Asia, especially in Nepal and parts of India where the Naxalite insurgency continues to seek the support especially of marginalized tribal peoples in peripheral but often mineral-rich areas, as well as some other states such as the Philippines.

People's war as a strategic approach, with its integral popular recruitment and mobilization, is still worth looking at in detail, both at staff colleges and in courses on counter-terrorism. The tendency to dwell on the tactical minutiae misses the profound insights into the construction of the counter-state which are the heart of the approach and its literature. The Vietnamese made this systematic in a way which produces nothing short of astonishment at the fact that their contributions remain completely ignored in Western warfighting (much less political) circles. The approach, though at heart a populist variant of Marxist-Leninism, moved far beyond the Bolshevik strategy of the urban putsch led by select groups of revolutionary soldiers and militant party followers. That the Maoist narrative was driven by Chinese internal politics to the point of hagiography, focused on the heroic myth of the 'Long March' to Yenan, should not obscure the power of what is contained in Mao's various works. Therein, he spelled out not only the specifics with which Western observers are so besotted but a sophisticated political approach to the building of counter-state challenge and the projection of its power so as to vanquish the state.

This is not to confuse mobilization with democratic empowerment. Mao's mass line was a feedback mechanism for exploitation of popular desire for justice and self-defence. Even some sympathetic Western observers, such as the Marxist historian V.G. Kiernan, recognized that there was a 'gigantic feat of sleight of hand' in Mao's project, in the sense that mobilizing the peasant masses was intended as the first stage in a guided transition towards a very different type of society.[22] Maoism was also a distinctive model of social revolution, aimed at other Third World societies, especially those that had experienced the full ravages of Western imperial rule or capitalist exploitation. In the 1950s and 1960s, this revolutionary guerrilla model was one that the Chinese regime was keen to try and export to revolutionary insurgencies across abroad as a way of offsetting the influence of the rival Soviet Union as well as the *focismo* of Che Guevara and Regis Debray in Central and South America.

A shift to post-Maoism?

Thus, we return to our final chapter. In the last few years, several analysts have begun to identify a phase of post-Maoism that includes some of the new jihadist insurgent formations in regions such as the Middle East, Afghanistan, and South Asia. This journal, in a recent contribution by Marks, has spoken directly to the matter.[23] It is possible that we have reached a historical turning point in the Maoist impact on global politics, identifiable as four main phases over the previous 75-odd years from the mid-1930s, when Mao emerged as the undisputed head of the Chinese Communist Party (CCP) in the aftermath of the Jiangxi debacle (Chiang Kai-shek's Fifth Encirclement Campaign), to the peace agreement signed in November 2006 between Kathmandu and its arguably victorious Maoist challengers. The first phase pivoted around the Chinese Revolution of 1949 and ran from the mid-1930s to the mid-1950s. It included Vietnam and the first period of war against the French that ended in 1954 after the defeat at Dienbienphu. The second phase pivoted around the Guevarist heresy rather than pure Maoism and ran from 1959, the start of the Cuban Revolution, to the late 1970s, when it expired with the victory of the Sandinistas in Nicaragua, a movement that had started with a focoist strategy but gravitated to a broadly based strategy of popular insurrection. The third phase started in 1980 pivoted around *Sendero Luminoso* in Peru. The movement was as much a terrorist as a Maoist one, though it emerged from a long tradition of rural discontent and marginalization in the Andes. Its defeat by the early 1990s, following the 1992 capture of its leader Guzman,[24] led to a fourth phase that has pivoted around exploitation of political negotiation and democratic politics rather than the violence line of effort of protracted people's war. As noted above, it is exemplified by the processes of political accommodation in Nepal and Colombia, but perhaps nowhere more so than the Bolivian case treated here.

The four phases suggest a trend within global Maoism away from protracted guerrilla war towards a more complex mix of strategies including selective guerrilla attacks, urban terrorism, protracted negotiations, as well as alliances with other powerful actors, such as drug lords. This is not particularly surprising when the peasant base of Maoist movements is taken into consideration. There are few classic peasantries left in the modern global system as were present in China and Vietnam. Decades ago, Farideh Farhi had already recognized the analogous role played in Iran of the previously rural masses that had taken up residence in urban space.[25] Most countries today have rural communities that have become increasingly linked to the towns and urban areas by modern transport and communications. Isolated rural peasant communities have largely become things of the past while modern methods of counterinsurgency, including satellite surveillance and drones, have led some analysts such as Joes to conclude that Maoist-type insurgencies and the creation of secure base areas are increasingly problematical.[26] As David Kilcullen, among others, has argued, insurgencies in the future are increasingly likely to take an urban form, picking up arguments that were initially developed in the Latin American context in the 1960s by revolutionary theorists such as Carlos Marighella. This urban guerrilla warfare, though, is likely to take an increasingly transnational form, with coastal cities (such as Mumbai in India) vulnerable to coastal attack.[27]

Post-Maoism, by contrast, stretches the Maoist categorization into the arena of contemporary jihadist global insurgency and terrorism. Mackinlay has suggested that the 'globalised insurgent' and the 'post-Maoist' are the same type, though post-Maoist insurgencies are ones that overlap with the previous Maoist era, even if those fighting in them are no longer local or regional peasantries but insurgents drawn from the 'global community'. These post-Maoist insurgents seem, to Mackinlay, to be engaged in a new type of protracted war even if its long-term objectives are 'unrealistic or intangible', while the insurgents fighting them span a range of global cultures and nationalities. Most importantly, the new post-Maoist global insurgency has no clear military centre of gravity making its defeat difficult and problematic.[28] In any case, Mackinlay suggests, the campaigns being fought by post-Maoist insurgents are as much in cyberspace as on the battle field, though they might well have the capacity to federate or form alliances with more conventional Maoist-type movements, locally or nationally.[29]

This reformulation of Maoist warfare for the modern age is certainly innovative and suggests that people's war is increasingly likely to be global in orientation, with battle sites in cyberspace as much as the local level. For many analysts, the theory is not fully supported by the evidence. 'The people' at the global level remains a nebulous concept and may in practice consist of an interlinking network of groups with varying forms of ideological commitment to global jihad. Equally, the relationship between global insurgents and local movements is also somewhat fractious, though much might be derived from looking at how some of these evolve over the years ahead. Mackinlay's designation of 'Maoist' is also broader than the category adopted in this collection, which is anchored on movements constructed around Maoist ideological and organizational precepts. Other insurgencies, though, of a non-Maoist type, might still ally themselves with the post-Maoist global jihad even if their various understandings of the end-state may well ultimately conflict. It will be hard for any would-be global insurgency to impose (so far at least) a global 'mass line' on its followers, though we should not presume that this will be impossible at some time in the future.

More likely, though, are the sort of post-Maoist movements illustrated by the Nepali and Bolivian cases, both of which have been mentioned several times over here, with the latter included in this volume. These are viable and dangerous precisely because they are grounded in objective consideration of the past and explicit consideration for leveraging the changed context of the twenty-first century. Their decision to emphasize what certainly were 'supporting forms' at one point in the Maoist trajectory has generally left states counter them either clueless or simply befuddled. Nepal survived in its democratic form due to a serendipitous combination of circumstances; Bolivia did not. Therein lies continuity with the past and a warning for the future.

Notes

1. Freedman, *Strategy*, 191.
2. Calder, *The Peoples War*, 1992.
3. Anderlini, "The Return of Mao."
4. Johnson, *Peasant Nationalism and Communist Power*; Wolf, *Peasant Wars of the Twentieth Century*, 103–55.
5. Some retired, others embarked on a second career as mercenaries in Africa; and a few others served as advisors to military regimes in South America, eager to develop their own draconian forms of counter-insurgency. Paret, *French Revolutionary Warfare from Indochina to Algeria*, remains an indispensable guide. For the influence of French advisors on South American military regimes see Robin, *Escadrons de la Mort*.
6. Teiwes, "The Chinese State during the Maoist Era," 107.
7. Girling, *People's War*, 50.
8. Gewirtz, "How Andy Warhol Explains China's Attitude Toward Chairman Mao."
9. Pfeffer, "Mao Tse-tung and Revolution," 281.
10. Chang and Halliday, *Mao*; see also Beckett, *Modern Insurgencies and Counter-Insurgencies*, 77.
11. Porch, *Wars of Empire*, 201; a point which likewise suffuses the argument of Thomas A. Marks in his *Making Counterrevolution: Wang Shheng and the Kuomintang*. London: Frank Cass, 1998.
12. For details see the early chapters of Marks, *Maoist People's War in Post-Vietnam Asia*.
13. Freedman op. cit., 186.

14. O'Dowd, "Ho Chi Minh and the Origins of the Vietnamese Doctrine of Guerrilla Tactics," 564 (in 561–87).
15. Ibid., 569.
16. Gubbins, *The Art of Guerrilla Warfare*, 32–4.
17. O'Dowd, 567.
18. Colvin, *Volcano Under Snow*, 86.
19. Ibid.
20. Pike, *Viet Cong*, 50.
21. Mason, "John McDonnell Under Fire for Quoting Mao Tse-tung in Commons"; for discussion of the book itself, see Cook, *Mao's Little Red Book*.
22. Kiernan, *Marxism and Imperialism*, 160.
23. See Marks, "Terrorism as Method in Nepali Maoist Insurgency, 1996–2016," 81–118.
24. Mandatory for appreciation of this entire period is the film, *The Dancer Upstairs* (20th Century Fox, 2003), directed by John Malkovich and based upon the novel of the same name by Nicholas Shakespeare (1995). Whatever its allowances to artistic licence to provide a compelling plot, the film is masterful in creating the atmosphere of sheer disorientation and helplessness that was engendered by Shining Path terrorism.
25. Fahri, *States and Urban-based Revolutions*.
26. Joes, *Urban Guerrilla Warfare*, 5.
27. Kilcullen, *Out of the Mountains*.
28. Mackinlay, *The Insurgent Archipelago*, 160–1.
29. Ibid., 162.

Disclosure statement

The views and opinions expressed by author Marks in this article are his own and do not necessarily reflect the official policy or position of any agency of the U.S. government.

Bibliography

Anderlini, Jamil. "The Return of Mao: A New Threat to China's Politics." *Financial Times*, September 29, 2016.
Calder, Angus. *The Peoples War: Britain, 1939–1945*. London: Pimlico, 1992.
Jung, Chang, and Jon Halliday. *Mao: The Unknown Story*. New York: Knopf, 2005; see also Ian Beckett, *Modern Insurgencies and Counter-insurgencies*. London: Routledge, 2001.
Colvin, John. *Volcano Under Snow: Vo Nguyen Giap*. London: Quartet Books, 1996.
Fahri, Faridesh. *States and Urban-based Revolutions: Iran and Nicaragua*. Champaign: University of Illinois Press, 1990.
Cook, Alexander C., ed. *Mao's Little Red Book: A Global History*. New York: Cambridge University Press, 2014.
Freedman, Lawrence. *Strategy: A History*. Oxford: Oxford University Press, 2013.
Gewirtz, Julian. "How Andy Warhol Explains China's Attitude Toward Chairman Mao." *The Atlantic*, December 23, 2013.
Girling, J.L.S. *People's War: The Conditions and the Consequences in China and in South-East Asia*. London: Allen and Unwin, 1969.
Gubbins, M.G. Colin. *The Art of Guerrilla Warfare*. n.p., n.d.
Joes, Anthony James. *Urban Guerrilla Warfare*. Lexington: University of Kentucky Press, 2007.

Johnson, Chalmers. *Peasant Nationalism and Communist Power*. Stanford, CA: Stanford University Press, 1962.

Kerttunen, Mika. "A Transformed Insurgency: The Strategy of the Communist Party of Nepal (Maoist) in the Light of Communist Insurgency Theories and a Modified Beaufrean Exterior/interior Framework." *Small Wars and Insurgencies* 22, no. 1 (March 2011): 78–118.

Kiernan, V.G. *Marxism and Imperialism*. London: Edward Arnold, 1974.

Kilcullen, David. *Out of the Mountains: The Coming Age of the Urban Guerrilla*. London: Hurst, 2015.

Mackinlay, John. *The Insurgent Archipelago*. London: Hurst, 2009.

Mahadevan, Prem. "The Maoist Insurgency in India: Between Crime and Revolution." *Small Wars and Insurgencies* 23, no. 2 (May 2012): 203–220.

Marks, Thomas A. *Counterrevolution in China: Wang Sheng and the Kuomintang*. London: Frank Cass, 1998.

Marks, Thomas A. *Maoist People's War in Post-Vietnam Asia*. Bangkok: White Lotus, 2007.

Marks, Thomas A. "Terrorism as Method in Nepali Maoist Insurgency, 1996–2016." *Small Wars and Insurgencies* 28, no. 1 (2017): 81–118.

Mason, Rowena. "John McDonnell Under Fire for Quoting Mao Zedong in Commons." *The Guardian*, November 25, 2015.

O'Dowd, E.C. "Ho Chi Minh and the Origins of the Vietnamese Doctrine of Guerrilla Tactics." *Small Wars and Insurgencies* 24, no. 3 (2013): 561–587.

Paret, Peter. *French Revolutionary Warfare from Indochina to Algeria*. London: Pall Mall Press, 1964.

Pfeffer, Richard M. "Mao Tse-tung and Revolution." In *National Liberation: Revolution in the Third World*, edited by Norman Miller and Roderick Aya. New York: The Free Press, 1971.

Pike, Douglas. *Viet Cong*. Cambridge, UK: MIT Press, 1966.

Porch, Douglas. *Wars of Empire*. London: Cassell, 2000.

Robin, Marie Monique. *Escadrons de la Mort: l'ecole francaise*. Paris: Editions La Decouverte, 2008.

Teiwes, Fredericak C. "The Chinese State during the Maoist Era." In *The Modern Chinese State*, edited by David Shambaugh. Cambridge: Cambridge University Press, 2000.

Wolf, Eric R. *Peasant Wars of the Twentieth Century*. London: Faber and Faber, 1971.

Revolutionary leadership as necessary element in people's war: Shining Path of Peru

David Scott Palmer

ABSTRACT
Though it is well understood that all internal upheaval within a polity is a consequence of agency interacting with structure, the importance of the former has perhaps become too pushed to the rear. In reality, as demonstrated by the case of *Sendero Luminoso* (Shining Path) in Peru, even cases which seem most determined by structural factors, in practice remain problematic, absent necessary revolutionary leadership. This leadership in turn, can make mistakes just as it guides successes.

Much that is written concerning mass mobilization insurgency – people's war – remains derivative and incomplete. It is derivative in that few any longer grapple with the actual works they purport to cite. It is incomplete in that the mechanics of mass politics remain increasingly less understood in Western societies given to out-sourcing democracy.

People's war remains a bracing corrective. Far from being the trite episode implied in most official literature – 'guerrilla warfare by well-behaved peasants' – it is the epitome of armed politics, a strategy for mobilizing the masses in support of revolutionary aspirations for a new societal ordering. Thus, it is leaders gazing at society, assessing imperfections, and advancing ideological solutions. It is followers being exhorted or compelled to participate in the realization of the solution. Violence is but one way forward, and it takes place alongside a host of other (often nonviolent) ways.

There is, then, as has always been the case, enormous danger in viewing past cases of people's war as quaint episodes of the Cold War. To the contrary, they are the very essence of the political process accompanied by violence to carve out the political space necessary for ideological action. Thus, there are lessons that are timeless. Nothing illustrates this more than the case of Shining Path in Peru.

Ironically, Peru (see Figure 1) in the 1980s appeared to provide infertile ground for the emergence of an insurgency threatening the state.[1] It, after all, was a functioning, if imperfect, democracy with significant representation of Marxist left parties. It could not be classified as authoritarian, dictatorial, or repressive. Yet radical Maoist 'people's war' emerged within democratic political context and expanded over time to include wide swaths of the countryside as well a significant urban presence. Even though rural areas had high levels of extreme poverty, and the insurgency concentrated its actions in these parts of

Figure 1. Peru. Source: Available at: http://www.zonu.com/imapa/americas/Peru_Shaded_Relief_Map.gif (accessed 4 March 2017).

the countryside, the revolutionary spark did not originate among the populations there. It was brought to them by outside agents who saw themselves as the revolutionary vanguard with a vision of a better and more equitable society based on the scientific application of Marxist–Leninist–Maoist principles.[2]

This is significant because many underestimate the capacity of a small group of determined leaders, totally convinced of the rightness of their cause, to pursue a people's war involving acts of terrorism in spite of generally unfavorable objective conditions. This suggests that the revolutionaries' own initiative or voluntarism may offer a better explanation for levels of political violence than structural factors such as type of government, economic or social system, or levels of poverty.[3]

Conversely, would-be revolutionaries are unlikely to win on their own. For success, they must be able to count on a government that pursues inappropriate and erroneous policies to respond to their threat. In short, revolutionary terrorism designed to force putative beneficiary acquiescence is counterproductive unless it occurs in combination with serious, continuing, and multiple mistakes by the government.[4]

Origins of the insurgent movement

Shining Path (*Sendero Luminoso* or *Sendero*) was born in the 1960s in an impoverished highland department, Ayacucho, 48 hours overland from the coastal capital of Lima. Its 566,000 people, 90% Quechua speaking, lived in isolated poverty.[5] It was logical, analysts concluded, that they would respond to the call for people's war declared in 1980 by the Communist Party of Peru in the Shining Path of Mariátegui (the father of Peruvian Marxism), or PCP-SL, and that their pent up anger would often take horrific forms, including torture and mutilation of terror victims. *Sendero*, in other words, was judged a logical outgrowth of its environment.[6]

In fact, this explanation foundered upon larger realities. Peru's national conditions were not those that should have led to insurgency in the 1980s. The national economy had expanded almost continuously from the 1940s through the mid-1970s. Peru in 1980 was returning to democracy after 12 years of reformist, not repressive, military rule (1968-80) that nationalized major foreign investments, established relations with the socialist world (especially the Soviet Union, which became Peru's chief source of military aid and advice), and carried out an extensive agrarian reform.[7] Furthermore, from the late 1970s through the 1980s, the Marxist left was both legal and the second largest political force. Illiterates (mostly indigenous) could vote. There seemed to be sufficient political space within the system for the resolution of grievances, however profound. Even so, *Sendero* chose this moment to begin in Ayacucho its people's war against the system.

What was to become by the 1980s 'the world's deadliest subversive movement',[8] first appeared in Ayacucho in 1962 in the presence of Abimael Guzmán

Reynoso. Taking up his first job as a university instructor, he served initially as a philosophy professor in the Education Program of the recently reopened (1959) National University of San Cristóbal de Huamanga (UNSCH – originally founded in 1677). Initially a member of the Stalinist wing of the mainstream, Soviet-oriented Communist Party of Peru (PCP), then of the breakaway Maoist party, Red Flag, established after the Sino-Soviet split in 1963, Guzman formed the PCP-SL between 1968 and 1970.[9]

In Ayacucho, Guzmán's organization seemed little more than 'coffee house' radicals limited to university politics.[10] Further, commitment of its members to action among the populace dovetailed neatly with the university's own orientation toward service. The school's various academic programs were tailored to meet the specific needs of the highlands and its Indian population. Nearly three quarters of the student body in the 1960s were Quechua-speaking natives of the region, for whom Spanish was a second language.

As they were trained to return in service roles to their communities, especially as teachers, they were indoctrinated by Guzmán, the first director of the university's teacher training school, and other PCP-SL members. As the university, with just 550 students and 40 faculties in 1962, grew to approximately 4,500 students and 200 teachers by the early 1970s, Guzmán emerged as the institution's personnel director (1971-74). As such, he was able to stack the deck and use the time to develop the cadre and organization of *Sendero*.[11]

Ironically, all of the top party leadership, including Guzmán himself and the original Central Committee of the PCP-SL, were outsiders to Ayacucho and did not speak Quechua. Faced with the suffering of the downtrodden, however, they threw themselves into the effort to prepare for a Maoist revolution. By April 1980, when they declared people's war, the party numbered at most 150 to 200 militants but had a network of sympathizers in the Ayacucho region and in some of Peru's other public universities.

Their first revolutionary act was to burn a ballot box in a small Ayacucho district capital on the eve of Peru's first national elections in 17 years. This seemed an inauspicious beginning. A decade later, however, political violence had caused about $10 billion in property damage and over 20,000 deaths. By the time the insurgency died down in the mid-1990s, deaths and disappearances had exceeded 69,000 and property damage, up to $25 billion.[12]

Latin American university traditions

Such a trajectory demands greater examination of the role of leadership – of voluntarism – in this case. A logical point at which to begin is with the larger intellectual context that produced the minds involved.

The Latin American university has long played a major role in the preparation of generations of political leaders and has served as a center of social protest as well. A tradition going back as far as medieval Spain and Portugal defined the university student as one who is there to be educated to serve his family and society but also to protest against social evils. As a result, institutions of higher education in the Iberian Peninsula as well as its diaspora, most especially Latin America, have long been havens for challenges to the status quo, generally protected by this centuries-old principle of inviolability from interventions by the military or police forces of the state.[13]

As education shifted from control by the Catholic Church to control by the state in Latin America during the latter decades of the nineteenth century, student opposition to social and political forces gathered momentum. This change from religious to public higher education was part of a larger political process in almost every country of the region that pitted longstanding Conservative traditions originally brought from Spain and, to a lesser degree, Portugal, against more modern Liberal theories from England. The core differences included the separation of Church and State, as well as equality instead of hierarchy, individualism instead of communitarianism, and free trade instead of mercantilism. Such core differences provoked civil wars in many countries of the region between the 1840s and the 1880s, with Liberalism emerging victorious in almost every case.

With Liberal principles taking root in most of Latin America, by the turn of the twentieth century public higher education had also been widely established. In addition, since the higher education reforms proposed in 1918 in a meeting of students in Córdoba, Argentina spread throughout the region over the next decade, universities have institutionalized principles of autonomy as well as decision-making power by both students and faculty. These include the right of each sector to elect a third of representatives to central university councils as well as to the individual schools within the institution.[14]

Through the 1950s, higher education was the province of the sons of the elite, gradually including some daughters as well, who tended to adopt anti-establishment positions during their student years but usually returned to the establishment fold after graduation.[15] However, beginning in the late 1950s and 1960s, higher education in most Latin American countries expanded rapidly to include the youth of middle and lower classes as well, due to quickening social change which brought an ever increasing proportion of the hitherto marginalized population onto the national economic and political scene for the first time. This process was occurring during the same period that left ideologies were becoming more prominent in the wider body politic of the region and beyond.[16]

The role of the cold war

Growing ideological consciousness during these years was strengthened by Cold War considerations, in which the Soviet Union played an important role in contributing to Communist Party organizing in national politics, labor unions, and student organizations. To counter such initiatives, the United States pursued an active anti-communist agenda throughout the region in support of alternative student and labor groups, along with a number of interventions to thwart the advance of radicalism. Between the 1950s and the late 1980s, national security considerations dominated US policy toward Latin America and produced growing hostility among nationalists and progressives, especially in such institutions as the public universities.[17]

The Cuban Revolution led by Fidel Castro, which overthrew the US supported dictatorship of Fulgencio Batista in 1959, was a watershed event. It served as an inspiration to generations of students throughout Latin America. The Revolution and its charismatic leader fostered an anti-American and anti-capitalist orientation that mobilized legions of student sympathizers to compete in and often win university elections. Once in control, they could pursue more radical approaches to governance, including greater student control, open admissions, and hiring policies favoring faculty members who shared their ideological views. Such an anti-US perspective became more pronounced after the rupture in diplomatic relations between the United States and Cuba (in late 1960), and particularly following the failed invasion of Cuba by US-supported anti-Castro Cubans in April 1961.[18]

Even though President John Fitzgerald Kennedy generated a great deal of enthusiasm among Latin Americans from all walks of life due to his charisma, Catholic religion, and policy initiatives like the Alliance for Progress economic assistance program and the Peace Corps, Fidel Castro and his revolutionary partner Ché Guevara became equally prominent as icons of the left. In the face of the implacable hostility of the United States, the Cuban regime turned to Marxism as its guiding ideology and allied with the Soviet Union as both a model and an economic lifeline, and very soon began to expand its efforts to foster other revolutionary movements throughout Latin America.[19]

Such efforts included invitations to selected Latin American university students to come to Cuba to observe the Revolution first hand and participate in short-term seminars on Marxism, which served to further expand political radicalism within their home institutions upon their return.[20] Furthermore, for most of the 1960s and 1970s Cuba actively trained and supported guerrilla movements of national liberation in several Central and South American countries, the largest portion of whose members came from the ranks of university students and professors. Although the communist guerrilla groups which emerged in Uruguay (the Tupamaros), Colombia (the Revolutionary Armed Forces of Colombia – FARC), and Argentina (the Montoneros) were home grown, all were inspired by the example of Cuba. However, most of the others (as in Guatemala, El Salvador, Nicaragua, Venezuela, Brazil, and briefly in Peru, Ecuador, and Bolivia) were trained as well as inspired by Cuba.[21]

The major exception was the case we are considering, the particularly virulent Shining Path of Peru, which turned to Maoism after the Sino-Soviet split in the early 1960s. Members of Shining Path's Central Committee made multiple trips to China for their training, which happened to coincide with that country's Cultural Revolution (1966–1976). The party's maximum leader, university professor Abimael Guzmán Reynoso, found the Chinese Cultural Revolution's more radical forces, led by Mao and then Madame Mao, to be more compatible with his extreme Marxist views. Until the split, Guzmán had been a fervent Stalinist within the Moscow-oriented Communist Party of Peru – PCP – and had helped to revitalize the local branch once he moved to Ayacucho.[22]

After Madame Mao's faction lost out in 1976 to the so-called 'moderates', in which Deng Xiaoping emerged as leader, Guzmán and Shining Path were cut adrift. Instead of fading away after losing their foreign mentor and sponsor, however, they continued to prepare on their own for a radical Maoist revolution in Peru, which they launched as a 'Peoples War' in May 1980. Their origins and evolution represent a significant example of how a small, isolated, and provincial public university served as the incubator of radical revolutionary fervor and a guerrilla war that soon convulsed the Peruvian countryside and came alarmingly close to overthrowing the government within a decade.[23]

The university which gave rise to Shining Path[24]

The University of San Cristóbal de Huamanga where Abimael Guzmán taught for 12 years, starting in 1962, is located in what was then a remote capital, Ayacucho, connected to the outside world by a one-lane road in the indigenous heartland of the Peruvian *sierra*. For a number of reasons, this university would have appeared to be a very unlikely place for preparing what was to become the most violent guerrilla war in the history of the Peruvian republic.

Founded in 1679, the country's second oldest institution of higher learning, it functioned for some 200 years to serve the local elite before being shut down in 1880 due to Peru's economic collapse after the War of the Pacific (1879–1883). But in 1959, through the efforts of Ayacucho's congressional delegation, the university was relaunched with a totally new purpose, unique in South America at the time. The goal was to establish an institution that would reach out to serve the needs of the population of the highland region in which it was located; Peru's poorest and most isolated.[25]

Instead of being organized around traditional fields of study, such as law, medicine, engineering, and literature and the arts, the University of Huamanga set up programs attuned to preparing students from the area for professions closely related to its most pressing deficiencies. These included education, rural engineering, nursing and obstetrics, applied anthropology, and mining engineering, to be chosen after two years of broadly-based required foundational courses. In addition, students and their faculty mentors would engage in a variety of service activities in fieldwork among the area's indigenous communities and marginal settlements within the small city of Ayacucho, with a population of less than 20,000 in 1960.[26]

The faculty recruited to fill positions included some of Peru's most distinguished academics, many of whom came because they shared the vision of an institution dedicated to improving the condition of the local population, with the added benefit of enjoying salaries based on full-time employment, a rarity in the country at the time. Political orientation was not a consideration initially, as the first generation of professors included a wide range of views, representing virtually every political party as well as such international entities as Fulbright, a Danish government ceramics program, the missionary organization Summer Institute of Linguistics, and the US Peace Corps. The university was quite small during the first years after its refounding, with a total of about 40 faculty members and 400 students, and functioned in a very small city with few amenities. As a result, everyone knew each other, socialized together, and shared the view that they were part of a significant innovation in Peruvian higher education.[27]

About 70% of the students came from the most humble of backgrounds. In a region in which some 90% of the population of approximately 500,000 was rural and Quechua speaking, for the majority Spanish was their second language. The fact that they had gained entrance to the university at all meant that most had overcome a daunting set of obstacles to achieve this objective. These included deficient primary schools in their communities, the need to move to a provincial capital for their secondary school education, and poor parents who made enormous sacrifices to help them stay in school. After succeeding where most of their peers had not, they viewed the University of Huamanga and its mission as the opportunity for them to gain the tools they needed to give back to the communities from which they had come.[28]

Explaining university radicalization and Shining Path

In spite of such a promising beginning, this university could not isolate itself from what was happening in the world around it. Enthusiasm for the Cuban Revolution and the figure of Fidel Castro made its presence felt. Some of the most able students were invited to Cuba and returned with a more ideological orientation. The Cuban missile crisis brought home the challenge of the Cold War and sensitized many at the university to the need to take sides. Within Peru, the election of a more reformist administration after a military intervention and decades of conservative governments, both civilian and military, generated a more open political climate and an expansion in party activity, especially on the left.[29] In addition, in the 1960s and 1970s, Peruvian students in secondary and higher education expanded rapidly, from 17 to 52%.[30]

Given such developments, it was not surprising that even the University of Huamanga would be affected by them. One manifestation was the increasing politicization of elections for student organizations and university governing bodies among the members of this community. Ideological orientation began to compete with perceived competence for support, fostered by a growing presence of Peru's Communist Party (PCP) and its financial support of the Revolutionary Student Federation (FER). Although still a minority within the university in 1963, it nevertheless was able to wage a successful campaign to force a reluctant administration to request the departure of the Peace Corps professors.[31] Years later, this FER faculty advisor, none other than Professor Guzmán himself, was to declare the action against the Peace Corps presence in the University of Huamanga as 'the first blow against international imperialism in Peru'.[32]

The leadership exercised by a single individual over more than a decade as a professor of education proved to be the most important factor in turning this university from a force for local development into an incubator for guerrilla war. Abimael Guzmán Reynoso arrived in Ayacucho in 1962 as a dedicated member of the Communist Party who identified with its Stalinist wing as the result of mentoring during his undergraduate years by two hard line Communists at his university in Arequipa, Peru's second-largest city. He was successful in reviving the then moribund Communist Party in Ayacucho as he began to use his classes and 'study groups' to proselytize among the students. Some of these were instrumental in agitating for the removal of Peace Corps faculty.[33]

After his appointment as the first director of the university's teacher training school, Guzmán was able to use his position to influence a generation of students in the most popular academic program (about one-quarter of the students at the time). Upon graduation, a large number of these returned as teachers to the indigenous communities from which they had come. Here, as respected members, they frequently used their positions to propagandize for radical political approaches. Over the course of the 1960s and 1970s, these teachers became a significant support network for the Communist Party in scores of rural communities throughout Ayacucho.[34]

As one born on the coast and educated in the cosmopolitan southern Peru city of Arequipa, Professor Guzmán was very much affected by the very different reality he found in the much poorer rural indigenous sierra of Ayacucho where subsistence agriculture predominated. As a result, after China's split with the Soviet Union in 1963–64, he found the Maoist ideological principles of peasant revolution more compatible with the reality he was then observing, and soon shifted his political allegiance and the source of his financial support accordingly.[35]

Over the course of the next decade, he made several extended trips to China where he and most of the leading members of his followers received training in party organization and guerrilla war techniques. Given his ideological formation at the radical fringes of communism, he was attracted to the more extreme tenets of permanent revolution advocated by Mao and his wife during the Cultural Revolution in China, which was taking place during the years he was traveling there.[36]

Back at the University of Huamanga, the ideological ground work Professor Guzmán had been carrying out produced results in the 1968 university elections, which his supporters won. During the 1968–1972 period of university control by his now Maoist group, the last vestiges of the original principles of the institution were abandoned. Guzmán was named Secretary General, a position which enabled him to name his supporters to key positions and open the university to all, which produced a chaotic mix of Maoist ideological orthodoxy and facilities overwhelmed by underprepared students.[37]

Although eventually defeated in subsequent elections, the legacy of a politicized institution in which ideological criteria overrode quality education remained. Many of the original members of Guzmán's central committee leading his now fully Maoist party, known as the Communist Party of Peru – Shining Path (PCP-SL), came from the faculty and students of the University of Huamanga. Guzmán himself left the university in 1974 and went underground where he continued to prepare his organization for a future guerrilla war.

In spite of these developments, which would normally have attracted the attention of central government authorities and quite possibly have led to steps to restore the educational mission of the University of Huamanga and undermine the PCP-SL, it didn't happen. In part, this was due to the isolated location of the university in Ayacucho, largely out of view of national officials in the coastal capital of Lima. Inaction was also the result of an institutionalized military coup in 1968, which overthrew the elected president and brought to power a self-titled Revolutionary Military Government (GRM) determined to effect change along socialist principles, including nationalization of private and foreign companies, agrarian reform, and worker self-management.[38]

As a result, the GRM was less interested in stemming the influence of left political parties than with reducing the role of traditional elites. Such a perspective by this military government favored socialist and communist parties and unions, strange as that may seem. Over the course of the 12 years of military rule, then, all of them, including the PCP-SL, continued to function and to grow largely unimpeded. In fact, by the time the military realized that its reformist agenda was much too ambitious given available resources, and moved to turn the political system back over to elected civilian government, the multiple parties of the largely Marxist–Leninist–Maoist left had become Peru's second largest political force.[39]

With one exception, the Peruvian left political organizations decided to participate in the electoral process, including a constitutional convention that produced the progressive Constitution of 1979 and, in 1980, the country's first national elections based on universal suffrage. Over the course of the 1980s, in fact, most left parties joined forces in the United Left (IU) and retained their number two position in national as well as municipal elections. Only Shining Path chose a different route.

The University of Huamanga was the incubator and facilitator of the PCP-SL under the leadership of Professor Guzmán in the 1960s and early 1970s, and provided the institutional cover for the continuous proselytization of faculty and students. By the mid-1970s, after Shining Path's founder, leader, ideologist, and organizer had gone into hiding, he had succeeded in using his university position to create a regional network of supporters. Over the next several years, this network became the foundation of what was to become his guerrilla organization.

It included not only radicalized UNSCH graduates who returned to their communities but also some who took up positions in other public universities in the highland provinces. Many of these were founded in the 1960s as part of a major government expansion of post-secondary school institutions and needed to be staffed quickly from what was initially a limited pool of candidates. Even with a very small number of Shining Path militants in their faculty ranks, given the tolerant atmosphere for left ideological perspectives in universities at the time, several soon became producers of radicalized student recruits as well.

The combination of isolation from the center, determined and charismatic leadership, a congenial university environment, the presence of a variety of Communist states in the international arena, Cuba's support of guerrilla movements in Latin America, training in China, and a tolerant military regime in Peru, all contributed to Abimael Guzmán's ability to slowly build a significant political force over a 17-year period. At each critical juncture, he chose the more radical ideological option, from his student days in Arequipa to the Cultural Revolution in China.

When Guzmán's Chinese mentors, Madame Mao and her fellow extremists, lost out to the more pragmatic moderates in 1976, both he and Shining Path were cut off from their financial and ideological support. Instead of fading away, however, he spent the next four years in Peru preparing to launch a guerrilla war based on his own exhaustive study of Marxist–Leninist–Maoist ideology. He concluded that only the proper application of these ideological principles could produce the pure revolutionary state that every other Communist regime had failed to generate once in power.

Strategy and tactics for people's war

The progressive expansion of the people's war throughout Peru was due to two key factors. One was Shining Path's strategic finesse and ability to recruit new cadre. The other was the inability of the government to respond appropriately and effectively. The strategic acumen came directly from China. Between 1969 and 1974, virtually every Central Committee member made at least one extended trip to the People's Republic of China (PRC). Guzmán made three. There, amidst the Cultural Revolution, the Shining Path elite was trained in 'Gang of Four' Maoism and in the mechanics of people's war. When the radical Maoists ultimately lost influence in China in 1976, Guzmán, bereft of his party's international sponsor, took the *nom de guerre* President Gonzalo and became the self-appointed heir to the 'true' Marxist legacy.[40]

In Guzmán's view, the communist revolutions in China and elsewhere had become revisionist dictatorships and had lost their legitimacy by failing to remain true to original ideological principles. He now saw himself as the one to assume the responsibility for leading a revolution that would be ideologically pure. To accomplish this goal for the people's war in Peru, PCP-SL had to obtain its resources locally and not depend on any other outside assistance. The party also had to retain an internal tension based on the operation of the dialectic, so that there would be a continual internal process of ideological purification through creation of new syntheses, determined, of course, by President Gonzalo himself. This assured that the most radical line would always prevail within the party, and that its fundamental ideological principles would revolve around the thought of Marx, Lenin, Mao, and President Gonzalo.[41]

An extensive political organization worked hand-in-glove with a 'Popular Guerrilla Army', which maintained the classic tripartite division into main, regional, and local forces. Numbers were never *Sendero's* strength. In its Ayacucho heartland, for instance, in mid-1989, the principal and local forces fielded only about 250 personnel each, and the base force, about 750. The counter-state this armed force was intended to protect was much larger, of course, but never exceeded more than 20 to 30% of the population.[42]

Where Shining Path excelled was in organization, strategy, and ideological commitment. During the early 1980s, the leadership established seven regional committees in major areas of operations around the country, all, like the central committee, made up of university-educated individuals committed to radical Maoist principles. Regional committees operated with small annihilation squads to carry out operations against key targets, especially local officials. Larger groups of armed cadre operated against police and military targets, especially in isolated and more vulnerable areas.

At the same time, popular committees of sympathizers or intimidated locals, mostly poor and less educated indigenous farmers, were established in hundreds of so-called 'liberated zones' opened up by the organization's military operations. They also set up a finance committee to gather resources from 'people's taxes' on coca leaf growing and cocaine paste transporting operations in the Upper Huallaga and Apurímac valleys. These resources, estimated to be at least $10 million per year in the late 1980s, were channeled to the central and regional committees in order to pay cadre and to carry out operations.[43]

Shining Path's strategy was designed to create through voluntarism the objective conditions that did not exist when it began the people's war. The intent was to bring about the generalization of political violence, the gradual encirclement of the cities, the eventual collapse of the government, and the establishment of 'New Democracy'. For almost a decade, such a strategy was almost diabolical in its effectiveness. The main elements included the following:

- Carrying out selective attacks and assassinations to provoke the gradual elimination of government 'contact points' at the local level.

- Provoking intemperate government responses by carefully planned operations against key facilities; symbolic actions designed for maximum psychological impact, such as illuminating huge hammers and sickles on prominent hillsides overlooking major cities; and destruction of key electrical and communications infrastructure.
- Gathering of arms and dynamite by attacks on isolated police posts or individual police or military figures and operations against scores of small mines scattered throughout the highlands.
- Cutting off power, water, and overland communications to important cities, including Lima, to demonstrate the organization's operational capacity and government's weakness.
- Utilizing, cynically, Peru's democratic institutions to publicize their activities in the press, to free captured militants through the judicial system, and to organize their jailed comrades, in combination with threats and selective assassinations against reluctant officials.[44]

Initial government response

Successive democratic governments of the 1980s – Fernando Belaúnde Terry (1980–85) and Alan García Pérez (1985–90) – responded just as the Shining Path leadership had hoped. By their actions against the insurgents and by ineffective governance, they contributed in significant ways to create the conditions favorable to the insurgents' advance. Among the government's most counterproductive responses were:

- President Belaúnde, because he had been ousted by the military in its 1968 coup, was reluctant to use it against Shining Path for fear it might gain in strength and influence and again turn him out of office. So he downplayed the importance of the guerrilla actions, calling them 'cattle rustlers'. In the two years before he declared Ayacucho an emergency zone and committed the military, Shining Path gained precious time for increasing its organizational strength and operational capacity.
- When the military did respond, it used massive and brutal force against insurgents and innocent civilians alike, inflicting over 7,500 casualties in 1983 and 1984, mostly among the rural indigenous population. The result was predictable. Tens of thousands fled, and many others who stayed were convinced or were coerced into concluding that their future lay with Sendero.
- Brutal state response highlighted a longstanding feature of Peruvian social reality, the division of the country between urban whites and *mestizos* and rural indigenous communities. This racial divide blinded the center to the needs of the periphery, producing actions that only served to create conditions more favorable for the expansion of Shining Path.

- Making matters worse was a set of ineffective macroeconomic policies in the 1980s that eroded the fiscal capacity of the government, provoked hyperinflation (a cumulative two million percent between 1985 and 1990), massive unemployment, and economic contraction (over 20% in 1989 and 1990 alone).[45]

The 1990 election to president of a political outsider, academic Alberto Fujimori, was widely seen as an act of popular desperation. His measures to restore economic stability initially made matters worse. When he administered an *autogolpe* (self-coup) against his own government, seizing control in April 1992 and sparking a cutoff in most foreign aid, even optimists feared the worst was soon to come. At that point *Sendero* had become a nationwide force, seemingly financially secure, and in the driver's seat strategically. Its infrastructure was growing in the capital itself. Shining Path leadership had become convinced that it was on the verge of triumph, and began to plan for the final offensive against the beleaguered state.

What had happened over 12 years of people's war in Peru was the progressive expansion of political violence through *Sendero* actions that took advantage of structural weaknesses and contextual factors to open up spaces in the periphery by destroying the contact points of government and establishing liberated zones for creating local popular committees of New Democracy. Their strategy, ideology, and selective terrorism created an aura of invincibility that further eroded the legitimacy of a weakened and now unconstitutional government. Its actions had indeed produced the favorable objective conditions that had not existed in 1980.

For its part, the government, through its multiple mistaken actions, both against the insurgents and in its national economic and social policies, contributed in various ways to making the situation worse. This combination had produced a dynamic by mid-1992 in which the Peruvian state teetered on the verge of collapse and Shining Path advanced toward what appeared to many to be an almost inevitable victory. While specific elements and dynamics vary, the situation in Nepal a decade later mirrors quite closely Peru's in the early 1990s for many of the same reasons.

Peruvian systemic response to the insurgent challenge

With its back against the wall in the early 1990s, Peru's government began to take measures that in combination produced positive results at various levels in a relatively short time. While some political violence has continued and Shining Path has never been completely eliminated, over the course of three or four years the insurgents ceased to be a threat to the state. Some of the explanation for such a dramatic turnabout may be found in the errors and oversights of the guerrillas themselves; however, most has to do with a set of government initiatives that was put in place between 1989 and 1993.

Refloating the economy

President Alberto Fujimori (1990–2001) addressed the governance problem first. He began by carrying out a number of moves that strengthened the national political and economic system as a whole and thus its capacity to respond to Shining Path. His financial measures – particularly an economic 'shock' program – brought inflation down from 2,600% in 1991 to 15% by 1994. Combined with significant economic restructuring, the result was that the confidence of both domestic and foreign private investors was restored, and private investment soared.[46]

Revamping security

This dramatic government policy turnabout served as the foundation for the second set of initiatives relating to counterinsurgency policies that involved both security and support measures working to reinforce each other. On the security side, changes included six key components:

- A more robust legal framework for counterterrorism was established, enhanced by speedy trials and a repentance law. These measures went hand-in-hand with judicial reforms, including a system of 'faceless judges'. This measure was deemed necessary at the time both for protection from insurgent threats and assassinations, even though it often constrained due process (and was declared unconstitutional in 1999 by the Inter-American Human Rights Court).[47]
- Intelligence operations were dramatically improved by joining eight separate agencies into one, thereby diminishing inefficiency and duplication of effort. In addition, a much smaller police organization, the Special Intelligence Group (GEIN), was formed within the National Agency Against Terrorism (DINCOTE), specifically to track the PCP-SL leadership.[48]
- The military, after years of failure in stemming insurgent advance, rethought its strategy in 1989 and began to implement a 'hearts and minds' campaign built around successive domination of areas supported by elite reaction units.[49] Although these changes began before Fujimori's election in 1990, his government continued their implementation. A previously unused step, due to fear of local cooptation, was to begin to assign military personnel from a target area to serve in that same area, in order to get eyes and ears on the ground. This was particularly important in the highlands due to the significant differences in languages and accents as well as customs and cultures.[50]
- With the implantation of the first two steps above – a more focused military response based on more accurate intelligence – the human rights record improved. This occurred as Sendero was sliding into ever greater human rights abuses as the guerrillas tried to retain control over local populations by force

and intimidation. The combination reinforced popular willingness to provide information and to cooperate with government operations and programs.[51]
- The military also began to engage in civic action. Engineer units, for example, were used to cut roads and to address other pressing local needs. Military personnel now went into local communities to provide basic health and dental services, offer free haircuts, and rebuild schools and community offices destroyed by Shining Path. Immediate local concerns drove implementation and quickly garnered local support.[52]
- Finally, the military began to support systematically local popular opposition that had developed to Shining Path. Insurgent terrorist attacks and actions against local officials and communities alike had increased substantially over the decade of people's war, provoking significant increases from the mid-1980s onward in instances of spontaneous organized local resistance. Previously resistant to the idea of arming civilians, lest weapons be lost to the guerrillas or turned against them by indigenous recipients, the military moved to provide significant support for local civil defense, beginning in May 1991.[53] Eventually, such civilian groups, officially known as Civil Defense Committees (CDC), and locally as *rondas campesinas*, dominated local security in the insurgent heartland.[54]

Targeting resources at the local level

Lima moved vigorously to address the structural basis for *Sendero's* ability to recruit at the local level, poverty and lack of opportunity. A new set of semi-autonomous agencies, run from the Office of the President, was established to respond to development needs. Guided by an updated 'poverty map' of Peru's 200 poorest districts, the campaign pursued microdevelopment that emphasized a variety of small programs targeted particularly for those districts identified as being characterized by 'extreme poverty'. In many cases, these were the very areas where Shining Path had been most active.

Personnel commitments were minimal, as were resources for individual projects – fewer than 300 individuals implementing programs in each agency; most projects, $2,000 or less. Yet personnel were handpicked on merit, largely decentralized to regional offices, and responsible for overseeing programs generated by local demand from several options. These included access roads or trails, electrification, potable water, reforestation, dams, and irrigation projects, among others. Local demand, in turn, was accomplished by community vote, with locals providing both oversight and labor. As a result, most allocated funding was delivered directly to the target areas for a variety of small projects that the residents had identified as their highest priorities, had organized locally to implement, and had committed themselves to completion.[55]

Results were impressive. In 1994, 31% of the population (or 9 million of 24 million) was categorized as living in 'extreme poverty'. Four years later, with an input of $2–2.5 billion in resources for all the agencies nation-wide (over half of which from international financial institutions), this figure had dropped to 15%.[56] Such dramatic progress, providing as it did tangible evidence of government interest – and results – led not just to heightened popular backing in the abstract but a willingness to provide information and to participate in self-defense. This led directly to increases in the strength of local organizations, community empowerment, and the perception by marginal local citizens that they had a stake in the political system.[57]

Results and implications

Perhaps predictably, it was the intelligence coups, notably the capture of Guzmán, which occupied the limelight. Having revamped its approach to dealing with the insurgency in multiple ways, the government was able to turn the tables on Shining Path rather quickly. These events showed up the weaknesses of the guerrilla organization, including its hydrocephalic nature with Guzmán's multiple roles as founder, chief ideologue, strategist, and party organizer; its hubris due to overconfidence in the imminent success of the revolution; its terror actions to coerce the revolution's presumed beneficiaries to continue to be loyal to Sendero; and the lack of adaptability of its highly centralized decision-making machinery to new challenges.[58]

Sendero remnants remain active in Peru. Whether or not the organization or something similar will rise again in Peru should not obscure the fact that there will in all likelihood be replication of such a phenomenon in other venues. What needs to be firmly grasped, particularly from the internal security perspective, is the degree to which terror-driving insurgency, a virtual straw man in analytical constructs, became a reality. In Shining Path we see terror deliberately used by a ruthless group to create the objective conditions that will combine with its assaults to enable it to seize power. *Sendero's* success demonstrates the frightening potential for victory if the target – the government itself – is unable to respond in an appropriate, timely fashion.

Conclusions

The Peruvian case demonstrates quite clearly the havoc that can be wreaked by a small number of individuals totally committed to 'making revolution' irrespective of objective conditions. In neither case is the leadership's class or caste identification with the presumed beneficiaries of their effort relevant. Much more important is the degree to which they have become committed to the most radical approaches through their university educations, exposure to radical mentors, and participation in political organizing. Through these experiences, they have taken on a one-dimensional and all-encompassing vision of history that they truly believe offers humanity's only hope for the future. They see themselves as ideologically pure and complete, and combine their convictions with intelligence, charismatic personalities, and strong strategic capacities.

Party leaders' political participation was limited to provincial university politics. They were upwardly striving products of the bottom rung of the provincial middle class, succeeded intellectually in the periphery rather than the center, and were educated almost exclusively in provincial universities (but with brief and significant forays to China during the Cultural Revolution to hone their ideologies and practical skills in making revolution). From the outset, in addition, the PCP-SL was very dependent on one individual to provide ideological coherence, motivation, and strategic vision – Professor Abimael Guzmán Reynoso – who went so far as to articulate the necessity of a cult of personality for success.[59]

The voluntarism of revolutionary leadership produced over time the generalization of political violence and the creation, through such violence and inappropriate government response, of more favorable conditions for the continued pursuit of the people's war. Strategy and tactics were driven by purposive initiatives that worked to snip off the contact points of central government in poorer and more isolated parts of the country through attacks with superior forces on police posts, municipal buildings, and infrastructure. Rudimentary people's committees were established under their direction in the spaces that opened up. The growing counter-state served as the basis for the projection of power to defeat the military, once it was deployed. Following Mao, the effort progressed from the first to the second phase of revolutionary war. Both used carrots and sticks to gain support of local populations, with no hesitation in employing terror to ensure acquiescence.

Negotiation was never an option. Guzmán and his key followers, never a part of the national political or social scene, were so committed to the purity of their revolutionary course and so blinded by their progressive successes against the state through the early 1990s that they saw their final triumph as inevitable. They failed to consider that the Peruvian government was capable of changing its counterproductive strategy. Thus, they were unprepared for the counteroffensive that rounded up Guzmán, the master files, and key leadership in 1992. *Sendero's* top-down hierarchy, its all-encompassing ideology, its coercive approach to maintain support, and its use of terror to advance the revolution, long seen as advantages in the people's war, became key components of its defeat. Only from jail, after being sentenced to long terms in prison, including for life, has the *Sendero* leadership begun to consider a more pragmatic approach in its dealings with the government.

In the Peruvian case, government officials were capable of rethinking their strategy and changing course, but only after years of failure. What may finally have provoked the new approach was the belated realization that Shining Path might succeed after all, after it began to cut off Lima from water, electricity, and even food in 1998–1989 and started a campaign of car bomb attacks on Lima city streets.

Whatever the motivation, the steps taken to reorganize the intelligence services and give them greater resources and autonomy; to revamp military operations in the shanty towns and countryside; to make justice swift and effective, if sometimes arbitrary (but which included a repentance law to encourage defections); and to train and provide some arms to the long-suffering *rondas campesinas*, all served to turn the tide. When combined with tough measures that revived the economy and a new array of small, efficient government agencies operating in response to local citizen to reduce extreme poverty in the countryside, the Peruvian state moved beyond short-term counterinsurgency measures toward reducing the structural incentives and opportunities for revolutionary action.

What emerges from consideration of the Peruvian case is evident: voluntarism is as critical a component as objective circumstances, with deliberate action actually able to shape those circumstances in a weak state setting. Further, inappropriate state response is itself a key factor in contributing to this dynamic.

The implications are sobering in an era when states worldwide are faltering in the difficult transition to democracy even as they are challenged by development demands exacerbated by heightened popular expectations. In such settings, terror is able to tip the scales in situations which otherwise would hang in the balance, thus allowing voluntarist actors to engage in activity not unlike that envisaged in *foco* theory where Ché Guevara posited that guerrilla action itself could produce the conditions for the revolution. As the cases make clear, when governments are able to be more effective in dealing with such initiatives, as well as to be more responsive to the basic needs and demands of their citizenries, they are likely to overcome the challenges of determined adversaries willing to use terror and violence even when only a small minority.

Notes

1. Portions of the discussion in this article have appeared previously in numerous efforts by the author; but see in particular two works co-authored with Thomas A. Marks: "Radical Maoist Insurgents and Terrorist Tactics: Comparing Peru and Nepal," *Low Intensity Conflict and Law Enforcement* [now incorporated in *Small Wars and Insurgencies*] 13, no. 2 (Autumn 2005), 91–116; and "Lessons From Peru," *Counterterrorism* 13, no. 2 (2007), 18–25.
2. Numerous works shed light on this phenomenon. Particularly useful is David P. Chandler, *Brother Number One: A Political Biography of Pol Pot*, rev. ed. (Boulder: Westview, 1999).
3. An overview that illuminates well the structure/voluntarism issue is Jack A. Goldstone, ed., *Revolutions: Theoretical, Comparative, and Historical Studies*, 2nd ed. (New York: Harcourt Brace, 1994).
4. David Scott Palmer, "Rebellion in Rural Peru: The Origins and Evolution of Sendero Luminoso," *Comparative Politics* 18:2 (January 1986), 142.
5. For background, among others, see Palmer, "Rebellion in Rural Peru," 127–46.

6. Among others, see Senado del Perú, Comité Especial sobre las Causas de la Violencia y las Alternativas de Pacificación en el Perú, *Violencia y pacificación* (Lima: DESCO and Comisión Andina de Juristas, 1989).
7. There are a number of excellent studies of this period; one of the best is Cynthia McClintock and Abraham Lowenthal, eds. *The Peruvian Experiment Revisited* (Princeton: Princeton University Press, 1982).
8. Simon Strong, *Sendero Luminoso: El movimiento subversivo más letal del mundo* (Lima: Peru Reporting, 1992).
9. Particularly good for this period is Gustavo Gorriti, *Sendero: Historia de la Guerra milenaria en el Perú* (Lima: Editorial Apoyo, 1990). For summary details of Guzmán's life, see Gustavo Gorriti, "Shining Path's Stalin and Trotsky," in David Scott Palmer, ed., *Shining Path of Peru*, 2nd ed. (New York: St. Martin's Press, 1994), 149–70.
10. Including author Palmer, who served as a Peace Corps Volunteer in Ayacucho and taught at UNSCH in 1962 and 1963.
11. Palmer, "Rebellion in Rural Peru;" Carlos Iván Degregori, *Ayacucho 1969–1979: El surgimiento de Sendero Luminoso* (Lima: Instituto de Estudios Peruanos, 1990).
12. Comisión de la Verdad y Reconciliación Perú, *Informe Final: Tomo I: Primera Parte: El proceso, los hechos, las víctimas* (Lima: Navarrete, 2003). The complete report covering all aspects of the Commission's work is contained in nine volumes. Previously, official casualty and disappearance figures had been set at 35,000.
13. Hubert Herring, *A History of Latin America* (New York: Knopf, 1955), 40.
14. Rock, *El radicalismo argentino 1890–1930* (Buenos Aires: Editorial Amorrotu, 1977), Ch. 4.
15. The author recalls a government functionary, a former radical student leader and pupil of his at the University of Huamanga, who said in a conversation some years after graduation, "I've already done my part for the cause."
16. See Daniel C. Levy, *Higher Education and the State in Latin America* (Chicago: University of Chicago Press, 1986), *passim*.
17. Jorge Balan, "Latin American Higher Educational Systems in a Historical and Comparative Perspective," in *Latin America's New Knowledge Economy* (New York: International Institute of Education, 2013), xiv.
18. Esteban Morales Dominguez and Gary Prevost, *United States-Cuban Relations: A Critical History* (Lanham, MA: Lexington Books, 2008), Ch. 2.
19. Rex A. Hudson, *Castro's Americas Department Coordinating Cuba's Support for Marxist-Leninist Violence in the Americas* (Miami: Cuban American National Foundation, 1988).
20. As a concrete example, two or three of the author's best students at the University of Huamanga were invited to Cuba in 1963, and went. One later became a leading member of the Shining Path.
21. Ibid.
22. Gustavo Gorriti Ellenbogen, "Shining Path's Stalin and Trotsky," in David Scott Palmer, ed., *Shining Path of Peru*, 2nd ed. (New York: St. Martin's Press, 1994), 154–5.
23. Gustavo Gorriti Ellenbogen, *Sendero. La historia de la Guerra milenaria en el Perú* (Lima: Editorial Apoyo, 1990).
24. The author served as a Peace Corps Volunteer Leader in Peru between 1962 and 1964, and was invited to join the University of San Cristóbal de Huamanga faculty as a visiting professor of English and social studies, where he taught in 1962 and 1963 During this time, he shared an office with his colleague Abimael Guzmán Reynoso and interacted regularly with him. Such a first-hand experience contributed to an early article on the university and the challenges of accomplishing its academic goals given the political agenda of Guzmán, as well as

ongoing research and writing in an effort to explain Shining Path and its leader's role over the course of the 'People's War'. See David Scott Palmer, "Expulsion from a Peruvian University," in Robert B Textor, ed Cultural Frontiers of the Peace Corps (Cambridge: MIT Press, 1966), 243–70.

25. See Fernando Romero Pintado, "New Design for an Old University: San Cristóbal de Huamanga," *Américas* (December 1961), 9–16.
26. Palmer, "Expulsion from a Peruvian University," 244–7.
27. Ibid., 249–53.
28. Gustavo Gorriti Ellenbogen, *Sendero*, 41–7.
29. McClintock, Cynthia, "Theories of Revolution and the Case of Peru," in Palmer, ed., *Shining Path*, 234–5.
30. Gustavo Gorriti Ellenbogen, "Shining Path's Stalin and Trotsky," 60.
31. Palmer, "Expulsion from a Peruvian University" 255–61.
32. Abimael Guzmán Reynoso, English translation and transcription of his interview in prison after his capture, Foreign Broadcast Information Service (FBIS), U.S. Government, 1993.
33. Degregori, "The Origins, 52–3."
34. David Scott Palmer, "Rebellion in Rural Peru: The Origins and Evolution of Sendero Luminoso," *Comparative Politics* 18, no. 2 (January 1986), 127–46.
35. Gustavo Gorriti Ellenbogen, *Sendero*.
36. Gustavo Gorriti Ellenbogen, "Shining Path's Stalin and Trotsky," 173–4.
37. Carlos Iván Degregori, *Ayacucho 1969–1979*.
38. David Scott Palmer, "Rebellion in Rural Peru," 127–46.
39. Peter F. Klarén, *Peru: Society and Nationhood in the Andes* (New York: Oxford University Press, 2000).
40. Most fully developed in Gorriti, *Sendero*. Also see Cynthia McClintock, "Theories of Revolution and the Case of Peru," in Palmer, *Shining Path*, esp. 247–9.
41. Such interpretations come from Guzmán's own unpublished but privately circulated musings; one published exception is his interview by Luis Arce Borja and Janet Talavera Sánchez, "La entrevista del siglo: El Presidente Gonzalo rompe el silencio," *El Diario*, 24 July 1988, 2–48.
42. From interviews and fieldwork by Palmer and Marks in Ayacucho, July 1998, with additional information subsequently provided by one of the military officers interviewed. See also the earlier findings of Thomas A. Marks, "Making Revolution with Shining Path," Ch. 10 in Palmer, *Shining Path*, 191–205. Marks had first conducted fieldwork in Ayacucho in summer 1989.
43. Gabriela Tarazona Sevillana, "The Organization of Shining Path," in Palmer, ed., *Shining Path, op.cit.,* 189–208. Also see David Scott Palmer, "Peru, the Drug Business, and Shining Path: Between Scylla and Charybdis?" *Journal of Interamerican Studies and World Affairs*, 34:3 (1992), 65–88.
44. Detailed in Palmer, "Revolutionary Terrorism."
45. Among various excellent discussions of this turbulent period, see especially Steve J. Stern, ed., *Shining and Other Paths: War and Society in Peru, 1980–1995* (Durham: Duke University Press, 1998).
46. David Scott Palmer, "'Fujipopulism' and Peru's Progress," *Current History*, 95:598 (February 1996), 70–5.
47. Comisión de Juristas Internacionales, *Informe sobre la administración de justicia en el Perú* (Washington, DC: International Jurists Commission, 30 November 1993), Typescript.

48. Benedicto Jiménez Bacca, *Inicio, desarrollo y ocaso del terrorismo en el Peru* (Lima: SANKI, 2000), three volumes, provides a comprehensive summary and analysis. Jiménez was the deputy chief of GEIN.
49. Carlos Tapia, *Las Fuerzas Armadas y Sendero Luminoso: Dos estratégias y un final* (Lima: Instituto de Estudios Peruanos, 1997), esp. 43–55. Also Orin Starn, "Sendero, soldados y ronderos en el Mantaro," *Quehacer* 74, November-December 1991, 64–5.
50. Interviews by Palmer and Marks with military personnel in Ayacucho, July 1998.
51. Starn, "Sendero, soldados y ronderos," 64; Tapia, *Las Fuerzas Armadas*, 47–8.
52. Lewis Taylor, "La estratégia contrainsurgente: El PCP-SL y la guerra civil en el Perú, 1980–1996," *Debate Agrario*, 26, July 1997, 105–6. Based also on Palmer's observations in Ayacucho rural areas, June-August 1998.
53. Objections were overridden, and in 1991, 10,000 *Winchester Model 1300* shotguns were distributed, as well as a larger number of pistols. A 1992 change in the law recognized the people's right to self-defense. Fieldwork by Palmer and Marks, Ayacucho, July 1998. For an overview of the impact of the *rondas campesinas*, see Orin Starn, ed., *Hablan los ronderos: La Búsqueda por la paz en los Andes*, Documento de Trabajo 45 (Lima: Instituto de Estudios Peruanos, 1993).
54. The force-multiplication effect is evident in the figures for the key departments of Ayacucho and Huancavalica, which together were the area of operations for the army's 2nd Division. In mid-1998, while the division had but 2,500 of its own personnel, the militiamen, or *ronderos*, numbered 142,000. This figure, by early 2000, had increased to some 200,000. Field work in Ayacucho by Palmer and Marks, July 1998, and by Palmer, July 2000.
55. David Scott Palmer, "FONCODES y su impacto en la pacificación en el Perú: Observaciones generales y el caso de Ayacucho," in *Concertando para el desarrollo: Lecciones aprendidas del FONCODES en sus estratégias de intervención* (Lima: Fondo Nacional de Compensación y Desarrollo Social – FONCODES, 2001), 147–80.
56. As presented in internal documents of FONCODES and in the annual statistical compendium prepared by Richard Webb and Graciela Fernández Baca, *Perú en números*.
57. The force-multiplication effect is evident in the figures for the key departments of Ayacucho and Huancavalica, which together were the area of operations for the army's 2nd Division. In mid-1998, while the division had but 2,500 of its own personnel, the militiamen, or *ronderos*, numbered 142,000. This figure, by early 2000, had increased to some 200,000. Field work in Ayacucho by Palmer and Marks, July 1998, and by Palmer, July 2000.
58. Palmer, "Revolutionary Terrorism," 301–5.
59. As articulated in his long interview in *El Diario*.

Bibliography

Altamirano, Teófilo. *Exodo: Peruanos en el exterior* [Exodus: Peruvians abroad]. Lima: Pontificia Universidad Católica del Perú, 1992.

Altamirano, Teófilo. *Liderazgo y organizaciones de peruanos en el exterior* [Leadership and peruvian organizations abroad]. Lima: Pontificia Universidad Católica del Perú, 2000.

Arce Borja, Luis and Janet Talavera Sánchez. "La entrevista del siglo: El Presidente Gonzalo rompe el silencio." *El Diario*, July 24 1988, 2–48.

Balan, Jorge. "Latin American Higher Educational Systems in a Historical and Comparative Perspective." [The interview of the century: president Goinzalo speaks.] In *Latin America's New Knowledge Economy*, i–xiv. New York: International Institute of Education, 2013.

Chandler, David P. *Brother Number One: A Political Biography of Pol Pot*. rev ed. Boulder: Westview, 1999.

Comisión de Juristas Internacionales, *Informe sobre la administración de justicia en el Perú* [Report on the rule of law in Peru]. Typescript. Washington, DC: International Jurists Commission. November 30, 1993.

Comisión de la Verdad y Reconciliación Perú, *Informe Final: Tomo I: Primera Parte: El proceso, los hechos, las víctimas*. [Final report, volume 1, part 1: process, events, victims] Lima: Navarrete, 2003.

Degregori, Carlos Iván. *Ayacucho 1969–1979: El surgimiento de Sendero Luminoso* [The rise of shining path]. Lima: Instituto de Estudios Peruanos, 1990.

Degregori, Carlos Iván. "The Origins and Logic of Shining Path: Return to the Past." In *Shining Path of Peru*, 2nd ed., edited by David Scott Palmer, 33–44, 1994.

Dominguez, Esteban Morales and Gary Prevost. *United States-Cuban Relations: A Critical History*. Lanham, MA: Lexington Books, 2008.

Goldstone, Jack A. (ed.). *Revolutions: Theoretical, Comparative, and Historical Studies*. 2nd ed. New York: Harcourt Brace, 1994.

Gorriti Ellenbogen, Gustavo. *Sendero. La historia de la Guerra milenaria en el Perú* [Shining path: The history of millenarian war in Peru]. Lima: Editorial Apoyo, 1990.

Gorriti Ellenbogen, Gustavo. "Shining Path's Stalin and Trotsky." In *Shining Path of Peru*, 2nd ed., edited by David Scott Palmer, 149–170. New York: St. Martin's Press, 1994.

Guzmán Reynoso, Abimael. "English translation and transcription of his interview in prison after his capture." Foreign Broadcast Information Service (FBIS), U.S. Government Printing Office, February 21–23, 1993.

Herring, Hubert. *A History of Latin America*. New York: Knopf, 1955.

Hudson, Rex A. *Castro's Americas Department Coordinating Cuba's Support for Marxist-Leninist Violence in the Americas*. Miami, FL: Cuban American National Foundation, 1988.

Hunefeldt, Christine, Carmen Rosa Balbi, and Francisco Durand in Maxwell A. Cameron and Philip Mauceri, eds. *The Peruvian Labyrinth: Polity, Society, Economy*. University Park: Pennsylvania State University Press, 1997.

Jiménez Bacca, Benedicto. *Inicio, desarrollo y ocaso del terrorismo en el Peru* [The onset, growth, and decline of terrorism in Peru], 3 vols. Lima: Sanki, 2000.

Klarén, Peter F. *Peru: Society and Nationhood in the Andes*. New York: Oxford University Press, 2000.

Levy, Daniel C. *Higher Education and the State in Latin America*. Chicago, IL: University of Chicago Press, 1986.

Marks, Thomas A. "Making Revolution with Shining Path." Chap. 10 in *The Shining Path of Peru*, 2nd ed., edited by David Scott Palmer, 191–205. New York: St. Martin's Press, 1994.

Marks, Thomas A. and David Scott Palmer. "Radical Maoist Insurgents and Terrorist Tactics: Comparing Peru and Nepal." *Low Intensity Conflict and Law Enforcement [now incorporated in Small Wars and Insurgencies]* 13, no. 2 (Autumn 2005): 91–116.

Marks, Thomas A., and David Scott Palmer. "Lessons From Peru." *Counterterrorism* 13, no. 2 (2007): 18–25.

McClintock, Cynthia. "Theories of Revolution and the Case of Peru." In *Shining Path Peru*, 2nd ed., edited by David Scott Palmer, 243–258. New York: St. Martin's Press, 1994.

McClintock, Cynthia, and Abraham Lowenthal, eds. *The Peruvian Experiment Revisited*. Princeton: Princeton University Press, 1982.

Morales Domínguez, Esteban and Gary Prevost. *U.S.-Cuban Relations: A Critical History*. Lanham MD: Lexington Books, 2008.

Palmer, David Scott. "The Authoritarian Tradition in Spanish America." In *Authoritarianism and Corporatism in Latin America*, edited by James Malloy, 377–412. Pittsburgh: University of Pittsburgh Press, 1977.

Palmer, David Scott. "Citizen Responses to Crisis and Political Conflict in Peru: Informal Politics in Ayacucho." In *What Justice? Whose Justice? The Latin American Experience*, edited by Susan Eckstein and Timothy Wickham-Crowley, 233–254. Berkeley: University of California Press, 2003.

Palmer, David Scott. "Countering Terrorism in Latin America: The Case of Shining Path in Peru." In *Essentials of Counterterrorism*, edited by James J. F. Forest, 251–270. Denver: Praeger, 2015.

Palmer, David Scott. "Expulsion from a Peruvian University." In *Cultural Frontiers of the Peace Corps*, edited by Robert B. Textor, 243–270. Cambridge: M.I.T. Press, 1966.

Palmer, David Scott. "'Fujipopulism' and Peru's Progress." *Current History* 95, no. 598 (February 1996): 70–75.

Palmer, David Scott. "FONCODES y su impacto en la pacificación en el Perú: Observaciones generales y el caso de Ayacucho." In *Concertando para el desarrollo: Lecciones aprendidas del FONCODES en sus estratégias de intervención* [The National Compensation and Social Development Fund (FONCODES) and its impact on pacification in Peru: General comments and the case of Ayacucho." In promoting development: Lessons learned from FONCODES and its aid strategies], 147–180. Lima: Fondo Nacional de Compensación y Desarrollo Social – FONCODES, 2001.

Palmer, David Scott. *Peru: The Authoritarian Tradition*. New York: Praeger, 1980.

Palmer, David Scott. "Peru, the Drug Business, and Shining Path: Between Scylla and Charybdis?" *Journal of Interamerican Studies and World Affairs* 34, no. 3 (1992): 65–88.

Palmer, David Scott. "Rebellion in Rural Peru: The Origins and Evolution of Sendero Luminoso." *Comparative Politics* 18, no. 2 (January 1986): 127–146.

Palmer, David Scott. "The Revolutionary Terrorism of Peru's Shining Path." In *Terrorism in Context*, edited by Martha Crenshaw, 249–308. University Park: Pennsylvania State University Press, 1995.

Palmer, David Scott. *The Shining Path of Peru*. 2nd ed. New York: St. Martin's, 1994.

Rock, David. *El radicalismo argentino 1890–1930*. Buenos Aires: Editorial Amorrotu, 1977.

Romero Pintado, Fernando. "New Design for an Old University: San Cristóbal de Huamanga." *Américas* (December 1961): 9–16.

del Perú, Senado. *Comité Especial sobre las Causas de la Violencia y las Alternativas de Pacificación en el Perú, Violencia y pacificación* [Senado del Peru...violence and pacification]. DESCO and Comisión Andina de Juristas: Lima, 1989.

Skcopol, Theda. *States and Social Revolutions: A Comparative Analysis of France, Russia, and China*. New York: Cambridge University Press, 1979.

Skcopol, Theda. *Social revolutions in the modern world*. New York: Cambridge University Press, 1994.

Selbin, Eric. *Modern Latin American Revolutions*. 2nd ed. Boulder: Westview, 1999.

Starn, Orin. "Sendero, soldados y ronderos en el Mantaro." [Shining path, soldiers, and civil defence committees in the Mantaro calley.] *Quehacer* 74 (November–December 1991), 60–68.

Starn, Orin (ed.). *Hablan los ronderos: La Búsqueda por la paz en los Andes* [Civil defence committee members speak: The search for peace in the Andes], Documento de Trabajo 45. Lima: Instituto de Estudios Peruanos, 1993.

Stern, Steve J. (ed.). *Shining and Other Paths: War and Society in Peru, 1980–1995*. Durham, NC: Duke University Press, 1998.

Strong, Simon. *Sendero Luminoso: El movimiento subversivo más letal del mundo* [Shining path: The world's deadliest subversive movement]. Lima: Peru Reporting, 1992.

Tapia, Carlos. *Las Fuerzas Armadas y Sendero Luminoso: Dos estratégias y un final* [The armed forces and shining path: Two strategies and a result]. Lima: Instituto de Estudios Peruanos, 1997.

Tarazona Sevillana, Gabriela. "The Organization of Shining Path." In *Shining Path Peru*, 2nd ed., edited by David Scott Palmer, 189–208. New York: St. Martin's Press, 1994.

Taylor, Lewis. "La estratégia contrainsurgente: El PCP-SL y la guerra civil en el Perú [Counterinsurgency strategy: Shining path and civil war in Peru], 1980–1996." *Debate Agrario* 26 (July 1997): 81–110.

Véliz, Claudio. *The Centralist Tradition in Latin America*. Princeton, NJ: Princeton University Press, 1980.

Webb, Richard, and Graciela Fernández Baca. *Peru en números 2000* [Peru in numbers, 2000]. Lima: Cuánto, 2001.

Wiarda, Howard J., and Harvey F. Kline. *Latin American Politics and Development*. 3rd ed. Boulder: Westview Press, 1990.

People's war antithesis: Che Guevara and the mythology of *Focismo*

Paul B. Rich

ABSTRACT
This paper re-evaluates the role and significance of Che Guevara and *focismo* in the strategic debate on insurgent warfare. It argues that Guevara's approach to making revolution in Latin America and the Third World emerged out of his own earlier escapades as a restless tourist travelling through South and Central America in the early 1950s. Guevara's life was one marked by a struggle to define an identity in a continent that he saw as dominated by the informal imperial power of the US. *Focismo* crystallised in the years after the Cuban Revolution in 1959 into an ideological concept supportive of the Castro regime's claims to provide a distinctive new model of Third World revolution in opposition to those of the Soviet Union and China. *Focismo* has survived in the contemporary era as an approach that partly describes some modern terrorist and Jihadist movements in the Middle East.

Che Guevara was once viewed as one of the major 'guerrilla theorists' of the Twentieth Century along with other notables such as T.E Lawrence, Mao Zedong, and Vo Nguyen Giap.[1] In more recent years, his importance in the strategic debate on modern insurgencies has declined markedly, though he can yet be viewed as a figure worthy of inclusion in the historical evolution of guerrilla warfare.[2] Assessing Guevara's legacy has been hampered, though, by a wider political mythology focused on his role as a Twentieth Century revolutionary dying, Shelley-like, at a young age. It is an important discussion since the *foco* strategy offers a very different approach from that of people's war. Linked in oppositional time and space to people's war, it was criticised in its day and remains spectacular only in its image and lack of success.

Compared to Mao's rather brief claims to 'revolutionary immortality' in the years of the Chinese Cultural Revolution in the 1960's, Guevara has transcended his own time.[3] Analysts examining Che's place in the pantheon of twentieth century guerrilla theorists find that discussion quickly becomes complicated by this global mythology, especially in Central and South America, where, since the thirtieth anniversary of his death in 1997, there has been a resurgence of Che memorabilia. Tourists can buy Guevara mugs, drawings, paintings, T-shirts, and CD recordings of the song *Comandante Che Guevara*.[4] The Che myth is an interesting example of masculine hero worship, somewhat at odds with Guevara's commitment to Marxist revolution. Here the myth reinforces an image of Che as a modern-day saviour, made only too redolent by an early death in Bolivia pictorialized world-wide in images of a bearded Christ-like corpse being ignominiously poked by army officers.[5] At other levels, fascination with Che reflects the commercialisation of a myth-metaphor forged in the late 1960's by a radical trans-Atlantic student counter-culture but also embraced by some South American urban insurgent movements such as the Tupamaros in Uruguay.[6]

The Guevara revolutionary myth derives from a personality cult forged around him in the early 1960s in the aftermath of the Cuban Revolution. Guevara started his career as a kind of radical tourist before his dramatic death in Bolivia. The Che myth that emerged after 1967 transformed him into a global celebrity, dovetailing with the emergence of a backpacker generation keen to traverse continents in search of adventure and self-knowledge. Guevara's career was one of continuous and rapid movement, starting with journeys that traversed the South American continent in the early 1950s in a restless quest for a new identity. In 1954 he briefly encounters an American-organised counter-revolution in Guatemala; then he meets up with Fidel and Raúl in Mexico City before setting out in the *Granma* on a campaign of guerrilla war in Cuba at the end of 1956, leading to the rapid overthrow of the Batista regime at the end of 1958. This background shaped and inspired his own thoughts on guerrilla warfare and *focismo* as part of a quixotic programme of continental and even global Third World revolution, leading eventually to a miserable end in southeast Bolivia in 1967.

I will examine these themes in three parts: In the first part, I will look at the evolution of Che's political outlook during the 1950s, and their disconnection with Maoist ideas of protracted war will be treated. In the second part, I will discuss how *focismo* emerged in the 1960's with a critical contribution from the French Marxist Regis Debray. In the third part, I will examine the impact of this guerrilla doctrine in the context of American strategy towards Central and South America. Finally, in some concluding remarks, I will briefly examine the longer-term significance of the Che myth and explore how far *focismo* can be seen to have been reinvented by more recent jihadist insurgent movements.

Evolution of Che's revolutionary thought

Che's political outlook is usually viewed in terms of a rebellious medical student abandoning his secure bourgeois background in Argentina to travel across the continent in two trips in 1950 and 1953–1956. In 1954 in Guatemala, he became a fervent Marxist inspired by his Peruvian communist lover Hilda Gadea, whom he eventually married in Mexico. This view tends to underplay the role of the journeys across South America in the early 1950s, a period that has often been relegated to a sort of juvenile background before the real action begins in Cuba. Travelling across Latin America gave Che an identity as a tourist that he continued to maintain as a cover after moving into revolutionary politics. Right up until the time he embarked on the *Granma* for Cuba at the end of 1956, Guevara was essentially a tourist adventurer, raising serious questions about whether *focismo* is really a form of deviant revolutionary tourism.

Tourism is a complex pattern of human behaviour infused with varying ideological assumptions.[7] Unless tourists are well informed about the places they visit, they are highly prone to viewing them in terms of dominant myths about peoples, places, and cultures, often of a static and outdated kind. From the time of his first travels in 1950, Guevara took more and more trouble to find out about the locations he visited, and his diaries are full of observations of Inca, Aztec, and Maya ruins. Sometimes, these sites seem to be more important to him than the current politics of the societies he was passing through, despite his broad commitment to revolutionary change in South America. Being a 'tourist' provided a convenient cover when Guevara found himself in trouble with state authorities, such as in Mexico City in 1956, after he was arrested by the police after training as a guerrilla.[8] Even after the Cuban Revolution, travel appears to have been one of his main aims. When he was asked by the undercover CIA agent David Atlee Phillips in a Havana bar, sometime in 1959, what he planned to do next in life, he remarked, 'I will travel and take the revolution with me.'[9] While clearly a joke, the remark confirmed that there was a link, in Guevara's mind at least, between travelling and promoting revolution in some form or other.

The Motorcycle Diaries, together with the more recently published diary *Back on the Road* covering the period 1953–1956, provides considerable insight into Guevara's adventurist approach to politics and the societies of Latin America. He came from the predominantly white upper-class society of Buenos Aires that had emerged in the late nineteenth century as another version of 'settler colonialism' comparable to Australasia, South Africa, French Algeria, and modern Israel. This variant of colonialism is defined less in terms of the domination of a colonised majority by a small colonial minority (for example the Indian Raj) than the expropriation of land from the indigenous inhabitants and their progressive marginalisation or even total liquidation by communities of settlers embarking on the creation of a new kind of society.[10] As recently as the 1880s, the native Indian cultures on the pampas had been conquered and destroyed by a ruthless class of gaucho cattlemen backed up by the Argentinian army, who systematically massacred the Indian population in Patagonia. Though Argentina had evolved a sophisticated civil society by the 1930s and 1940s, Guevara rebelled against the restrictions of a social order that retained many colonial features. The country was, after all, governed by a quasi-colonial upper-class highly beholden to Britain and the United States until the emergence of the populist nationalism of Juan Peron after World War II. Guevara developed an intense loathing for US influence and power in South America, whilst maintaining a very American form of radicalism that led him to replace the 'American Dream' with a quixotic myth of continental Marxist revolution. While he spent his life in such a quest, it was also the case, as one biographer, Jorge Castaneda, points out, that 'the poor, the proletarians and Communists might be brothers – but they were essentially foreign to him.'[11]

Moving beyond his native Argentina led Guevara to question the very idea of Latin American statehood. The states that had emerged from the imperial retreat of Spain and Portugal in the nineteenth century seemed superficial European constructions imposed on the continent. Guevara developed a wider idea of a South American *patria grande*, a form of Pan Americanism bearing some resemblance to Pan Africanism and Pan Arabism. He continued to identify culturally with his native Argentina, especially its literature and music, though his preoccupation with establishing an identity led him to avoid investigating too deeply the histories and cultures he encountered, confirming Zeldin's observation that people searching for roots often end up only scratching the surface of the world around them.[12]

Certainly, Guevara imagined that, by travelling across Latin America, he could, in some way, create a new relationship to the continent and its plethora of peoples, about which he knew little. He was shocked by the level of poverty he encountered and blamed much of this on exploitation by American capitalist concerns. Unlike Mao writing about Chinese peasant culture in the context of the Japanese invasion of the 1930s, he could not look back to some indigenous Latin American culture capable of being easily mobilised in the continent's defence. He found the Araucanian Indians silent and defensive towards white men such as himself, 'shrugging their shoulders and saying "don't know" or "maybe", quickly ending the conversation.'[13] Later, when he encountered the Aymaras in Peru, he viewed the valley where they lived as lost in time, where 'evolution had been suspended' and the people were 'tame, almost fearful, and completely indifferent to the outside world'. Yet, these same people would become one of the key centres of the Maoist guerrilla insurgency in Peru three decades later.[14]

There is little recognition here that Che and his companion would be treated as anything less than visiting tourists, short of staying for a long period, learning the local language, and winning the trust and confidence of the 'defeated race.' He comes across as uninformed about the debate in Peru since the 1920s over 'indigenismo' and the place of its native peoples in the forging of a distinct Peruvian culture. Neither did he seem aware of a tradition of peasant unrest in the rural areas, although most opposition by the early 1950s was in the cities following the crackdown on the left-leaning populist American Popular

Revolutionary Alliance (APRA) by the military regime of General Odria, a movement he came to loath even though his lover and eventual wife, Hilda Gadea, had been prominently involved in it before she went to Guatemala.[15]

Guevara was certainly an inquisitive traveller in his tourist adventures; but even as he become better informed about the archaeological sites he was visiting, he tended to be locked into a static and ahistorical view of South American indigenous cultures. When he visited Mayan ruins in Mexico in 1956, for instance, he viewed them through the work of the archaeologist Sylvanus Griswold Morley, a towering figure in American archaeology in the 1930s and 1940s (he was also an agent for US naval intelligence in the First World War, and some have seen him as a possible model for Steven Spielberg's Indiana Jones) but already partly displaced by more historically-focused work.[16] Morley's pioneering work reinforced the idea that Mayan culture was a static pacifist theocracy standing outside time. This suggests that Guevara tended to see the remains, along with those of the Incas and Aztecs, as symbols of the continent's ancient greatness and capacity to stand up for itself in the future, though this would only occur within the context of continental-wide revolution. Guevara's thinking evolved in the early 1950s in a Marxist-Leninist direction, though he was careful to avoid joining a communist party, mainly, it seems, because this might threaten his chances of getting a visa to travel to the US and Europe. He was, for a period, closely involved with the radical figure Hilda Gadea, though her influence has been rather overstated. Another sporadic influence was the Marxist American scholar Harold White, again in the chaotic circumstances of Guatemala in 1954. The most important systematic Marxist influence would not really come until after the Cuban Revolution when Guevara became acquainted with the French philosopher Regis Debray, though by then the basic idea of *focismo* had already formed in his mind.

Guevara's political radicalism stemmed initially from his shock at the plight of the continent's poor, whom he met on his first journey in 1950. His sympathy resembled other outsiders such as missionaries, especially American Protestants, eager to save lost and demoralised communities. At another level, travelling as a tourist confirmed only too starkly the dichotomy between an apparently static Indian and indigenous past and the exploitative features of modernity. The dichotomy had evolved since the early Twentieth Century as part of the wider impact of what Ricardo Salvatore has termed the 'representational machine' of US informal imperialism on the continent. South America has experienced since the early Nineteenth Century, Salvatore has suggested, not one but two separate informal imperial influences: first, a British one experienced mainly through a commercial nexus anchored in shipping, insurance, and the export of commodities. This was relatively superficial and defined mainly in terms of the accumulation and classification of knowledge about the continent and its peoples. US informal imperialism, on the other hand, was far more penetrating given that it was driven by the demands of a corporate capitalism, such as mining companies in South America and United

Fruit in Central America. This informal imperialism became defined by wide-ranging patterns of information disseminated through popular magazines such as *National Geographic*, the Hollywood movie industry, the nascent tourist industry, and the strategic need, by the time of the Cold War, to define 'South America' geopolitically as part of the Americas but different in kind to 'Central America', where the US maintained a far more interventionist, quasi-colonial presence.[17]

Guevara's relationship to the continent was thus inherently ambiguous. He displayed a marked engagement for the Latin American poor without wishing to get too closely involved in understanding the peoples and cultures of the continent in any depth. He never attempted any serious sociological or historical approach, comparable, for example, to T.E Lawrence's efforts to understand the cultures of the Arab tribes he sought to mobilise against the Turks, though he did vaguely toy with the idea of taking up 'anthropology' (a word that also in the 1950's embraced archaeology). But he rejected the idea, mainly because he could not accept that 'the lodestar of my life could be the study of what is now dead beyond recall.'[18] Instead, he adopted an all-encompassing Marxist theory to navigate through complex cultural and sociological issues. This would lead him to avoid any serious sociological or anthropological examination of how to win over and sustain the support of suspicious peasant communities, often speaking little or no Spanish, for the project of rural guerrilla war. The approach led him to talk with enormous confidence about the continent. By mid-1955, he wrote to his mother in Buenos Aires that he felt able to write a book about 'The Function of the Doctor in Latin America,' because he now had 'Latin America sized up.'[19]

This outlook bears some similarities to what the Tunisian intellectual Albert Memmi termed the 'coloniser who refuses.' Cutting himself adrift from the largely white colonial society of Argentina, Che attempted to empathize with the plight of the poor and oppressed in Latin America even as he found that he encountered these communities mostly as an outsider and often ended up being treated as a social superior capable of gaining concessions unimaginable to ordinary Chileans or Peruvians.[20] There are difficulties, Memmi suggests, in trying to maintain such a stance. On the one hand, the revolting coloniser wants to obtain the 'love' of the colonised; on the other, he finds it difficult to maintain this standpoint given that it is little different from that of a tourist. 'As a tourist one can become enamoured and perhaps interested in it for a time,' Memmi points out, 'but one ends up tiring of it and shielding himself (*sic*) from the original attraction.'[21]

Sooner or later, the refusing coloniser needs to make some sort of distinct life-style choice to avoid becoming a 'remittance man' dependent on money sent from his wealthy family lest he slip down into the roving underclass of semi-panhandlers living off the tourist industry. Guevara faced a crisis of this kind following his second tour through the continent, when he arrived in Guatemala in January 1954, a few months before the CIA-backed military overthrow of the left-leaning Arbenz government. He did receive, somewhat ungratefully, some financial support from his family back in Buenos Aires, and he also undertook temporary forms of income, including photographing tourists in Mexico City, while also undertaking various forms of low paid medical research. But it was during this period that he began a systematic reading of Marxist texts along with continued tourist trips to local attractions. Indeed, tourism appears to have provided an outlet for his energies as he found it difficult to relate to the circles of exiled South American radicals. Che continued with this tourism even after he became aware, by early February, that some sort of US-backed military incursion was imminent. He failed to immerse himself in the politics of the opposition in Guatemala, 60% of whose population was descended from Maya Indians. It also appears that one of the main reasons for eventually leaving the country was as much his failure to find paid employment as the turn of political events, though the local CIA station did get as far as starting a file on him.[22]

Guevara's six months in Guatemala in 1954 epitomised his approach to revolution, rooted as it was in myth rather than any serious understanding of the historical trajectory of individual societies. Guatemala was one of the closest examples that the US came to running an actual colony in Central America. It was one of the most backward of the 'banana republics,' where the United Fruit Company owned not only large tracts of land but much of the transport infrastructure. It also enjoyed a close relationship to senior figures in the Eisenhower administration, rendering it comparable to earlier examples of monopolistic imperial trading companies such as the British East India Company in the Eighteenth Century. The country lacked a developed rural guerrilla movement, which only emerged in the wake of the downfall of Arbenz. Indeed, the place was gripped, Richard Gott has suggested, by a myth that no revolution could ever succeed while the US could topple governments at will, a myth that was only broken with the Cuban Revolution five years later.[23]

The few months Guevara spent in Guatemala were crucial in fomenting a Marxist revolutionary commitment. Rather than trying to learn the local Mayan language, he spent some of his scarce funds learning English from a radical American professor, Harold White. Guatemala City played host to a variety of Latin American political exiles in a heady atmosphere of political discussions and debate, though Guevara also wrote to a friend that, while being 'interesting,' Guatemala 'like all revolutions…loses something with intimacy.'[24] Revolution was, at this stage, still another stimulating attraction to be added to the roster of tourist sites that Che had already encountered. It would take a few more years to evolve over time into a more refined concept of guerrilla warfare.[25]

But Guevara's rudimentary commitment to Marxism-Leninism became intertwined, after 1955, with the one serious revolutionary project in town: Castro's plan to invade and overthrow the Batista regime in Cuba. It was in Mexico City that Che first met the charismatic figure of Fidel, who had fled there after being released from prison by Batista where he had been lodged due to his involvement in the attack on the Moncada barracks in 1953. Fidel had moved from being an urban *Moncadista* towards becoming a guerrilla fighter, though the exact form this was to take remained vague. Taking up arms to fight the guerrilla war in the Sierra Maestra provided Guevara with a new identity as a revolutionary struggling for a just cause, even though he knew at this stage little about Cuba and its peoples. By 1956, he had become a firm Marxist-Leninist in outlook and had largely broken from Hilda Gadea, whom he described as a 'misguided representative of the worthy anti-communist party, the APRA'.[26] Broadly sympathetic to the Soviet Union, he had at this stage no fervent commitment to guerrilla war and was mostly drawn to the Cubans by shared language and cultural outlook. They offered a route out of Mexico which, like Guatemala, remained a largely foreign culture that Guevara had made no serious attempt to understand. The Cuban exiles were Spanish-speaking revolutionaries, though Fidel's approach was at this stage more one of Jose Marti than Marx immersed, as he was, in coordinating the activities of his 26th July Movement. The relationship between the two men was captured in a photograph taken while they were held in prison for a few weeks in mid-1956. As Simon Red-Henry has pointed out, the picture reveals an evolving relationship between Fidel on the left, dressed as a rather brash urban city slicker and bourgeois nationalist, and Guevara, on the right, who appears as an unkempt student radical, peering curiously towards Castro's composed and self-contained figure (see Plate 1).[27]

Guevara was desperate to escape Mexico, and the Cuban expedition was clearly the best option available. It not only enabled him to leave Hilda (now with a small child) but was attractive for the way it at least had some money behind it, even if the actual planning left much to be desired. Castro sought

Plate 1. Fidel and Che in prison in Mexico. 1956.

funding from wealthy opponents of Batista, wading on one occasion across the Rio Grande into Texas to meet the former Cuban president Rafael del Pino in McAllen where he secured USD 50,000, funds – some observers have speculated – that really came from the CIA, keen at this stage to keep its options open towards Castro's movement.[28] The decision to embark with some 82 men for Cuba on the grossly over-laden *Granma*[29] a few months later was not based on any sort of *focista* concept, since Castro maintained close links at this stage with the urban underground (the *llano* or plains-based groups) in Cuba.[30]

The Cuban adventure seemed to Che to be one step beyond tourism, writing to his mother sometime in November 1956, 'Now, when I get to a new country, it won't be to look around and visit museums or ruins, but also (because that still interests me) to join the people's struggle.'[31] The *Granma's* landing was timed to coincide with an insurrection to be organised by the student leader Frank Pais in Santiago. The boat, though, landed further down the coast from Santiago and was spotted by Batista's coast guard, leading the plan to go awry. The small party of some 22 men who survived the landing (not the New Testament 12 of the official revolutionary myth) made their way conveniently into the Sierra Maestra. More were quickly recruited from the *llano*, as well as a few semi-peasant squatters inhabiting one of the poorest and most disadvantaged regions of Cuba.

There was little here that resembled the Maoist peasant revolutionary model. Castro had initially taken the initiative by having the squad intended for the *Granma* trained in some basic guerrilla techniques by a Spanish civil war veteran, General Alberto Bayo, at the Rancho San Miguel some 35 miles east of Mexico City. Bayo found Guevara was of the ablest of the student guerrillas in a training programme that involved long night hikes with little food and learning navigational skills.[32] The training provided Guevara with an opportunity to rise quickly as a guerrilla leader, despite his asthma attacks, and this would continue once the party found themselves in the Sierra Maestra.

At this stage, Guevara and Castro attached little importance to Maoist concepts of guerrilla war. Guevara had never displayed any real desire to visit Cuba before he went there with Castro and cautioned Hilda Gadea against doing so herself when he was in Guatemala.[33] Regis Debray has asserted that neither man read Mao's *Problems of Strategy in Guerrilla War Against Japan* until late 1958.[34] Guevara would eventually visit China in the 1960's, but he never attempted to get to know Maoism at first hand by talking to former guerrillas; and Boot is incorrect when he asserts that he came to 'embrace Maoist China as his model.'[35] He sporadically referred to events such as the Long March, but the Chinese model of peasant-driven revolution remained a distant one, and the impression is that he tended to view the whole Asian experience of insurgency, Chinese and Vietnamese alike, as inherently ill-suited to South American conditions. He also avoided any emphasis on a revolutionary vanguard party, though Lacquer is incorrect to suggest that he attached little importance to ideology and political education. *Focismo* often involved intense political discussion on the various experiments tried out in the 1960s, though these were conducted more through collective group-think than formal education instilled by party cadre.[36]

There were strong political reasons, before the revolution at the end of 1958, to play down any sort of Marxist theory of insurgency. Castro needed to maintain close links with the *llano* groups, both to sustain the guerrillas as well as avoid upsetting the Eisenhower administration or the more conservative elements of the anti-Batista opposition. The image he endeavoured to present was one that appeared to draw most of its inspiration from the earlier nationalist struggle against Spain at the end of the Nineteenth Century and the heroic figure of Jose Marti, campaigning for some nationalisation of land and redistribution of wealth, in a programme that was in no obvious way Marxist.

Castro, after all, had initially attempted an urban insurrection with the attack on the Moncada Barracks in 1953, and the strong links to the *llano* groups suggested that any future attempt to overthrow Batista could hardly be an entirely rural one. To the extent that it is possible to talk of a 'Sierra Maestra model' in Cuba, the strategy combined rural insurgency with urban insurrection and strike action that ended up surprising both Castro and Che by the speed of Batista's collapse. This was as much an urban as a rural revolt, but neither man had any interest in playing up the *llano* groups' role. In terms of Maoist theory, the Sierra Maestra venture was 'adventurist' and heretical, though the divergence became evident only as the Cuban 'model' of the *foco* became ideological doctrine during the early 1960s.

In the process, the exponents of *focismo* found themselves departing markedly from the Maoist 'line.' In 1938, Mao had warned in *Problems of Strategy in Guerrilla War Against Japan* that guerrilla war, in the first instance, is defensive. While guerrilla warfare might provide, on occasions, some opportunities for tactical offensives in the form of surprise attacks against the enemy, it was, first and foremost, part of a wider defensive strategy encompassing more regular forms of war. Guerrilla war, for Mao, was secondary in a strategy of 'protracted war' that required patience and endurance. He warned against waging peasant type wars of the 'roving rebel' type which were never likely to lead to long-term military victories, especially as 'in the minds of guerrilla commanders it becomes the view that base areas are neither necessary or important.'[37]

It was Castro rather than Guevara who drove strategy in Cuba from the *Granma*'s landing to Batista's eventual departure at the end of 1958. While urban insurrection of the Trotskyist kind had clearly not worked, he recognised that protracted guerrilla war was not necessarily inevitable given the relatively small size of Cuba and the difficulties of maintaining a Yenan-type base area for a long period. What emerged was a rural insurrection that quickly became inter-connected with the *llano* groups given the relatively efficient transport and communications links across the island. Most of the inhabitants living in the rural areas of Cuba by the late 1950s were no longer peasants in the classic sense of autonomous small landholders but a rural proletariat working seasonally for the large, and mainly American-owned, agri-businesses. The population living around the Sierra Maestra were exceptions to this general trend, being in the main poor farmers known colloquially as *guajiros* (hillbillies), while others were illegal squatters called *precaristas*. Over most of the rest of the island, by contrast, there resided rural working class communities tied as clients to the Batista regime by what Eric Wolf has termed a 'quasi syndicalist' type bureaucracy.[38]

Fighting in the Sierra Maestra and Oriente province in eastern Cuba plunged Castro's force into an insurrection reminiscent of Nineteenth Century bandit struggles, requiring from the start little mass political mobilisation. The *quajiros* were recruited to work on the large estates owned by absentee landlords. They were chosen by tough *mayorales* who were especially hostile towards the *precaristas*. Thomas has pointed to a state of near-civil war between the *mayorales* and the *precaristas* that had been going on for years before Che and Fidel arrived, ensuring the insurgency developed out of an ongoing rural insurrection.[39] Assassinating the *mayorales* was an easy way to gain the support of *precaristas* and *quajiros*, some of whom were eager to join the guerrillas. The campaign, certainly in the early stages, resembled the sort of rural insurrection envisaged by the veteran French revolutionary Auguste Blanqui, based as it was on a small group of well-organised and -motivated group of men taking over the state when the right moment presented itself.[40] By so doing, the revolution effectively became its own justification, though in the process it also generated some peasant resistance that eventually took a counter-revolutionary form in the early 1960s, especially in the Escambray Mountains of Oriente, a rebellion that became forgotten both by the Cuban government propaganda and right wing exiles in Miami alike.[41]

Castro's guerrillas were also never that isolated, since they were constantly supported by the *llano* groups, which also arranged for the visit of the veteran American news reporter Herbert Matthews to the *sierra* in March 1957.[42] Both Castro and Guevara had a joint interest in promoting a mythology around rural guerrilla warfare, Castro because he saw the guerrillas as providing a power base he could control as opposed to the 26th July Movement which threatened to undermine his control over the new revolutionary Cuban state. Guevara, by contrast, had a rather more ideological commitment to the guerrilla myth. It was, after all, a form of war in which he had felt he had excelled as a guerrilla leader, and he felt instinctively close to the rural recruits who joined the guerrillas rather than to those from the cities. Fighting as a guerrilla not only confirmed for Guevara his identity as a revolutionary but one that led him to distrust urban radicals. Indeed, the revolutionary commitment of many of the activists in the 26th July Movement seemed to Guevara highly questionable, as it had been the urban resistance which had proved crucial in the latter phases of the revolution when Bastista's demoralised army started to collapse. Fighting in the *sierra* gave Guevara an opportunity to present himself as Latin America's own home-grown version of Mao. From 1962 onwards, he began to refine the idea of guerrilla warfare from the experience gained in the Sierra Maestra and to plan a new series of revolutionary *focos*, starting in South America but expanding to Africa, as part of a global strategy of insurgent-based revolution.

The emergence of *Focismo*

The theory of *focismo* has been associated as much with the French Marxist philosopher Regis Debray as with Guevara.[43] Debray's book, *Revolution in the Revolution*, certainly became a favourite text among the Western New Left in the late 1960s. It appeared to offer a quick path to revolution without the attendant dangers of a Leninist party vanguard, though some analysts on the right suggested that *focismo* was little more than a transitional doctrine between rural guerrilla warfare and later patterns of urban terrorism.[44] Both these interpretations tend to neglect the evolution of *focismo* by Guevara and Debray in the context of several guerrilla forays prior to the Bolivian fiasco in 1966–1967.

Che was gradually attracted to *focismo* in the years after the Cuban Revolution. By 1963, he saw it as a useful concept to demonstrate how guerrillas could attain tactical superiority as well as to exemplify the inherent moral virtue of rural guerrilla struggle, involving as it did rigorous discipline, self-reliance, and a suspicion that too much external aid that might well dilute revolutionary commitment. The widely read book *Guerrilla Warfare* (1960), however, avoided using the term specifically; and Paret, in his essay on guerrilla warfare in 1962, does not use the term either when examining Guevara's thinking.[45] Indeed, Guevara seems initially to have viewed the rural guerrilla fighter more as an armed missionary than an ideologically inspire *focoista*, urging that he needed to be like a 'guiding angel who has fallen into the zone, helping the poor always and bothering the rich as little as possible.'[46]

Much of what Che had to say about guerrilla insurgencies still amplified the works of Mao, as he pointed to the need to build up the guerrilla organisation, to look to the training and indoctrination of recruits, and to establish secure supply lines. He also envisaged popular forces eventually winning a guerrilla insurgency, though this was a form of war that should be mainly fought in the countryside. He departed from an orthodox Maoist perspective by avoiding the issues of base areas, and the book lacked any distinct trajectory for a guerrilla war and its transformation into positional war. He simply remarked that 'the enemy falls when the process of partial victories becomes transformed into final victories, that is to say, when the enemy is brought to accept battle in conditions imposed by the guerrilla band; there he is annihilated and his surrender compelled.'[47]

This was a highly optimistic conception of guerrilla war and its role in wider strategy. The implication was that guerrilla warfare, on its own, might defeat a regular army and provoke the revolutionary overthrow of states far more advanced than Batista's Cuba. Some Western analysts, though, studying what was then called 'internal war,' were struck by the way Che distinguished *focismo* from terrorism.[48] Che's approach began to diverge between 1960 and 1963 from the Maoist model of 'peoples war' of mass political mobilisation, the training of guerrillas to accept lengthy or 'protracted' war, the creation of base areas, and the projection of a national appeal through 'united front' tactics.[49] There were growing political imperatives for Guevara to spell out more precisely the differences between the Cuban revolutionary 'model' and Maoist 'people's war.' As the Sino-Soviet split intensified, Maoist 'people's war' became simplified by China into a propaganda model suitable for export, especially to states in Southeast Asia such as Malaya, Indonesia, and Thailand. Maoist 'people's war' became a robust ideological concept increasingly well-known around the 'Third World' and would be eventually linked, via the writings of Lin Biao, to the Cultural Revolution in the years after 1966.

Marks has noted how the people's war concept stresses the need for what the Vietnamese came to call a 'war of interlocking,' in which war was waged simultaneously through a series of forms – political, military, rural and urban, violent and non-violent – rather than fighting exclusively a rural guerrilla war.[50] In Cuba, the struggle to establish the legitimacy of the Castroite revolution worked against support for such a symbiosis. The shift to the left in the early 1960s heightened domestic class conflict and led to the exodus of a considerable section of the Cuban middle class, some of whom had supported the left-leaning *llano* groups in the period prior to Batista's departure. Guevara's claim to the legitimacy of the revolution thus came through support for rural guerrilla warfare as he increasingly opposed the *llano* groups.

It was cinema, as much as anything, that proved crucial in the early stages of the revolution for dissemination of the *foco* guerrilla myth. Guevara started a military cultural school in Havana as early as 14 January 1959 in the La Cabana fortress, where he also interrogated and executed political prisoners. The school made several propaganda documentaries, moving into features the following year.[51] One of the most notable of these was the 81-min neorealist *Historias de la revolucion*, directed with considerable verve by the Cuban director Tomas Gutierrez Alea. It had three interlocking narratives, recalling Roberto Rossellini's 1946 film *Paisa*.[52] The first narrative was *el herido* (the wounded man), dealing with the resistance of the *llano* groups; the second, *Rebeldes*, focused on the insurgency in the Sierra Maestra; the third, *La batailla de Santa Clara*, covered Guevara's great battle in Santa Clara before the collapse of the Batista regime. The movie was a propaganda triumph for *focismo*. It portrayed the *llano* groups as nervous, divided, and disorientated by Batista's security forces, engaged in an increasingly desperate struggle as they flee through the back alleys of Havana. Although they shoot one policeman, two bodies of the *llano* group portrayed are left out in the street to warn others of the dangers of tackling Batista's brutal regime, which appears to be in its element in the city. One of the *llano* radicals manages to secure the help of a compassionate working class milk-man in evading arrest, but the overall message is that these bourgeois radicals are simply not very good in standing up to Batista's well-armed police.

The second narrative, by contrast, reveals a considerably different situation in the *sierra*, where a group of bearded, Guevara-like guerrillas blow up an army truck with an IED before hiding out in the forest. Compared to the *llano* groups, they are composed and highly focused, mainly trying to save the life of a wounded man and seemingly unconcerned about the shots of advancing troops. The guerrillas confidently make their way to safety up steep mountain slopes and emerge as a self-reliant and competent *foco*, though the narrative avoided outlining how they gained fresh equipment and supplies beyond those captured from the enemy.

The third narrative complements the second by bringing the story forward to late December 1958. The revolutionary movement that is now apparently unstoppable as it reaches Santa Clara. It is also well versed in fighting in the town as much as the *sierra* and once again shows up the limitations of the disorganised *llano* groups.

Historias de la revolucion began the steady mythologization of the *sierra* struggle, even though the film was not seen widely outside Cuba and the Soviet Union, where it was shown at the Second Moscow International Film Festival. It laid the foundations for a narrative that Guevara would continue in his own *Reminiscences of the Cuban Revolutionary War* in 1963, based on notes he had made during the guerrilla campaign of 1956–1958. Che distinguished two separate and opposing 'tendencies' prior to the revolution. Those in the *sierra*, he claimed, fought a guerrilla struggle that led to the encirclement of the cities and 'by strangulation and attrition' managed to 'destroy the entire apparatus of the regime.' The *llano* groups, in contrast, had an 'ostensibly more revolutionary position' based on 'armed struggle in all towns, culminating in a general strike which would topple Batista and allow the prompt taking of power.' This conception, Che argued, was 'too narrow,' exemplified by the failure of the general strike called in Havana on 9 April 1958.[53]

Che accused the *llano* groups of a syndicalist approach to revolutionary change, although he overlooked how support from the *llano* groups had been crucial in the struggle in the Sierra Maestra. Even if Che's argument against the strike strategy of the *llano* groups was true, it still ignored one of the basic precepts of Maoist people's war of a united front and suggested that he really had another agenda of his own at a time when Cuba was falling ever more closely into the Soviet sphere of influence. In Cuba, the struggle to establish the legitimacy of the Castroite revolution worked against support for such united front tactics. The shift to the left in the early 1960s heightened domestic class conflict and led to the exodus of a considerable section of the Cuban middle class, some of whom had supported the left-leaning *llano* groups in the period prior to Batista's departure. Guevara's claim to the legitimacy of the revolution came through support for rural guerrilla warfare, and he increasingly opposed the *llano* groups. By 1963, the issue became starkly evident when Guevara first published *Reminiscences of the Cuban Revolutionary War*.

For Guevara, there was a growing appeal in *focismo* as the basis for a revolutionary myth that was, in part, an apparent doctrinal breakthrough in the Marxist theory of guerrilla war and, in part, a means to project his own role as a new kind of Latin American, if not Third World, Mao. He did not, as J. Bowyer Bell suggested in *The Myth of the Guerrilla*, 'misunderstand' a doctrine of Third World revolution disseminated by Frantz Fanon but forged one anew to accord with Cuban government policy as well as his own restless desire to promote revolutionary struggle wherever possible against American power and influence.[54] Guevara acknowledged that the main actors behind the Cuban Revolution, such as Fidel, Raúl, and himself, had 'no coherent theoretical criteria' even if they were not ignorant of 'the various concepts of history, society, economics and revolution.'[55] Within two to three years of Batista's overthrow, he began to find this a political hindrance, while more widely *focismo* became one of the core underlying principles behind Cuban government policy in international forums such as the Organisation of Latin American Solidarity (OLAS) and the Tricontinental. What might be termed a 'Guevarist line' now became a major component in Cuban efforts to combat isolation as well as distinguish itself from the more 'revisionist' line of the Soviet Union, even though it was the Soviets who were supporting the Cuban economy by purchasing the bulk of its sugar crop. Childs has suggested that this pattern continued right up to Che's death in 1967.[56]

Despite distinguishing itself from the Soviet ideological position on Third World revolution, the *foco* theory was also considerably different from the Maoist line of the Chinese. There is little in Che's speeches and articles in the early 1960s praising either Mao or the Maoist revolution, though he urged 'solidarity' with North Vietnam, since the war there was a 'great laboratory of Yankee imperialism for preparing all their equipment for a battle, perhaps more awesome, may be more important, which will have to take place in the back yard of *their colonial possessions* on the whole American continent (my emphasis).'[57] For Guevara, it was the peasantry that would 'provide the great liberation army of the future, as it has already done in Latin America,' though it would be 'based on the ideological force of the working class, whose great leaders discovered the social laws that govern us.'[58]

This was a heretical Maoism that continued to look to the 'peasantry' as the main revolutionary force across the developing world, even though Guevara acknowledged that many of the Cubans who had flocked to the revolution had been rural proletarians rather than real peasants. If Che had visited Vietnam and observed closely the struggle being waged there, he might also have realised that the war being prosecuted in the South by the supposed peasants of the NLF (Viet Cong) was being increasingly buttressed by regular troops of the

North Vietnamese Army (NVA). Indeed, a conventional confrontation between US forces and the NVA occurred at la Drang in November 1965 – depicted in the 1992 movie, *We Were Soldiers*.[59]

Nevertheless, Guevara's anti-urban leanings became increasingly prevalent in the early 1960s as he championed the virtues of rural guerrilla war along with its privations and hardships. 'The more uncomfortable the guerrilla fighter is,' he noted, 'and the more he feels himself at home, his morale is higher; his sense of security, greater. In general, as a result of this kind of combat, it matters little to the individual guerrilla whether he survives or not.'[60] Che had by the 1960s become, very possibly, addicted to armed combat in some form or another. The Chilean poet Pablo Neruda recalled visiting him in Havana after the publication of *Guerrilla Warfare* and being rather shocked by his remark, 'War…war…We are always against war, but once we have fought in a war, we can't live without it. We want to go back to it all the time.'[61] There was also a strong sense of urgency in Che's thinking: Time did not necessarily appear to be on the side of Castro's brand of revolution, given the rapidly shifting pattern of global power politics. This was not the moment to get bogged down in any sort of Maoist protracted war, though Che never seems to have understood the full array of forces against him, including Latin American armies trained in American (and sometimes French) counterinsurgency techniques. The deepening Sino-Soviet split in the early 1960s suggested that the Third World could not look easily to just one socialist patron to advance the interest of a single revolution against 'American imperialism.' Equally, the agreement between Kennedy and Khruschev over Cuba in 1962, and the Test Ban Treaty the following year, reinforced the stance of pro-Moscow communist parties in opposing 'adventurist' guerrilla campaigns in favour of slower processes of political mobilisation.

Between 1962 and 1964, Che became increasingly demoralized with the trajectory of Cuban politics, which seemed to be increasingly bureaucratised as the country fell into the Soviet sphere. By 1964, Fidel had begun to marginalise him from decision-making and sent him off on numerous international visits as a colourful ambassador for the Cuba Revolution, including a speech at the UN in New York. It is during this period of 1964–1965 that the global myth about Che began to take hold, though he had already begun to set in motion a series of guerrilla *focos* in several South American states. All failed, one of the most spectacular being the foray into Argentina organised by Che's fellow Argentinian Jorge Ricardo Masetti, otherwise known as 'Commander Segundo,' in 1963–1964.

Masetti had been the only Argentinian journalist to enter the Sierra Maestra during the guerrilla war against Batista and maintained close links with Che. After the revolution, he formed a news agency in Havana called *Prensa Latina*. Splits within the agency drove Masetti into training for guerrilla warfare organised by Che.[62] Guevara urged the *foco* leaders to avoid descending into a terrorist formation by robbing banks; they should also avoid being too dependent on outside supplies, a tactic markedly at odds with the way that the guerrillas in the Sierra Maestra had been so dependent on the *llano*. He did not even appear to hold out much hope for the *foco's* long-term success, telling the men that 'death is the only certainty in this; some of you may survive, but all of you should consider what remains of your lives as borrowed time.'[63] Guevara by this time, evidently, had a strong desire for martyrdom.

After a long period of training in Czechoslovakia and Algeria, Masetti's *foco*, known as the *Ejercito Guerrillero del Pueblo* (Peoples Guerrilla Army) or EGP, began its theatrical foray in June 1963. Starting with a tiny force of five men, contacts were made outside the remote region of the Salta Chaco in northwest Argentina, reaching as far as the city of Cordoba and the sympathetic editorial board of the left-wing magazine *Pasado y Presente*. The foco managed to gain more recruits, bringing its numbers to around 30, though the region it was in was more depressed that Oriene province of Eastern Cuba. There were scarcely any sharecroppers and gaining popular support proved extremely hard-going. Eventually news of the guerrillas leaked out to local landowners who informed the local Argentinian border police, while Masetti grew impatient with the slow progress being made and sent another *focista*, Ciro Bustos, to Buenos Aires carrying a letter to the democratically elected President Illia. All this did, though, was to galvanise a security crackdown. Eventually in March 1964, the Argentinian gendarmerie established contact with the guerrillas and arrested some, while two others died of hunger and two more fell into a gorge. Masetti himself disappeared without a trace in April 1964 and was never seen again.[64]

The dramatic failure of the *foco* might have led searching questions to be asked about the strategy that was being adopted, but this does not seem to have occurred. Ciro Bustos returned to Cuba and was called to a meeting with the ever-busy Guevara, where Che expressed puzzlement over how any of the men could have died of starvation in the jungle. Bustos explained that in such a small group it was hard to dedicate men for farming or for hunting for food while being tracked by the police. In any case, there was little food to be had in this sort of terrain, and one tapir that was shot made them sick because it was not cooked long enough, while wild turkeys proved difficult to shoot.[65] Masetti had also failed to develop an alternative plan for moving the group out of the Chaco region once it was discovered to be so unfruitful, though this suggested poor prior intelligence.[66] Overall the experience gained from the failed *foco* suggested a careful programme of training not only in guerrilla warfare but bushcraft skills necessary for survival in remote jungle terrains.

The Argentinian embroglio was not the only one, for there were several other attempts in Latin America, though its spectacular failure might well have served as a warning to Guevara of the logistical difficulties with the *foco* concept.[67] However, he appears to have ignored any lessons from Masetti's campaign. Indeed, there is a sense that the whole campaign was planned from the start as a Shakespearean drama in which the *focistas* started acting out the early scenes of a dramatic narrative before the main character, Che, made his long-awaited grand theatrical entry, sometime in Act 3 or 4, to take things through to its inevitable climax: a pattern consonant with Castaneda's assessment of Guevara as a man who 'not only flees contradiction; his is a role in search of tragedy.'[68]

By 1964 Guevara was increasingly interested In Africa in the wake of the French withdrawal from Algeria in 1962 and the collapse of central government in the Congo following its independence from Belgium in 1960. The *foco* failures in South America appeared to confirm, in Che's mind at least, that Africa was now the most potentially important arena for revolutionary insurgency. He started planning a venture into Central Africa – this time a *grand foco* – running alongside those in South America. Che knew even less about the cultures and history of the peoples in Central Africa than those of South America, though he saw an apparent opportunity to mobilise rural and peasant peoples into revolutionary struggle against the forces of 'neocolonialism' which 'has shown its claws in the Congo' though this, he felt, was 'a sign not of power but of weakness.'[69]

In Africa, Guevara soon found that the cultures he was working amongst had almost no conception of the 'people', and there was little prospect for any success – in the short to medium term at least – for guerrilla war.[70] His timing was also very poor: by the time he arrived in Dar es Salaam, in early 1965, the insurgent forces in the eastern Congo had been largely defeated in the aftermath of 'Operation Dragon Rouge' in November 1964, when a squad of Belgian paratroopers, supported on the ground by white mercenaries, relieved the regional capital of Stanleyville and rescued some of its beleaguered inhabitants from a violent group of rebel 'Simbas'. The same month as this operation, Che had visited Beijing to rally Chinese support behind his African venture, though this too ended in disaster. Mao Zedong initially refused to meet the Cuban delegation, and the discussions appeared to confirm how much the Chinese opposed Che's revolutionary strategy. Eventually, Chou-en-Lai sent one boat load of weapons to the rebels, quite a generous act given that the country was on the brink of the Cultural Revolution.[71]

Guevara also became frustrated by the intense rivalry among the various African political leaders of the National Liberation Committee he was supposed to be supporting. Some, such as Gaston Sumaliot and Pierre Mulele, had received training in insurgent warfare in mainland China, though the main figure leading the insurgents, Laurent Kabila, was absent for most of the time and reluctant to take any serious part in the proposed struggle. The guerrillas lacked weapons and were low in morale, and Guevara soon realised that a *grand foco* would be very difficult in such difficult circumstances. Sumaliot, he found a 'a big mystery', and outside the area held by his guerrillas there were only 'isolated bands surviving in the jungle'.[72] The Simbas (often viewed in the Western press as savage cannibals) were several thousand strong and managed to seize control of the regional capital of Stanleyville. They had emerged from an abortive revolutionary movement in 1963–1964 following the return from China of Mulele, one of the radical followers of Lumumba, and the movement has been viewed by one

Congolese analyst, Georges Nzongola-Ntalala, as the first national liberation in Africa against neo-colonial rule. Emphasising the need for strong discipline, Mulele's followers launched a guerrilla insurgency in early 1964, armed mainly with knives, shotguns, and any other weapons that came to hand.[73] But organising such a force into a disciplined revolutionary guerrilla army would have required immense patience and strategic skills that Guevara appears to have lacked. This was a region where his global role as charismatic revolutionary counted for very little, doubtless compounding his doubts on its potential as a significant Third World revolutionary force.

Returning to Cuba on 15 March 1965, Che was at a turning point. It is really from this time that the figure of Regis Debray starts to become important in developing the concept of *focismo*. Childs has suggested that *focismo* went through three distinct phases conceptually during the 1960s, beginning, first, with a phase of 'Sierraisation' in which Guevara exaggerated and romanticised the role of the *sierra* against the *llano* (i.e. mountains versus plains); second, 'Marxianisation' of the *foco* from 1963 to 1965 as Guevara attempted to initiate various *focos* in South America and Central Africa; and, third, the 'internationalisation' of the *foco* in which Debray's role proved increasingly important as Guevara embarked on his final guerrilla foray into Bolivia. There was obviously considerable overlap between the three phases, and all were broadly Marxist in orientation, even though each phase exhibited a difference of style and language.[74]

There was clearly a role that Debray could play in projecting Guevara's own revolutionary image, which was in danger of flagging in the aftermath of the Congo debacle. Debray, though, tended to play the role of backroom strategist to Guevara's political and strategic project, to some degree a forerunner of the role he would later play as adviser to President Mitterand in the 1980s. Nevertheless, Debray managed to disseminate a more intellectually rigorous variant of *focismo* to an audience in the West, especially among the New Left, at a time when Che's political position was under attack by both the Soviets and the Chinese and he no longer had any position in the Cuban government. Such support might, at one level, seem rather curious given that Debray was a philosopher rather than an active revolutionary, though he had studied under Althusser at the *Ecole Normale Superiore* in Paris and later played an important role in the development of 'mediology' in the 1970s and the theory of transmission of cultural meanings. Moving to Cuba in the early 1960s, he became professor at the University of Havana and established close links with Guevara. He was perhaps the most important Marxist influence on Guevara's thinking following the rather eclectic impact of Hilda Gadea and Harold White in the mid-1950s, and he gave *focismo* a distinctly French philosophical aura.

Debray's conception of the strategic purpose of *focismo* also underwent some change between 1965 and 1970, during which time he was arrested in Bolivia in 1967 and kept in prison until 1970, when he was released following an international appeal. He first spelt out the *foco* doctrine in an article in 1965 entitled 'Latin America: The Long March.' This was later published in Britain, along with a second article, 'Marxist Strategy in Latin America,' in *New Left Review* numbers 33 and 34 of 1967. This formed the basis of the 1968 Penguin book, *Revolution in the Revolution*, published simultaneously by Monthly Review Press in the US, Maspero in France, and Feltrinelli in Italy.[75] Debray proved to be an excellent self-publicist and supplied a Marxist input into the global mythology surrounding Guevera following his capture and execution in Bolivia in October 1967. Over the longer term, Debray's Marxist rationalisations of Guevara's guerrilla strategy were undermined by his later auto-critique, his departure from the South American arena to become an adviser to President Mitterand in the 1980s, and his eventual embrace of fervent Gaullism in the 1990s. For the moment, though, he was Che's ideal partner.

A student of Louis Althusser, Debray approached guerrilla insurgency from a strong commitment to the concept of agency conditioned by structuralist analysis. Sartre's existentialist idea of the 'possible' in history came under attack in the early 1960's by the Althusserian structural Marxists, who saw history conforming to certain clear laws defined by the dialectic of class struggle. The debate surfaced briefly when Sartre gave a lecture (unpublished) at the Ecole Normale that many of the students present never forgot.[76] Debray was a refugee from the Sorbonne, which he later declared in his autobiography to be 'too foggy and uncertain for my taste.'[77] He fled into intellectual exile, emerging as an intellectual tourist adventurer only too ready to find a common cause with Che, though, for Debray, it was some global philosophical ideal of revolution that he sought rather than more ruins of some dead Latin American culture. 'In effect,' he later declared, '"Marxism-Leninism" had the privilege of being spoken from Hanoi to Caracas by way of Rome and Brazzaville, unifying a multilingual diaspora of believers in the illusion of a shared destiny. I continued to practice this dead language long after I had lost the faith, at least partly to explain the need for losing it.'[78]

The strategy was heavily shaped by a Marxian theory of history that was averse to getting too bogged down in the minutiae of detail. 'History advances in disguise,' he observed, 'It appears on stage wearing the mask of the proceeding scene, and we tend to lose the meaning of the play.'[79] The metaphor doubtless appealed to Guevara, given his own theatrical approach to initiating and managing revolution, though this did not prevent Debray himself serving up historical examples to support his arguments when the occasion required it, even stretching back to the campaigns of Simon Bolivar in the early Nineteenth Century.

Revolution in the Revolution reinforced Guevara's own deviation from Maoist ideas of protracted war. Base areas and 'armed self-defence' had never really worked in South America, Debray argued, and he pointed to various examples such as the 'June Days' of the Tin Miners' insurrection in La Paz Bolivia in

1952, who were easily isolated and destroyed at will by government forces. The later example of the 'peasant zone of self-defence' of the so-called republic 'Marquetalia' in Colombia in the early 1960s also proved to be illusory since it provided the central government with the space and time to reorganize and to pose as 'guardians of national unity' against a 'cancerous growth' in the nation's midst (though the end of this ill-fated peasant 'republic' led, eventually, to the creation of FARC in the mid-60s).[80]

Debray also widened the arguments behind *focismo* by launching a vitriolic attack on Trotskyite exponents of urban class war. The problem with Trotskyism, he wrote, was that it was a 'metaphysic paved with good intentions' that had 'nothing to learn from history.' It assumed that there was a 'proletarian essence within peasants and workers alike which cannot be altered by circumstances,' though 'for them to become aware of it themselves, it is only necessary that they be given the word, that objectives be set for them which they see without seeing and which they know without knowing.'[81] Trotskyites were comparable to proponents of 'self-defence' with their attachment to trade unions as their main organizational base and did not really understand the basic principles of armed guerrilla struggle. Here, Debray cited as an example the failure of Yon Sosa's Trotskyite MR-13 movement in Guatemala in the early 1960s – though by the time he had published his book, MR13 had taken a markedly Maoist line, before Sosa was eventually killed by Mexican border police in 1970.[82]

The commitment by Debray to the voluntarist approach of *focismo* hardened between 1965 and 1967. He originally argued that *focos* should only be launched in states without any serious democratic political structures. By the time of *Revolution in the Revolution*, however, this was replaced by a far more wide-ranging commitment to *focoist* insurgencies throughout South America, whether the states were democratic in orientation or not. The guerrilla *foco*, was now, for Debray, a superior form of political activity for 'guerrilla warfare is to peasant uprisings what Marx is to Sorel.'[83] The significance of the *foco* lay in the way that rural guerrillas reduced their ties to the surrounding peasant population as they prepared to enter a phase of 'absolute nomadism,' which ensured both a 'hardening and seasoning' of the combatants as well as the development of their own autonomous infrastructure.[84] Debray supplied a sophisticated, if romantic, Marxist rationalisation for Guevara's approach to guerrilla war and used language that doubtless struck a chord given that Che's own career had been both nomadic and rootless as well as prone to theatrical image-building. *Revolution in the Revolution* further helps explain Guevara's decision to launch his final *foco* venture in the remote jungle wilds of southeastern Bolivia rather than linking up with the urban movement in the mining region to the west. While warning of the dangers of US support for South American regimes combatting guerrilla insurgencies, Debray's analysis avoided discussing the form that the American 'imperialist' enemy took. A rather crude Leninist view of capitalist imperialism continued, in effect, by default, reinforcing Che's belief that guerrilla incursions in South America would lead the US into military intervention on lines comparable to those in Korea and South Vietnam. This, in turn, would prompt a nationalist reaction that could be harnessed through mobilisation occasioned by guerrilla inspiration.

Some South American radicals began to point to the weaknesses of the theory from as early as 1968. Andre Gunder Frank observed the failure of guerrilla war on its own to achieve French withdrawal from Algeria, while the Cuban Revolution's apparent success was due in part to the easy way that the Cuban middle class had been able to withdraw to Miami, an escape route not open in most South American states. Moreover, he had been unable to show how a guerrilla band could be transformed into a guerrilla army, and 'military actions require adequate political direction and support, lest like a house built on weak foundations the first storm destroy both foundation and superstructure.'[85] Such criticisms became largely academic in the context of Guevara's death in Bolivia and Debray's departure for Europe. Within two years the election of Salvador Allende in Chile ushered in a new and darker phase of South American politics, while *focismo*, as we shall see at the end of this paper, evolved into a model of insurgent warfare applicable to societies and situations markedly different from those encountered by Guevera and Debray in the 1960's

America, counter-revolution and military intervention

The drift of Guevara's speeches and writings during the 1960s indicated just how far he had misunderstood the general trajectory of US strategy towards South and Central America. Travelling extensively around the globe, he became something of a celebrity figure in radical political circles and increasingly lauded as an iconic symbol in the fight of 'national liberation' forces against US and Western 'imperialism'. However, unlike Mao Zedong urging reconciliation in the late 1930s with Chiang Kai-shek's Nationalists in the face of Japanese invasion, he did not speak a language of national mobilisation even if the Vietnam War stood out as a major example of military resistance to US power.[86] In a widely publicised message to the Tricontinental in April 1967, Che championed a more internationalist stance, urging the body to act as the 'voice of the vanguard of its peoples' by creating 'a Second or a Third Vietnam, or the Second or the Third Vietnam of the World.' The message suggested that *focismo* was now the basis for a global revolutionary strategy with an internal dynamism strong enough to overcome local political, cultural, or class obstacles. The speech was a redolent example of how far sections of the South American left were willing to live outside rather than inside history, ensuring that political judgements would be guided by the patterns set by previous revolutions, such as Mexico earlier in the century, in addition to Cuba.[87]

At the time of his death, Guevara remained remarkably uninformed about the historical diversity of the South American continent or the parameters of US strategy. In the same message to the Tricontinental, he had asserted that there was emerging an *'international americano* type, much more complete than in the other continents,' while the growth of increasingly well-armed and trained guerrilla insurgencies would force the US into escalating its military involvement in the continent, leading to 'military aids' being substituted by 'regular troops to ensure the relative stability of a government whose national puppet army is disintegrating before the impetuous attacks of the guerrillas.'[88]

Guevara's analysis of US power in South America amounted to a simplistic application of Leninist theory, based on the idea that US policy was almost entirely driven by the interests of corporate capitalism and that there was a process of increasingly 'unequal exchange' as capital was exported from South to North America. Such a dynamic appeared to Che to impel the US inexorably into defending its interests through the increasing resort to military power.[89] In this regard, Guevara began the discussion of the economic links between the US and Central and South America which would continue after his death. He used concepts that would be developed by academic Marxists such as Andre Gunder Frank as well as the dependency school theorists in the 1970s into general theories concerning the 'development of underdevelopment' and continuing South American 'dependency' on US capitalist power, though, broadly speaking, these schools increasingly recognised the autonomy of South American statehood. This became evident, too, in the work of Immanuel Wallerstein on world-systems theory in the 1970s and 1980s. Wallerstein suggested that the functioning of the capitalist world economy led to a differentiation between core, semi-peripheral, and peripheral states, with semi-peripheral states being highly prone to political authoritarianism.[90]

Guevara's simplistic Leninist theoretical imperialism also led him to misunderstand US relations with South and Central America over the previous half century. The United States had traditionally manifested an ambiguous political stance towards the two regions. Imperial mission and a championing of American values often went hand in hand with periods of racist anti-imperialism and isolationism. Generally, the US preferred to acknowledge the sovereignty of states in the hemisphere and only intervened when there was marked intransigence among the governing elite or a serious threat of revolution.[91] Even then, there was a marked distinction between Central America and the Caribbean, on the one hand, and the states of South America on the other. South American states were geographically too far for any serious form of direct military intervention, and it was Central America and the Caribbean which were most subject to US military incursions in one form or another, such as Pershing's incursion into Mexico in pursuit of Pancho Villa in 1916 or the various Marine interventions into the Dominican Republic (1916–1922), Haiti (1915–1934), and Nicaragua (1912–1933). These latter examples were not so much attempts at formal colonial annexation as incursions by relatively small military contingents to support the remodelling of state structures on Progressivist lines and the building of national constabularies.[92] This in fact often led to brutal dictatorial regimes such as those of Trujillo in the Dominican Republic, Batista in Cuba, and 'Papa Doc' Duvalier in Haiti. Before the 1960s, these were usually viewed as capable of getting on with the job of suppressing opposition dissent, and it was only the rapid downfall of the Batista regime at the end of 1958 that forced a rethink, leading to a progressive escalation of military training and assistance over the next couple of decades

Thus, while the US broadly followed a counter-revolutionary strategy towards Central and South America during the Cold War, this did not lead inextricably to military intervention. Snyder has pointed out that the US, despite becoming embroiled in two Asian land wars in Korea and Vietnam, did not allow itself to become a victim of 'imperial over-stretch' in the way this term has been used by Paul Kennedy. Compared to the serious overstretch of the Nazi and Japanese empires, the US eventually extricated itself from both these 'quagmires' through diplomatic negotiation, while on a wider level, it is possible to observe an impetus for local control by reliable allies long before this became official policy in the form of the Nixon Doctrine in 1969.[93] The US relied far more on informal influence even in the Caribbean and only resorted to one military intervention during Che's lifetime – the Dominican Republic in 1965 – followed later by the intervention into Grenada in 1983, both to pre-empt possible revolutionary turns to the left that might have expanded Cuban influence in the region.

The US was certainly involved, though, in a pattern of counter-revolution against various forms of violent revolutionary upsurge, including guerrilla warfare on *focoist* or Maoist lines. As a term, 'counter-revolution' is one that needs to be taken far more seriously by military analysts and historians. Mayer has suggested that the term has a rather shorter history than the word revolution to which it is opposed, emerging in the wake of the French Revolution of 1789. It tends to be rather more ideologically driven than revolution, since it is very often not based on mass movements from below that drive revolutionary change such as those in France at the end of the Eighteenth Century, Mexico after 1910, and later Russia and China. Counter-revolution tends to be bound up with reaction and extreme conservatism and rallies those individuals and groups who sooner or later feel disappointed, affronted or betrayed by the revolution."[94]

Counter-revolution started to define US policy and strategy with the Cuban Revolution. The rapid shift to the left and the move of Castro's regime into the Soviet sphere of influence shocked US policy-makers like no other until the revolution that overthrew the Shah of Iran in 1979. Indeed, it was one of the principal factors in transforming post-war US policy of general cooperation with South and Central American regimes, broadly ignoring whether these were democratic in orientation, towards a more systematised policy of containment given the fear that Castro's revolution could spread more widely through the continent. For the first time since the Guatemala coup in 1954, the US seriously engaged, by the latter part of 1960, with the idea of overthrowing the Castro regime. The project went awry with the Bay of Pigs the following year and forced Castro's regime further into the Soviet sphere, helping, in the process, to consolidate a monolithic myth of revolution in Cuba belied by the pattern of resistance at the local level.

US counter-revolution was framed in no formal strategy, certainly in the era of Che's revolutionary publicising and *focist* adventures. The Cuban Revolution had indeed been unnerving for US policy-makers, especially as it underwent an increasingly radical definition in the early 1960s. Lillian Guerra has suggested that it was the profoundest shock in the Western Hemisphere since the revolutionary overthrow of slave planter rule in Haiti at the end of the Eighteenth Century. For it attacked US exceptionalism and the myth of American democratic intentions towards the continent.[95] The US was plunged into a multi-faceted crisis that nearly led to nuclear confrontation with the Soviet Union in 1962, though at the local level the revolution exposed the relative tardiness and incoherence in US counterinsurgency training. Batista's army had been left poorly trained and equipped to fight any sort of serious counterinsurgency, and it was not altogether clear whether either the US Department of State or the CIA were that interested in supporting it indefinitely at a time when there was much positive talk in liberal circles of neutralism. The concept continued to guide policy towards some states such as Laos in the early 1960s, but both South Vietnam and Cuba between 1960 and 1963 exposed the limitations of the strategy.

From the time of the first of Guevara's insurgencies in 1963–1964, it is possible to detect a hardening of policy that would continue throughout the 1960s until the election victory of Salvador Allende in Chile in 1970. The more popular trend of revolutionary politics in Chile between 1970 and 1973 acted as a new pivot in South American history, one largely unforeseen by the Latin American left in the 1960s, including the *focistas* around Guevara and Debray, as well as US intelligence.[96] It ushered in a new phase of revolutionary challenges that took the continent's politics to a violent new level as a series of military regimes came to power, such as Chile and Uruguay in 1973 and Argentina in 1976. The US applied a revamped version of its earlier military assistance programmes in Central America stretching back to the 1920s, involving the training of military officers and the supplying of a raft of new weaponry to enhance the capacity of states throughout South America to engage in counterinsurgency. In 1963, the US Caribbean School in Panama was revamped as the School of the Americas and ultimately trained over 13,000 students in the decade following the Cuban Revolution.[97]

This did not conform to a US grand strategy, and a considerable part of the initiative for counterinsurgency came from within South America itself, especially from the Chilean military regime after 1973, which took a leading part in the organisation of Operation Condor. Something like a continental pattern of military counter-revolution ensured during the 1970s and 1980s, ensuring by the end of the Cold War a cost approaching if not exceeding that of Soviet control in Eastern Europe: the overthrow of 24 governments between 1948 and 1990, 4 by direct US military intervention, 3 by CIA-managed revolts, and 17 by military coups; while between 1975 and 1990, the death toll was some 300,000 out of a population of 30 million with 1 million refugees.[98]

How significant is Guevara's theory of insurgency?

The global mythology surrounding Guevara markedly contradicts his achievements as a revolutionary, especially as a guerrilla fighter. He is more a bridging figure historically between the era of national liberation insurgencies in the two decades after 1945 and the later phase of urban-based terrorism in the 1970s and 1980s in Europe, Latin America, and the Middle East. His link to more recent phases of guerrilla insurgency is, at best, questionable.

Guevara was emphatic that *focismo* should not involve random terrorist attacks. He specifically condemned Jose Antonio Acheverria's *Directorio Revolucionario* as a *grupo terrorista* for its attempt in 1957 to assassinate Batista.[99] Nevertheless, it is possible to see *focismo* as a method of warfare involving terrorist features: a group of men hiding out in the countryside with weak attachments to the surrounding civilian population and prone to killing or stealing if the need requires; men often resorting to random attacks on whatever forces of the state they encounter as cases of 'armed propaganda'; and the apparent desire by Guevara as a *focista* for martyrdom in the cause of revolutionary struggle. The latter serves as an early example for the fanatical devotion to a cause displayed by many terrorist leaders and followers who have effectively burned their boats with the societies from which they came.

Guevara's career trajectory as a wandering tourist drawn eventually into the world of Cuban revolutionary politics also has some parallel with modern recruits drawn into the world of jihadist insurgencies. Like Guevara, some aspirant jihadist recruits into Al Qaeda and ISIS have had some experience of travel, though their radicalisation normally occurs less through reading prescribed (and at times, proscribed) revolutionary texts than the impact of various social networks, social media, and radical sermons in mosques. The recruitment network to handle these recruits is larger and more complex than the small revolutionary circles of South and Central American exiles whom Guevara encountered in Guatemala and Mexico. Yet Guevara's pattern of radicalisation replicates some modern jihadis, with a decisive spill-over occurring when the would-be recruit seeks to go beyond travel to identifying more firmly with an insurgent or terrorist network. Guevara, though, looked to the Inca, Aztec and Mayan archaeological remains he encountered as symbols of a South and Central American continental identity. He embarked on an ill-formed, and rather quixotic, quest for a continental myth, one that he never found and that has only begun to be realised in the decades since his death, especially through the literary contributions of authors such as Gabriel Garcia Marquez and Mario Vargas Llosa. Marquez's *One*

Hundred Days of Solitude, published in 1965, is particularly interesting for the way it drew attention to the absence of historical consciousness in the continent, colourfully exemplified by the allegory of the amnesiac plague that hits the town of Macondo.

Modern jihadis, by contrast, have no interest in this sort of historical retrieval given that the radical readings of Islamic texts provide a self-contained revolutionary mythology to rebuild society completely afresh. Any archaeological sites encountered, such as Palmyra, are thus obstacles against the true interpretation of the ideology and must be destroyed. There are major differences, though Guevara's career and radicalisation suggests that analysts in the arena of terrorism and security studies can derive useful insights from work done in tourism studies on various 'tourist imaginaries' to understand different patterns of terrorist radicalisation.

Ironically, *focismo* does serve up a good example of a distinctive branding effort by a *government-backed* insurgent campaign. As we have seen, the Che myth emerged gradually during the early 1960s, propelled by considerable propaganda in Cuba that included cinema, Guevara's speeches and writings, and his extensive travelling in distinctive revolutionary garb as a Cuban government emissary. Some of these visits were not only important for projecting the image of the new regime in Havana but also for galvanising the local population around a revolutionary myth. This appears to have been true, for instance, for Guevara's June 1959 visit to Gaza, then under the control of the Egyptian government. He was the first real revolutionary leader to visit this small territory wedged between Egypt and Israel, and he was welcomed by the leader of the *Fedayeen*, Abdullah Abu Sitta, at a time when the PLO had not yet been founded. Guevara urged the population to 'liberate' the territory, though cautioned that any Cuban help would only go via Nasser's government in Cairo.[100] The visit linked the cause of the Cuban Revolution with a wider revolutionary impulse and illustrated the propaganda payoffs from what might be broadly termed revolutionary tourism. Guevara's image has lived on, interestingly, in some Palestinian propaganda posters (see Plate 2), though largely as a minority political discourse.

Guevara, then, was an astute political figure managing and manipulating a myth of revolutionary action that secured a widespread following in parts of the developing world, as well as among the New Left in the West. As a brand, *focismo* was a form of Maoism-lite or protracted war without the tears. It promised an easy and quick approach to organising a revolutionary effort and one that did not need the long-term Maoist-type mobilisation of popular support among rural peasantries, sometimes speaking unfamiliar languages and with religious belief systems inscrutable to non-anthropological experts. Despite such obvious problems, Guevara was adept at projecting *focismo* as a form of heroic revolutionary struggle around the Third World. By the early 1970s, this strategy was increasingly at odds with the radical populism of the continent's politics in the wake of the election victory of Salvador Allende in Chile in 1970.

Plate 2. Guevara as an icon for 'Palestina Libre' – the caption in Arabic says 'Freedom for Palestine'.

Focismo became even further marginalised by the onset of a Maoist insurgency in Peru in the 1980s (see Palmer contribution in this issue). This was a markedly different kind of insurgency from those elsewhere in South America and probably had more in common with the Maoist upsurge in Nepal than the *focos* briefly attempted in states such as Argentina and Bolivia in the 1960s. It was, in part, a result of the land reforms of the military government of Juan Velasco Alvarado between 1968 and 1975, with the programme of the latter illustrating that the pattern of South American military regimes in the 1970s did not conform to a simple neo-liberal trajectory. In its extreme voluntarism, Shining Path resembled *focismo*; but it was explicitly Maoist in its claims to speak for the marginalized masses and in its efforts to mobilise them, first in the Ayacucho department, which was itself a hinterland, then later throughout the country, even in impoverished urban spaces.[101] There was a rural-urban alliance here that Castro and Guevara had largely fought against in the early 1960s, replicating the same sort of rural urban alliance that Masetti's foco attempted to forge in Argentina in the early 1960's.

But the eventual defeat of *Sendero Luminoso* hardly led to any sort of rehabilitation for *focismo*. By the 1990s, the term was seen by many analysts as largely redundant in the world of growing international terrorism. When Western states such as the US, Britain, and France did find themselves fighting new forms of rural insurgency in Afghanistan and Iraq, the focus was on newer forms of 'post-Maoist' protracted guerrilla war involving the progressive radicalisation of the peasantry on jihadist rather than Marxist lines.

As a model of insurgency, though, *focismo* has come to be viewed by some analysts as useful when examining movements such as Al Qaeda and ISIS. Payne has suggested that AQ developed a 'coherent strategy' of a *focoist* kind by planting groups of fighters on the margins of territories under enemy control who could then progressively expand their influence. The strategy accords with a wider thesis of 'leaderless jihad' to explain modern jihadist movements, one that has been strongly contested by some military analysts. It also implies that terrorist violence and the cult of the warrior can have significant ideological impact in mobilising disaffected Islamic communities.[102] Other analysts, by contrast, have seen *focismo* as more relevant to understanding the strategy of ISIS. Gartenstein et al., for instance, have recently suggested that the Al Qaeda rivalry with ISIS can be interpreted in terms of two contrasting models of war. It is now AQ which is the more Maoist type of insurgency, as it seeks to avoid direct military engagement with the enemy in favour of long-term political mobilisation, while ISIS, in contrast, is now the successor to Guevara with its commitment to military action to achieve effects, especially spontaneous mobilisation of the masses.

Both these analyses treat *focismo* as little more than a military 'model' available to modern insurgent leaders, divorced from the political, ideological, and cultural context of the original *focos* of the 1960s and early 1970s. There are some advantages to be derived from proceding in this analytical manner, though whether *focismo* can endure as a worthwhile concept in strategic studies remains to be seen. Guevara and Debray's concept of the *foco* presupposed a group of trained and ideologically committed guerrillas implanting themselves in remote terrain and spreading outwards as they gained new recruits and embedding themselves in peasant and rural communities. With modern forms of communication, latter days *focos* are likely to be far less autonomous that those of a fifty years ago, while at the same time any potential anonymity can be compromised by technological means and subject to devastating attacks, for instance by drones. It is possible to imagine a highly purified version of Islam supplying the ideological bond for the modern jihadist *foco*, though few, if any, of the modern ISIS practitioners of guerrilla war appear to have absorbed Guevara's warnings against terrorising civilian populations.

It is also possible to imagine a beleaguered ISIS in Syria and Iraq sending out a series of jihadist *focos* over new terrains, in which constant contact can be maintained by encrypted cell phones. The open desert terrain of large parts of the Middle East and North Africa will ensure that these operations will be considerably different from those of the Sierra Maestra or rural Bolivia and Argentina. Any such *focos* will be little different from the existing pattern of warlord-type militias moving rapidly across both rural and urban terrains in pick-up trucks and other captured military hardware. It is unlikely that any of these formations will learn much from consulting the works of Guevara from a past era. The past indeed has become a foreign country. Therein, Guevara's idea of guerrilla *focos* seems to be a conclusion of sorts at the end of long tradition of peasant insurrections and banditry stretching back, in both Europe and Central and South America, to the Seventeenth and Eighteenth Centuries, rather than to be what he and others thought it would be: the ushering in of a new form of insurgent war.

Notes

1. A term used by Peter Paret, *Guerrillas in the 1960's*. New York and London: Praeger, 1962, 31 and *passim*.
2. Beatrice Heuser's recent study of strategic thought, for instance, attaches little importance to Guevara's ideas, certainly compared to those of Mao. See Beatrice Heuser, *The Evolution of Strategy*. Cambridge: Cambridge University Press, 2010, 412–6. Heuser sees his writings being of interest for the way he dispenses advice on winning the confidence of peasants in the development of revolutionary struggle. Lawrence Freedman also notes that Guevara's approach to guerrilla war was a "romantic model ... based on a misreading of the Cuban revolution." Lawrence Freedman, *Strategy*. Oxford: Oxford University Press, 2013, 400.
3. Robert Jay Lifton, *Revolutionary Immortality: Mao Tse Tung and the Chinese Cultural Revolution*. Harmondsworth: Penguin Books, 1968; James Chieh Hsiung, *Ideology and Practice: The Evolution of Chinese Communism*. New York: Praeger, 1970, 103–5.
4. The song has been sung in several versions across the world. One recent video by the French actress and singer Natalie Cardone sees it as one that empowers women, as she walks across a sugar cane field holding a baby with an AK47 strapped to her back. See Alvaro Vargas Llosa, "The Killing Machine: Che Guevara, from Communist Firebrand to Capitalist Brand," *The New Republic* July 11 2005; Michael Casey, *Che's Afterlife*. New York: Vintage Books, 2009.
5. See Lucy Hughes Hallett, *Heroes: Saviors, Traitors and Supermen*. London: Knopf, 2004.
6. One of the activists from that period, Bill Ayers, recalled, "Our metaphors were constructed on other barricades: the metaphor of world revolution, for example, imperialism in decline, of the US as an ultimately doomed and helpless but temporarily deeply destructive giant." Bill Ayers, *Fugitive Days: Memoirs or an Antiwar Activist*. Boston: Beacon Press, 2001, 151. Arthur Schlesinger recalled a visit to the Cambridge (Boston) headquarters of the Students for a Democratic Society (SDS) in May 1967 and seeing a photograph of Che Guevara "hung in the hall of a studiously bare and dreary apartment." Arthur Schlesinger Jr., *Journals, 1952–2000*. London: Atlantic Books, 2008, 260. Freedman has pointed out that

Guevara was important for providing "a theory for the defeat of US imperialism that did not depend on the efforts of those living in its midst." Freedman *op.cit.* 402.
7. See for instance Cynthia Enloe, *Bananas, Beaches and Bases: Making Feminist Sense of International Politics*. Berkeley: University of California Press, 1990, 28.
8. Jon Lee Anderson, *Che Guevara: A Revolutionary Life*. New York: Bantam Books, 1997, 196.
9. David Atlee Philips, *The Night Watch: 25 Years in the CIA*. London: Robert Hale, 1977, 81.
10. See for instance Donald Denoon, *Settler Capitalism The Dynamics of Dependent Development in the Southern Hemisphere*. Oxford: Oxford University Press, 1983; Caroline Elkins and Susan Pederson (eds, *Settler Colonialism in the Twentieth Century*. New York and London: Routledge 2005.
11. Jorge Castaneda, *Companero: The Life and Death of Che Guevara*. London; Bloomsbury, 1997, 47.
12. Theodore Zeldin, *An Intimate History of Humanity*. London: Vintage, 1998, 43–51.
13. *Motorcycle Diaries*, 43.
14. Ibid., 92–3.
15. Marisol de la Cadena, "From Race to Class: Insurgent Intellectuals de provincia in Peru, 1910–1970" in Steve J. Stern (ed) *Shining and Other Paths: War and Society in Peru, 1980–1995*. Durham (NC) and London: Duke University Press, 1998, 22–55. In April 1954 Guevara wrote to his mother that he was trying to persuade Gadea to "leave that dump of a party." *Back on the Road*, 43.
16. *Back on the Road*, 101–8. For Griswold see Jason S. Shapiro, "Sylvanus Griswold Morley: A Life in Archaeology and Elsewhere". www.elpalacio.org. Accessed 21 January 2017.
17. Ricardo D. Salvatore, "The Enterprise of Knowledge: Representational Machines and Informal Empire" in Fernando Coronill (ed) *Close Encounters of Empire: Writing the Cultural History of US-Latin American Relations*. Durham (NC) and London: University Press, 1998, 93.
18. Guevara to mother April 1954 in *Back on the Road*, 59.
19. Guevara to mother n.d (1955) in *ibid.*, 91.
20. Anderson, 80.
21. Albert Memmi, *The Coloniser and the Colonised*. New York: Orion Press, 1965, 26.
22. Mike Gonzalez, *Che Guevara and the Cuban Revolution*. London and Sydney: Bookmarks, 2004, 28–33. Philipps op. cit , 54.
23. Richard Gott, *Rural Guerrillas in Latin America*. Harmondsworth: Penguin Books, 61.
24. Quoted in Ibid., 126.
25. Though Cuba was by no means the only possible context in which to pursue this, since Guevara also found that he had much in common with some of the radicals from Puerto Rico residing in Guatemala City.
26. Letter to mother October 1956 in *Back on the Road*, 114.
27. Simon Reid-Henry, *Fidel & Che: A Revolutionary Friendship*. London: Hodder and Stoughton, 2009, 144.
28. Ibid., 148.
29. K.S Karel, *Guerrillas in Power: The Course of the Cuban Revolution*. New York: Hill & Wang, 1970, 164–5. Interestingly, the *Granma* is on show behind a large glass case in a museum in down-town Havana. It has been immaculately renovated and looks as though it has just come from the 1956 Boat Show at Earls Court,

raising interesting questions about why the protectors of the revolutionary myth would want to show it in such a clean and pristine condition.
30. *Llano* or plains groups – as opposed to the guerrillas in the mountains or *sierra* – were mostly urban cells in the cities, where they could find security. They did carry out sabotage elsewhere in the 'plains,' though, for instance against sugar mills and other targets.
31. Letter to mother (probably late November 1956) in *Back on the Road*, 112.
32. Anderson, 193–5.
33. *Back On the Road*, 49.
34. Regis Debray, *Revolution in the Revolution*. Harmondsworth: Penguin Books 1968, 21 n.
35. Max Boot, *Invisible Armies: An Epic History of Guerrilla Warfare from Ancient Times to the Present*. New York and London: Norton, 2013, 441.
36. Walter Lacquer, *Guerrilla: A Historical and Critical Study*. London: Weidenfeld and Nicolson, 1977, 331.
37. Mao Tse Tung, "Problems of Strategy in Guerrilla War" in *Selected Works of Mao Tse Tung, Volume II*. Peking, Foreign Languages Press, 1967, 94.
38. Eric R. Wolf, *Peasant Wars of the Twentieth Century*. London: Faber and Faber, 1971, 265–6.
39. Hugh Thomas, *Cuba: A History*. Harmondsworth: Penguin Books, 2001, 751.
40. Ibid., 268–9, 273; James Joll, *The Anarchists*, London: Eyre and Spottiswoode, 1964, 139.
41. Lillian Guerra, "Beyond Paradox: Counterrevolution and the Origins of Political Culture in the Cuban Revolution, 1959–2009" in Grandin and Joseph, *op. cit*. 199–230.
42. Anthony De Palma, *The Man Who Invented Fidel: Castro, Cuba and Herbert L. Matthews of the 'New York Times'*. New York: Public Affairs, 2007.
43. See for example Robert Moss, *Urban Guerrillas*. London: Temple Smith, 1971, 141.
44. Walter Lacquer, *Terrorism*. London: Sphere Books, 1978, 217.
45. Paret, *op.cit*.
46. Che Guevara, *Guerrilla Warfare*. Harmondsworth: Penguin Books, 1969, 46.
47. Ibid., 83.
48. Thomas Perry Thornton, "Terror as a Weapon" in Harry Eckstein, *Internal War: Problems and Approaches*. London: Collier-Macmillan, 1964, 87. Roland Gaucher, *The Terrorists*. London: Secker & Warburg, 1965, 305; Gerard Chaliand, *Revolution in the Third World*. Harmondsworh: Penguin Books, 1978, 43.
49. J.L.S Girling, *Peoples War: The Conditions and the Consequences in China and South East Asia*. London: Allen and Unwin, 1969, 49–109. Missing from Girling's list, of course, is the regularization of the guerrillas that was integral to the Maoist approach; that is, the gradual turning of most guerrilla formations into regular formations capable of challenging their military opposites in the war of movement (or mobile warfare).
50. Thomas A. Marks, *Maoist People's War in Post-Vietnam Asia*. Bangkok: White Lotus Press, 2007, 41.
51. Michael Chanan, *The Cuban Image*. London: BFI Pub, 1985, 89.
52. See my discussion of this film in Paul B Rich, 'Rossellini, Pontecorvo and the neorealist cinema of insurgency,' *Small Wars and Insurgencies* 26, no. 4, March 2015, 640–64.
53. Che Guevara, *Reminiscences of the Cuban Revolutionary War*. London and New York: Harper Perennial, 2006, 210.
54. J. Bowyer Bell, *The Myth of the Guerrilla*. New York: Knopf, 1971, 42.

55. Che Guevara, "We Are Practical Revolutionaries", *Verde Olivo* October 8 1960 in John Gerasi (ed), *Vencemeros: The Speeches and Writings of Che Guevara*. London: Granada Books, 1969,182.
56. Matt D. Childs, "An Historical Critique of the Emergence and Evolution of Che Guevara's *Foco* Theory," *Journal of Latin American Studies*, 27, 1995, 196–8.
57. Che Guevara, "On Solidarity with Vietnam" speech delivered at the Ministry of Industry, November 20 1963 in Gerasi, 405.
58. Che Guevara, "Cuba – Exception or Vanguard?", *Verde Olivo* April 9 1961 in Gerasi, *op. cit*, 203–4.
59. Harold G. Moore et at, *We Were Soldiers Once and Young*. New York: Random House 1992.
60. Che Guevara, 'We Are Practical Revolutionaries,' *Verde Olivo* October 8 1960 in Gerasi, 188.
61. Pablo Neruda, *Memoirs*. Harmondsworth: Penguin Books, 1978, 323.
62. Gott, *op. cit,* 469–71; Castaneda, *op. cit.*, 247.
63. Anderson, 543.
64. For an account of the failed *foco* operation see Ciro Bustos, *Che Wants to See You*. London and New York: Verso 2013.
65. Bustos, 185.
66. Ibid., 176.
67. For a brief survey of the *focos* see Thomas C. Wright, *Latin America in the Era of the Cuban Revolution*. Westport (CT) and London: Praeger, 2001, 76–80.
68. Castaneda, 43.
69. Che Guevara, 'On Our Common Aspiration – The Death of Imperialism and the Birth of a Moral World' Speech delivered in Algiers February 26th 1965 in Gerasi, 530.
70. Castaneda, 282.
71. Ibid., 287–8.
72. Cited in ibid., 284.
73. Georges Nzongola-Ntalala, *The Congo: From Leopold to Kabila*. London and New York: Zed Books, 2007, 128–9.
74. Childs, 606.
75. Penguin Books, 1968.
76. Annie Cohen-Sodal, *Jean Paul Sartre*. New York and London: The New Press, 1985, 450–1.
77. *Praised Be Our Lords*, 14.
78. Ibid., 18.
79. Ibid., 19.
80. Ibid., 31.
81. Ibid., 39.
82. Ibid., 40–1. For the MR 13 see Gott, *op cit*, 106–7.
83. Ibid., 28.
84. Ibid., 51.
85. Andre Gunder Frank, 'Class, Politics and Debray' in Leo Huberman and Paul M. Sweezy (eds), *Regis Debray and the Latin American Revolution*. New York and London: Monthly Review Press, 1968. 16.
86. Stuart Schram, *Mao Tse Tung*. Harmondsworth: Penguin Books, 1966, 212; Dick Wilson, *China's Revolutionary War*. London: Weidenfeld and Nicolson, 1991, 83–101.
87. Greg Grandin, 'Living in Revolutionary Time: Coming to Terms with the Violence of Latin America's Long Cold War' in Greg Grandin & Gilbert M. Joseph (eds),

Insurgent and Counterinsurgent Violence During Latin America's Long Cold War. Durham and London: Duke University Press, 2010, 20.
88. Che Guevara, "Message to the Tricontinental: 'Create two three…many Vietnams'" April 16 1967 In Gerasi *op cit* 579.
89. Che Guevara, 'On the Alliance for Progress' Speech delivered at the Punta del Este Conference of the OAS August 16 1961 in Gerasi, 264–74.
90. Immanuel Wallerstein, *Geopolitics and Geoculture: Essays on the Changing World System.* Cambridge: Cambridge University Press, 1991.
91. Jane Burbank and Frederick Cooper, *Empires in World History.* Princeton and Oxford: Princeton University Press, 2010, 323–4.
92. Eric R. Rittinger, 'Exporting Professionalism: US efforts to Reform the Armed Forces in the Dominican Republic and Nicaragua, 1916–1933," *Small Wars and Insurgencies* 26, 1 February 2015, 136–51.
93. Jack Snyder, *Myths of Empire: Domestic Politics and International Ambition.* Ithaca and London: Cornell University Press, 1991, 255–6.
94. Arno Mayer, *The Furies: Violence and Terror in the French and Russian Revolutions.* Princeton and Oxford: Princeton University Press, 2002, 50.
95. Lillian Guerra, 'Beyond Paradox: Counterrevolution and the Origins of Political Culture in the Cuban Revolution, 1959–2009' in Grandin and Joseph, 201.
96. As late as 1969, the Trotskyite 'revisionist' analyst of the Cold War, David Horowitz, argued that Cuba continued to serve as a 'third revolutionary dentre' for the third world and the Latin American left in particular after the Soviet Union and China. David Horowitz, *Imperialism and Revolution*, Harmondsworth: Penguin Books, 1971 (1 ed 1969), 226.
97. Lesley Gill, *The School of the Americas: Military Training and Political Violence in the Americas.* Durham and London: Duke University Press, 2004, 73–4.
98. Perry Anderson, *American Foreign Policy and Its Thinkers.* London: Verso, 2017, 103 n. 8.
99. *Che Guevara: A Revolutionary Life.*, 246.
100. Salman Abbu Sitta, "Che Guevara in Gaza: Palestine becomes a Global Cause," *Middle East Monitor*, August 2015, 3–12.
101. Ivan Hinojosa, "On Poor Relations and the Nouveau Riche: Shining Path and the Radical Peruvian Left" in Stern, *op. cit.*, 60–78.
102. Kenneth Payne, "Building the Base: Al Qaeda's Focoist Strategy." *Studies in Conflict & Terrorism* 34, 2, 2011, 124–43.

Acknowledgement

I am grateful to Tom Marks for commenting on an earlier version of this paper.

Disclosure statement

No potential conflict of interest was reported by the author.

Bibliography

Anderson, Jon Lee. *Che Guevara: A Revolutionary Life.* New York: Bantam Books, 1997.
Anderson, Perry. *American Foreign Policy and Its Thinkers.* London: Verso, 2017.
Ayers, Bill. *Fugitive Days: Memoirs of an Antiwar Activist.* Boston, MA: Beacon Press, 2001.

Bell, J. Bowyer. *The Myth of the Guerrilla*. New York: Knopf, 1971.
Boot, Max. *Invisible Armies: An Epic History of Guerrilla Warfare from Ancient Times to the Present*. New York: Norton, 2013.
Burbank, Jane, and Frederick Cooper. *Empires in World History*. Princeton, NJ: Princeton University Press, 2010.
Casey, Michael. *Che's Afterlife*. New York: Vintage Books, 2009.
Castaneda, Jorge. *Companero: The Life and Death of Che Guevara*. London: Bloomsbury, 1997.
Chaliand, Gerard. *Revolution in the Third World*. Harmondsworth: Penguin Books, 1989.
Chanan, Michael. *The Cuban Image*. London: BFI Pub, 1985.
Childs, Matt D. "An Historical Critique of the Emergence and Evolution of Che Guevara's Foco Theory." *Journal of Latin American Studies* 27 (1995): 593-624.
Cohen-Sodal, Annie. *Jean Paul Sartre*. New York: The New Press, 1985.
Debray, Regis. *Revolution in the Revolution*. Harmondsworth: Penguin Books, 1968.
Debray, Regis. *Praised be our Lords.: The Autobiography*. London: Verso, 2007.
de la Cadena, Mariso. "From Race to Class: Insurgent Intellectuals de provincia in Peru, 1910-1970." In *Shining and Other Paths: War and Society in Peru, 1980-1995*, edited by Steve J. Stern, 22-55. Durham, NC: Duke University Press, 1998.
De Palma, Anthony. *The Man Who Invented Fidel: Castro, Cuba and Herbert L. Matthews of the 'New York Times'*. New York: Public Affairs, 2007.
Enloe, Cynthia. *Bananas, Beaches and Bases: Making Feminist Sense of International Politics*. Berkeley: University of California Press, 1990.
Frank, Andre Gunder, A. S. Shah. "Class, Politics and Debray." In *Regis Debray and the Latin American Revolution*, edited by Leo Huberman and Paul M. Sweezy, 12-17. New York: Monthly Review Press, 1968.
Freedman, Lawrence. *Strategy*. Oxford: Oxford University Press, 2013.
Gerasi, John (ed.). *Vencemeros: The speeches and writings of Che Guevara*. London: Granada Books, 1969.
Gill, Lesley. *The School of the Americas: Military Training and Political Violence in the Americas*. Durham, NC: Duke University Press, 2004.
Girling, J. L. S. *Peoples War: The Conditions and the Consequences in China and South East Asia*. London: Allen and Unwin, 1969.
Gonzalez, Mike. *Che Guevara and the Cuban Revolution*. London: Bookmarks, 2004.
Grandin, Greg. "Living in Revolutionary Time: Coming to Terms with the Violence of Latin America's Long Cold War." In *Insurgent and Counterinsurgent Violence During Latin America's Long Cold War*, edited by Greg Grandin and Gilbert M Joseph. Durham, NC: Duke University Press, 2010.
Guerra, Lillian. "Beyond Paradox: Counterrevolution and the Origins of Political Culture in the Cuban Revolution, 1959-2009." In *Insurgent and Counterinsurgent Violence During Latin America's Long Cold War*, edited by Greg Grandin and Gilbert M Joseph. Durham, NC: Duke University Press, 2010.
Guevara, Che. *Guerrilla Warfare*. Harmondsworth: Penguin Books, 1969.
Guevara, Ernesto Che. *The Motorcycle Diaries*. New York: Ocean Press, 2003.
Guevara, Che. *Reminiscences of the Cuban Revolutionary War*. London: Harper Perennial, 2006.
Hersch, Seymour. *The Dark Side of Camelot*. London: Harper Collins, 1998.
Heuser, Beatrice. *The Evolution of Strategy*. Cambridge: Cambridge University Press, 2010.
Horowitz, David. *Imperialism and Revolution*. Harmondsworth: Penguin Books, 1971 (1 ed 1969).
Hsiung, James Chieh. *Ideology and Practice: The Evolution of Chinese Communism*. New York: Praeger, 1970.

Hallett, Hughes, and Lucy Heroes. *Saviors, Traitors and Supermen*. London: Knopf, 2004.
Immerman, Richard H. *The CIA in Guatemala: The Foreign Policy of Intervention*. Austin: University of Texas Press, 1982.
Joll, James. *The Anarchists*. London: Eyre and Spottiswoode, 1964.
Lifton, Robert Jay. *Revolutionary Immortality: Mao Tse Tung and the Chinese Cultural Revolution*. Harmondsworth: Penguin Books, 1968.
Mao Tse Tung. "Problems of Strategy in Guerrilla War" *in Selected Works of Mao Tse-tung*. vol. II. Peking: Foreign Languages Press, 1967.
Marks, Thomas A. *Maoist People's War in Post-Vietnam Asia*. Bangkok: White Lotus Press, 2007.
Mayer, Arno. *The Furies: Violence and Terror in the French and Russian Revolutions*. Princeton, NJ: Princeton University Press, 2002.
Memmi, Albert. *The Coloniser and the Colonised*. New York: Orion Press, 1965.
Moore, Harold G., et al. *We Were Soldiers Once and Young*. New York: Random House, 1992.
Moss, Robert. *Urban Guerrillas*. London: Temple Smith, 1971.
Neruda, Pablo. *Memoirs*. Harmondsworth: Penguin Books, 1978.
Nzongola-Ntalala, George. *The Congo: From Leopold to Kabila*. London: Zed Books, 2007.
Paret, Peter. *Guerrillas in the 1960's*. New York: Praeger, 1962.
Payne, Kenneth. "Building the Base: Al Qaeda's Focoist Strategy." *Studies in Conflict & Terrorism* 34, no. 2 (2011): 124–143.
Philips, David Atlee. *The Night Watch: 25 Years in the CIA*. London: Robert Hale, 1977.
Porch, Douglas. *Counterinsurgency: Exposing the Myths of the New Way of War*. Cambridge: Cambridge University Press, 2013.
Reid-Henry, Simon. *Fidel & Che: A Revolutionary Friendship*. London: Hodder and Stoughton, 2009.
Rich, Paul B. "Rossellini, Pontecorvo and the neorealist cinema of insurgency." *Small Wars and Insurgencies* 26, no. 4 (March 2015): 640–667.
Rittinger, Eric R. "Exporting professionalism: US efforts to reform the armed forces in the Dominican Republic and Nicaragua, 1916–1933." *Small Wars and Insurgencies* 26, no. 1 (February 2015): 136–157.
Schlesinger, Arthur, Jr. *Journals, 1952–2000*. London: Atlantic Books, 2009.
Schram, Stuart. *Mao Tse Tung*. Harmondsworth: Penguin Books, 1966.
Snyder, Jack. *Myths of Empire: Domestic Politics and International Ambition*. Ithaca, NY: Cornell University Press, 1991.
Stern, Steve J. (ed.). *Shining and Other Paths: War and Society in Peru, 1980–1995*. Durham, NC: Duke University Press, 1998.
Sweezy, Paul M. (ed.). *Regis Debray and the Latin American Revolution*. New York: Monthly Review Press, 1968.
Tanham, George K. *Communist Revolutionary Warfare: The Vietminh in Indochina*. New York: Prager, 1961.
Thomas, Hugh. *Cuba: A History*. Harmondsworth: Penguin Books, 2001.
Thornton, Thomas Perry. "Terror as a Weapon." In *Internal War: Problems and Approaches*, edited by Harry Eckstein. London: Collier-Macmillan, 1964.
Vargas Llosa, Alvaro. "The Killing Machine: Che Guevara, from Communist Firebrand to Capitalist Brand." *The New Republic*, July 11, 2005.
Wallerstein, Immanuel. *Geopolitics and Geoculture: Essays on the Changing World System*. Cambridge: Cambridge University Press, 1991.
Wilson, Dick. *China's Revolutionary War*. London: Weidenfeld and Nicolson, 1991.
Wolf, Eric R. *Peasant Wars of the Twentieth Century*. London: Faber and Faber, 1971.
Wright, Thomas C. *Latin America in the Era of the Cuban Revolution*. Westport, CT: Praeger, 2001.

Zeldin, Theodore. *An Intimate History of Humanity*. London: Vintage, 1998.
Warren, Hinckle, and William Turner. *'The Fish Red': The Story of the Secret War Against Castro*, 311–313. New York: Harper and Row, 1981. The CIA used Beechcraft operated by a Missouri-based firm, Mark Hurd, which also did work for oil and construction companies and some governments.

FARC, 1982–2002: criminal foundation for insurgent defeat

Thomas A. Marks

ABSTRACT
Recent controversy during the conclusion of peace talks has renewed discussion as to the nature of the effort by *Fuerzas Armadas Revolucionarias de Colombia*, or FARC (Revolutionary Armed Forces of Colombia), to seize state power. FARC presents itself as an insurgency produced by societal imperfections and purports to speak for the marginalized and alienated of Colombia. Critics contend that FARC is a ruthless narcoterrorist organization that has targeted the people. In fact, FARC comes closer to the latter than the former, because its critical decision to privilege criminality for generation of means destroyed execution of a viable people's war strategy. Ultimately, *means* devoured *ways* in such manner as to make *ends* unachievable. Criminality, though it made FARC perhaps the richest insurgent group in the world during its heyday, laid the foundation for its defeat by ceding legitimacy, and thus mass mobilization, to the democratic state.

Introduction

Recent agreement by *Fuerzas Armadas Revolucionarias de Colombia*, or FARC (Revolutionary Armed Forces of Colombia), to join normal political society has resulted in considerable media treatment of what ostensibly occurred during the decades of insurgency and terrorism. Much of this reporting is inaccurate, and its accompanying figures have often lacked foundation. This matters a great deal, because the incorrect portrayal of the past has been used to support a FARC frame and narrative that is a gross distortion of the movement's essence. Particularly misguided is the effort by some to present Colombia's ordeal as a 'civil war', when, from first to last, a relatively small political group supported by criminality made the population its target. In contrast, legitimacy and mobilization belonged to the state.

Misrepresentation of the past has been accompanied by an effort to frame FARC's project as a quest for social justice extending from *La Violencia* to the present. Supporting this frame has been a narrative claiming that the insurgency reflected the marginalization of entire social strata, with FARC the necessary self-defense impulse stemming from this alienation. In reality, FARC became a viable entity only when its involvement with criminality allowed it to ignore gaining support of the population and to function as a parasitic counter-state whose funding was garnered by exploiting and attacking the population, not representing – much less protecting – it. That element of FARC's funding profile which particularly illustrated this was its kidnapping, a criminal tactic which began early in FARC's history and continued for the entire period of insurgency.

Any one of the issues just raised would support a stand-alone work. Necessarily, these will not be offered here. Instead, it is the intent of this contribution to revisit the critical years of the FARC insurgency's rise and failed effort to seize power, 1982–2002, using kidnapping as a compass to guide elucidation of the strategy at work. Though state response was ultimately to prove decisive, this subject has been covered elsewhere and will enter into the discussion only as necessary to the analysis of the insurgency.[1] What is central is that by relying upon criminality to gain strength, FARC laid the foundation not for victory but defeat.

Criminality as insurgent foundation

From the mid-1960s to the near-present, Colombia (see Figure 1) has been confronted by a FARC project to seize power for the purpose of instituting a Marxist-Leninist regime (more recently referred to as 'Bolivarian'). Initially driven by terrorism and guerrilla warfare, the threat reached a new level in 1996 with the initiation of mobile warfare, whereby large units sought to neutralize the military and sweep to victory. Unlike Vietnam, what followed was a regaining of the strategic initiative by the government and decimation of the insurgent threat.[2]

FARC's expansion was thus arrested even as it sought the intensification of operations and fundraising necessary to implement its Strategic Plan (*Plan Estratégico*), originally a phased assault which was to unfold in the 8-year period 1982–1990 and culminate in the seizure of Bogotá. Unveiled at FARC's VII National Congress held in May 1982, the plan remained the basic strategic document toward which FARC activities were directed during the period under examination. It was amplified and revised at the May 1989 Plenum, principally as concerned shifting the original timeframe to 1989–1997, but remained in essence what it had been all along: a classic people's war approach to be waged by 'dominating the countryside to surround the cities in order to galvanize a mass uprising to seize power. Crucial to the implementation of the strategy was adequate funding, a matter FARC addressed at length at the 27 December

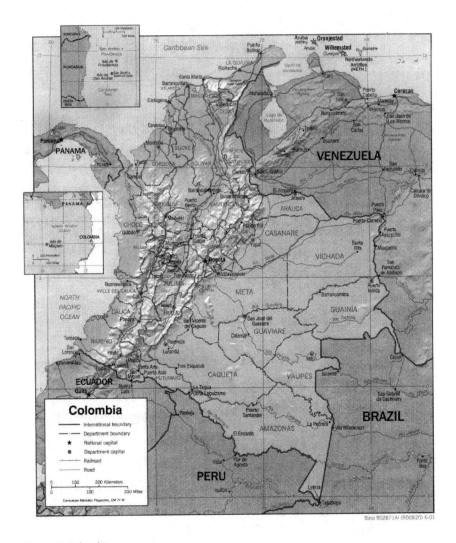

Figure 1. Colombia.

1984–2 January 1985 Plenum, then returned to in great detail at its 11–18 April 1993 VIII Conference.[3]

Paramount to understanding FARC, therefore, is recognition that it became a viable organization and hence a threat to the state only after the aforementioned May 1982 VII Conference, which both promulgated the Strategic Plan, with its attendant organizational structure and operational requirements, and also directed more robust fundraising, particularly through exploitation of criminality (in our terms) – or, in FARC's terms, attacking the financial oligarchy. Central to this criminality was kidnapping ostensible enemies of the people, levying revolutionary taxes upon businesses, and taxing the drug trade. In practice, efforts to prevent contamination of the political by the criminal quickly collapsed, and the three pillars of FARC's economic position became, in ultimate order of funds generation, drugs, kidnapping, and extortion, augmented by involvement in various licit and illicit enterprises, from the gold trade to cattle rustling and car theft. This reality increasingly estranged FARC from its purported social base – those ostensibly marginalized and alienated by a democratic but imperfect state.

Though FARC as a threat group emerged from the era of the Vietnam War, its roots lay in the colonial past of that imperfect state. An economy based upon mineral extraction and agricultural products[4] had struggled to industrialize and generate a trajectory capable of providing adequate employment. Social conservatism, a legacy of Spanish colonialism, increasingly clashed with the inability of the political opportunity structure to mediate grievances. A history of internal violence, which included a major civil war in the period 1899–1902,[5] peaked with a 1948–1960 social explosion labeled simply, *La Violencia* – 'The Violence' – which cost several hundred thousand lives and unleashed consequences with which Colombia continues to struggle.[6]

In the 1950s during *La Violencia*, Liberal and PCC (Communist Party of Colombia) guerrillas linked up, especially in Tolima (southwest of Bogotá; see Figure 1).[7] It was an effort to take the capital, Bogotá, by a combined Liberal/PCC 'column' that produced the terminology for what remains the basic tactical organizing structure for FARC (i.e. *columna*). Meantime, the organization of self-defense groups, *autodefensas*, exploded nationally, to include in the area of frontier colonization south of Bogotá that would become the so-called 'independent republics'. When there was a falling out between the Liberals and PCC over opposing goals (reform versus revolution), FARC was eventually founded in Tolima in 1963 by consolidating both existing guerrilla forces and various *autodefensas* that had left-wing leadership. Growing out of the Southern Bloc of the combined Liberal-PCC forces and ultimately (decades later) forming its own PCCC, or Clandestine Communist Party of Colombia, the new 'Popular Army' (*Ejército Popular* or EP) that was FARC grew steadily. FARC formally linked the two terms at its May 1982 National Conference to become FARC-EP, though reference simply to FARC continues to dominate the literature. That is, while FARC through the new title claimed to be but the armed forces of a larger social movement, ultimately realized in the party (PCCC) and a nationwide political organization, 'the Bolivarian Movement for a New Colombia', in reality, FARC *was* the movement (and has remained so to its present reincorporation).[8]

Government action proceeded in the early 1960s, more or less simultaneously, against all remaining pockets of guerrilla influence, which led to movement into final concentrations.[9] The most famous of these, Marquetalia, became associated in myth and reality with FARC's 'founder' and longtime head, Manuel Marulanda Vélez (actual name, Pedro Antonio Marín Marín), alias *Tirofijo* or 'Sure Shot' (12 May 1930–26 March 2008).[10] Indeed, it was the military's *Operation Marquetalia* in May 1964 which drove Marulanda and FARC to the national margins of the sparsely populated tropical plains of the *llanos* and deep jungle of *amazonas* in eastern Colombia (refer to Figure 1).[11] There, in areas that comprised a traditional Colombian frontier zone, they survived as national order was restored through a political power-sharing arrangement between Liberals and Conservatives, the National Front (*Frente Nacional*, 1958–1974), at the expense of other political forces.

FARC consolidation over the following decades in eastern Colombia would produce the extensive base complex that became the insurgency's 'strategic rearguard'. Other would-be revolutionary groups came and went on the national scene, such as M-19 and EPL, with only the Guevarist-inspired group *Ejército de Liberación Nacional* (ELN or National Liberation Army),[12] based principally in the northeast, joining FARC in demonstrating staying power. FARC had its main bases in the southeast throughout the conflict but was able to become a potent force in areas where colonization created opportunities for penetration.[13] Led throughout this process by Marulanda, FARC's overall command fell to a seven-man Secretariat (the equivalent of a politburo), which nominally reported to a central committee or central command (*Estado Mayor Central*) of 25 members (strength varied). In many ways, the central command functioned as would any higher level military staff, providing both analytical and administrative support, which was increasingly important as FARC became a national organization.

Its warfighting approach and doctrine, unlike those that dominated Latin America at the time, were derived from Maoist and Vietnamese 'people's war', with the ultimate filter the FMLN (*Farabundo Martí National Liberation Front*) of El Salvador. In the 1960s and early 1970s, the Colombian military regularly captured, from prisoners and in caches, Spanish language versions of Mao and the Vietnamese theorist, Truong Chinh, whose concepts are much the same (but keep alive the romance of the great urban uprising to accompany the surge from the rural areas). The Vietnamese worked with FARC directly to a limited degree, but eventually FMLN became the vector for transmission of the Vietnamese version of people's war, since the FMLN used Spanish-language versions of Vietnamese manuals. The physical location for this transmission was Cuba, and all major Marxist-Leninist groups (FARC, ELN, EPL, and M-19) worked closely with Havana.[14]

Just as the entire upper levels of command of *Sendero Luminoso* (Shining Path) of Peru were trained in China, so the same levels of the FMLN were trained in Vietnam. FARC benefited from this reality further, because eventually it also established links with *Sendero*. The importance of FARC's embrace of people's war doctrine cannot be underestimated. Its essence was a symbiotic 'combination of all forms of struggle' (*combinación de todas las formas de lucha*) doctrinally, the 'war of interlocking' which had so vexed Western response in Southeast Asia. As the insurgents thought strategically, the state continued to think tactically. Hence, prior to the Pastrana administration (1998–2002), FARC (as well as other

Marxist-Leninist groups) was rarely analyzed but rather described, especially its atrocities and its criminality.

In a sense, this served a useful purpose for FARC, because it focused analytical attention upon the most sensational but the least important aspects of its revolutionary project, its tactical outrages. Assessment of FARC's strategic thinking was carried out only at the individual level within the security forces and larger polity. Such development would take decades. Kidnapping (and extortion) could produce income that at times rose into the tens of millions in USD, but it was labor intensive and slow to generate a war chest. In altering the situation, the key intervening variable was the growth of the narcotics trade during the 1970s and 1980s. Success of the US-sponsored eradication effort in the main producer states, Bolivia and Peru, accompanied by interdiction of product movement to Colombia for processing, led to relocation and vertical integration within the latter.[15] The result was a concentration of leaf production in the *llanos*, with urban-based semi-legendary drug lords controlling cocaine production and smuggling. Principal markets were in the US and Europe, but Colombian society staggered under the violence and disruption of normal processes of administration and justice.

Pablo Escobar, still the most widely known figure associated with the cocaine trade,[16] would ultimately be killed in a December 1993 counter-narcotics operation in Medellín.[17] Yet he was already a prominent figure in 1982, at which time he was influential enough to be elected to the Colombian lower house (the Chamber of Representatives). This same year, as noted above, FARC held the significant VII Party Congress at which it outlined its Strategic Plan. This was to unfold in three phases – offensive, governance, defense of the revolution – over a period of eight years (1982–1990). As further noted, to fund this project, which it much later was to frame as 'the Bolivarian Revolution', and to gain manpower, FARC opted to exploit narcotics (and to increase its existing involvement in kidnapping and extortion). By taxing all facets of the drug trade, it would dramatically increase its war chest. By protecting and controlling production areas, it would not only secure its income but recruit from the marginalized.

This was known to state figures, principally within the security forces. Captured shortly after the VII Conference, the official FARC text of the proceeding was thereafter available to all desiring to work their way through the combination of colloquial and Marxist-Leninist prose.[18] Significant numbers of such FARC documents fell into the hands of the authorities over the decades of the conflict. Summaries and assessments were put in circulation.[19] The VII Conference itself was closely analyzed, as was the Strategic Plan. Though not well understood by most, it was straightforward enough. It called for the systematic building of a new world to challenge the existing world, of a FARC counter-state to challenge the state.

FARC's version of people's war was to unfold initially by creating 48 'Fronts of War' (*Frente de Guerra*; also termed *Cuadrilla*), wherein the combatants would eliminate government presence so that the new Marxist-Leninist order could be constructed. The result was that FARC, which began as a remnant group in the eastern *llanos*, built there substantial base areas (called in aggregate, the strategic rearguard) and eventually created a force which fielded nearly 17,000 combatants. These it deployed under the command and control of (eventually) 67 rural Fronts (and 4 urban Fronts), areas of physical and human terrain where the 'liberation movement' was active. The Fronts, in turn, were grouped under the seven larger *Bloques* (see Figure 2,[20] wherein two of the *Bloques* were actually Joint Commands or *Cdos. Conjuntos*, in effect, proto-*Bloques*). At this stage of the conflict, each of the seven Secretariat members commanded (often at a distance) one of the *Bloques*, which embraced in their assigned areas all of Colombia's 32 departments (*departamentos*[21]) – with the national capital district, Bogotá, its own entity – which were comprised of a total of 1,119 *municipios* (municipalities[22]). Major cities in the *Bloque* area of operations (see Figure 3) were to be isolated by having their lines of communication cut and their sources of sustenance blocked, to include power and water. This required systematic domination of mobility corridors (*corredores de movilidad*) between Fronts and between the *Bloques* (respectively, operational and strategic mobility corridors), producing an insurgent version of the well-known 'oil spot' technique. Domination of towns and population within or along 'corridors' allowed FARC free movement of men and supplies. Certain Fronts or groups of Fronts

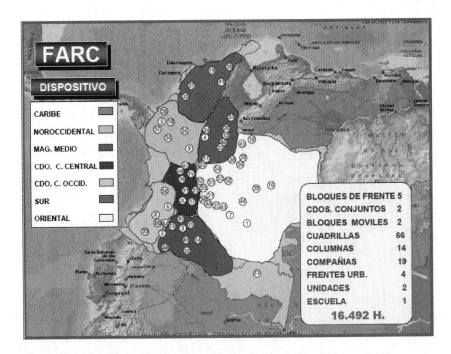

Figure 2. Principal FARC organizational structures.

PEOPLE'S WAR

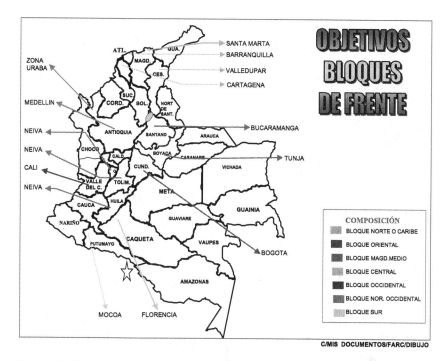

Figure 3. FARC Bloque primary objectives.

developed and controlled key base areas where organizational functions were carried out (e.g. training) and supplies were stockpiled. As new Fronts of War were opened and linked, all fused as the emerging counter-state.

For a ground level understanding of this reality, move through the 1st Front base area of Figure 4, lower right circle containing numeral 1, to the same area as positioned within its mobility corridor web, reflected at the numeral 2 on Figure 5; to the detailed mapping of that same base area in Figure 6. The illustration is taken from IV Division area of operations, but it applies to all areas of the country. The visualization, of course, is that of the state; there appear to be no equivalent FARC visuals, only documents that discuss implementation of the reality portrayed.[23]

Central to the actual development and functioning of this growing counter-state was FARC's organizational culture, particularly the relationship between the central leadership and the Fronts. The turning point for FARC as a force, as has been mentioned several times, was the VII National Conference in 1982. The setting forth of the Strategic Plan and the need for implementing forces (which required increased manpower and funding) meant that FARC expanded. As noted, the initial goal was to grow to 48 Fronts, and the procedure to do so was quite straightforward. FARC's existing Fronts, as they became larger, split and sent manpower into new areas ('Fronts of War', hence the terminology). Location of a new Front was determined by the Secretariat

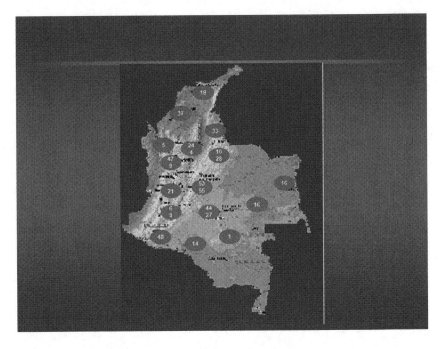

Figure 4. Farc major base areas.

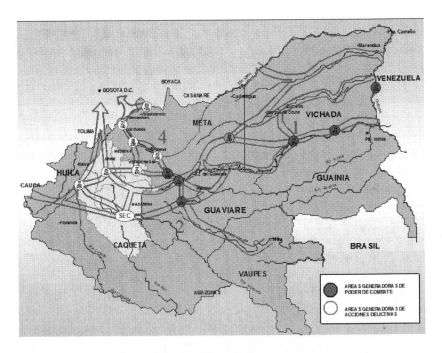

Figure 5. Farc base areas & mobility corridors - IV division

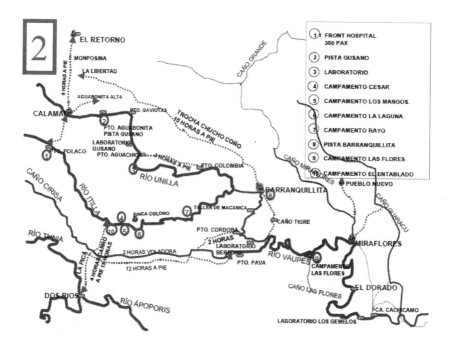

Figure 6. Base area - 1 front.

through a careful balancing of sustenance (i.e. availability of potential manpower and money) and local access (created by the unique dynamic of locality) with strategic calculation. The 5th Front, for example (return to Figure 4), was one of the oldest FARC 'structures', because the Secretariat sought very early to secure the mobility corridor to Darien while local particulars in Urabá allowed it to grow in manpower and funding.[24] It is reflected in academic and analytical work (see Figure 7 below) as early as the administration of President Turbay (1978–1982).[25] As its manpower increased, it served as the parent of the 34th Front (see Figure 8), which was formed at the end (1986) of the administration of President Betancur (1982–1986).[26] Finally, the 57th Front (see Figure 9) was formed in the same manner in 1991 during the administration of President Gaviria (1990–1994).[27] This process was repeated throughout the country, eventually arriving at the national structure discussed earlier. The Urabá case illustrates perfectly FARC's focus for expansion upon areas of frontier expansion, which offered ideal circumstances and contradiction for insurgent growth.[28]

Though FARC's rival, ELN operated in different areas. The state, savaged by the consequences of the narcotics trade compounded by multiple insurgencies, increasingly lost its coercive capacity in large swaths of the country. It would not re-emerge as a credible counter until the Pastrana administration (1998–2002). Hence, FARC was able to steadily become a more dangerous foe as it acquired means, manpower and resources, with the latter strongly impacting recruiting

PEOPLE'S WAR

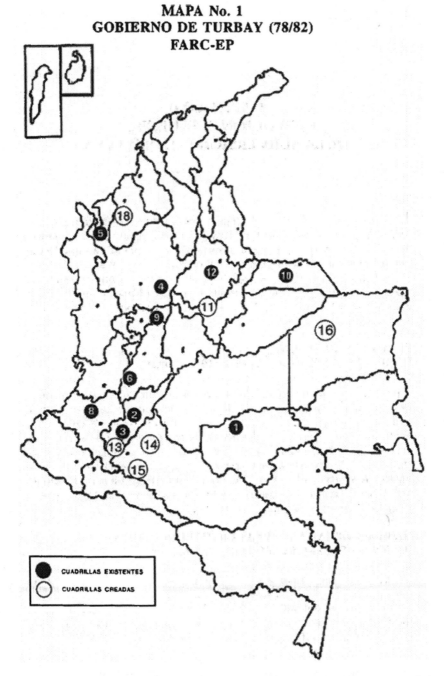

Figure 7. Fronts already existing (*Cuadrillas Existentes*) and those formed (*Cuadrillas Creadas*) during the administration of President Turbay, 1978–1982; 5th Front at upper left.

PEOPLE'S WAR

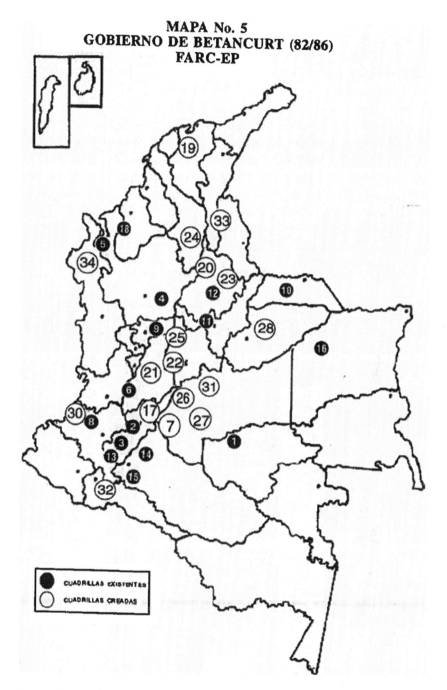

Figure 8. Fronts already existing (*Cuadrillas Existentes*) and those formed (*Cuadrillas Creadas*) during the administration of President Betancurt [*sic*], 1982–1986; 34th Front is below 5th Front, with location during the (later) 1998–2002 period reflected on Figure 2.

PEOPLE'S WAR

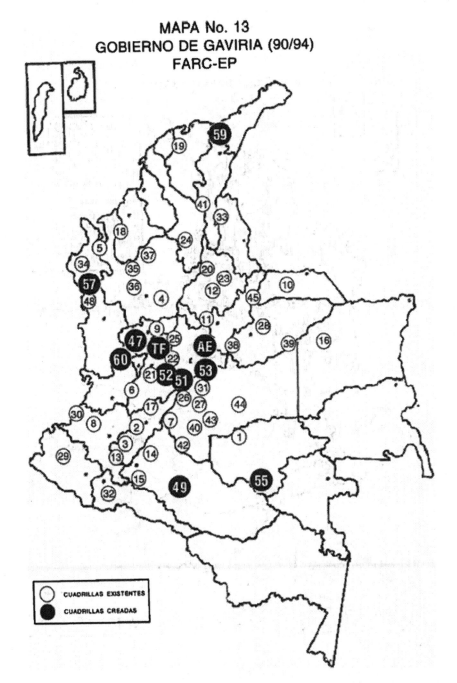

Figure 9. Fronts already existing (*Cuadrillas Existentes*) and those formed (*Cuadrillas Creadas*) – note the reversal of the black/white coding scheme – during the administration of President Gaviria, 1990–1994; 57th Front is below 34th and 5th Fronts, with location during the (later) 1998–2002 period reflected on Figure 2.

and retention. The modification of the 8-year Strategic Plan called for expansion to 60 Fronts, as well as the formation of mobile companies. In effect, FARC was duplicating the structure of the Colombian Army (COLAR), which fielded area domination forces and mobile or strike forces. In its functions, too, FARC duplicated the Colombian military. The crucial distinction was that FARC was forming a new world, a counter-state, while the Colombian military represented an existing state. That state provided the wherewithal to wage war, while FARC's emerging counter-state had to both grow and sustain itself.

This elevated the importance of the Financial Commissions of the center and the Fronts. A new Front could expect logistics support for a year from the larger FARC organization, by which time it was expected to be on its own. Each Front was in a command and control relationship with the center, yet at the same time, Colombia's sheer size and topography dictated that Fronts functioned semi-autonomously. This was true in all aspects, most particularly operations and generation of manpower and funding. FARC central authorities, recognizing that the latter was their linchpin, moved at the 27 December 1984–2 January 1985 Plenum of the Central High Command to establish more specific financial procedures. These asserted central control for the purposes of strategic coordination and prevention of free-lancing. The procedures were expanded at the VIII National Conference in April 1993, which published policies that have remained in effect to the present.

Generation of funds remained in the hands of the Fronts, but it was expressly noted that excess operational funding was to be forwarded to the center 6–12 months after the conclusion of the operation for which the funds were designated. Targets for funds generation were more carefully examined, with the economic growth of the country seen as offering myriad opportunities for exploitation, by which FARC meant demanding the payment of 'revolutionary taxation' (i.e. extortion payments) to support its operations. Fronts were enjoined to exploit the opportunities that were produced by their local circumstances.

Kidnapping was one form of funds generation which, though driven by local circumstances (i.e. the wealth of an area determined ransom possibilities), was explicitly adopted as a means of generating revenues for FARC; and the fact that most victims paid meant it was a steady generator of income.[29] Kidnapping had become a national scourge as the drug trade boomed, and both FARC and ELN were foolish enough to kidnap relatives or acquaintances of narcotics figures, thus opening up what became an intense struggle between the forces. It was the assassination of the Castaño brothers' father at a time when his eldest son, Fidel, was apparently involved in the drug trade, which led to a deeper family relationship with Pablo Escobar and a vendetta by the Castaño family that ultimately all but wiped out both FARC and ELN in key operational areas such as Urabá and the Upper Magdalena.[30] Pablo Escobar, the seminal figure associated with the cartels, it has previously been noted, would be killed only in December 1993, by which time Colombia was in chaos. It was to slide into what many called a 'failed state' status during the administration of President Samper, 1994–1998, and it emerged to lead the world in kidnapping.[31] The practical consequence, mentioned above, is that FARC exploited the vacuum created by the destruction of the dominant players to become the leading force in the drug trade.[32] This altered its funding profile but did not eliminate other contributors. Most prominent in terms of human tragedy, kidnapping remained a lucrative activity. [33]

A major source of funding and a significant strategic communications weapon when foreigners were victims, kidnapping was for FARC but one action to gain funding for implementation of its strategy. The criminal act was not intended for personal enrichment. Though exploitation of the drug trade eventually dominated the FARC funding profile, in the decades before 1982, kidnapping, extortion, and other traditional fundraising activities were central. Selection of victims was driven by a variety of factors, with prominence given to targeting individuals who were identified in FARC ideology as enemies – Americans and 'capitalists' were high on the list, as were members of the larger polity and economy – but the point of holding them was not for propaganda, as often imagined, but for the ransoms they could generate. These were normally substantial, particularly when converted to Colombian pesos.

It is noteworthy that well-known memoirs of Americans kidnapped by FARC speak directly to this point,[34] highlighting the ideological inspiration of leaders that caused indoctrinated followers (the majority of the movement) to label victims as 'enemies' but to understand little about them personally or contextually. FARC leaders, though burning with resentment at the alleged historical and present crimes of the United States, were less interested in the 'scoring of ideological points', except in a tactical sense, and remained focused upon ransom generation.[35] Whether the victims were foreigners or Colombians, at this point in time, the motivation was the same: generation of means to enable ways to seek ends, as strategy would formulate the issue.

Contingency was always a factor in victim survival and treatment but also in a victim's final disposition. For each constituent element of FARC was not only semi-autonomous with respect to the Secretariat but also necessarily highly decentralized operationally and geographically, which gave those physically possessing captives at any moment in time considerable sway over their fate and the specifics of their treatment. Memoirs are consistent in their descriptions of the awful conditions of captivity.[36] Though held under the same general circumstances accepted by the insurgents personally in response to operational requirements, these were invariably exacerbated for victims by measures taken by the insurgents to prevent escape, such as isolating and physically securing captives (e.g. keeping them bound). Implementation of the measures was left to the 'commissions' assigned 'guard duty'. These were normally of roughly squad-strength (approximately a dozen individuals), with all the resulting consequences of boredom and varied guard personalities. Medical treatment was rudimentary, as it was for the insurgents, with the ultimate goal only to keep the prisoner alive to the extent 'proof of life' (real-time confirmation that the prisoner was still alive) could be rendered. In the event rescue appeared eminent, execution was the normal course of action by FARC.[37]

If the actual manner in which captivity played itself out was contingent upon a host of factors, the same can be said for the process whereby targets were identified. The memoirs cited above reinforce a critical point: where foreigners were concerned, FARC as an organization generally viewed them as US agents (normally, as 'CIA agents'). Particular suspicion fell on missionaries since the central facilities that served as hubs for missionary activity had characteristics, such as communications equipment and organic transportation, that to the FARC mind indicated intelligence work. These central facilities could in and of themselves be assessed as strategic, a fact could not have escaped FARC suspicions; an assessment that was further solidified by the fact that they communicated with missionary sites which also had communications equipment and the coming and going of aircraft for resupply and the movement of personnel. The sites of missionary activity themselves were of concern to FARC, because the calling to bring the Gospel to marginalized populations necessarily placed the missionaries in peripheral areas largely devoid of significant or any state presence. These, as driven by FARC strategic doctrine, were the very areas in which the group sought local domination through its bases and corridors of movement and supply (i.e. mobility corridors or *corredores de movilidad*). The location of American Special Forces ('Green Berets') teams during the Vietnam War was driven by this same dynamic – making common cause with marginalized tribal populations, the imprecisely named *Montagnards* in South Vietnam and the *Meo* (actually *Hmong*) in Laos – though for an altogether different reason: to disrupt North Vietnamese mobility corridors by monitoring and raiding them but more significantly bringing to bear superior American combat power, often airpower. The comparison was not lost on FARC, particularly as its relations with the Vietnamese and Cubans grew.[38]

If the well-known cases cited in n.34 are augmented by analysis of the kidnappings of other missionaries and their acquaintances, as discussed in available memoirs,[39] it can readily be seen that all cases involve locations connected with FARC's structure and operations. Kidnapping, therefore, remained prominent throughout FARC's history. Indeed, it is remarkable that the important kidnappings of foreigners discussed above all occurred shortly after the 1982 and 1993 National Congresses, both of which validated the use of kidnapping for generation of funds. The wording of the 1993 conclusions is especially telling:

> The enemies of the people and of the revolution remain financial targets for the movement, [and are to be targeted] through generation of the previously [noted] political and economic intelligence [and in such manner] as to achieve [our objectives] while not creating problems with the masses, [simultaneously] avoiding investments that in many cases only generate costs and serious political damage to relationships with potential allies.[40]

Though it was also stated that

> in choosing a target to satisfy an economic requirement, [a unit] should communicate to its superior the data necessary for the evaluation of the case, so that the superior can make a decision whether to authorize or prevent the effort.[41]

there is little evidence that this procedure was followed. Perhaps most revealing in this respect was the kidnapping by FARC on 25 February 1999 of three international indigenous environmental activists in Arauca, their subsequent murder, and the dumping of their bodies across the border in Venezuela. Intercepted radio transmissions made clear that local initiative, in both instigating the episode and then seeing it through to its grisly conclusion, caught the central leadership by surprise. Nevertheless, so great was the error – the activists, not surprisingly given their presence in a highly contested, resource-rich area, were initially fingered as American intelligence – and so severe the consequences that the Secretariat felt compelled to deceive, denying all knowledge of the activists. FARC's second leading figure, Raul Reyes, in fact, simply lied, claiming no knowledge of the killings. Privately, Mono Jojoy, whose Front commander brother had ordered the killings, astutely termed them, 'The mistake from hell'.[42]

The killings, as they illuminate the previously noted tenuous balance between central desires and local initiative, also serve to highlight the points raised early on as to the prominent role played by parochial features and contingency in FARC's organizational culture. FARC's central command treated the incident very much as one of collateral damage. There was no disciplinary action of any substantive sort, because the local FARC commanders had the authority to make on-the-spot decisions. Their radio banter makes clear that, in this case, operational security was the driving factor, not kidnapping. Had the local commanders acted from a kidnapping motive, though, there would have been little different in the behavior revealed by the episode. Further, had events dictated that the captives – in the opinion of those holding them – needed to be executed, that too would have been sanctioned. FARC policy was well-known and discussed by all sides: It stipulated that hostages on the verge of rescue were to be executed. This, in fact, was the norm, with only the most sensational cases making the news.[43]

Quite apart from policy, the nature of FARC manpower – overwhelmingly very young, marginalized youth (principally males[44]), who fit the same profile as those recruited into gangs throughout the region – all but guaranteed that orders to murder kidnapping victims would be followed if it seemed they were on the verge of being rescued.[45] If the ransoms demanded at times seemed absurd, they stemmed naturally from the worldview of a force of which Carlos Ospina (who served as both COLAR and COLMIL commander) has observed: 'A remarkable feature of the first generation of FARC leaders was its permanent isolation from the quotidian realities of everyday Colombian life'.[46] Further, the manpower-intensive nature of securing captives, reflected in the memoirs cited earlier, all but drove a need to make astronomical demands as though to justify the time and effort expended. In a large number of cases, once ransom was delivered, actual release was made contingent upon an agreement to make a later secondary payment.

During the administration of President Pastrana (1998–2002), FARC began to shift from an emphasis upon fiscal to strategic considerations in its kidnapping. It sought to achieve equivalency with the government through the exchange negotiations and mechanisms for release involving very high value targets, aiming even to a state of belligerency as was achieved by the FMLN. This was to come later. In the period under discussion here, FARC remained focused upon financial rewards. There was simply too much money to be made, with ransoms at times paid in the millions of dollars,[47] money that was essential for the implementation of the strategic plan.[48]

FARC as threat to the state

FARC planned, as its growing means and operational improvement shifted the correlation of forces in its favor, a national offensive. This was to be led strategically by *Bloque Oriental*. The eastern mountain range, *Cordillera Oriental* (return to Figure 1; Bogotá is at the approximate center of the range), was to serve as the central base from which the offensive would be launched; that is, it would serve in the plan as the 'center of strategic deployment' (*centro de despliegue estratégico*). As the senior *Bloque*, led by the charismatic Mono Jojoy (actual name, Víctor Julio Suárez Rojas), it was positioned to benefit from narcotics growth and production in the *llanos*. Throughout the conflict, it was the largest and most heavily armed component of FARC, the heart and soul of the 'strategic rearguard', dominating FARC's combat profile. By 2002, it alone fielded 44.3% of FARC combatants. Of the seven largest FARC combatant formations at the time, five were *Bloque Oriental* assets.[49]

FARC constantly sought a synthesis which would produce victory. As its early guerrilla bands gained strength and funding, a 'regularization' took place (the term is Mao's) that analysts had witnessed elsewhere in theaters such as China, Vietnam, and El Salvador. Ultimately, multiple battalion-strength columns (*columnas*) were capable of converging upon and destroying vulnerable targets, with diversionary attacks (at times in their dozens) occurring nationwide to conceal the main effort. Manpower was equipped with more powerful weapons and indoctrinated ideologically, with Marxism-Leninism an integral element of capacity development. Captured FARC unit libraries throughout this period and later were comprised nearly exclusively of Marxist-Leninist works (in Spanish translation). Notebooks that had been carried by *male* combatants utilized the vocabulary and analytical framework of Marxism (e.g. always speaking of the state as 'capitalist') – even as the dominant 'doodles' in *all* such notebooks were sexual in nature, often graphically so.[50]

A harbinger of what was to come was the overrunning, on 30 August 1996 at Las Delicias in eastern Putumayo on Rio Caquetá (in 48th Front area as displayed earlier in Figures 2 and 4), of a company base of 120 men, killing or wounding half, capturing the remainder. Forces from *Bloque Sur* were joined by *Bloque Oriental* forces to execute the operation.[51] Significantly, in order to conceal this main attack, FARC struck simultaneously at nearly two dozen other areas. Security forces were quite unclear as to what was happening but sought to go onto the tactical offensive.

Elsewhere in the country, there followed other actions, often coordinated with demonstrations by coca growers in municipal areas.[52] Concurrently, a stepped-up campaign sought to clear entire areas of government presence. Mayors and policemen were particular targets, for once they were killed or driven away, a region became ripe for control. Special attention was paid to localities which would serve to isolate the national capital, Bogotá. Clandestine urban militias were formed to multiply the combat power of FARC Fronts. Simultaneously, Colombia itself was hammered by the US which decertified the country in both 1996 and 1997 for its poor counter-narcotics posture, thus denying it aid and advice even as the insurgents moved to exploit weaknesses in security force organization, doctrine, and deployment. Just how far FARC had progressed was brought home in late February 1998 when the under strength 52nd Counterguerrilla Battalion (52 BCG) of the newly formed 3rd Mobile Brigade (3 BRIM), deploying only 154 men in three of its companies, was lured into a prepared ambush and decimated at El Billar, Caquetá. As the Colombian presidential election campaign went on in August 1998, FARC launched a nationwide series of attacks. The most significant saw an estimated 1200 insurgents attack a company of the Joaquin Paris Battalion and the co-located counter-narcotics police base at Miraflores, Guaviare. Overrun, government forces again took heavy casualties: 30 killed, 50 wounded, and 100 taken prisoner. Again, response was difficult as more than two dozen other attacks occurred throughout the country as this one unfolded.[53]

It is important to reiterate how little of this was understood by either the Samper (1994–1998) or Pastrana (1998–2002) administrations. Even for the military, the key meeting at which top leadership came to comprehend what was occurring strategically did not occur until August 1999.[54] With a note of desperation – and anxious to act upon popular sentiment for 'peace' – the president-elect, Andrés Pastrana Arango, personally met with FARC leaders, then ceded to them, on a 'temporary' basis, a demilitarized zone (*Zona de Despeje* or *Area de Distensión*; see Figure 10 below[55]), as the price for entering into negotiations.[56] Centrally located in the heart of the country, the size of Switzerland (though with a limited population of perhaps 100,000), and within easy striking distance of both Bogotá and other major targets, it was ostensibly an area where military activity was prohibited. FARC not only violated such prohibition immediately, but subsequently used the *Zona*, as it came to be called, as a

Figure 10. Demilitarized Zone (i.e. *Zona de Distensión*); shows also areas of coca cultivation.

coca production base and recruiting zone, and as an unsinkable aircraft carrier from which to launch repeated strikes against government targets during the Pastrana administration, 1998–2002.

Dramatic as such action was, however, the ultimate danger lay in FARC's recognition of its relative political underdevelopment and its continued efforts to rectify the situation. Most interesting was its explicit assumption of the communist mantle, not just in-country via the Clandestine Colombian Communist Party (PCCC) but also internationally, where it sought to present itself in much the same fashion as did *Sendero Luminoso* in Peru, as the torchbearer for the wounded international Marxist-Leninist forces. Thus it stood up party schools and worked to expand not only cadre but the political educational level of military commanders. The schooling system was intended to solidify the FARC Marxist-Leninist ideological position, with all commanders being required to pass through ideological indoctrination curricula. These were established, with programs of instruction and texts. To cast its net still further, FARC publicly advanced its national front, the Bolivarian Movement for a New Colombia. Hand-in-hand with this went expansion of the militia, to protect 'liberated' territory, to the point that some of these local forces in the *llanos* were armed with high-powered firearms.

FARC in a sense saw itself as the next generation of the Viet Cong.[57] Where the analogy broke down was that the combatants *were* essentially the movement.[58] In a more ideologically sound insurgency – e.g. the Communist Party of the Philippines (CPP), which reached its peak in 1986–1987 – most manpower would be cadre and political operatives, with the combatant strength as necessary to facilitate political mobilization and governance of liberated areas. Ironically, despite having adopted the people's war approach in preference to the *focismo* of Che Guevara, FARC, from first to last, remained a large *foco* in search of a popular following.[59] *Foco* has the same essential meaning as al-Qaeda, the base: From a nucleus of determined, ideologically motivated and guided combatants, a revolution will come. The realization of this process was *focismo*. Set forth by Che Guevara in Cuba, the approach is the antithesis of people's war, which sees popular mobilization as producing the combatants, who, in essence, are but the tip of the spear. Both approaches, though, advocated a symbiotic relationship with the people, a reality negated by FARC's all but complete reliance upon criminality to generate the manpower and money needed to carry out its strategic approach. This involvement had distorted ways to the point that revolutionary ends were in question. Kidnapping and extortion continued, and despite its professed determination to the contrary, the deeper FARC was drawn into what had begun as a protection racket for drugs production, the more the organization morphed into a vertically integrated cartel in and of itself. The inevitable result was less contact with the population and more gang-like behavior.[60]

Thus FARC's military progress toward the goal of state power concealed a starker strategic reality. The 'combination of all forms of struggle' did not unfold. From its earliest years, FARC adopted terrorism as a primary way to achieve its operational goals. Citizens who resisted or even simply crossed the wrong FARC individuals at the wrong time were killed, often in the most hideous of ways. Captives, especially policemen, were frequently tortured and executed; from 1990 to late 2001, more than 5,000 policemen were killed in the conflict (most by FARC). Kidnapping, rather than being driven primarily by ransom concerns, as in the past, became a hybrid weapon with which to pressure the government for concessions; for example, by kidnapping VIPs and then demanding that the government either negotiate with FARC as an equal or involve outside organizations and countries (with the ultimate aim to achieve a legal status of belligerency). In 2000, kidnappings (not all FARC) peaked at 3572, making the country one of the most dangerous in the world.[61] Motorists could not drive out of Bogotá as the highways in the mountains were constantly attacked. Combined with widespread extortion and attacks on infrastructure, FARC essentially held the country for ransom, with entire towns attacked and left in shambles. The cumulative figure for displaced in the two-decade period, 1985–2005, was 3,940,314.[62]

FARC's brutality offered the logical opening for response, yet no coherent strategy came from Bogotá. Instead, it told the security forces to deal with the rebels, to engage in operations designed to maintain 'public order' (*orden público*). This they did by engaging in the tactics of counterguerrilla warfare as opposed to a strategy to implement counterinsurgency. There was little else they could do, for they found themselves quite on their own – at the very time when policy makers, both Colombian and American, had little knowledge as to the realities of insurgency/counterinsurgency, particularly the philosophy and mechanics of irregular much less revolutionary war.[63] Further, the diversion of the police into a focus upon counter-narcotics (CN) thrust the burden of formulating and conducting national response squarely upon the shoulders of the military, which in practice meant the Colombian Army (COLAR).[64]

In the absence of anywhere near the troop concentrations required for area domination and popular security, a vacuum developed – particularly in the areas where FARC focused its depredations. The result was a surge in self-defense groups (*autodefensas*), as had been the norm throughout Colombian history. They were linked in an umbrella organization, the AUC (*Autodefensas Unida Colombia*, or United Self-Defense Groups of Colombia), which was led for much of this period by the previously discussed, charismatic Carlos Castaño Gil.[65] In many cases, *autodefensas* emerged as a legacy of past state efforts to sponsor local forces. Even when they were judicially declared subject to restrictive legal interpretations, many of these groups were able to maintain linkages with military individuals and some units. Such was their explosive growth, though, that temporal sequence alone served to highlight the demand for popular protection and a willingness to both sponsor and join *autodefensas*. This mushrooming growth continued even after criminal linkages – often achieved in pursuit of enhanced funding, as was the case with FARC – led to their being declared illegal and targeted by the same security forces that they themselves refused to attack.[66]

The *autodefensas* engaged in savage battle with FARC (and ELN), clashing both with its units and brutally eliminating the organization's human support base. This contributed significantly to popular displacement and greatly complicated state response, forcing upon overextended units the thankless task of prioritizing foes and missions. For reasons stemming from ideological affinity or skewed priorities, cause-oriented groups, especially foreign, demanded that operations focus upon the AUC despite the reality that the major threat to the state was FARC. The predictable result of Bogotá's resistance was the widespread use of *Lawfare* against the security forces,[67] with the army again bearing the brunt of assault.

This was particularly ironic, since surveys consistently showed the armed forces to be the most respected institution in the country. In contrast, as has been previously noted, FARC had little to no popular following. The support it had achieved stemmed from its enhanced presence due to resource expansion. In particular, it worked to generate support from the drug production cultivators and workers themselves. Its cash-rich position had allowed it to recruit, as would any criminal gang, from among the margins of Colombian society. What was significant, following the creation of the *Zona*, was not the increase in the number of FARC combatants – almost 100% in some units – rather the growth of the counter-state behind this increase. This counter-state had been slowly developing but began to show signs of dangerous vitality in the strategic space provided by unfocused state approach.

Conclusions

As events actually played themselves out, military reform produced a powerful counter to the FARC general offensive. The strategic initiative was regained *militarily*, though overall the situation remained fluid.[68] The population continued to be largely unprotected, and remote regions were still under the control of FARC units. As his presidency drew to a close, Pastrana certainly recognized that his efforts had not produced the results he sought. Therefore, on 23 February 2002, he ordered that the *Zona* be retaken even as peace negotiations ended. One month later, in an unprecedented first round victory, a third party candidate, Álvaro Uribe, former governor of Antioquia, swept into the presidency. His administration, 2002–2010, was to decimate FARC and pave the way for the agreement that is now to demobilize FARC and reintegrate its manpower into the polity.

The strategy of the Pastrana government is considered by at least some credible observers as intermediate, a necessary prelude to the *Democratic Security* strategy that followed the period under consideration and which saw FARC's defeat. An opposing body of thought asserts that the lack of understanding of the strategic situation evinced by the president and his advisors unnecessarily permitted the insurgents to utilize the privileged opportunity provided by the peace negotiations and the sanctuary of the *Zona* to reach an even more powerful level. In reality, it becomes increasingly clear that the state approach in the 1998–2002 period was important in fostering the legitimacy of the polity while simultaneously building the capacity and capability of the security forces (especially the military). When Uribe took office, the state had regained the strategic initiative.

Central to the Uribe effort, particularly during his first term (2002–2006), was national mobilization grounded in popular legitimacy, the very foundation which FARC, though its reliance upon criminality to generate and sustain its insurgency, had increasingly ignored. This proved a fatal error, for the Melgar meeting had already recognized that only the violence line of effort of FARC's people's war was being implemented at the operational level. It was failing to pay more than lip-service to all nonviolent lines of effort integral to winning legitimacy. This allowed Bogotá to concentrate upon FARC's operational centers of gravity – structures (FARC units) and funding – in such manner as to produce success despite the disconnect between military and national strategy. When Uribe integrated all levels of strategy in support of democratic empowerment and mobilization, FARC, absent a popular foundation, shattered.

There is danger, though, in turning this reality into tautology. Legitimacy produced victory, but only because it served as the basis for warfighting mobilization. Building its revolutionary project upon a foundation of criminality indeed led to FARC's defeat. Yet it was a very near-run thing. All war, whether irregular or regular, is a contest of mobilization and skill. Power goes to the side that is first past the post. Once in power, a political force has any number of tools and techniques to ensure it stays there and to reshape the world in a manner that responds to its ideological essence. That Colombia could have lost may be a counter-factual bridge too far, but it is safe to say the state placed itself in a very dangerous position by forgetting the strengths inherent to any democracy built upon rule of law and popular empowerment. Once politics restored memory, the conflict's outcome appeared all but inevitable

Rather different lessons emerge from examining FARC's project. As the challenger, it was always in an asymmetric position of vulnerability. It sought to amass combat power through criminal resource mobilization. Kidnapping, as a salient component of the resulting resource profile, highlights just what an astonishingly inept choice criminality was for a political force that claimed to speak for the people. For kidnapping – like drugs and extortion – has but one target, the people, and as victims multiplied, so, too, did atrocities. Uribe's third party electoral victory in 2002 was an utter rejection of FARC*ismo* and all it had come to stand for in the popular mind. As the state pursued it, FARC could not hide amongst the people, who would have protected it had its strategy been pursued differently. Instead, the FARC remnants became a band on the run. In such circumstances, seeking peace was a wise strategic decision.

Notes

1. A large number of works treat this effort. See for example, article by Carlos Ospina in this number of the journal; also Ospina and Marks, "Colombia: Changing Strategy Amidst," 354–71.
2. See Marks, "Colombia: Learning Institutions," 127–46.
3. Single best assessment of this strategic decision-making process is Spencer, "The Evolution and Implementation of FARC Strategy," 73–98.
4. Colombia is well endowed with a variety of minerals, but only in the last decade of the 20th Century did oil exports replace coffee as the dominant (legal) export. The latter had been in top spot at least since 1860; in 2001, it was pushed to third (in export earnings) by oil and coal. Useful is Palacios, *Coffee in Colombia, 1850–1970*.
5. Sánchez and Aguilera, *Memoria de un País en Guerra, Los Mil Dias*.
6. See esp. Sánchez and Meertens, *Bandits, Peasants, and Politics*; also, Ramsey, *Guerrilleros y Soldados*. Excellent local study is Roldán, *Blood and Fire: La Violencia*. For background to the explosive violence: Caballero et al., *El Saqueo de Una Ilusión*; Sharpless, *Gaitán of Colombia*; Braun, *The Assassination of Gaitán*; and Green, *Gaitánismo, Left Liberalism, and Popular*.
7. See Henderson, *When Colombia Bled*; for *La Violencia* connection to FARC, Molano, *Trochas y Fusiles*.
8. This and other issues concerning FARC's history are discussed thoroughly in Ospina Ovalle, *A la Cima Sobre los Hombros del Diablo*.
9. Best source presently available on the American role in this process is Rempe, *The Past as Prologue?*
10. For a partial biography focused on, among others, this early period, see Alape, *Tirofijo: Los Sueños y las Montañas*; for FARC during this period, Pizarro Leongómez, *Las FARC (1949–1966)*.
11. Essentially, the *llanos* comprise the entire eastern half of Figure 1 above *amazonas* (true jungle), which conveniently for orientation has a department indicated with the same name. FARC was concentrated in the southern half of the *llanos*. Superb treatment of the region is found in four volumes by Jane M. Rausch; most germane to our discussion here is her *Territorial Rule in Colombia*.
12. See Medina Gallego, *ELN: Una Historia de los Orígenes*; also Medina Gallego, *ELN: Una Historia Contada*; for a substantial paired history, Medina Gallego, "FARC-EP y ELN."
13. The role of geography in fostering Colombian national disunity is a central point made in Safford and Palacios, *Colombia: Fragmented Land*; for further insightful commentary on the matter (referencing Safford and Palacios), see Coatsworth, "Roots of Violence in Colombia."
14. For details of the approach, see Spencer and Moroni Bracamonte, *Strategy and Tactics of the Salvadoran FMLN Guerrillas*, as well as my *Maoist People's War in Post-Vietnam Asia*, 1–55 and 353–67. Following the end of the conflict in El Salvador, interaction of the Colombians (and at times, this author) with FMLN personalities confirmed the details of their training and education in Vietnam.
15. For overview, Gootenberg, *Andean Cocaine*.
16. Early service in the Escobar organization and later battles against it were central to the rise of the Castaño brothers, Fidel and Carlos, who ultimately became the most powerful figures in the self-defense movement represented, in the first instance, by Castaño's own ACCU (*Autodefensas Campesinas de Córdoba y Urabá* or Peasant Self-Defense Forces of Córdoba and Urabá), apparently formed in 1994; in the second instance, by the umbrella group of self-defense forces Carlos Castaño

headed, the AUC (*Autodefensas Unidas de Colombia* or United Self-Defense Forces of Colombia), apparently formed in the mid-1990s. Though not the subject of this article, the role of the ACCU and AUC was central to events as they unfolded from the mid-1990s to the years after the period under consideration here. For the AUC, in a sense, fought fire with fire, returning FARC's terrorism with terror of its own, particularly against communities it deemed implicated in supporting FARC.

17. Though not necessarily the best or most accurate work on the operation, certainly the most widely read by English-speaking audiences is Bowden, *Killing Pablo*. Among the most detailed accounts of the actual mechanics of the Medellín cartel is a volume by Escobar's brother and administrator; see Escobar, *The Accountant's Story*, published under a slightly different title in UK. Useful, as well: Thoumi, "Why the Illegal Psychoactive Drugs."

18. Copy examined by author decades ago was mimeographed, 41 pages on legal-size paper and titled simply, *Informa Central a la Septima Conference* [Central Reports of the Seventh Conference]; see also the useful FARC publication, *Historia de las FARC-EP* (no publications data), which discusses the conferences and plenums from the II Conference to the 25–27 December 1987 Plenum. National Conferences were meetings between the leadership and the representatives of the local and regional groups to develop future plans. Originally designed to be held annually, they became quite infrequent due to practical and security concerns. Decision-making was carried out by the previously mentioned Secretariat and central command, which met formally in Plenums. The advantage for outsiders was that all such sessions were documented and their decisions distributed to FARC units. Such details could be and regularly were captured and analyzed.

19. Throughout much of the period under discussion, major Colombian security force units had access to a 'Power Point Paper' titled *Conferencias-Plenos*, which presented the main conclusions and directives of important FARC congresses and plenums (both regular and enlarged). Reduced over time to virtual boilerplate for widespread, continuous dissemination, the 'paper' lost all original identification and publications data.

20. Figures 2 through 6 are Colombian military graphics obtained during 1998–2000 fieldwork and are also reproduced in my "Colombian Army (COLAR) Counterinsurgency," 77–105.

21. The equivalent of states in the American political system; excellent maps, with numerous links, to include to *municipios*, available at: https://en.wikipedia.org/wiki/Departments_of_Colombia (accessed 29 November 2016). All levels of governance in Colombia have elected officials as a consequence of the 1991 constitution that led to the demobilization of M-19 and EPL. This is important, because officials in most sub-national entities before 1988 were appointed; after 1991 in particular, as noted, they were elected. Ultimately, as will be discussed later in this article, this was to play a powerful role in isolating FARC from those it claimed to represent. In a phrase, FARC lost the battle for legitimacy.

22. 'Counties' would be the most accurate English descriptive translation; the figure used is current (it was slightly less during the years under discussion).

23. Though not our subject at this point in the narrative, it was, of course, such assessment which ultimately allowed successful security force action against the clandestine world portrayed.

24. To my knowledge, FARC's role in the Darien has received no serious media or academic treatment; for Urabá, see Clara Inés García, *Urabá: Políticas de Paz*; Botero Herrera, *Urabá: Colonización, Violencia y Crisis*; and Plamondon, *Changing*

Social Relations of Production in Urabá. The latter is of particular interest for its examination of class structure development as a consequence of local, regional, and international forces, with insurgency an important element. The previously mentioned FARC 5th Front makes its appearance in the text on page 10.

25. La Rotta Mendoza, *Las Finanzas de la Subversion Colombiana*, 46.
26. Ibid., 54.
27. Ibid., 71.
28. For discussion of long-term trajectory, see the benchmark work Catherine Legrand, *Frontier Expansion and Peasant Protest*; for a specific case relevant to later FARC position in the *llanos*, Alfredo Molano, *Selva Adentro: Una Historia de la Colonización del Guaviare*; for specific discussion of FARC exploitation within and exploiting the colonization dynamic, Alfredo Molano, "Violence and Land Colonization," 195–216.
29. For later overview, see especially Cook, "The Financial Army of the FARC-EP."
30. Of the numerous works available, a number are particularly useful in revealing the intense battle for local security. See especially a trio of works by Romero: "Changing Identities and Contested Settings," 51–69; *Paramilitares y Autodefensas 1982–2003*; and (an edited work) *La Economía de los Paramilitares*. For the two major figures of the paramilitary movement, first and second in commands of the AUC during the period under discussion, see: Aranguren Molina, *Mi Confesión*; and Glenda Martinez, *Salvatore Mancuso, Su Vida*.
31. See Spencer, *Lessons From Colombia's Road to Recovery*, 24–37.
32. See Henderson, *Colombia's Narcotics Nightmare*.
33. See e.g. Luis Alberto Villamarín Pulido, *The FARC Cartel*. Particularly useful is the detailed assessment visually displayed at page 169. It presents FARC's funding profile for 1991–1993 and highlights that while taxing the drug trade had emerged as the dominant source of FARC income, kidnapping remained a healthy contributor, both in actual and proportional terms (e.g. $8 million in 1993 or 7.6% of the whole). Drugs, the author notes, continued to grow in importance as, in the aftermath of the major cartels' downfall, FARC moved beyond taxation to involvement in production and marketing. By 1995, of FARC's then-62 Fronts, 38 (61%) were active to some extent in the drug trade. That year, captured documents for the seven Fronts in Caquetá alone led to an estimate of approximately $36,780,000.
34. Among the most prominent American memoirs of this period, all available through Amazon, are: Johnson, *God at the Controls*, which treats the October 1985 kidnapping by FARC of four NTM (New Tribes Mission) missionaries (two on-site and two pilots) in Morichal, Guainia; Chad and Pat Stendal, *The Guerrillas Have Taken Our Son*; and Stendal, *Rescue the Captors*, which treats the August 1983 kidnapping by FARC of SIL (Summer Institute of Linguistics/Wycliffe Bible Translators Center) missionary (and pilot) Russell Stendal but also, in some depth, the FARC kidnapping (several months before Russell) of their intensely religious (though not missionary) neighbor, Ricky Kirby, both in Caquetá Department; Siino, *Guerrilla Hostage: 810 Days in Captivity*, which treats the 31 March 1994 kidnapping by FARC of SIL missionary (and mechanic) Ray Rising in Lomalinda itself; and Thomas R. Hargrove, *Long March to Freedom*, which treats the 23 September 1994 kidnapping by FARC of agricultural researcher Thomas Hargrove outside Cali, Valle del Cauca. In all of these cases, ransom was paid, and the hostages were recovered alive. Nancy Mankins, wife of one Panama NTM kidnapping victim, has also published a memoir, *Hostage*.

35. The point is well illustrated by the notoriety associated with kidnap victim Patty Hearst's participation in the string of California bank robberies executed by the Symbionese Liberation Army (SLA) in the mid-1970s. Though there was propaganda value in the now-iconic image of Patty as 'Tania' wielding a firearm in the Hibernia 'expropriation combat operation,' 15 April 1974, the point of all such actions was funds not propaganda. For useful discussion of the episode, see Wilmers, "Patty and Cin," 8, 9.
36. That of Tom Hargrove is of particular value. He spoke Spanish, was a Vietnam veteran with an advanced degree in agriculture (in which field he worked as a local advisor in the Mekong Delta and later in Colombia), and was familiar with the circumstances of Colombian insurgency and of insurgent personalities. He was also able to bring out intact his concealed diary. These factors combined to provide astute and measured analysis of what he details as a horrific experience. He was treated as one might expect from the minimally competent owners of a dangerous pet. His captors understood that he was useless unless alive, but beyond actions necessary to achieve this, concern for his physical and psychological wellbeing did not figure into the process. The personal ordeal created by isolation, restraint, constant movement, and fear, at times deliberately heightened by abusive guards, was peripheral to FARC calculations.
37. *Proof of Life* (Castle Rock, 2000) established widespread recognition of the term. Much in the film, based upon the kidnapping of Tom Hargrove (see n.34 and n.36 above), has been hyped for dramatic effect. The actual mechanics of establishing 'proof of life' – that is, that the victim being ransomed is actually alive – are reasonably well done. Deviating most from reality, according to Hargrove in personal discussions, was not 'the Hollywood,' which was to be expected, but the inserting into the film of blatant acts of defiance by the captive to establish a certain moral or even physical ascendance (or simply maneuver space) over his captors. Hargrove emphasized that such actions would likely have resulted in death and tended to misrepresent the sheer helplessness of prisoners in the overwhelming power mismatch experienced by the victim, both in human and physical terms. Colombia itself, in its stunning size and domination by tropical growth, was an overwhelming and formidable obstacle to survival, he noted, which further reinforced compliance with the rules of captivity.
38. For details on the former case, see Kelly, *US Army Special Forces 1961–1971*.
39. See e.g. a later episode involving two Britons, who were kidnapped on 16 March 2000 by FARC while seeking rare orchids in the Darien Gap: Dyke and Wilder, *The Cloud Garden*. The particulars are in their essentials in agreement with the American cases of n.33.
40. *Política Financiera de las FARC-EP*, 79; original is 5 pp hard copy in author possession as extracted from the much larger *FARC-EP Documentos*, a Colombian military compilation of FARC documents (obtained during fieldwork); my translation (with brackets indicating the sense of the text). The Spanish is: *Los enemigos del pueblo y de la revolución siguen siendo objetivos financieros para el movimiento, hacienda previamente la inteligencia politica y económica que es básica para poder alcanzar los objetivos sin crearnos problemas con las masas, evitando inversions que en muchos caso solo generan gastos y grave daño en las relaciones políticas con los potenciales aliados.*
41. Ibid., 79, 80; the Spanish is: *Al tener un objetivo elegido para hacerle la exigencia económica debe comunicarse al organism inmediatamente superior para que con los datos que suministren, más los que considere necesario solicitor, puedan hacer*

el análisis del caso y sobre esos elementos se autorice o se impida la ejecución del trabajo.

42. For details, to include transcripts of the intercepts, see Henao Ospina, *¿Asesinados por Error?* For the quote, 209.
43. For a particularly poignant, *recent* case, where the victims had been held more than a dozen years yet were executed with shots to the head and body when their captors feared they were on the verge of rescue, see Bajak, "Colombian Official: Rebels Executed 4 Captives."
44. During the peace negotiations, several media reports claimed as much as 40% of FARC was comprised of women. There is no convincing evidence that would support such a figure, and 15% is probably more correct, though it is possible that particular Fronts or *Bloques* reached higher female percentages. My own fieldwork on female combatants in Nepal has sensitized me to alteration of manpower profiles that can occur due to recruiting surges compressed into short periods (e.g. several years) and in particular localities. Nevertheless, that the '40%' figure surfaces regularly as media describe various insurgent groups globally suggests a lack of actual assessment.
45. Hargrove, *op.cit.* is especially observant and insightful on this matter, noting at one point (page 25), 'Most are, simply, not very bright.' This echoes my own experience in the several dozen interviews I have had with FARC prisoners.
46. Carlos Ospina, "Colombia and the FARC," 161.
47. In my work as a freelance journalist and political risk consultant, I became acquainted with kidnap and rescue operatives working in Colombia who had delivered cash ransoms in excess of a million USD.
48. *Política Financiera de las FARC-EP* makes this point abundantly clear. Throughout, it exhorts the Fronts, operating under the *Bloques*, to avail themselves of the ample opportunities available for accumulating the means to see the political project through to its conclusion. Nothing, from 'the buying and selling of cattle' to 'kidnapping enemies of the people,' to arranging for 'contributions from the oil, power, and mining sectors,' is beyond consideration.
49. Figures and calculations were done by author at the time based upon Colombian military order of battle figures.
50. Though I have interviewed female prisoners, I have never encountered a female personal notebook. Worth consideration in examining the lives of FARC combatants is @ Johnny, *In Hell: Guerrillas That Devour Their Own*.
51. For a discussion of this period, to include the attack on Las Delicias, see Spencer, "A Lesson for Colombia," 474–77.
52. For a nuanced treatment of the coca-population interface, Ramírez, *Between the Guerrillas and the State*.
53. See Spencer, "Bogotá Continues to Bleed as FARC Find Their Military Feet," 35–40. FARC's own treatment of these years may be found in FARC-EP International Commission, *Historical Outline FARC-EP*; timeline in text extends to 6 May 1999, which would indicate a publication date shortly thereafter.
54. Held at Melgar (some 90 km south of Bogota), the meeting was small and chaired by the commanding generals of the joint force (Tapias) and army (Mora). Most attendees were COLAR and included division commanders and key staff.
55. Available at: http://images.nationmaster.com/images/motw/americas/colombia_coca_density_2002.gif (accessed 29 November 2016).
56. For details, see Kline, *Chronicle of a Failure Foretold*; also, Édgar Téllez, Óscar Montes, and Jorge Lesmes, *Diario Íntimo de un Fracaso: Historia no Contada del*

Procedo de paz con las FARC (Bogotá: Planeta, 2002); for wider context, see Charles Bergquist et al., *Violence in Colombia 1990–2000*.

57. The most outstanding works on the subject remain those of Pike, *Viet Cong: The Organization and Techniques, PAVN: People's Army of Vietnam*, especially Chapters 9 and 10 of Section IV, 'Strategy.'
58. Though few, there are some who challenge this assessment. Not even giving a nod to nuance, they continue to hold that FARC, from first to last, has been an authentic expression of Colombian state imperfections and resultant popular grievances, representing a significant social base. See e.g. Britain, *Revolutionary Social Change in Colombia*.
59. For discussion of the Philippine case, with figures and maps to illustrate the point made in the text here, see Marks, *Maoist People's War in Post-Vietnam Asia*, 125–202; for comparison of people's war and *foco* approaches, 1–55.
60. This statement is accurate, but it is the very complexity of the situation that contributes in no small part to its intractability, with intertwining interests often approaching symbiosis. Of particular interest for the nuanced manner in which it approaches this reality is Gutiérrez and Barón, "Órdenes Subsidiarios: Coca, Esmeraldas," 102–29. For an equally fascinating discussion, comparing the drug ecosystems of FARC and the Afghan Taliban as they impinge upon ideological project, see Puentes Marín, *El Opio de Los Talibán y la Coca de las FARC*; as well as Colectivo Maloka, ed., *La Economía de las Drogas Ilícitas. Escenarios de Conflictos y Derechos Humanos* (Barcelona: Generalitat de Cataluña, September 2009); available at: http://www.gencat.cat/drep/ipau/sumaris/economia_drogas.pdf (accessed 28 February 2017). For FARC relations with the drug trade at this moment in the discussion, Luis Alberto Villamarín Pulido, *op.cit.*, as well as Jesus Enrique La Rotta Mendoza, *op.cit.*
61. For an effort to portray the horror and anguish inflicted upon victims and their families, see Posada, *Colombia's Kidnapping Industry*. Therein, the author uses selected case studies to highlight the terror attendant to having a loved one disappear, the shock for the victim himself/herself, and the toll exacted by unremitting fear at an uncertain fate, greatly exacerbated by often brutal conditions of captivity.
62. Rochlin, *Social Forces and the Revolution in Military Affairs*, 79 (Table 4.2). The cumulative total is useful in gauging the impact of the war, but in a country of some 40 million the size of California, Nevada, Utah, and Idaho, even figures in the hundreds of thousands annually must be used with caution, particularly since final disposition seems to be indifferently studied. There are no refugee camps in Colombia. Indeed, the subject of the displaced (*desplazados*) produces some of the most abused statistics of the conflict, because the total invariably appears in aggregate rather than annually or in any relationship to final disposition of the individuals concerned. For a solid treatment of the issue, see Stirk, *Colombia: Resources for Humanitarian Response*. It should further be noted that conflict violence of whatever form was (and is) but a subset of the more horrific legacy and criminal violence that battered the country. In my own fieldwork e.g. I estimated that of the 38,820 'violent deaths' experienced in Colombia in 2000, 3600–5000 deaths were directly a consequence of 'the war.' This is not to downplay the impact, when combined with the other factors discussed above, but it does urge caution. A solid discussion of intertwining threads of violence in the country during the years under discussion is Mauricio Rubio, "Es Desbordamiento de la Violencia en Colombia," 103–71; for details (with excellent maps and graphics) of only conflict-related violence, see Echandía Castilla, *Dos Décadas de Escalamiento*; for attempt,

as part of a larger approach to peacemaking, to examine the manner in which socio-economic-political costs of conflict in Colombia have been quantified, see for their useful data and graphics, Álvarez and Rettberg, "Cuantificando los Effectos Económicas del Conflicto," 14–37.

63. At this time, as implied in the text, there were no Colombian policymakers who were known to have any particular expertise on matters of irregular warfare. This was also true in the US. Even amongst the military, there was a lack of in-depth knowledge, though various components of the government had endeavored to remain engaged with the theory and practice of irregular warfare, notably the intelligence and special operations communities. The armed forces themselves (specifically, the army) were not altogether different but did not publish the 'interim COIN manual' until October 2004; see Headquarters, Department of the Army, *FMI [Interim Field Manual]*, 1–1 to 1–11. The much-discussed 'COIN manual' itself did not appear until two years later in December 2006; an official version is available at: http://usacac.army.mil/cac2/Repository/Materials/COIN-FM3-24.pdf (accessed 29 November 2016). A 'government COIN manual' was not published until January 2009; see United States Government Interagency Counterinsurgency [colored emphasis in original] Initiative, *US Government Counterinsurgency Guide*. These dates are well past the main events to be considered in this article. It may be noted that I wrote Chapter 1, 'Overview,' for the 'interim manual' and included Colombian examples in the discussion, having by that time been quite influenced by that conflict. The chapter was reprinted in a number of places, under various titles, notably as "Insurgency in a Time of Terrorism." It was cited in the 'government COIN manual' bibliography. The circle came round when a slightly updated version was published in the journal of the Colombian joint war college, *Escuela Superior de Guerra*. Its first section is: 'Insurgency is Armed Politics.' For the work in its entirety, see "Insurgency in a Time of Terrorism," 10–34.

64. For general discussion of the situation, Vargas, *Las Fuerzas Armadas en el Conflicto Colombiano*; for details on composition and budget of the security forces, see an article as notable for its misunderstanding of the rudiments of irregular warfare as for its excellent data, "Fuerzas Publicas: Una Empresa," 26–35; for linkage between past and present security situation, Tovar, *Inseguridad y Violencia en Colombia*.

65. Much discussed when it appeared for its frank, brutal assessment of the national situation was the earlier noted *Mi Confesión: Carlos Castaño Revela sus Secretos*. Similar impact was registered by a Castaño interview given to Kirk, included in *More Terrible Than Death*. Following his death, Castaño (born 16 May 1965, he was assassinated on 16 April 2004) was succeeded by his second, Salvatore Mancuso, who was eventually extradited to the US; see the earlier cited work by Glenda Martínez Osorio.

66. No subject is more fraught with analytical peril than that of the *autodefensas*. Yet little serious work in English was conducted on them at the time, even as they grew in a matter of half a dozen years to (apparently) outnumber FARC combatant strength (and dwarf that of ELN). The work in Spanish by Colombian analysts, only a portion of which I have cited earlier, was much better.

67. *Lawfare* can have any number of plain text meanings, but it is most often applied to the efforts of *sub-state* actors, both legal and illegal, to use the law as a weapon to impose their will upon others – hence the play on 'warfare'; see Marks, "Lawfare's Role in Irregular Conflict." A growing body of discussion and scholarship is available on the topic, to include a blog (jointly sponsored by the Lawfare Institute and Brookings) that adopts the more expansive

definition; i.e. the use of law as a weapon of war (irrespective of user). See: http://www.lawfareblog.com/ (accessed 29 November 2016).
68. See e.g. my assessments: Marks, *Colombian Army Adaptation to FARC Insurgency*; and Marks, "A Model Counterinsurgency," 41–56.

Disclosure statement

The views and opinions expressed in this article are those of the author and do not necessarily reflect the official policy or position of any agency of the U.S. government.

Bibliography

Alape, Arturo. *Tirofijo: Los Sueños y las Montañas 1964–1984*. 4th ed. Bogotá: Planeta, 1998.

Álvarez, Stephanie, and Angelika Rettberg. "Cuantificando los Effectos Económicas del Conflicto: Una Exploración de los Costos y los Estudios Sobre los Costos del Conflicto Armado Colombiano." *Colombia Internacional* 67 (2008): 14–37. Accessed November 29, 2016. http://otramiradadelconflicto.wikispaces.com/file/view/CUANTIFICANDO+LOS+EFECTOS+ECON%C3%93MICOS+DEL+CONFLICTO-+una+exploraci%C3%B3n+de+los+costos+y+los+estudios+sobre+los+costos+del+conflicto+armado+-colombiano.pdf

Aranguren Molina, Mauricio. *Mi Confesión: Carlos Castaño Revela sus Secretos* Bogotá: Editorial Oveja Negra, 2001.

Bajak, Frank. 2011. "Colombian Official: Rebels Executed 4 Captives." *AP*, November 26. Accessed November 29, 2016. https://www.yahoo.com/news/colombian-official-rebels-executed-4-captives-213725853.html

Bergquist, Charles, Ricardo Peñaranda, and G. Gonzalo. *Violence in Colombia 1990–2000: Waging War and Negotiating Peace*. Wilmington, DE: Scholarly Resources, 2001.

Botero Herrera, Fernando. *Urabá: Colonización, Violencia y Crisis del Estado*. Medellin: Editorial Universidad de Antioquia, 1990.

Bowden, Mark. *Killing Pablo: The Hunt for the World's Greatest Outlaw*. New York: Atlantic Monthly Press, 2001.

Braun, Herbert. *The Assassination of Gaitán: Public Life and Urban Violence in Colombia*. Madison, WI: The University of Wisconsin Press, 1985.

Britain, James J. *Revolutionary Social Change in Colombia: The Origin and Direction of the FARC-EP*. New York: Pluto Press, 2010.

Caballero, Antonio, et al. *El Saqueo de Una Ilusión: El 9 de April: 50 Años Después*. Bogotá: Revista Número Editores, 2003.

Coatsworth, John H. "Armed Actors in Colombia." *ReVista: Harvard Review of Latin America (Colombia: Beyond Armed Actors, A Look at Civil Society)* (2003). Accessed February 26, 2017. http://www.revista.drclas.harvard.edu/book/roots-violence-colombia

Cook, Thomas R. "The Financial Army of the FARC-EP: A Threat Finance Perspective," *Journal of Strategic Security* 1, no. 4 (2011): 19–36. Accessed November 29, 2016. http://scholarcommons.usf.edu/cgi/viewcontent.cgi?article=1072&context=jss

Dyke, Tom Hart, and Paul Wilder. *The Cloud Garden: A True Story of Adventure, Survival, and Extreme Horticulture*. Guildford, CT: Lyons Press, 2005.

Echandía Castilla, Camilo. *Dos Décadas de Escalamiento del Conflicto Armado en Colombia (1986–2006)*. Bogotá: Universidad Externado de Colombia, 2006.

Escobar, Roberto. *The Accountant's Story: Inside the Violent World of the Medellín Cartel*. New York: Grand Central Publishing, 2009.

"Fuerzas Publicas: Una Empresa de Billones de Pesos Que No Marcha." *Poder & Dinero* 47, no. 5 (1997): 26–35.

Gootenberg, Paul. *Andean Cocaine: The Making of a Global Drug*. Chapel Hill: The University of North Carolina Press, 2008.

Green, W. John. *Gaitánismo, Left Liberalism, and Popular Mobilization in Colombia*. Gainesville: University Press of Florida, 2003.

Gutiérrez, Francisco, and Mauricio Barón. "Órdenes Subsidiarios: Coca, Esmeraldas: La Guerra y la Paz." *Colombia Internacional* 67 (2008): 102–129. Accessed November 29, 2016. http://www.redalyc.org/pdf/812/81206706.pdf

Hargrove, Thomas R. *Long March to Freedom: The True Story of a Colombian Kidnapping*. College Station: Texas A&M University Press, 1995.

Headquarters, Department of the Army. *FMI [Interim Field Manual] 3-07.22 Counterinsurgency Operations*. Ft. Leavenworth, KS: US Army Combined Arms Center, 2004. Accessed November 29, 2016. https://fas.org/irp/doddir/army/fmi3-07-22.pdf

Henderson, James D. *Colombia's Narcotics Nightmare: How the Drug Trade Destroyed Peace*. Jefferson, NC: McFarland, 2012.

Henderson, James B. *When Colombia Bled: A History of the Violencia in Tolima*. Tuscaloosa: The University of Alabama Press, 1985.

Henao Ospina, Evelio. *¿Asesinados por Error? El Caso de los Indigenistas Estadounidenses*. Bogotá: Intermedio Editores, 2002.

Historical Outline FARC-EP. Canada: FARC-EP International Commission, 1999. ISBN 0-9686802-0-8.

Inés García, Clara. *Urabá: Políticas de Paz y Dinámicas de Guerra*. Medellin: University of Antioquia, n.d. Accessed February 26, 2017. http://aprendeenlinea.udea.edu.co/revistas/index.php/estudiospoliticos/article/viewFile/16150/14001

@ Johnny. *In Hell: Guerrillas That Devour Their Own (The Story of a Former Member of the FARC, Colombian Revolutionary Armed Forces)*. Colombia: Centro de Análisis Sociopolíticos, 1996.

Johnson, Jean Dye. *God at the Control*. Sanford, FL: New Tribes Mission, 1990.

Kelly, Francis J. *U.S. Army Special Forces 1961–1971*, Vietnam Studies. Washington, DC: Center of Military History, 2004. Accessed November 29, 2016. http://www.history.army.mil/html/books/090/90-23-1/CMH_Pub_90-23-1.pdf

Kirk, Robin. *More Terrible Than Death: Massacres, Drugs and America's War in Colombia*. New York: Public Affairs, 2003.

Kline, Harvey F. *Chronicle of a Failure Foretold: The Peace Process of Colombian President Andrés Pastrana*. Tuscaloosa: The University of Alabama Press, 2007.

La Rotta Mendoza, Jesus Enrique. *Finanzas de la Subversión Colombiana: Una Forma de Explotar Una Nación*. Bogotá: Editorial Ultimos Patriotas, 1996.

Legrand, Catherine. *Frontier Expansion and Peasant Protest in Colombia, 1850–1936*. Albuquerque: University of New Mexico Press, 1986.

Mankins, Nancy. *Hostage*. Nashville, TN: W Publishing, 2001.

Marks, Thomas A. "A Model Counterinsurgency: Uribe's Colombia (2002–2006) vs FARC." *Military Review* 87, no. 2 (2007): 41–56. Accessed November 29, 2016. http://www.au.af.mil/au/awc/awcgate/milreview/marks2.pdf

Marks, Thomas A. "Colombia: Learning Institutions Enable Integrated Response." *Prism* 1, no. 4 (2010): 127–146. Accessed November 29, 2016. http://cco.ndu.edu/Portals/96/Documents/prism/prism_1-4/Prism_127-146_Marks.pdf

Marks, Thomas A. *Colombian Army Adaptation to FARC Insurgency*. Carlisle, PA: Strategic Studies Institute, Army War College, 2002. Accessed November 29, 2016. http://www.strategicstudiesinstitute.army.mil/pdffiles/PUB18.pdf

Marks, Thomas A. "Colombian Army (COLAR) Counterinsurgency." *Crime, Law and Social Change* 40 (2003): 77–105. Accessed November 29, 2016. https://www.researchgate.net/publication/227087962_Colombian_army_counterinsurgency

Marks, Thomas A. "Insurgency in a Time of Terrorism." *Desafíos* [Bogotá] 12 (2005): 10–34. Accessed 29 November 2016. http://www.redalyc.org/pdf/3596/359633157002.pdf

Marks, Thomas A. "Insurgency in a Time of Terrorism." *Joint Center for Operational Analysis and Lessons Learned (JCOA-LL) Bulletin* VIII/3 (2006): 33–43. Accessed November 29, 2016. http://oai.dtic.mil/oai/oai?verb=getRecord&metadataPrefix=html&identifier=ADA521486

Marks, Thomas A. "Lawfare's Role in Irregular Conflict." *Focus* 4, no. 2 (2010): 12–14. Accessed November 29, 2016. https://www.jewishpolicycenter.org/infocus-summer-2010-counter-terrorism/

Marks, Thomas A. *Maoist People's War in Post-Vietnam Asia*. Bangkok: White Lotus, 2007.

Marín, Puentes, and Angela María. *El Opio de Los Talibán y la Coca de las FARC: Transformaciones de ka Relación Entre Actores Armados y Narcotráfico en Afganistán y Colombia*. Bogotá: Universidad de los Andes, 2006.

Martinez, Glenda. *Salvatore Mancuso, Su Vida: "Es Como si Hubiera Vivido Cien Años"*. Bogotá: Grupo Editorial Norma, 2004.

Medina Gallego, Carlos. *ELN: Una Historia Contada a dos Voces (Entrevista con "el Cura" Manuel Pérez y Nicolás Rodríguez Bautista, "Gabino"*. Bogotá: Rodriguez Quito Editores, 1996.

Medina Gallego, Carlos. *ELN: Una Historia de los Orígenes*. Bogotá: Rodríguez Quito Editores, 2001.

Medina Gallego, Carlos. "FARC-EP y ELN: Una Historia Politica Comparada (1958–2006)." PhD diss., in History, Universidad Nacional de Colombia, 2010. Accessed February 26, 2017. http://www.bdigital.unal.edu.co/3556/1/469029.2010.pdf

Molano, Alfredo. *Trochas y Fusiles*. Bogotá: El Áncora Editores, 1994.

Molano, Alfredo. *Selva Adentro: Una Historia de la Colonización del Guaviare*. Bogotá: Al Áncora Editores, 1987.

Molano, Alfredo. "Violence and Land Colonization." In *Violence in Colombia: The Contemporary Crisis in Historical Perspective*, edited by Charles W. Bergquist, Ricardo Penaranda, and Sanchez G. Gonzalo, 195–216. Wilmington, DE: Scholarly Resources, 1992.

Ospina Ovalle, Carlos Alberto. *A la Cima Sobre los Hombros del Diablo* [To the Top on the Shoulders of the Devil]. Saarbrücken: Editorial Académica Española, 2012.

Ospina, Carlos. "Colombia and the FARC: From Military Victory to Ambivalent Political Integration?" In *Impunity: Countering Illicit Power in War and Transition*, edited by Michelle Hughes and Michael Miklaucic, 161. Washington, DC: NDU Press, 2016. Accessed November 29, 2016. http://cco.ndu.edu/Portals/96/Documents/Impunity/Impunity%20FINAL%20for%20Web.pdf

Ospina, Carlos, and Thomas A. Marks. "Colombia: Changing Strategy Amidst the Struggle." *Small Wars and Insurgencies* 25, no. 2 (2014): 354–371. Subscription: Accessed November 29, 2016. http://www.tandfonline.com/doi/pdf/10.1080/09592318.2014.903641?needAccess=true

Palacios, Marco. *Coffee in Colombia, 1850–1970: An Economic, Social, and Political History*. New York: Cambridge University Press, 1980.

Pike, Douglas. *PAVN: People's Army of Vietnam*. Novato, CA: Presidio, 1986.

Pike, Douglas. *Viet Cong: The Organization and Techniques of the National Liberation Front of South Vietnam*. Cambridge, MA: MIT Press, 1966.

Pizarro Leongómez, Eduardo. *Las FARC (1949–1966): De la Autodefensa a la Combinación de Todas las Formas de Lucha*. Bogotá: Universidad Nacional de Colombia, 1991.

Plamondon, Olivier. *Changing Social Relations of Production in Urabá: Social Forces and the Colombian Form of State*. Montreal: CEIM and IEIM, 2008. Accessed February 26, 2017. http://www.ieim.uqam.ca/IMG/pdf/OPlamondon.MRP.pdf

Política Financiera de las FARC-EP ["Financial Policy of the FARC-EP"], VIII Conference (11–18 April 1993); hard copy extract (in author possession) from *FARC-EP Documentos*, Colombian military compilation (no publication data) containing important FARC captured documents.

Posada, Lia. *Colombia's Kidnapping Industry*. 2nd ed. Bogotá: Centro de Análisis Sociopolíticos, n.d.

Pulido, Villamarín, and Luis Alberto. *The FARC Cartel*. 2nd English ed. Bogotá: Editions The Pharaoh, 1996.

Ramírez, María Clemencia. *Between the Guerrillas and the State: The Cocalero Movement, Citizenship, and Identity in the Colombian Amazon*. Durham, NC: Duke University Press, 2011.

Ramsey, Russell W. *Guerrilleros y Soldados*. 2nd ed. Bogotá: Tercer Mundo Editores, 2000.

Rausch, Jane M. *Territorial Rule in Colombia and the Transformation of the Llanos Orientalales*. Gainesville: University Press of Florida, 2013.

Rempe, Dennis. *The Past as Prologue? A History of US Counterinsurgency Policy in Colombia, 1958–1966*, Special Series – Plan Colombia. Carlisle Barracks, PA: US Army War College-Strategic Studies Institute, 2002. Accessed March 1, 2017. https://www.bing.com/search?q=The+Past+as+Prologue%3F+A+History+of+US+Counterinsurgency+Policy+in+Colombia,+1958-1966&FORM=EDGENA

Rochlin, James F. *Social Forces and the Revolution in Military Affairs: The Cases of Colombia and Mexico*. New York: Palgrave Macmillan, 2007.

Roldán, Mary. *Blood and Fire: La Violencia in Antioquia, Colombia, 1946–1953*. Durham, NC: Duke University Press, 2002.

Romero, Mauricio. "Changing Identities and Contested Settings: Regional Elites and the Paramilitaries in Colombia." *International Journal of Politics, Culture and Society* 14, no. 1 (2000): 51–69. Subscription; Accessed November 29, 2016. http://www.jstor.org/stable/pdf/20020064.pdf

Romero, Mauricio. *La Economía de los Paramilitares: Redes de Corrupción, Negocios y Política*. Bogotá: Random House Mondadori, 2011.

Romero, Mauricio. *Paramilitares y Autodefensas 1982–2003*. Bogotá: Editorial Planeta Colombiana, 2003.

Rubio, Mauricio. "Es Desbordamiento de la Violencia en Colombia." Ch.3 in *Asalto al Desarrollo: Violencia en America Latina*, edited by Juan Luis Londoño, Alejandro Gaviria, and Rodrigo Guerrero, 103–171. Washington, DC: Banco Interamericano de Desarrollo, 2000.

Safford, Frank, and Marco Palacios. *Colombia: Fragmented Land, Divided Society*. New York: Oxford University Press, 2001.

Sánchez, Gonzalo, and Mario Aguilera, eds. *Memoria de un País en Guerra, Los Mil Dias: 1899–1902*. Planeta: Bogotá, 2001.

Sánchez, Gonzalo, and Donny Meertens. *Bandits, Peasants, and Politics: The Case of "La Violencia" in Colombia*. Translated by Alan Hynds. Austin: University of Texas Press, 2001.

Sharpless, Richard E. *Gaitán of Colombia: A Political Biography*. Pittsburgh, PA: University of Pittsburgh Press, 1978.

Siino, Denise Marie. *Guerrilla Hostage: 810 Days in Captivity*. Grand Rapids, MI: Fleming H. Revell, 1999.

Spencer, David. "A Lesson for Colombia," *Jane's Intelligence Review* (1997): 474–477. Accessed November 29, 2016. http://search.proquest.com/military/docview/198214510/D0A0A5C6EDEA4254PQ/4?accountid=12686

Spencer, David. "Bogotá Continues to Bleed as FARC Find Their Military Feet." *Jane's Intelligence Review* (1998): 35–40. Subscription; Accessed November 29, 2016. http://search.proquest.com/military/docview/198071637/D0A0A5C6EDEA4254PQ/5?accountid=12686

Spencer, David E., ed. *Lessons From Colombia's Road to Recovery: Security and Governance 1982–2010*. Washington, DC: Center for Hemispheric Defense Studies, 2011, 24–37. Accessed November 29, 2016. http://chds.dodlive.mil/files/2013/12/pub-OP-spencer.pdf

Spencer, Dave, and Jose Angel Moroni Bracamonte. *Strategy and Tactics of the Salvadoran FMLN Guerrillas: Last Battle of the Cold War, Blueprint for Future Conflicts*. Westport, CT: Praeger, 1995.

Spencer, David. "The Evolution and Implementation of FARC Strategy: Insights from Its Internal Documents." *Security and Defense Studies Review* 12, no. 1 & 2 (2011): 73–98. Accessed February 24, 2017. https://digitalndulibrary.ndu.edu/cdm/compoundobject/collection/chdspubs/id/18640/rec/45

Stendal, Chad and Pat. *The Guerrillas Have Taken Our Son*. Burnsville, MN: Ransom Press, 1989.

Stendal, Russell. *Rescue the Captors*. Abbotsford, WI: Life Sentence, 1984.

Stirk, Chloe. *Colombia: Resources for Humanitarian Response and Poverty Reduction*. Bristol: Global Humanitarian Assistance, 2013. Accessed November 29, 2016. http://www.globalhumanitarianassistance.org/wp-content/uploads/2013/04/Colombia-final-draft.pdf

Tovar, Alvaro Valencia. *Inseguridad y Violencia en Colombia*. Bogotá: Universidad Sergio Arboleda, 1997.

United States Government Interagency Counterinsurgency [colored emphasis in original] Initiative. *U.S. Government Counterinsurgency Guide*. Washington, DC: U.S. Department of State, 2009. Accessed November 29, 2016. http://www.state.gov/documents/organization/119629.pdf

Vargas, Alejo. *Las Fuerzas Armadas en el Conflicto Colombiano: Antecedentes y Perspectivas*. Bogotá: Intermedio, 2002.

Wilmers, Mary-Kay. "Patty and Cin." *London Review of Books* 4 (8) (1982): 8–9. Accessed February 28, 2017. https://www.lrb.co.uk/v04/n08/mary-kay-wilmers/patty-and-cin

Was FARC militarily defeated?

Carlos Alberto Ospina Ovalle

ABSTRACT
The concept of military victory has become opaque and quite different from the days of the industrial wars. Full military victory through total annihilation of the enemy has yielded to more complex ways of achieving political objectives. Eventually the understanding of the fact that the war is unwinnable on martial terms shifts insurgent strategy to one of survival, normally peace talks. It is this very shift of strategy, albeit the absence of insurgent annihilation, that constitutes the core of military victory for the government. Politicians and decision makers, if not military forces, blinded by the victory idea of the past, are unable to understand this reality. Hence, when peace talks are held, they are approached as the end of conflict rather than a shift to war by other means. This gives the upper hand to the insurgents.

Introduction

In the wake of the political debates that emerged during the peace agreement discussions in Havana, several government negotiators took the position that 'the FARC were not defeated militarily' and therefore a variety of concessions were both necessary and justified. This was reinforced by a member of the FARC Secretariat, who observed, 'We could not beat the state but neither did it beat us'.[1] Such positions, if considered from the point of view of partisan politics or even journalism, could have some speculative validity. Considered from a strategic perspective, though, such stances are without merit. It is possible to proceed objectively. There were political issues that gave rise to the conflict, and both sides had objectives that were sought. The strategies decided upon were the ways to apply means to reach ends. Either this occurred or it did not.

How, then, should the concept of victory be understood? What has been its evolution over time? In what way should strategic concepts be applied to revolutionary doctrines and theories and, on the other hand, to current military strategies? Is it possible to identify a decision and therefore a winner? How can this logic be applied to what happened in Colombia?

The present article will analyze each one of these questions to arrive at a conclusion based on the weighting and the analysis of each, with strategy considered scientifically and as an intermediate step between politics and war. This eminently deductive procedure results in a clear strategic conclusion: FARC was defeated militarily. Simultaneously it will be necessary to highlight the difference between two concepts that are often confused, defeat and annihilation, which can lead to conflicting interpretations and misunderstanding of the difference between ends, ways, and means as central elements of strategy. In order to obtain a more solid conclusion, we will also analyze two variables that are unfailingly present, the use of time as an unbalancing factor and the degree and intensity of the contestants' will to fight within the uncertain, changing, and unpredictable environment that governs the passage of contemporary times.

The concept of military victory

The definition of the concept of victory has as one of its starting points the Clausewitzian idea of 'an act of force to impose our will on the enemy'.[2] No doubt this idea could have many interpretations and could be framed at different levels. In the first one, it may be suggested that the essence of the Clausewitzian approach is directed to the act of force itself and that this constitutes the central part of the idea. Thus understood, no doubt its conception will be tactical and by association would implicitly imply the idea of destruction or perhaps of annihilation. This way of thinking leads to another of the Clausewitzian concepts, indispensable for victory, the center of gravity. Understood under this view and interpreted in the traditional way, it would be defined as 'the center of power and movement on which everything depends and without which nothing is possible'[3] and could be identified in 'those places where the mass is dense.'[4] Under this idea emerged the single point strategy according to which the outcome of a confrontation depends on a confrontation in which one of the two contestants imposes himself forcefully upon the other, totally neutralizing his ability to continue the struggle and, in this way, ending the war.

The term 'decisive battle' emerges naturally, then, in reference to obtaining 'decisive victory'. And there is no shortage of illustrations from history whereby, indeed, a key battle has produced a critical turn that has led to victory. The concept of victory followed a logic. Feudal or perhaps monarchical or imperial interests were threatened; deployment of armies looking for a total confrontation and the 'decisive victory'; maneuvers, counter-maneuvers, and fires. Ultimately, one of the contestants lost his internal cohesion, his ability to continue the struggle, and retreated hastily or surrendered. In contrast to the victor's achievement, the loser was decisively 'defeated'.

Matters become more complicated when the emergence of nation-states brings with it the concept of *national* interests. Conflict now proceeded as per the raison d'être of the state, to protect national interests and not those of the monarch. The new national armies fought for the former even if symbolically represented by the latter. Still, while professionalism in the officer ranks interjected another layer of complexity, the maneuvers in the field remained much the same (Alexander and Napoleon, for instance, may be usefully compared despite the intervening centuries). What did change was that the spirit of nationalism brought the strength and passion of the people to those in uniform, who defended with fury what was now considered to be their own interests, their nation's interests – the state.

It is likely this ingredient plus the effects of the first industrial revolution[5] contributed to the more aggressive confrontations witnessed, and thus the concept of victory was associated even more with the destruction of the enemy forces. The conduct of the world wars flowed naturally from this orientation. Even in the confrontations between less developed countries, the concept of victory was based on the idea of the destruction of the enemy. The Nineteenth Century War of the Triple Alliance, for example, that saw Paraguay confront Argentina, Brazil, and Uruguay, ended with the annihilation of the Paraguayan forces, and its commander and president of the country, Mariscal Solano López, perished in battle in the battle of Cerro Cora.

Ultimately, the threat posed by mutually assured destruction[6] forced the Cold War superpowers to displace their confrontation to the so-called Third World, with support being given to agency that sought either to hold or to seize power put up for grabs by structural contradictions and a modicum of contingency. Thus Latin America became one theater of battle among several, with no geographic area immune in the post-World War II era. This development occurred even as guerrilla war had been lifted from the tactical to the strategic level through its incorporation in Mao Tse-tung's 'people's war', which was closely followed in time and space by the Vietnamese variant and the altogether different Cuban approach.[7]

Mao's defeat of the Kuomintang began a new generation of war that raised a new concept of victory – though this would only become evident much later, since for the actual Chinese insurgency (as with the Vietnamese and the dissimilar Cuban approach), the ends remained the same as with regular warfare: decisive victory. Yet in its strategy, it replaced the idea of conquering the maximum space in the minimum of time, the fundamental characteristic of conventional war that leads to the 'decisive victory', with the use of time to wear down, to demoralize, and to discredit to the state, obtaining not the type of traditional victory but that which came after wearing down his enemy, ending his will to fight, without needing to defeat him in a single battle.[8] In order to execute this approach, two conditions were indispensable: to demoralize the military force and to make it appear that the armed insurgency was undefeatable. This was accomplished through partial offensives that would wear down the opposition to the point of breaking its will to fight and simultaneously through a series of organizations of social appearance that served to mobilize the civilian population to support 'the revolution' and simultaneously isolated the state, a task not difficult because as in many Third World governments, the misery of an important sector of the population, corruption of officials and dignitaries, and state incapacity remained constant over time and gave little hope of change.[9] In this way, the state loses its legitimacy and its ability to defend itself.

Thus did the Kuomintang gradually lose popular support, and its armed forces were defeated on the battlefield, though there was no 'decisive victory' on the part of Mao. It was time that decided the outcome. The fundamental variables had been altered in their priority and thus the structure of war. Time, as a consequence, assumed the central role in the process of revolutionary war, for it was around it that politicization and mobilization of the civilian population took place, especially the rural population,[10] as a state was built within the state in a confrontation that could last for years, thus the very name, 'protracted people's war'. Feedback on the progress of the process was structured politically, so that it was possible to measure the degree of mobilization of the civilian population and its link to the insurgency. The progress strategically within the three basic phases (defensive, balance, and offensive)[11] determined the degree of progress as time went by and the popular mobilization intensified. An intense mobilization brings the war ultimately to the war of position, the counteroffensive of the third phase. If mobilization is not accomplished, it is quite possible that the insurgent movement does not pass out of the initial phase, defensive strategy or guerrilla warfare.[12]

Years later in Cuba, Fidel Castro took advantage of the unpopularity of the dictator Batista to organize an insurgent movement in the mountains of the Sierra Maestra. There, he organized what came to be called the *foco*, a guerrilla center which leads the confrontation with the forces of the state. This initial *foco* gives rise to others, which gradually strengthens the insurgent scheme. In contrast to the method implemented by Mao, no integral attempt is made to politicize in order to mobilize the civilian population. Rather, successfully combating the unpopular government troops is intended to stimulate popular emotions in order to achieve their attachment to the movement. After each successful bout, the villagers are invited to join. It is a mobilization through demonstration.

While the two approaches of Mao and the Cubans are divergent as to how the civilian population should be mobilized, they have some points in common. The first of them is in the way to obtain the victory. It is not necessary for decisive battle but for the destruction of the will of the opposition. The concept of victory is thus transformed for both. Elements that make up the roots of the problem, such as inequality,[13] authoritarianism, exclusion, corruption, and the like facilitate the beginning and development of the process. Ultimately, it is their transformation into a new synthesis which is intended as victory. This, too, is achieved through time.[14]

State response

It is the roots – the contradictions – which in Latin America and elsewhere have given root to a plethora of insurgencies. In a first wave, enthusiastic would-be revolutionaries sought to emulate the success of the *foco* theory. In their eagerness, they overlooked the necessity for authoritarian structures to sharpen contradictions to allow exploitation. Where a state retained legitimacy, the *foco* approach found itself mired in miscalculation. Only Nicaragua, with a dictatorship operating in unique conditions of isolation alongside insurgent external reinforcement, proved vulnerable. Government strategy in such circumstances was based on maintaining certain degrees of security in the population and simultaneously confronting the armed uprisings without allowing them to expand their popular support. Thus failed the insurgencies in Argentina, Dominican Republic, Bolivia,[15] Venezuela, Honduras, and some attempts in Brazil and Ecuador. There were no 'decisive victories' even as the insurgent groups were decimated and their members killed or fled.

Those revolutionaries who adopted the Maoist approach, more painstaking and drawn out in time, achieved different results. Among these, the most important case was Vietnam. There, the insurgent leaders[16] not only welcomed the idea of Mao's protracted war but, unlike Guevara, had the mental capacity to adapt the ideas to their own situation. The Vietnamese brought to the task an explicit interweaving of the phases so that they 'interlocked'. Local time and place became the drivers, with growing state incapacity ultimately inviting a 'final offensive' of a great popular strike and insurrection that would paralyze the country and create an immense vacuum of national power and bewilderment. Power would then be seized.

The strategy used by the Americans failed, and although the revolutionary process was not carried out as initially planned by the insurgent leaders, the victory was won. The prolonged nature of the fight and its cost in what increasingly seemed a secondary global theater caused the Americans to withdraw nearly completely and then stand by as all of Indochina collapsed. Though decisive battle against the South Vietnamese sealed the victory, in reality it was the protracted effort against the Americans which determined the correlation of forces so profoundly favored the communists that when collapse came it was rapid and total.

The American strategy was influenced by the mentality of the previous wars[17] in which they had succeeded in destroying the enemy armies, thanks to the tremendous military capacity of that country and the idea that its troops would prevail as in all previous cases. Therefore, the main effort was directed in two basic lines: to destroy the Vietnamese forces of the North by constant and effective attrition using all available means; and to support a government that managed to stabilize the country and prevent it from being taken over by the communists of the North. In the years of commitment, these two goals were not only not achieved but to the contrary affected the cohesion of American society to the extent that military withdrawal proved necessary. Undoubtedly, the strategy was not appropriate, as it did not give due focus to the legitimacy of the state and mobilization of the people, thus denying political value to the military actions that were executed in the field and that, although in their vast majority favorable to the United States, had little significance on the outcome of the conflict.[18]

From the doctrinal point of view, Vietnam contributed a significant transformation to the concept of center of gravity. With no enemy formations to be destroyed, US forces were frustrated and, as part of that frustration, many rejected the Clausewitzian concepts that hitherto had been dominant. Nevertheless, some,[19] far from rejecting them, understood that the environment of war had changed. The character of the concepts had been transformed by generating an asymmetry that made them inapplicable.

The traditional concept of center of gravity was as the epicenter of force, but there was no definite power center upon which everything depended in the Vietnamese scheme and upon which the immense American power could be concentrated. Unlike previous conflicts, the fight was not for national interests but internal power and thus the center of gravity had to be found at that level. The point from which the legitimacy of the state was generated and upon which 'gravitational forces' of a political, military, social, and economic order converged was undoubtedly the center of gravity. A political opportunity structure accepted by the people as legitimate became the center of gravity.

This conclusion led to another. There were two ways of interpreting the war: the results it produced on the battlefield, which was not unlike a conventional conflict; and the effects generated in the area of legitimacy. The challenge was that the latter could not be definitively measured as could be the former, creating uncertainty. Further, since it was not a decimal, the former could through sheer power vanquish the latter if the state lacked either capacity or capability.

From 2002, the Colombian military adopted both concepts to the serious situation the country faced as a consequence of the effects of the FARC strategic plan for the seizure of power. This allowed it to produce a fundamental change in tactical dynamics but more especially in the strategic approach. As a consequence, the center of gravity in Colombia was identified as the legitimacy of the government, which in practice meant enhancing and expanding the processes of governance as well as popular mobilization, the latter much dependent upon the former. Local security[20] was combined with economic and social uplift within the political framework of democracy. Military focus was upon long-term effects upon FARC, to inflict blows of such nature and consequence as to make it give up in its attempt to take the government by force.[21] This concept of victory was captured in the strategic plans of the time. Effort by the military, therefore, was directed not at annihilating FARC but at ending its will to fight.

Vietnamese people's war variant in Colombia

FARC began its existence in the mid-1960s linked to the Communist Party of Colombia (PCC).[22] The PCC was not Maoist and thus incorporated rural effort as but one of its forms of struggle.[23] After indoctrinating them and legitimizing their actions, FARC understood their incompatibility with the party. The PCC was more sophisticated at this moment in its approach to seizing power. Hence armed struggle was but a line of effort. In contrast for FARC, it was a strategic approach. There were to be no alternatives except as supported violent seizure of power. These two views grew yet further apart when, after 1982, FARC formally opted to exploit the drug trade to enhance its means.

Indeed, FARC saw two direct benefits from the growing narcotrafficking (see Marks chapter in this edition for greater discussion): to provide finances for implementing the strategic plan promulgated in 1982, even as some FARC individuals benefited personally; and to weaken the state, both tangibly and morally (intangibly).[24] This would set a precedent for means generation in the era of 'new war'. That is, by relying upon what came to be called the 'terror-crime nexus', FARC was able to achieve complete strategic independence through control of means generated by exploiting the opportunities provided by globalization. Other groups, ranging from Hezbollah to Taliban to ISIS, would pursue the same course of action. In fact, ironically, the very predictability and sustainability of the drug trade allowed a degree of long-range calculation that would otherwise be impossible.

This long-range calculation took the form of a strategic plan for the seizure of power. By the December 1987 Plenum, this would be called the 'new way of operating',[25] but the plan had been outlined as early as the VII Conference in 1982 and was essentially an adaptation of the Vietnamese variant. Three ideas of this 'new way of operating' came from experience in that country.

First and most important was the shift from 'guerrilla warfare' to 'people's war' – in a sense, definitively rejecting the *foco* approach for the protracted war approach. This involved building a counter-state within the state, establishing 'Fronts of War' (normally termed simply 'Fronts', the idea of dividing the insurgent force to accomplish two specific missions, which should not be confused with front organizations in a united front sense) wherein local armed action disrupted and demoralized the state, even as mobile columns (of various strengths) answering to higher headquarters – *Bloques* had by 1990 been established as the higher command and control headquarters incorporating the Fronts – exploited the opportunities that emerged as the state sought to deal with local disruption. In terms of operational art of a traditional military but irregular warfare form, tactical action caused state forces to be placed in a position where the coordinated assaults could defeat them in detail. All such operational acts, in turn, responded to the strategic plan. This simply could not be more different from what most seem erroneously to envision is contained in the various works by Mao and the Vietnamese.

Second, the idea of carrying out a final offensive against the military forces protecting Bogota was incorporated just as it was in the Vietnamese planning for the now almost legendary 'Tet of '68' offensive. The FARC offensive was to coincide with a general strike and insurrection of the inhabitants of the most important cities to create a generalized chaos that would lead to a power vacuum, which in turn would give rise to a transitional government that would later give its place to FARC.

Finally, integral to the first and second borrowings just discussed, FARC explicitly adopted the mass mobilization approach as practiced in Vietnam (there was less direct understanding of what had occurred in China). Rather than leading with guerrilla action as in the *foco* theory, FARC opted to mobilize the civilian population through a series of organizations structured as nuclei of solidarity cells[26] directed to mass work. That its actual conduct on the ground would prove nearly the polar opposite of this would ultimately expose profound vulnerability, but that was for the future and later discussion below.

The concept of victory proposed by FARC, therefore, did not contemplate the destruction or annihilation of the military force of the Colombian state in an important and definitive action. Rather, this was to be achieved through regional offensives dispersed in time and space. This would achieve the objectives of demoralizing the military forces through a constant succession of blows and of delegitimizing the state by showing its inability to provide even a minimum of local security. The result would be a pre-insurrectional situation which would lead to the final or general offensive directed at the capital. In case of setbacks, what was at hand was not defeat but only the dropping back to an earlier strategic stage for reconstitution of power and rebuilding of the assault.

It can be seen that the two key pillars of this approach are the destruction and demoralization of the military and the mobilization of the civilian population. If these are not accomplished, the FARC plan is not viable. Comparatively, it was what the North Vietnamese were looking for, demoralizing the US military (especially the army), something that they achieved to the extent necessary by going through the society as a whole, and mobilizing the population in their favor, an objective more than fulfilled as documented copiously in various local studies and other works. The result, as is well known, is that the virtuoso nature of American tactical (and operational art) finesse was quite irrelevant to the outcome. As such, the approach, complete with its Tet offensive (no matter that it was decimated on the ground) served as a model not only for FARC but also for other insurgent movements such as the CPP/NPA in the Philippines and, especially, the FMLN in El Salvador.[27]

In order to fulfill the objective of shattering and demoralizing the Colombian military, FARC, starting in 1995–1996, initiated its war of movement,[28] seeking a balance of forces in certain regions, particularly those it considered as part of its strategic rearguard. These offensives had very particular characteristics, because they were carried out by massed forces of several battalion-equivalents, more than 1000 guerrillas and in some cases 2000, which struck isolated military units of but company strength even as diversionary attacks launched nationwide concealed the main effort.[29]

The high number of casualties suffered by the Armed Forces and the National Police began to cause an effect intended and desired by FARC. Police stations located in regions difficult to access or too far away to be supported had to be abandoned. In total, 154 municipalities of the country were without stations or presence of Police by 2002. Similarly, military locations in the same position had to be reinforced and their tactical activities curtailed, thus achieving the same effect. Some of the more remote patrol bases, such as Pedrera and Tarapacá in the Amazon, had to be abandoned altogether. Without security, in some departments, 39–41% of the municipal heads did not perform this important service.[30] FARC filled the resulting vacuum and created zones that it mistakenly considered liberated but nonetheless served the gradual expansion of the counter-state.

The mobilization of the civilian population should have gone into overdrive with the withdrawal of the security forces from various areas. Yet this did not happen, and even in the meetings of the insurgent group, this aspect was analyzed, because it would prevent their campaign from being sustainable.[31] FARC's self-examination could not discern that it was its very essence that repelled the populace. Its militarized posturing and quick slide into ignoring popular concerns were made possible by a funding profile dominated nearly exclusively by criminality. Despite all its surface efforts and mass actions, therefore, there was no acceptance of FARC by the civilian population, and only those directly related to the organization for geographical or personal reasons (notably, convenience) backed them. It was very difficult to replace casualties and to complete the formation of planned units, even as alienation from the populace deepened and took the form of fear by the latter. The inability of the state to offer protection would seemingly have cost it legitimacy, but FARC's brutality and violence served to more than offset this possibility.

This dramatically impacted FARC's center of gravity. Like all such mass mobilization insurgent movements in this period, FARC hoped to enjoy a certain degree of legitimacy in rural areas in order to mobilize the population. This perhaps was the fundamental aspect in Cuba and in Nicaragua where the illegitimacy of the government legitimized the insurgency. But FARC, having lost legitimacy, saw its center of gravity exposed and its operational critical vulnerabilities looming as operational centers of gravity in and of themselves. Ironically, FARC's effort to become viable through criminality had brought it internal cohesion in a military sense at the expense of legitimacy at the political, strategic level.

This caused FARC to cross the line of inversion discussed in the literature of terrorism.[32] It structurally isolated itself from the populace it claimed to represent, turning FARC itself into a self-referential organization that struggled for struggle's sake. Its terrorism – which was abundant and horrific (to include skinning victims alive) – was not a method, one among many, but had become the logic of the organization. The population was not represented but assaulted, with the notion of the enemy becoming universalized to all those who were outside the organization.[33] This took at times absurd (and obscene) forms, such as indiscriminate shelling with insurgent-manufactured mortars and the placement of mines in schools. The spirit of terrorist logic was reflected in utterances, such as 'giving the pistol to whoever opposes [us]'[34] or (explaining indiscriminately placing bombs) 'thus the rich are punished.'[35]

It can be argued, therefore – and the administration of President Uribe (2002–2010) did so – that FARC had transformed itself into a terrorist organization,[36] driven to structural estrangement by the conflation of ends-ways-means. That is, the means to implement strategic design to achieve the objectives had all fused into violence that was executed, because that was the purpose of violence. The resulting combination of ruthlessness and criminality delegitimized FARC and exposed its center of gravity. Strategically, its center of gravity had become the equivalent of a black hole, with the government mobilizing the masses through democratic process and enhanced mechanisms of governance. Operationally, FARC existed because of its 'structures' (or insurgent counter-state, especially its armed units) and its illicit funding. It sought to be like the Vietnamese but ended up not only a *foco* but a *foco* with the characteristics of that which Che Guevara launched in Bolivia. That, as already noted, led to disaster, and so it was with FARC.

Reformulation of the concept of military victory

By 1998, the turmoil of the state and the lack of comprehension of the strategic approach of the insurgents had allowed FARC to seize the strategic initiative. Military response was overwhelmingly tactical, and there was no political or strategic integration of counter. The regaining of the strategic initiative during 1998–2002 has been amply discussed in this journal. What only needs reiteration is the point raised above. As FARC was knocked back to the first phase of strategic framework, matters went much further, from bad to worse for it, because the nature of the project it had become meant not a return to first principles of popular mobilization but rather of criminality. This only heightened popular fear and estrangement from the ostensible revolutionary movement that claimed to represent the masses.

By 2002, the state had regained the strategic initiative, but there remained the need to go on to the offensive and to build upon the foundation of legitimacy through mass mobilization. Thus the Colombian military adopted a new strategy based on the government's overarching Democratic Security Policy, which stated directly that the protection of the civilian population was the point of the exercise. Strategically, what President Uribe was doing was the very opposite of FARC's approach, which had relegated the population to a position subordinate to the dictates of criminal fundraising. The result was a contrast of centers of gravity. Ironically, it was FARC that embraced force even as it had traditionally been the state that had behaved in this manner. With legitimacy, the state could proceed from a position whereby it was strongly supported by the civilian population. FARC, without this support, depended almost exclusively on its combat capacity, something that was politically untenable and militarily unsustainable.

Strategically, the Colombian military supported Democratic Security through *Plan Patriota* ('Plan Patriot'; see Barrios contribution in this issue for further details), the ultimate aim of which was to break FARC's will to fight and force it to negotiate on terms favorable to Colombian society represented by the government.[37] It is evident that this concept of victory, aligned with the parameters of fourth generation of war, allows us to appreciate how the idea of destroying or annihilating in order to overcome does not correspond to the environment of post-modern confrontation. Given the irregularity of methods and state-insurgent asymmetry that usually prevails, and which forces the triumph to manifest itself in adequate terms with the characteristics of the confrontation, the traditional idea of annihilating the 'enemy' is itself eliminated. Under this premise and with reference to the confrontation in Vietnam, other parameters determine the basis upon which the idea of victory is based. It is almost unthinkable for an insurgency to act as strategically irrationally as the Tamil Tigers did in Sri Lanka, with their hubris leading to their annihilation in 2009.[38]

In contrast, for most insurgents today, the loss of the will to fight is perhaps the most important parameter, and it manifests itself as the political objective of the insurgency becomes increasingly distant and difficult to reach, rendering useless even the use of time as a strategic weapon. After several years of struggle during which this altered reality is evident, the revolutionary war reaches the point highlighted by ex-M-19 guerrilla and Colombian congressman Antonio Navarro Wolf in a recent interview on Colombian television: 'It is a road without point of arrival, without meaning'.[39] The loss of the will to fight leaves only three options: surrender; loss of internal cohesion that exposes the insurgent group to destruction or annihilation; or flight, abandoning the struggle to search for what can be saved politically, normally through a peace process, an option increasingly adopted and producing quite unexpected results. Often, there is a general amnesty (normally backed by the same cause-oriented groups which make their main object of attack the state and focus their outrage upon state actors 'escaping accountability', not the insurgents). Through it is achieved political positioning without limits in the heart of the very state the group normally remains committed to combating, albeit by a different combination of forms. In EL Salvador, for instance, FMLN, which had been quite weakened by the time of the end of the offensive, still managed to achieve a resurgence through the peace process, to the point that today Salvador Sanchez Ceren,[40] one of the insurgency commanders, is president of the country. It can hardly be said that his ascendance has been the product of untainted democratic process.

In Colombia, the military effort that implemented *Plan Patriota* established very important parameters that were definitive over time and had a cumulative effect that led to those currently termed terrorists losing their will to fight and their desire to carry on with their struggle, something they had proclaimed would never happen. On the one hand, the very scheme of maneuver of the insurgent group was both a strength and a weakness. The Fronts and *Bloques* were dispersed throughout the Colombian national space ostensibly to mobilize the masses while avoiding concentrations of forces that would make them vulnerable. This dispersion, while protecting these structures, also caused them to be isolated from each other and attacked successively, concentrating sufficient military force on each one, with the aim of demoralizing them and gradually destroying their will to fight. This ultimately would be reflected in the reduction of their numbers through desertions and deaths in combat, as well as in the loss of territorial control that would accompany FARC flight and withdrawal from areas. At the same time, the civilian population was protected, as was the national infrastructure. Repeated time and again, the components of *Plan Patriota* had a significant psychological effect upon the insurgents. Security and fear became their companions. Such a sensation was the first step to demoralization.[41]

In such a dynamic, the attempt by the insurgents to use time was turned against them, because in general the actions that were taken to combat them were limited in time. This parameter suffered a significant alteration and was prolonged by the presence of military personnel in the areas occupied by FARC, controlling communication channels and attacking the structures, not only for days but for months. Political space compressed. The remnants were forced to abandon their dens and seek to survive far from them. Even their elementary activities, such as securing supplies, were seriously affected.

Plans carefully prepared by the Secretariat, which had hitherto been fulfilled, could no longer be executed. For example, the kidnapping of members of the military forces, politicians, and citizens – who were used as bargaining chips in political negotiations – was neutralized by a continuous effort to locate and rescue them from even the most remote jungle places where they languished in the hands of their captors. This effort could also be made against the members of the Secretariat, attacking them where they felt safe and protected, for in truth up to that point nothing had been attempted directly against them. Perhaps that was the origin of the haughty attitude they displayed until circumstances were permanently altered.

Military victory of the state

Assessments embodied in the analysis above were transferred to the operational field and materialized in three lines of military effort that unfolded over several years after 2002 and would produce a definitive effect on FARC that would lead to a loss of its will to fight. The way out, of course, was to seek an opportunity to survive politically. The expectation at the initiation of *Plan Patriota* was that the three lines of effort, carried out consistently, simultaneously, and efficiently, in all areas where the armed group was deployed, would have definite effects. These would not be measured through metrics of destruction or annihilation of FARC but of the neutralization of its capacities and capabilities to the point of forcing it to a strategic and tactical defensive[42] equivalent to a negative purpose.[43] This would result in invalidation of its political project and lead to the rational understanding of the futility of continuing the struggle against a steady-state reality of military victory (or domination, if you will). This was precisely what was achieved in Colombia.

The first line of effort of *Plan Patriota* was aimed at closing the capacity gaps in a grid of self-defense. The goal of various programs was to link defensive and offensive action, to protect the civilian population, its resources, and the national infrastructure, thus to consolidate legitimacy as a center of gravity and as a basic element of the civil status–population relationship. A notable feature was the novel (for Colombia) program of home guard defense termed 'peasant soldiers',[44] later called 'soldiers of my pueblo [home]', which used a slice of the national draft levy to form locally-based platoons to buttress protection of vulnerable small towns that were attacked regularly as FARC objectives. Until 2003, 116 towns had been attacked with little purpose other than to terrorize. Some were partially destroyed, others bombarded indiscriminately with explosive cylinders, area weapons launched from insurgent-manufactured tubes that caused deaths among the population. Such a case was Toribio in Cauca, which, according to *Semana*,[45] was attacked more than 400 times, of which 14 assaults had been major. More than a 100 homes had been destroyed and the inhabitants displaced. From the arrival of the peasant soldiers, the situation experienced a positive change. The peasant soldiers, organized into platoons of 41 men, nearly 600 such platoons in all, with the units tied into a grid comprised of the larger regular command, began to provide local area security and changed the force ratios on the ground. The civilian population experienced a sense of ownership, since the soldiers were from within. The deterrent effect was impressive, and over the course of a year, the attacks on the towns declined dramatically until they disappeared altogether.

Similarly, to end the rampant kidnapping on the roads and highways, which served both to generate funds and to terrorize – as well as to extract large 'taxes' on the transportation industry – a national *Plan Meteoro* ('Plan Meteor') was established with assigned units coordinated by central command. It took away, in particular, the problem of boundaries and limited local resources being exploited by FARC. In like fashion, special units were committed under centralized command to the protection of the national energy infrastructure. The point was not tactical protection alone, which was important, but buttressing government presence, reputation, and responsiveness in a system where all levels of governance were elected.

All this led FARC to withdraw from the outskirts of the urban areas and to enter the jungle, where it sought safety. This was a hard blow to absorb, because it meant objective limitations to any efforts at mass mobilization, regardless of past mistakes. In this manner, great regions of the state were restored to normalcy as measured by the metrics of daily life that one would associate with democratic governance assessing its effectiveness. State legitimacy was strengthened, and as a consequence, the center of gravity of the government prevailed over that of the terrorist force. The transcendence of this action was such that it had two immediate and definitive consequences. The first to deny a base of social support for FARC, which continued its descent into terrorism as a logic; and second, the idea of popular mobilization in favor of the self-proclaimed revolution was buried. It was through this line of effort that Colombia began to regain faith in itself.

The second line of effort envisaged under *Plan Patriota* sought to neutralize and dismantle FARC's armed structures, reducing their combat capacity and forcing them to disperse or abandon the regions in which they acted. The ultimate aim was to neutralize FARC's strategic plan for the seizure of power by eliminating the armed means necessary for implementation. To achieve this goal, the national army used one of its most important resources, the mobile brigades. Colombian force structure had long included very flexible mobile units with high firepower and self-sustaining capacity. These were expanded, first to battalions (called counter-guerrilla battalions or BCG, from the Spanish acronym), then to groups of battalions, the mobile brigades or BRIM (from the Spanish acronym).[46] Their characteristics allowed them to deploy even in the most difficult terrain such as the intricate Amazon jungle for long periods of time, permanently stalking FARC's units, forcing them to fight, wearing them down, preventing them from resting, and especially making them see that this action would be permanent. This seriously affected the morale of members of FARC. The number of individual guerrillas who deserted increased considerably, as did the number of killed in combat with mobile brigades and other military units.

As FARC's capability for popular mobilization, already limited, declined further, replacing its high casualties began to pose a serious problem. The solution was to increase the forced incorporation of children into the ranks as well as people who were not completely clear that it was the armed group they were joining. Such measures notwithstanding, a process of steady and inevitable decline had set in. One of the critical years was 2004, during which an average of seven FARC members per day were reported as casualties in combat[47] even as the number of deserters per day reached 7.8 on average. Such a rate of decline was very difficult to contain, especially given the lack of any possible mobilization from the population in general. By the time of the peace talks, FARC said it had just 6700 combatants. Given that in 2002, the insurgent peak strength was placed at 20,766, there had been a decrease of 66%.[48] From the point of view of the Vietnamese model adopted by FARC, these figures, far from showing the qualitative and quantitative rise required to obtain victory, demonstrated failure in two ways: from the political, a poor capacity for mobilization; from the military, a loss of cohesion and possibility of physical extinction with the accompanying loss of morale and will to continue.

The third line of effort in *Plan Patriota* was directed at neutralizing the strategic plans of FARC by eliminating those who generated them and by rescuing the military and civilian hostages who were being used as attempted bargaining chips for political negotiations. That is, while FARC implemented its strategic plan, it sought to become an equal, perhaps even to achieve a state of belligerency, by making demands concerning exchange of prisoners which would establish that it was a state equal to Bogotá. It built pressure by holding its hostages deep in the jungle in circumstances of indescribable physical and human suffering.[49] The means to attack both ends of the equation, perpetrators and release of victims, was a new special operations command that would dedicate itself to the task, supported by high technology and a much higher degree of training and capabilities than had previously been the norm for Colombia. Integration of superior, all-source intelligence was vital and accomplished. Between 2003 and 2010, most of the kidnap victims were rescued. The centerpiece of this effort, as the world came to know it, was the spectacular *Operation Jaque* in 2008, which used deception and capabilities to rescue three long-held American contractors and a Colombian presidential candidate.[50]

Using the same resources, the most important members of the FARC leadership, especially those in the Secretariat, were killed in combat. A new generation, whose will to fight was seriously affected, assumed leadership, but no longer with the same conviction as the generation decimated by the Colombian military. The extent to which the situation was changed was evidenced by FARC's inability to hold physically its X Conference. Ambushes and targeting of personalities forced a decentralized virtual conference to be held instead. As a consequence, without a clear idea of the way forward, FARC decided to welcome the idea of a peace process with the government.[51]

Thus the simultaneous, permanent, and effective action of the three lines of effort had a profound effect on FARC. The organization, accustomed to a certain passivity (in its eyes) of the government, suffered what amounted to strategic surprise since its analysis and appreciation of the situation were both based on false premises and approaches that in reality did not correspond to that mapped out in doctrine as the 'existence of a pre-insurrectional situation'. Marxist analysis, in other words, was providing a false picture of the state and its forces, and FARC was paying the price in blood and decimation. In a decade, 2002–2012, most of which were the two terms of the Uribe administration (2002–2010), FARC lost nearly everything it had built in the previous 40 years.

In fact, after the initial actions of *Plan Patriota* in the south of the country (2004), FARC leader Tirofijo was reported to have assessed, 'We need another four or five years from the moment the troops retire to recover [from] our losses'. The Fronts and *Bloques* were forced to consolidate the survivors simply to survive. Movement was constant to avoid strikes, and the ability for offensive action was lost. The Vietnamese model remained on paper, but all of its components, especially its fundamental grounding in mass mobilization, were gone. FARC had reached a state where it was on both the tactical and strategic defensive.

As noted earlier, the planning and leadership capabilities of the organization's top leaders were seriously interrupted by deaths and the inability to issue new policies. *Operation Jacque* had revealed that even FARC's fundamental and hitherto most secure communications processes had been not just penetrated but turned against it, with no way for units to ascertain the authenticity of orders received. The planned X Conference of key personalities to produce strategic innovation had also collapsed, leaving in place a strategic design that had been essentially unchanged since 1993. The result was a vacuum that the Secretariat tried to fill with temporary instructions. This was not successful for strategy.

FARC's initial reformulation of strategy was a plan for renewal, *Renacer* (rebirth), promulgated in 2010. It featured a return to the level of guerrilla warfare, abandoning mobile warfare, which would be combined with the political action of Front organizations to bring about not a martial final offensive but a popular insurrection against the government. This approach was contrary to what had been proclaimed by the founder of FARC, Tirofijo, but he had died on 26 March 2008, shortly after FARC's number two, Raul Reyes, had been eliminated in a precision strike upon his camp in Ecuador on 1 March 2008. With the similar death of FARC's premier combatant, Mono JoJoy, on 22 September 2010, the way seemed clear for a revision of past approaches. Here, too, reality caused FARC to stumble, as a November 2011 military operation killed Tirofijo's successor, Alfonso Cano.

This action caused FARC not only to renounce armed action as a means to reach power but also to open the third political moment of its political project: to opt for a peace process with the government and to try to obtain maximum political advantages. In this course of action, it was aided by the extreme left-wing elements of the FMLN, still active in El Salvador, Fidel Castro, and the usual assortment of radical foreigners (primarily Spanish-speaking Europeans). Taking advantage of the fact that the civilian population still feared the havoc and destruction that FARC had unleashed in its assault upon them, it represented its shift as one of the heart rather than of circumstance. By adopting an outwardly conciliatory position, FARC could advance further than it had in the field and could yet plot to secure its criminally-generated funds for future political action within the very system it had sought for so long to destroy. A nation desperate for peace, cut corners in both the negotiations and terms of reincorporation into the polity. A Nobel Peace Prize was awarded, and the process is ongoing.

All this allows us to return to the concept of military victory. FARC indeed had been defeated. Its insurgent project based on the seizure of power by arms had failed, neutralized to the point that it could evince no current effects with no prospect (save wishful or dogmatic thinking) for realization in the future. The death of personalities ultimately allowed the bubble at the top to be pierced in a manner which joined its reappraisal with the already rampant loss of morale at the base. That base, to be clear, was the organization itself. There was little else, for the Vietnamese approach had not been realized.

It was Colombian military action that produced this 'effect', one of such proportions that it significantly affected the will of the insurgency to the point of forcing it to retire from the field of battle. In modern terms or the fourth generation of war, such action is in fact 'military victory'. The conditions of a globalized, technologically advanced, and interconnected world, with a democratic mentality (regardless of the apparent romance with authoritarianism in some circles), makes anachronistic the idea of insurgent triumph and, to the contrary, provides conditions for military defeat as happened in Colombia. The challenge within this somewhat uplifting message is that, as was seen much earlier in the Vietnamese and El Salvadoran cases (or even that of Nepal as discussed recently in this journal[52]), peace is not at hand – only a shift to a different form of struggle.

Notes

1. "Interview with Timoleon Jimenez, Leader of the FARC."
2. Echeverria, *Clausewitz and Contemporary War*, 64.
3. Ibid., 177.
4. Ibid., 180.
5. Sigman, *1848: The Romantic and Democratic Revolutions of Europe*, 43.
6. The Cold War concept, aptly abbreviated MAD, whereby the use of nuclear weapons by one or several of the contenders would trigger massive retaliation and the destruction of both sides.
7. See Marks, *Maoist People's War in Post-Vietnam Asia*.
8. See *Selected Works of Mao Tse-tung*.
9. See Skocpol, *States and Social Revolutions*.
10. Mao used Lenin's ideas to organize and inform his revolutionary war. However, due to the rural nature of his country, he replaced the idea of mobilizing workers, unions, and associations to obtain a social explosion with the mobilization of

the peasantry to develop 'people's war' or 'popular protracted war.' This type of war has been taken as a model by numerous groups to include some of today's jihadist groups in the Middle East.
11. The way Mao's war has been structured with an initial guerrilla phase has given affected governments the false idea that what they are facing are only small and dispersed gangs of criminals. They are unaware that what actually is going on is an ascendant strategy which is designed to transition to the war of movement (i.e. maneuver or mobile warfare involving rival military units). Thus several armies have been surprised. In El Salvador and arguably in the Philippines, both armies were taken to the brink of defeat, forcing their governments to introduce radical changes in their strategies, policies, and budgets.
12. Each phase is characterized by the way the insurgent armed force is applied. During the first phase, this force is utilized in the form of small guerrilla groups accompanied by 'struggle' in local areas, which is terrorism, though not termed as such by the perpetrators. With time, these groups, having through political action mobilized manpower, 'regularize', become copies of government units. This allows them to exercise force-on-force in maneuver warfare (also rendered by the Chinese as the war of movement, by the Vietnamese as main force warfare). Eventually, as required, light units will become heavy units, and conventional warfare will allow the seizing of territory, the war of position. If the situation reaches this level, it is very likely the insurgency will defeat the government and will seize power.
13. Called 'objective conditions' in the Marxist theory. According to the same theory, they are complemented by the 'subjective conditions' produced by the radicalization of the masses through the political action of the insurgent group.
14. See Debray, *Revolution in the Revolution*.
15. In this country, the failure of the revolutionary process was total. The failure included the death of the revolutionary icon, Ernesto 'Che' Guevara, the originator of the *foco* theory. Guevara performed poorly, not only at the tactical but also at the strategic level. He showed little understanding of such basic principles of irregular war as adaptability, flexibility, and modernization *despite* his previous failure in the Congo. There, he had been forced to flee after his men became demoralized and useless for combat. Later, in Bolivia, he became isolated from any kind of support; and in his final combat, he was captured and later executed by his Bolivians captors.
16. Ho Chi Minh was the real leader of the Vietnamese revolutionary process. However, the writing part was done by Truong Chinh, and in the field, operations were conducted by the famous Vo Nguyen Giap, the same general who defeated the French at Dienbienphu.
17. The American general William Westmoreland commanded the troops in Vietnam between 1964 and 1968. He implemented a strategy that sought to push the main forces away from the populated areas while the Vietnamese forces engaged in counterinsurgency. Often misunderstood as a strategy of 'Search and destroy,' the attrition phase was necessary in a situation that had already reached 'war of position' prior to U.S. main force intervention in March 1965.
18. A much repeated anecdote was reported at the time of the signing of the treaty between the US and Vietnam, in which the withdrawal of the American troops from that country was agreed. An American representative, Harry Summers, told the North Vietnamese representative that the Vietnamese had never defeated the American troops in battle. The Vietnamese officer answered to the effect 'that might be true, but in war it is irrelevant.'

19. One of the most insightful of them is Professor Antulio Echavarria, who, in spite of his opposition to the concept of fourth generation war, defined with great clarity the strategic concept of center of gravity in a new dimension. For further information see his *Clausewitz's Center of Gravity*.
20. The rampant insecurity that affected the countryside in Colombia was reflected in the permanent fear amongst much of the peasantry. According to the Colombian Defense Ministry, during 2002, 2885 citizens were abducted in the countryside, an average of 8 per day.
21. Local newspapers, in particular *el Tiempo* from Bogota, were more concerned with making headlines and breaking news than in understanding the government's strategy, and for this reason, they misguided their audiences, focusing upon the tactical, ignoring the strategic effects obtained through that strategy.
22. In 1961, during the IX Congress of the Communist Party of Colombia – and following the directives of the Communist Party of the Soviet Union that encouraged peaceful coexistence – this approach was adopted as part of further conspiratorial action. It was given priority over guerrilla war, which was considered supporting rather than primary.
23. Eduardo Pizarro Leon Gomez (a well-known Colombian analyst) defines FARC as a guerrilla party 'working for a political project of a political party, which in turn has command and control over the guerrilla group.'
24. Ospina, *A la Cima sobre los hombros del diablo*, 228–30.
25. One of the conclusions of the FARC VII Conference was to implement massed actions against isolated detachments of the armed forces in order to obtain better results and demoralize the troops.
26. These are part of the conclusions of the FARC VII Conference. This was the most important of FARC's conferences. It called for a protracted war to seize power.
27. This offensive was launched mainly in the city of San Salvador. After some days of hard fighting, the FMLN suffered high casualties and withdrew. However, it was an important step leading to the signing of the peace in El Salvador, the demobilization of the FMLN, and the end of the conflict.
28. This is linked to the quality of popular mobilization. If a strong peasant rate of mobilization can be sustained for a prolonged time, the war of movement can be prolonged. If it fails, the process will fail.
29. Through this technique FARC surprised and defeated military units in places such as las Delicias (Caquetá), el Billar (Caquetá), la Carpa (Guaviare), Paramo de Alizales (Nariño), San Juanito (Meta), Pavarando (Antioquia), and Mitu (Vaupes). During these actions, the military units were not only defeated but FARC was able of seize hundreds of troopers as hostages. Some of them spent prolonged periods of captivity that lasted a dozen years before they were rescued by the Colombian Army.
30. Orlando Restrepo, "Municipalities Without Police Stations Fight Back." *El Tiempo* [Bogota], 9 July of 2000.
31. FARC's leader, aka Tiro Fijo (Sure Shot), during several of FARC's guerrilla conferences, complained about the lack of mobilization capacity showed by leaders and members of this insurgent organization.
32. This concept was developed by the French professor Michel Weiviorka in *The Making of Terrorism*. Therein, he explains 'inversion' as a process of evolution of an insurgent organization into a terrorist one.
33. Without enjoying popular support, the insurgents begin to see everybody as hostile and as potential enemies.

34. In this way, the deceased FARC guerrilla leader aka Mono Jojoy used to encourage his men to kill without further investigation those persons they considered as enemies of FARC.
35. Following this logic, a bomb was placed in the social club *El Nogal* in Bogota on 7 February 2003, killing 36 innocent civilians.
36. Several countries, such as the U.S. and the European Union, classified FARC as a terrorist organization because of these actions against innocent civilians.
37. In spite of this, during the peace process in Havana (Cuba) between the government and FARC, the terms were overwhelmingly favorable to FARC, to the point that the agreement was rejected in a plebiscite called by the president.
38. Thomas A. Marks has observed that the defeat and extermination of the Tamil Tigers was caused at least in part by the extreme radicalization of some of its militants, in particular of LTTE leader Prabhakaran. His determination to confront the Sri Lankan military frontally ultimately ceded to it the advantages of mobility, surprise, and flexibility. The result was LTTE's decimation and, like Che, his own death.
39. Antonio Navarro, a former guerrilla leader of the also defeated M-19 insurgent movement, admitted that he and some of his guerrilla mates understood that fighting against the government was useless. He demobilized himself, was admitted as part of a political process, and sometime later was elected as mayor of a Colombian city, and further on as congressman.
40. He has been accused by his own guerrillas of authorizing the killings of approximately 300 of his men that were accused (but never proven) of being infiltrators.
41. To try to counter this problem, FARC leadership ordered the killing of those who displayed these symptoms. In this way, discipline was restored in some of the FARC Fronts and *Bloques*. There are no statistics on these killings, but some sources claim they were in the thousands.
42. Baron Colmar Von der Goltz, a well-known German Army strategist before the First World War, explained in *The Conduct of War* that as soon as both tactical and strategic defensive situations obtain for one of the parties, defeat is unavoidable. That was the situation that FARC was in after 2006 and the reason why it accepted peace talks in 2012.
43. This point is reached when one of the parties loses its strength. From that moment on, further efforts are useless, forcing the attacker to adopt a defensive posture to avoid the destruction of his forces. U.S. forces in Vietnam reached that point due to the reality that none of their military actions could change the fate of the war. FARC was in a similar situation after 2004.
44. The peasant soldiers program was structured to avoid the use of paramilitary forces or armed civilians. Normally, individuals were young males of the town or municipality they were entrusted to defend. They joined the army according to Law 1 of 1945 and were trained in a battalion, normally located close to the town or municipality. There, they became part of a regular company under military leadership. Their training lasted for 3 months, and when done they returned to guard their village for 18 months under military regulations and as part of the area control mission of their battalion. In case of attack, they were supported by the superior unit.
45. "Toribio, the People of War Who Do Not Sleep."
46. Each was comprised of 1300 volunteer personnel who received much more intensive training than is the norm for draftees. Such units have as a defining characteristic mobility at both the strategic and tactical levels. A BRIM, with four

line battalions, was assigned its own air mobility assets. Mobile brigades are perhaps one of the most remarkable products of Colombian doctrine in the struggle against irregular threats, especially FARC.
47. According to official statistics, the number of FARC casualties in 2004 was 5400, which included dead and deserters or captured. This trend continued in subsequent years until the opening of the peace talks in Havana (Cuba) in 2012.
48. Data researched by RCN (National Radio Company). Military figures said 17,000.
49. Some of hostages held by the FARC, such as Police general Herlindo Mendita, had to endure 12 years of captivity in the middle of the jungle while suffering all possible type of disease and humiliations.
50. This operation was launched in 2008. Utilizing electronic intelligence, the Colombian forces were able to deceive FARC through interception and penetration into its communications to the point that members of the Colombian intelligence ordered one FARC's fronts to gather the hostages in an open area, where they would be transported via helicopter to FARC's general headquarters. Unaware of the army's maneuver, the guerrillas moved the hostages to the designated location, where an army helicopter and rescue team, posing as an international humanitarian commission in charge of the mobilization of the hostages, succeeded in putting all onboard, even inviting the group's leader and the guerrilla in charge of the hostages to join the trip, achieving not only the rescue but capturing the leader and his second-in-command without a shot being fired. Furthermore, when the helicopter was taking off, the complete guerrilla unit turned into a group of well-wishers, waving farewell with their hands. Twenty minutes after the takeoff, they learned through radio breaking news that they have been fooled by the army and had lost their valuable hostages.
51. The lack of strategic guidance from the Secretariat caused the plans and the objectives of this organization to devolve into confusion as each Front advanced its own interpretations. This was another factor that contributed to the demoralization of the guerrillas.
52. Refer to Marks, "Terrorism as Method in Nepali Maoist Insurgency, 1996–2016," 81–118.

Disclosure statement

The views and opinions expressed in this article are those of the author and do not necessarily reflect the official policy or position of any agency of the U.S. government.

Bibliography

Debray, Regis. *Revolution in the Revolution*. Paris: Maspero, 1967.
Echeverria, Antulio. *Clausewitz and Contemporary War*. New York: Oxford University Press, 2007.
Echavarria, Antulio. *Clausewitz's Center of Gravity: Changing our Warfighting Doctrine – Again*. Carlisle, PA: Strategic Studies Institute, September 2002. Accessed March 5, 2017. http://www.clausewitz.com/readings/Echevarria/gravity.pdf
"Interview with Timoleon Jimenez, Leader of the FARC." *El Espectador* [Bogota], June 24, 2016. Accessed January 3, 2017. https://farc-epeace.org/index.php/background/
Marks, Thomas A. *Maoist People's War in Post-Vietnam Asia*. Bangkok: White Lotus, 2007.
Marks, Thomas A. "Terrorism as Method in Nepali Maoist Insurgency, 1996–2016." *Small Wars and Insurgencies* 28, no. 1 (2017): 81–118.

Ospina, Carlos. *A la Cima sobre los hombros del Diablo* [To the Top over the Shoulders of the Devil]. Madrid: Editorial Académica, 2012.

Selected Works of Mao Tse-tung. Accessed March 8, 2017. https://www.marxists.org/reference/archive/mao/selected-works/index.htm

Sigman, Jean. *1848: The Romantic and Democratic Revolutions of Europe.* Madrid: Siglo XXI, 1985.

Skocpol, Theda. *States and Social Revolutions: A Comparative Analysis of Social Revolutions in Russia, France and China.* New York: Cambridge University Press, 1979.

"Toribio, the People of War Who Do Not Sleep." *Semana.* Accessed November 25, 2016. www.semana.com

Weiviorka, Michael. *The Making of Terrorism.* Chicago, IL: University of Chicago Press, 1993.

Critical ingredient: US aid to counterinsurgency in Colombia

Carlos G. Berrios

ABSTRACT
In assisting states facing insurgencies, few subjects are more vital than understanding the manner in which external aid can be applied in a sustainable manner. Colombia, touted by proponents as a case study for astute application of external reinforcement for democracy, is just as often held up by critics as an illustration of the misplaced priorities of the US. No part of the critique is more prevalent than assertions concerning the nature of US military assistance. American aid to counterinsurgency filled particular capacity gaps and enhanced capabilities that already existed. These were possible due to the Colombian ability to absorb input.

Faced with a situation where a long-time partner was challenged by an ostensibly mass mobilization insurgency, Colombia after 1998 received assistance from the US. A key component of this aid was military. This reality is much discussed but normally misrepresented, with few particulars offered in the public discussion being accurate. This requires rectification because few subjects are more vital than understanding the manner in which external aid can be applied in an appropriate, sustainable manner. This, the US did. Ironically, the effectiveness of US assistance has led to a narrative that asserts both decisive US military input and ineffective strategic consequences due to a focus upon counter-narcotics. Reality, as outlined herein, was more complex.

Strategic context

Throughout the 1980s and 1990s, Colombia (see Figure 1 in Marks, this issue) experienced a significant increase in illegal drug trafficking and production as a result of the successful interdiction and eradication efforts in Peru and Bolivia. This shift in illegal drug production and cultivation to Colombia led to the rise of the drug cartels and reinvigorated the nascent insurgency of *Fuerzas Armadas Revolucionarias de Colombia*, or FARC (Revolutionary Armed Forces of Colombia), which in 1982 had made a formal decision to exploit the drug trade for revenue generation. The exponential growth of the illegal drug trade and the relentless attacks by the drug cartels against the Colombian government brought unprecedented levels of violence and enabled the rapid growth of FARC in terms of fighters and war materiel.

The newfound home for drug trafficking and production for the cartels and new source of income for FARC was facilitated by a traditionally weak central state unable to exercise control over its territory and by public security forces too small and starved for resources to provide security throughout the country. So potent became the threat from the drug cartels and illegal armed groups, primarily FARC, that many analysts in Colombia and the United States began to describe Colombia as a state on the brink of failing.

Though the US has since World War II supported the Colombian military (COLMIL) and state, Washington's focus by the 1970s was counterdrug assistance. Most of the latter went to the Colombian National Police (CNP), which had the counterdrug mandate. COLMIL was also the beneficiary of security assistance in the form of International Military Education and Training (IMET),

Figure 1. Intended Plan Patriota Phasing.

Military Assistance Program (MAP) funds, Foreign Military Financing (FMF), 506 drawdown funds, and Department of Defense (DOD) Counternarcotics (CN) funding for training and equipment of military units involved in counterdrug missions. The decades of the 80s and 90s witnessed a US Government strategy focused on providing the Colombian government and other countries in the region the needed capacity to interdict and eradicate illegal drugs at source. In the meantime, the drug problem in Colombia was a manifestation of weak state institutions unable to wield authority throughout the national territory and of a political class unwilling to muster the will to deal with the problem. This set of factors created an untenable environment where FARC found itself well on its way of realizing its strategy of taking power.

When Andrés Pastrana assumed the presidency of Colombia in 1998, FARC had become a national security threat, and other illegal actors, such as the paramilitary umbrella body, *Autodefensas Unidas de Colombia* (AUC), had also mushroomed in strength as a result of the security vacuum left by the state. Faced with this complex challenge, the government of Pastrana attempted a peace process to address the FARC challenge, while simultaneously working to strengthen state institutions and military and police operational capacity through the enactment of Plan Colombia, to which increased US assistance was vital.

US assistance, 1999–2002: counterdrug focus

In 1999, the US Government approved a four-year USD 1.9 billion in assistance to supplement the Colombian government's political strategy called Plan Colombia. Plan Colombia was designed to combat narcotics trafficking, revive the economy, and strengthen human rights and democratic institutions. The US counterdrug assistance package had as a strategic objective the reduction of coca production by 50 percent in four years. The US assistance earmarked for the COLMIL under the supplemental package, funded through the Department of State, International Narcotics and Law Enforcement (DOS-INL) (see Table 1), although substantial in terms of funds, was focused on the purchase of 13 UH-60 Blackhawk helicopters and the training and equipping of the Colombian Army Counterdrug Brigade (CD BDE). The US supplemental package, although it covered a variety of programs designed to strengthen the state, was aimed primarily at combating drug trafficking. US policy toward Colombia spelled out in Presidential Decision Directive 73 (PDD-73) stated that the US Government *would not* support Colombian counterinsurgency efforts. The US Congress at the time had no appetite to fund counterinsurgency efforts. What resonated with the US Congress and the American people was the government's effort to reduce coca production and decrease the amount of illegal drugs entering the US from Colombia.

Thus US Government assistance funded through DOS-INL and DOD CN dollars provided to COLMIL under Plan Colombia was during this period focused

Table 1. U.S. Assistance to Colombia 1999–2002 (USD).

Military programs	1999	2000	2001	2002	Total
Aviation leadership program					
Combating terrorism fellowship program					
Emergency drawdown	58,000,000				
Excess defense articles	199,169			499,010	
Exchange training		580,000	395,014		
foreign military financing	440,788	24,524	4,492,628	7,684,274	
International narcotics and law enforcement-dpt of state	197,910,000	666,168,408	42,350,000	252,485,720	
International military education and training	917,000	900,000	1,040,000	1,180,000	
MAP(Now Unused)				80,712	
Regional centers for security studies	42,852	131,742	199,989	192,435	
Section 1004 DOD counter drug assistance	52,073,000	103,880,000	175,367,000	99,562,000	
Section 1033 DOD counter drug assistance					
Section 1207 security & stabilization assistance					
Service academies					
Total	309,582,809	771,684,674	223,844,631	361,684,151	1,666,796,265

Source: security assistance monitor (securityassistance.org)

on training and equipping three counterdrug battalions which became part of the CD BDE. The brigade's mission was initially to interdict drug base and HCl labs in the area of southern Putumayo, where the bulk of the coca was cultivated. Later, the brigade was reorganized to cover the entire country. The brigade was trained by US Special Forces personnel and equipped with funds from US Plan Colombia channeled through DOS-INL and DOD. Simultaneously, DOD began to train Colombian Army (COLAR) pilots, crew chiefs, and mechanics so COLAR would have the capacity to fly the UH-60 Blackhawks helicopters acquired specifically to support the CN BDE's mission.

Despite this substantial level of support, it was clear early on that there was strategic misalignment of the two countries' objectives. Policymakers in Washington, haunted by the ghosts of Vietnam, did not want to engage in what many analysts and people familiar with Colombia's problem believed had to be done, which was to support a counterinsurgency effort. Therefore, the only way to support Colombia was through a policy that would sever the drug supply coming from Colombia to the United States, thus impacting both the drug and security challenges. For COLMIL, though, especially under the presidency of Alvaro Uribe (2002–2010), the strategic objective lay in establishing security throughout the country. This required defeating FARC and securing the population. Extending the state's reach and securing the population would necessarily deprive FARC of its illegal funding source and ability to carry out terrorist activities.

Democratic security: Colombia's counterinsurgency strategy

After the failed attempt by the Pastrana administration (1998–2002) to reach a peace agreement with FARC, during which period there was significant fighting that included battles between the main forces of the two sides, the popular reaction in the 2002 presidential election swept a third party candidate to power, Álvaro Uribe. His new policy, *Democratic Security*, was based on three pillars: first, the protection of the rights of all Colombians; second, the protection of democratic institutions, their values, and plurality; and third, the solidarity and cooperation of all the citizens in the defense of democratic values.[1] In order to strengthen Colombia's democratic institutions, it was imperative to establish security throughout the country. This task became the primary mission of the CNP and COLMIL. Military implementation was through a campaign plan called Plan Patriota (the English translation merely drops the 'a').[2]

Plan Patriota: the COLMIL campaign

Plan Patriota was designed to re-establish security for all citizens throughout Colombia. FARC had grown significantly in terms of military capabilities and number of fighters during the peace process of the Pastrana administration.

The fact that President Pastrana granted FARC a demilitarized zone (*Despeje*; frequently termed simply, *Zona*) as a sign of good faith as part of the negotiations, this area the size of the country of Switzerland, gave FARC ample time and space to grow militarily. These circumstances led the COLMIL to design a military campaign, Plan Patriota, which focused on three key areas where FARC had to be dislodged in order to begin debilitating its ability to harm the population (refer to Figure 1). The first area was the department of Cundinamarca, where the capital of Colombia, Bogotá, is located. FARC had begun to encircle the capital, and it was imperative to clear the area in order to create the space for renewed economic activity and travel without fear of attacks.

COLAR's operational scheme of maneuver, which became COLMIL's campaign design, is shown in Figure 2.[3] Using the strategic concept of ends-ways-means, this operational concept was laid out by General Carlos Alberto Ospina Ovalle – COLAR Commander in 2003–2004 and subsequently Joint Forces Commander from 2004 to 2006, the architect of Plan Patriota – during a meeting with senior US military officers in Bogota in August 2003. General Ospina envisioned COLAR as having objectives for the campaign, to regain control of territory by establishing legitimate government presence and to kill or capture FARC leadership. The military campaign would be conducted through a two-pronged approach: first, by conducting area control with regular infantry and cavalry units and through the use of *Soldados de mi Pueblo* or local soldiers ('home guard' is a useful translation), recruited by the army as regular soldiers but allowed by law to serve their mandatory military service in their municipalities; second, by conducting offensive operations against FARC bases using counter-guerrilla battalions, mobile brigades, and Special Forces units. It was to be the Special Forces mission to kill or capture FARC leadership.

The success of this initial phase of the plan would bolster the confidence of the people in the government and its security forces. The second phase (refer again to Figure 1) focused on the areas of Meta, Caqueta, and Guaviare, an area in the southeastern part of the country used by FARC as its strategic rearguard. This was the area where its forces had established base areas and had created a state within a state, a counter-state. FARC used this area to replenish its combat power and also as a springboard to launch attacks against the urban population centers. The area was the heart of FARC's power, its operational center of gravity. As the Colombian political leadership captured the strategic center of gravity, legitimacy allowed for national mobilization and forced FARC to society's margins. COLMIL's campaign plan (see Figure 3[4]) was to destroy FARC's alternative world, its clandestine infrastructure, especially its leadership. The primary means to kill or capture the FARC leadership would be the Special Forces, who acting as guerrillas would infiltrate enemy territory to reach their high-value targets. In order to accomplish this mission, COLMIL created the Colombian Army Special Operations Command (COESE).

PEOPLE'S WAR

COLAR Scheme of Maneuver
Against Threat of Narcoterrorism

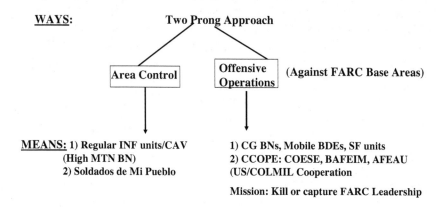

Figure 2. COLAR scheme of maneuver in Plan Patriota.

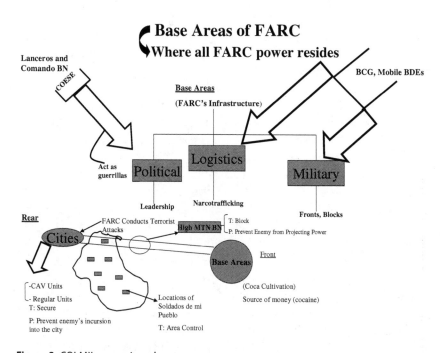

Figure 3. COLMIL campaign plan.

The logistics units of FARC, which dealt in the illegal drug trade, and the main fighting units would be handled by the counter-guerrilla battalions and mobile brigades. For FARC, its battlefront was made of the base areas and its effort to isolate and penetrate government centers of power, the cities. Areas around the cities became the focus of FARC terrorist, kidnapping, and extortion activities, the purpose of which was both to blockade them and to generate resources for insurgent expansion. In order to counter FARC's operational plans, COLMIL created and deployed Joint Task Force Omega (JTF-O), a force composed of over 18,000 soldiers distributed in over 13 mobile brigades. The mission of JTF-O was to disrupt and dismantle the FARC strategic rearguard and to kill or capture the FARC leaders who were located there (which included the FARC Secretariat and Estado Mayor or General Staff). In other words, to defeat FARC nationally, COLMIL had to dominate FARC's heartland.[5]

The third phase of Plan Patriota (see Figure 1) was to control Antioquia using the forces permanently assigned to that area. This area was critical to both Colombia – among other things, it was the source of one-third of the country's GDP – and FARC, due to its use of Urabá and the Darien Gap in Panama for resource generation and transit, as well as base area activity (refer again to Marks, this issue). Local resources proved largely sufficient to implement this component of the overall plan.

The beginning of the Plan Patriota military campaign nearly coincided with the post-9/11 change of US policy, which authorized the DOD to use CN funds for combating terrorism. As a result of this shift and a significant increase in DOD CN funds, the US Southern Command (US SOUTHCOM) began to focus its efforts and resources in support of JTF-O combat operations against FARC. The 'authorities' (i.e. legal parameters) granted to the US military to support the COLMIL campaign plan demonstrated well how an indirect approach to counterinsurgency, without committing US ground combat forces but instead providing operational support to a partner nation, could work successfully.

The operational support concept is assistance provided to fill certain warfighting *capability gaps* in a partner nation military or police force. Filling these gaps is intended to enable the partner nation security force to sustain itself on the battlefield and gain the upper hand. This operational support concept was executed in Colombia in conjunction with steady-state security cooperation activities. Below, this study discusses the various capacities the US military helped create to fill gaps, as well as existing capabilities that were enhanced in order for the COLMIL to achieve the objectives outlined in the Democratic Security Strategy.[6]

US assistance, 2003–2010: expanded authorities

The events of 9/11 led to reinvigorated thinking about the broader threat of 'terrorist groups' globally to US interests and brought US and Colombian strategic objectives into alignment. By 2002, the assessment shared by the US Government interagency community with respect to Colombia was that the country's problem was driven by an insurgency (FARC) that used the profits from the illegal drug trade to finance its terrorist activities and that Colombian security forces lacked key capacities and capabilities to achieve area control and to dismantle FARC's clandestine infrastructure (i.e. counter-state). In order to assist Bogotá to 'clear, hold, and build' in areas long held by FARC and other illegal armed groups, the US Government changed its policy to support democracy in Colombia as outlined in NSPD-18 in 2002.

NSPD-18 would recognize the need to assist the Colombian government establish security first in order to deny the illegal armed groups, primarily FARC as the major threat to the state, the space to carry out their attacks against the population. NSPD-18 also in combination with Congressional legislation granted the DOD expanded authorities, which enabled the Pentagon to use CN funds to combat the terrorist threat in Colombia. Congress approved a supplemental appropriation in 2003 for DOD to assist the COLMIL in its military campaign against FARC. The new policy also paved the way a significant increase in FMF funds starting in 2004 with USD 98.4 million for the COLMIL to support its efforts to reestablish security throughout the country (see Table 2).

Closing COLMIL capability gaps

With NSPD-18 in place together with new Congressional legislation, US SOUTHCOM had the necessary authorities to support COLMIL's military campaign, a key element of Colombia's larger Democratic Security strategy. As noted earlier, the US military began to provide operational support to the COLMIL in order to enable the sustainment of COLMIL offensive operations in Joint Task Force-Omega's area of operations (see Figure 1), FARC's heartland, and also to support the High Value Target (HVT) program aimed at killing or capturing FARC central (especially Secretariat) and mid-level leaders. US military support focused on filling COLMIL capacity or capability gaps in training, equipment, organization, infrastructure, and expertise in the areas of: Intelligence, Communications, Information Operations and Psychological Operations, Civil Affairs, Riverine Operations and Maritime Interdiction, Special Operations Forces (SOF), Planning Assistance and Training Team (PATT), Air Mobility (fixed wing and rotary wing), Combat Search and Rescue (CSAR), Logistics, Medical, and Engineer. In the aforementioned capabilities, it was assessed that COLMIL lacked sufficient capacity or capability to sustain the largest military campaign in its history, with over 18,000 troops deployed in an area inhospitable for its forces and strategically important to FARC.[7]

While providing operational support to the COLMIL campaign plan was US SOUTHCOM's main effort after 2003, with US MILGP-Colombia as its implementer, the operational capabilities provided to COLMIL became permanent fixtures at

Table 2. Enhanced U.S. Support to Colombia (USD).

Military programs	1999	2000	2001	2002	2003	2004	2005	2006	2007	2008	2009	2010	Total
Aviation Leadership program							27,267	59,383	23,840		38,092		
Combating terrorism fellowship program					930,000	543,665	310,200	222,659	434,590	481,949	789,505	1,280,885	
Emergency drawdown	58,000,000												
Excess defense articles	199,169		395,014	499,010									
Exchange training		580,000			3,104,177				3,961,200		2,364,935	4,949,803	
Foreign military financing	440,788	24,524	4,492,628	7,684,274	17,100,000	98,450,000	99,200,000	89,100,000	85,500,000	55,050,000	53,000,000	55,000,000	
International military education and training	917,000	900,000	1,040,000	1,180,000	1,165,000	1,676,000	1,700,000	1,673,000	1,646,000	1,421,000	1,400,000	1,694,000	
MAP (now unused)				80,712									
Regional centers for security studies	42,852	131,742	199,989	192,435	191,272	71,300	155,150	99,138	189,146	298,136	357,103	460,123	
Section 1004 counter drug assistance	52,073,000	103,880,000	175,367,000	99,562,000	148,572,000	178,229,000	155,313,000	140,552,000	115,430,000	109,635,000	117,007,000	122,874,000	
Section 1033 counter drug assistance									13,976,000	10,227,000	10,865,000	6,493,000	
Section 1207 security & stabilization assistance									4,000,000	5,000,000	4,800,000		
Service academies					52,140	100,995	220,995	227,725	481,636	424,310	502,801	430,314	
Total	111,672,809	105,516,266	181,494,631	109,198,431	171,114,589	279,070,960	256,926,612	231,933,905	225,642,412	182,537,395	191,124,436	193,182,125	2,239,414,571

Source: security assistance monitor (securityassistance.org)

COLMIL training and education institutions through the bilateral security cooperation programs. The following discussion will describe the implementation of the aforementioned capabilities and the effects they had on COLMIL as a warfighting force and as provider of training and education to other militaries in the region.

US intelligence support

Having the intelligence systems and being able to integrate them is paramount to successfully defeating an insurgent such as FARC. COLMIL had a growing knowledge and expertise about the FARC's strategic plans, disposition, composition, and strength, as well as its propaganda activities in the region and Europe. What it lacked was the ability to integrate intelligence information into the operational cycle in a timely manner. Intelligence collection as a matter of culture within COLMIL was designed to be pushed up to the senior military leadership rather than disseminated down to field commanders.[8]

Information and processed intelligence on FARC had become increasingly available, but COLMIL lacked the intelligence architecture to integrate all sources of intelligence as well as the culture to pull the information up to senior decision-makers and push it down to commanders in the field to act on the information.[9] This situation fostered a lack of collaboration where all sources of intelligence (human, technical, and imagery) failed to be integrated.

The inability of COLMIL to consistently fuse all the intelligence information it had and the stated desire by President Uribe to push for this drove the SOUTHCOM J2 to develop a program of 'Intelligence Integration.' Its intent was to provide COLMIL with the capability to process intelligence, fuse it, and disseminate it back to the field in support of Plan Patriota Operations.[10] In order to fuse COLMIL intelligence, SOUTHCOM J2 had to tie in all COLMIL intelligence sources, also known as 'centers of excellence,' which to that point did not habitually share information. The Combined Enterprise Information Exchange System (CENTRIXS) became the backbone of the secure architecture to enable the integration of all-source intelligence.[11]

CENTRIXS allowed secure communications between the COLMIL regional intelligence centers and the national COLMIL intelligence center (CIME). The intent of CENTRIXS was to foster a culture of information sharing among the COLMIL intelligence centers of excellence.[12] CENTRIXS further provided analytical tools such as imagery, access to tactical Intelligence, Surveillance, and Reconnaissance (ISR), and access to signals intelligence information. It was also a collaboration tool which enabled the user to send requests for information (RFIs). In addition to the CENTRIXS system, SOUTHCOM J2 embedded Intelligence Planning and Assistance Teams in key COLMIL intelligence nodes in order to enable the transfer of US intelligence tradecraft and norms of aggressive push-and-pull processing of information.[13] The US intelligence teams would assist in this process by participating in the validation of information through other intelligence sources and by enabling its fusion.

The Intelligence Integration Program designed by the SOUTHCOM J2 and funded with DOD CN dollars helped improve intelligence sharing within the COLMIL, to improve its Command, Control, Communications, Computer, and Intelligence (C4I), and to improve ISR operations. The CENTRIXS network went from an initial 10 nodes in 2005 to 65 nodes in 2010, allowing intelligence sharing in a secure environment between the US and Colombia, and between one place in Colombia to another. COLMIL was able to send information instantaneously through a secure intelligence network. Having intelligence planning and assistance teams in key intelligence nodes also enabled COLMIL to operationalize its intelligence and carry out operations against FARC units and HVTs.[14]

The success of the intelligence integration program demonstrated the need to share and fuse all-source information horizontally and vertically while having a secure means to do so. It also demonstrated how having a systems architecture allowed the COLMIL intelligence community to meet the needs of commanders in the field and at higher levels.[15] From the US perspective, the Intelligence Integration Program could also be used as an example of how Defense Attaché Offices (DAOs) and Security Cooperation Offices (SCOs) could work together to build the intelligence enablers for a host nation and be able to integrate all sources of information as well as the intelligence tradecraft to enable the process to work as efficiently as possible.[16] As a second-order consequence, the robust intelligence sharing and integration capacity now enjoyed by the COLMIL, through its enhanced infrastructure, expertise, equipment, training, and education can definitely be used to help other countries in the region build intelligence capacity to confront irregular threats.[17]

Communications

The enhancement of COLMIL's strategic communications network and the expansion of the COLAR signal corps with the assistance of communications experts from SOUTHCOM and the US Military Group enabled the fusion of intelligence and operations and provided greater battlefield situational awareness through enhanced connectivity to senior military commanders in Bogotá as well as those in the field. This increase in communications capability took place through the expansion of the main strategic communications architecture of COLMIL called the Integrated Communications Network or RIC, using its Spanish acronym (for *Red Integral de Comunicaciones*).

RIC is a high capacity strategic communications network, which covers over 70 percent of Colombia's territory by combining microwave, satellite, and fiber-optic systems. It serves as the main transport system that extends typical network services (e.g. data, video) to units in fixed locations (e.g. military bases and main command posts). This is similar to the way the Defense Information

Systems Agency (DISA) provides communications support to the US Armed Forces.[18] The main capability of RIC was that it provided reliable and sufficient communications bandwidth to COLMIL military bases and units throughout the national territory. It served as the main means of connectivity for the following data networks, which it did not have before: the Combined Enterprise Information Exchange System (CENTRIXS), the Cooperating Nations Information Exchange System (CNIES), the Colombian Imagery Library Archive (CILA), and the Automated Logistics System (SLOG). These data networks were added with the assistance of SOUTHCOM, US Military Group-Colombia, and other communications experts from the US military with relatively small amounts of DOD CN and Plan Colombia funds.[19]

The data networks mentioned above provided the following added capability to the COLMIL: First, CENTRIXS, a secure bi-lateral data system that allows the exchange of operational and intelligence information. This system was widely installed at critical Colombian command and control (C2) centers and military units to support operations and enhance the decision-making processes of commanders and staff officers. The system was similar to the secret network (SIPERNET) used by the US Armed Forces. Second, CNIES, a private network that served as an operational tool and assisted in producing extrapolations that primarily targeted narcotrafficking within Colombia and abroad. This system had an instant messaging service application that allowed sites to communicate through live chat. This network was sponsored by the Joint Inter-Agency Task Force- South (JIATF-S).[20]

The third data network was CILA, a private network that allowed COLMIL and CNP to share imagery products using an Image Product Library (IPL). CILA analysts received, screened, processed and exploited imagery, and posted exploited imagery and reports via a wide area network to the IPL. This network was sponsored by the US National Geospatial-Intelligence Agency (NGA).

The last data network was SILOG, which implemented and maintained the logistics and maintenance processes of the COLMIL and CNP in an integrated information system, using a common automated platform that maximized operational results. The software provided integrated tools (database management and reporting) to assist with maintenance, supply, warehouse, personnel, and financial management.[21]

RIC also provided connectivity for the COLMIL administrative data net, which was similar to the US NIPR net. It further connected COLMIL tactical radio nets, such as the Air to Ground Network, the Mobile Digital Network (MDN), Tactical Radio Nets, and Iridium satellite phones. RIC, according to Juan Soto, the US Military Group-Colombia Communications Advisor, provided COLMIL with capabilities it had never had. Mr Soto also stated that using DOD CN funds, SOUTHCOM assisted in extending the RIC into La Macarena, a remote area in south central Colombia with scant electrical infrastructure and once considered a FARC stronghold. The benefits were substantial because they provided tactical commanders and operation centers with access to sophisticated data and video applications they had never had before. This enabled provision of the latest operational and intelligence products within seconds of their being released, while at the same time having a secure voice capability to discuss and expand as necessary.[22]

Another successful program that enhanced the tactical communications capability was the placement in 2004 of seven 250-foot towers at selected locations within the JTF-Omega area. Erecting these towers extended COLMIL's tactical VHF-FM nets to cover the entire area of operations. At each tower, COLMIL communicators with US assistance installed TADIRAN high power VHF-FM repeaters. Rather than using 250-foot signal cables to link the repeaters to their antennas, COLMIL personnel constructed wooden boxes that housed the entire repeater and placed them at the very top of each tower. This method allowed the repeaters to radiate from a position right next to the tower antenna with minimum signal loss. The result of this initiative was the creation of a robust command net that connected every tactical unit within the JTF-Omega area of operations to include aircraft and riverine elements.[23]

While SOUTHCOM maintained its focus on enhancing the COLMIL strategic communications network, the US Military Group-Colombia Communications Advisors worked with COLAR to enhance the institutional capacity of the COLAR Signal Corps and its operational support units. Through sustained engagement in the form of SMEs (subject matter experts) and COLMIL senior leader visits to US Army Signal Center of Excellence and Fort Gordon, Georgia, as well as the commitment of US Army Signal leaders to serve as mentors to their COLAR counterparts, COLAR activated a signal brigade, which was clearly an indicator of the importance senior COLMIL leaders placed upon communications as a battlefield enabler. The numerous encounters between the US and COLMIL military leaders facilitated the sharing of information on doctrine, training, leader development, and equipment that led to the expansion of the COLAR signal branch, a branch capable of exporting its expertise to other partners in the region.[24]

Information and psychological operations

Just as the intelligence integration program enabled the COLMIL to improve the fusion of all-source intelligence, the operations conducted by JTF-Omega required the integration of information and psychological operations in order to influence the environment and defeat FARC. The integration of Information Operations (IO) into operations had not been systematically a feature of COLMIL planning and execution of operations before Plan Patriota. Aware of this shortcoming, SOUTHCOM, through the US Military Group-Colombia, urged COLMIL to have a dedicated Information Operations (IO) officer in its JFT-Omega staff. This officer, with the assistance and mentoring of the US Military Information Support Team (MIST), would ensure IO played an integral part in operations.[25]

At the tactical level, the MIST team assisted the JTF-Omega staff by providing a much needed graphic printer better known as RISO. This piece of equipment enabled the JTF-Omega staff to develop graphic products at its headquarters in support of tactical operations. In addition, the MIST team, with funds provided by DOD CN, purchased mobile radio stations and assisted the JTF-IO officer in the development of radio messages.[26] As part of JTF-Omega operational plan, the mobile radio stations were located in strategic areas within the JTF-Omega area of operations in order to target FARC activities.

Another example of integration of IO into operations was the establishment of demobilization sites in key areas of JTF-Omega battlespace. FARC demobilized fighters would come to these sites based on information provided through leaflets, radio stations, and loud speakers provided by the US and mounted on helicopters. The humane treatment provided by COLMIL at these sites would motivate FARC fighters to provide information on weapons caches and other information of value.[27]

IO activities within the JTF-Omega area also enabled the collection of battlefield intelligence, which was pushed to higher headquarters through the CENTRIXS node established at JTF-Omega headquarters. While MIST assistance had been valuable at the tactical level and at COLAR instructional facilities, the integration of IO at the strategic level was also critical to the success of the COLMIL military campaign. The SOUTHCOM IO LNO located at the US Military Group-Colombia ensured there was a strategic link between the COLMIL Joint Staff (*Comando General*) and all units responsible for executing the campaign plan on all matters related to IO. The SOUTHCOM IO LNO engaged with senior COLMIL leaders to enhance their knowledge of IO and the capabilities the COLMIL needed in order to successfully prosecute their military campaign in support of Democratic Security.[28]

The SOUTHCOM IO LNO also exposed several senior COLMIL officers to the US IO and Psychological Operations training and educational system in order to show them what it would take to sustain such a critical capability and to expand their knowledge of the value of IO to military operations. The effort undertaken by the SOUTHCOM IO LNO in enhancing the training and education of senior COLMIL officers on the benefits of IO enabled SOUTHCOM to influence the COLMIL Joint Staff to name a general or flag officer as the IO officer in its staff. This move enabled the integration of IO throughout the force. The first COLMIL general officer came from the Navy.

Having a Joint Staff IO flag officer ensured better synchronization of efforts among the services' IO officers and the Ministry of Defense, and paved the way for greater collaboration. As part of the overall SOUTHCOM IO and Psychological Operations plan, the SOUTHCOM IO LNO continued to coordinate workshops to enhance the skills and competencies of the services IO and Public Affairs (PA) officers. At the same time, refresher training and table-top exercises were provided to senior COLMIL leaders in order to continue with the education process of understanding and incorporating IO capabilities to military campaigns.[29]

While SOUTHCOM emphasized the importance of IO in support of COLMIL tactical operations and strategic objectives, the Narcotics Affairs Section (NAS) in the US Embassy and the US Military Group provided funds to support the Colombian government's IO efforts in support of the demobilization and reintegration program. With NAS funds, Bogotá purchased television advertisement during the 2006 World Cup to encourage demobilization. Knowing that FARC fighters would watch the games, FARC leaders were forced to turn off the TVs to deny their fighters exposure to the commercials.[30] This IO method proved to be very effective in inciting demobilizations.

In order to ensure that the transfer of IO and psychological operations capabilities endured within the COLMIL, the MIST team and SOUTHCOM IO LNO worked with (primarily) COLAR to revise its doctrine, revamp its training and education curricula, and upgrade its equipment. With DOD CN funds, the US Military Group-Colombia purchased a set of loud speakers capable of being used in manpack mode or mounted in a vehicle or aircraft. The intent of this purchase was to provide a set to each COLAR division and other major service components located in strategic areas of the country in addition to a RISO graphic printer, a trained IO officer, and an NCO trained on how to use and maintain the equipment.[31]

The IO program provided by SOUTHCOM to COLMIL demonstrates that for any capability to endure in a partner nation, a course of action must take into account training of the force, the provision of modern equipment, senior leader education, and the integration of all the services' IO efforts from the tactical to the strategic level. COLMIL now has a robust IO capability that can be transported in support of Peacekeeping Operations or other multilateral operations where additional partners could benefit from this valuable yet underappreciated capability.[32]

Civil affairs

The contribution of the US Military Civil Affairs (CA) community, in particular of the CA LNO assigned to the US Military Group-Colombia, must be explained within the context of Plan Patriota and the government's National Consolidation Strategy (*Plan de Consolidacion Nacional*), which began in 2007. US Military CA efforts focused on supporting both of these plans. At the onset of Plan Patriota, the US CA LNO worked with the COLMIL *Acción Integral* directorates from each of the services to integrate civic action into military operations. During this period, he provided advice, facilitated coordination among the services, and coordinated the resources provided by the US military in the form of funds for the construction of schools, health clinics, rehabilitation centers for civilian mine victims, libraries, and medical supplies for health clinics. He also coordinated (through SOUTHCOM) civil affairs training in the form of mobile training teams (MTTs) for all COLAR Divisions to include JTF-Omega, the Colombian Navy (ARC), and the Air Force (COLAF), as well as the CNP.[33]

The growth of COLMIL and CNP in terms of manpower and subsequent success in clearing and holding territory previously held by FARC led Bogotá to move into a new phase of the Democratic Security strategy in 2007. This new phase, the National Consolidation Plan, emphasized social and economic development, strengthening of local governance and the justice system, protection of human rights, expansion of the licit economy, assistance to displaced population and Afro-Colombian and Indigenous communities, and reintegration of ex-combatants.[34] The plan was the first civil-military, integrated, whole of government stabilization effort aimed at establishing state presence in key strategic zones of the country. These zones historically had been controlled by FARC and other illegal armed groups. The implementation of the National Consolidation Plan would be executed in large part through the Center for Coordination of Integrated Action (CCAI).[35]

During the execution of Plan Patriota and later under the National Consolidation Plan, the US Military Group-Bogota took the important step to support the creation of CCAI. CCAI was an interagency coordinating body created by the Office of the Presidency in recognition of the government's need for a mechanism to coordinate government actions in areas retaken by the military.[36] CCAI was responsible for ensuring unity of effort among 15 ministries including the military and police and directing them to support the government's consolidation efforts in 12 priority areas of the country. It conducted planning coordination, mobilized resources, and monitored developments in those priority areas.[37] The person in charge was a civilian accountable to the President with the Deputy Armed Forces Commander serving as the center's deputy.

The implementation model of CCAI consisted of: first, having the military clear and secure areas held by the illegal armed groups, allowing the establishment of police stations. Permanent police stations ensured local security and enabled the military to expand its operations to rural areas. Once security was established, coca fields were eradicated. With security and eradication completed, the area was considered part of the 'consolidation nucleus,' which meant the conditions were appropriate for the rest of the state to begin moving resources into the area.[38] During this phase, USAID and the US Military Group CA program provided assistance by quickly identifying and implementing small scale social infrastructure and productive activities on behalf of the government. These projects had the effect of increasing the confidence in the government's ability to respond to community needs as they began to transition from FARC control and illicit economies. They also created a greater willingness upon the part of the community to collaborate with the government, while giving CCAI the time it needed to mobilize government institutions and the private sector to establish a permanent presence in the newly stabilized zones.[39]

COLMIL played a central role in CCAI's implementation with its commitment of significant civic action resources and its enunciation of the importance of having a whole of government approach in order to re-establish permanent state presence. General Freddy Padilla, former Commander of COLMIL (following Carlos Ospina, who followed General Mora), spoke to the importance of *Acción Integral* (integrated action) or 'whole of government' approach when he commented to the US Military Group CA LNO: 'The COLMIL can have in its possession the best cannons, the best combat aircraft, and the best destroyers, but without *Acción Integral*, we are never going to defeat the enemy.'[40]

COLMIL incorporated Civil Affairs, Psychological Operations, Information Operations, and Public Affairs into *Acción Integral*. Moreover, 90 percent of the COLMIL CA assets were located in the *Profesionales de Reserva*, a type of military reserve program that brought doctors, engineers, and lawyers (among other professionals) to support COLMIL operations with civic action. COLMIL CA doctrine was based upon that of the US, which focused on unconventional warfare and counterinsurgency operations.[41] Thus COLMIL had all the CA capabilities it needed and was also capable of executing CA operations from the tactical to the strategic level. What it did lack at the time of execution of this plan was the monetary resources and materiel to support the significant number of civic action requirements outside the 12 priority zones designated by the CCAI.

The contributions of USAID and the US Military Group to the success of the CCAI are worth noting: First, both USAID and the US Military Group advised the government to maintain a permanent security presence in the communities retaken by the security forces. Second, both advised it to follow security efforts with a robust and unified civilian response.[42] Third, both advised it to sequence in an intentionally and coordinated way the actions of the military, the police, and eradication forces, as well as social services, to ensure each action built and supported the other. This coordination process became the responsibility of the CCAI.[43]

From a broader US Government policy perspective of supporting Colombia's democracy, the synergy achieved by the USAID mission and US Military Group in Bogotá led to three major achievements: First, it helped increase the perception of legitimacy and responsiveness of the Colombian state in recently recovered areas. Second, it helped increase the willingness of communities to interact and collaborate with their government. And third, it helped increase the capacity of national and local government entities to execute the planning, coordination, and implementation of socio-economic strategies in conflict zones.[44]

Riverine operations and maritime interdiction

The Colombian Marine Corps (COLMAR) grew exponentially in terms of operational capacity and professionalism after 1999. Prior to Plan Colombia, COLMAR had one operational riverine brigade on paper, but its personnel and equipment did not make a full brigade combat element according to the table of organization and equipment (TOE). This lack of operational capacity limited

COLMAR's ability to provide security and control to the thousands of square miles of navigable rivers and their tributaries. From the beginning of Plan Colombia and with significant funding support in FMF and DOD CN, COLMAR grew to more than three riverine brigades and was able to provide greater security along Colombia's major rivers.[45] This increase in riverine operational capacity disrupted FARC's ability to use the rivers to move fighters and materiel to sustain its force and enabled the growth of licit commercial activity due to greater government presence.

The US Marine Corps (USMC) invested significant resources in the COLMAR training facility located in Coveñas in the form of SMEs, MTTs, senior leader exchanges, and visits to USMC training and education centers. A visit to Coveñas revealed little visible difference between what USMC recruits went through in Parris Island and what COLMAR recruits went through at the training facility. The facility's transformation represents years of bilateral engagement resulting in a sustained transfer of a professional culture in terms of training, organizational values, and operational expertise from arguably the best marine corps in the world, USMC, to its partner, COLMAR. A positive consequence is that the Coveñas facility is also used to train regional security forces engaged in littoral operations inside their borders.[46]

COLMAR also has a riverine training facility located at Puerto Leguizamo. A significant number of the COLMAR instructors at this facility have been trained at NAVCIATTs, which is the US Navy (USN) Riverine Training Facility in Mississippi. The COLMAR riverine facility provides a capability available to USN and other partner nations in the region as NAVCIATTs reaches its own limited capacity in Spanish-speaking instructors.[47] At the same time, the COLMAR riverine facility could serve as a platform for USN to train its own operational riverine forces in a challenging environment such as that encountered in Colombia.

USN itself has long had a close security partnership with ARC. Both navies work together, for instance, to counter illicit trafficking in the Caribbean and in the waters along the Colombian Pacific coast. The US Military Group-Colombia through its Naval Mission provided security assistance to ARC to improve its maritime interdiction capability. With FMF funds, the US installed digital radars and upgraded FLIR systems in ARC maritime patrol aircraft in order to interdict illicit traffic along Colombia's vast coast. It also invested funds to assist in repairing an ARC maintenance support ship acquired from the US Coast Guard (USCG), which was capable of supporting counterdrug operations beyond the littoral coast. This support ship added additional operational days to smaller patrol boats engaged in interdiction operation.[48]

SOUTHCOM through the US Naval Mission also provided support to the Regional Maritime Training Center located in Cartagena. The idea for this school came out of the regional counterdrug conference held in Cartagena in 2007 that was attended by senior Navy and Coast Guard leaders from the hemisphere. At the conference, the leaders agreed that maritime illicit trafficking was a problem that affected all and that a regional school was needed to train personnel entrusted with conducting maritime interdiction and search and rescue. The Colombian Navy offered to host such school in Cartagena.

The mission of the Regional Maritime Training Center was to train Coast Guard and Navy personnel from other nations in boarding procedures, search and rescue operations, and other tasks related to countering illicit trafficking. USCG sent officers to serve as instructors and also sent officers as students to two courses. It contributed to the center with DOD CN funding for spare parts for boats, training aids, and USCG experts who taught maritime interdiction and search and rescue skills.[49]

Despite considerable progress, ARC capability gaps remained, primarily in the area of coastal patrol boats. ARC had 26 *Midnight Express* boats (fast boats), but many more were needed to cover the vast coastal area of Colombia.[50] As drug traffickers continued to find ways to evade maritime forces deep off-shore, the capability to patrol the littoral only increased, leading to a significant long-term US commitment.

US special operations forces

US Special Operations Forces (SOF) have been training COLMIL and CNP forces since the 1980s. The amount and scope of US SOF training varied due to Washington's counterdrug-centric policy in the 80s and 90s and the decertification of Colombia during the 1994–1998 Samper administration, labeling it a country unwilling to support US counternarcotics efforts. In fact, ever since the US launched the 'war on drugs' in Latin America in 1986, US SOF have been involved in training security forces to conduct interdiction and eradication and to kill or capture drug cartel leaders.

The reluctance of militaries in Latin America to assume the counterdrug mission led to the militarization of police forces through training and equipment support to fight the powerful cartels.[51] Colombia was a case in point. With the COLMIL adamant about not getting involved in counternarcotics missions, the US turned to the CNP. Beginning in 1990, US SOF took over the mission of training the CNP *Junglas* from the British SAS, who had begun the program in 1989.[52] At the time, the CNP *Junglas* was a 120-man (company size) unit tasked with conducting interdiction operations against base and HCl drug labs. Thereafter, with funding assistance from the Department of State, International Narcotics and Law Enforcement (DOS-INL) Bureau, US SOF trained and equipped this highly mobile paramilitary police. The *Junglas* grew to four company-size units with their own air wing capable of striking HVT and drug labs anywhere in the country.

Prior to Plan Colombia (1999), the US provided security assistance to COLMIL and thus US SOF trained two brigades of COLAR, the 12th and 24th, which were conducting counterdrug operations in the Putumayo-Caquetá (see Figure 1).

This area in southeastern Colombia, as indicated earlier, was a center of extensive illegal drug production and cultivation. In order to support these two units, the country team in Bogotá in coordination with SOUTHCOM identified a box of territory where both units operated in order to enable US military assistance in the form of equipment and training under the legal parameters of counterdrug policy.[53]

Additionally, prior to Plan Colombia, US SOF were involved in the development of plans and surveys for possible rescue operations should such be necessary for the US personnel located at five counterdrug radars in Marandua, Araracuara, Lago Agrio (in Putumayo), San Jose del Guaviare, and Rio Hacha.[54] At the time, COLMIL did not have the capability to launch a quick reaction force in case a radar site was attacked. These radars allowed the US to track suspected drug flights and therefore paved the way to provide military assistance to COLAF as long as 51 percent of the assets provided went to interdict drug flights.[55]

After the COLMIL commander agreed to the proposal that a Counterdrug (CD) Battalion be created using the US Army Table of Organization and Equipment (TO&E) model, US SOF began to train this 1st CD Battalion in April 1999.[56] While the training of the 1st CD Battalion continued, US Government officials began to look at increasing this newly created interdiction capability into a broader plan to assist Colombia. The result was the creation of a CD BDE, since US policy precluded any counterinsurgency assistance.

The CD BDE would come with its own organic rotary wing capability (i.e. helicopters). US officials offered ARC, which already had a robust rotary wing capability, a package of 18 Canadian UH-1 helicopters to support the CD BDE. ARC leadership rejected the offer because there was no maintenance package with it.[57] COLAR, however, agreed to take on the UH-1 helicopter fleet, which became the genesis of the COLAR aviation effort. Later, COLAR would also receive an additional 13 UH-60 Blackhawks under US support to Plan Colombia to enhance the CD BDE's air mobility.

The role of US SOF following the implementation of US support to Plan Colombia legislation in 1999 was to train only human rights-vetted COLMIL units. The 1999 and subsequent legislations also specifically stated that no US forces deployed to Colombia could be involved in ground combat operations. After NSPD-18 became US policy in 2002 and Congress granted expanded authorities, US SOF continued to train COLMIL units but also provided operational planning advice to Colombian SOF units and facilitated the fusion of all-source intelligence. In short, the number of US SOF forces deployed to Colombia increased considerably beginning in 2002 due to the expansion of their training mission to COL SOF, to COLMIL units participating in Plan Patriota, and to units from the 18th BDE of the COLAR under the Infrastructure Security Strategy (ISS).

Although US SOF trained the CD BDE to accomplish a counterdrug mission, the brigade soldiers trained on military tasks designed to fight an unconventional enemy heavily involved in the protection of all facets of the drug trade.

Significantly, though, deployment of the unit and its assets could only occur in specific areas and could only involve specifically cleared personnel. Authority for helicopter use was held at the Embassy level. This at times caused considerable friction between the Colombians and their American partners and led in many ways, until 2002, to the emergence of two conflicts: the counterinsurgency, which was a Colombian affair; and the counterdrug effort, which was often called 'the State Department's war.' Personnel involved on both sides were in a sense compartmentalized, though Colombian officers and skill-personnel necessarily had greater latitude in their deployment patterns. There is no evidence that the relatively short period involved from 1999 to 2002 saw rotation of personnel through US funded and advised units to the general population of COLMIL forces. Most troop instruction, in any case, was not unlike what the Colombians themselves offered. It was simply delivered by US SOF. US SOF continued to train units of the CD BDE until 2005.

Of perhaps greater moment, in 2002, the Commander of US Military Group-Colombia, Colonel Ken Keen, who later became the SOUTHCOM Deputy Commander (3-star general), developed the proposal to create a unit that could infiltrate deep into FARC territory and conduct direct action against FARC infrastructure and leaders. COL Keen's vision was to form a strike unit similar to a US Army Ranger Battalion. In essence, this unit, together with others that would be added later by COLMIL, would act as raiders (see Figure 2) and would focus on killing or capturing FARC leaders as specified in the COLMIL campaign plan. With support from SOUTHCOM and the US Ambassador in Bogotá, Keen presented the idea to General Mora, COLMIL Commander at the time, who agreed to carry out the project. As a result, the Commando Battalion was created with the support of US SOF and oversight of representatives of COLMIL, which already had its own plans to field a similar unit. Soldiers were called up from across COLAR units to take part in a selection process to become the new *comandos* (commandos).

The Commando Battalion enhanced the COLMIL's ability to penetrate deep into FARC's territory with stealth. Its organic units had the capability to conduct direct action as well as reconnaissance. The initial purchase of lethal and non-lethal equipment for the *comandos* was made with DOS INL funds under Plan Colombia in order to enable initial operating capability. Beginning in 2003, the Commando Battalion received FMF and DOD CN funds. These funds facilitated the purchase of additional equipment (lethal and non-lethal). The training and operational planning advice provided by US SOF along with the equipment provided through US security assistance increased the operational capacity of the Commando Battalion and provided a much reliable strategic asset to the GOC capable of dismantling FARC infrastructure (leadership, logistics and military units).

In 2003, COLMIL created a parallel battalion with similar capabilities to the Commando Battalion, the *Lanceros*, with manpower drawn from the *Lancero* school, an intense, 'jungle Ranger' course that had been in existence since the 1960s. With the addition of this battalion, COLMIL established the *Comando de Operaciones Especiales del Ejercito* (COESE) or COLAR Special Operations Command. The *Lanceros* provided the COLMIL an added capability to sustain its pressure against FARC leaders and logistics infrastructure. US SOF began to provide training to the *Lancero* battalion in 2003 and operational advice and facilitation of intelligence fusion to the COESE, its command and control (C2) headquarters.

While providing training and operational advice to COL SOF, US SOF forces' trained counter-guerrilla units of the COLAR 18th Brigade with headquarters in Arauca as part of the Infrastructure Security Strategy (ISS). The ISS program was designed to assist the government in the protection of the strategically valuable Caño Limon Oil Pipeline. The pipeline originates in the northeastern part of Colombia, in the department of Arauca located along the Venezuelan border, and ends at the port of Barranquilla. Due to excessive number of attacks on the pipeline (over 160 in 2001) by the illegal armed groups, primarily the National Liberation Army (ELN), the state was losing a significant amount of revenue. The intent of the ISS program was to provide training and equipment to two counter-guerrilla battalions of the 18th BDE that would function as rapid reaction forces. Along with training and equipment, the US provided a rotary wing capability (two UH60s and one UH-1) in order to facilitate the movement of the rapid reaction force along the 178 KM of pipeline protected by the 18th BDE.

US SOF trained counter-guerrilla units of the 18th BDE in small unit tactics, operational planning, air mobile planning and operations, and other military related tasks to enhance the units' capabilities. At the same time, US SOF worked with the 18th BDE staff to facilitate the integration of civil affairs, information operations, and psychological operations into the brigade's operational plans. The effort contributed to the significant reduction of pipeline attacks. By 2005, the ISS program had also run its course.

In 2004, US SOF also began training mobile brigades attached to JTF-Omega. These units conducted offensive operations against FARC Fronts and *Bloques* as well as against their narcotrafficking infrastructure. US SOF training included a variety of small unit tactical inputs. Though relatively mundane, these – together with the procurement of equipment and funding of special initiatives, such as transportation for unit block-leave-helped sustain the combat power of the JTF-Omega units operating under the extremely challenging conditions already mentioned. US SOF continued to train COLAR mobile brigades until 2008.

While US SOF expanded its training to other COLMIL units, its focus remained with developing COL SOF as a premier special operations force capable of conducting multiple operations anywhere within Colombian territory and interoperable with US SOF. In 2004, COLMIL expanded its special operations forces by adding the urban and naval commandos and creating the *Comando Conjunto de Operaciones Especiales* (CCOPE) or Joint Special Operations Command commanded by a COLAR Colonel. US SOF assisted the CCOPE leadership in organizing its headquarters element in coordination with US Military Group-Colombia. With the formation of the CCOPE, US equipment and training requirements for COL SOF began to be channeled through the CCOPE leadership.

In 2007, COLMIL leaders enhanced the capabilities of CCOPE and indicated the change by adopting a new acronym, CCOES, but keeping the name (in Spanish and English) the same.[58] Command, though, now resided in a COLAR general officer. The creation of this new command under a one-star general demonstrated the importance the Colombian civilian political leadership, specifically, the Minister of Defense (MOD) and the President, placed on COL SOF. COL SOF had demonstrated that with timely intelligence and proper amount of support it could successfully execute high risk operations to kill or capture FARC leaders or rescue hostages. The higher profile placed on the CCOES and close interaction with the MOD and President ensured greater integration of all-source intelligence. US SOF continues to this day to provide training, operational advice, and facilitation of intelligence fusion to CCOES leaders and subordinate units.

The expansion of US SOF training and operational advice led US Special Operations Command South (SOCSOUTH) in coordination with SOUTHCOM and with approval of the US Ambassador in Bogotá to establish in 2005 a C2 element called Special Operations Command Forward (SOC FWD). SOC FWD had the mission to provide C2 for all US SOF in-country, to serve as the interface with COLMIL leaders on matters related to SOF, to facilitate intelligence fusion, and to serve as baseline C2 headquarters to support a potential rescue operation in coordination with COLMIL of the three American hostages held by the FARC since February 2003. As such, SOC FWD facilitated the coordination of all US SOF activities within Colombia, served as the main coordination element for US SOF coming to Colombia, and provided counsel to the US Ambassador on matters related to the three Americans held hostage by FARC. The SOC FWD mission in Colombia ended in 2009 after the three Americans were rescued and US SOF training missions drew down.

The contribution of US SOF in Colombia in terms of training, operational planning advice, and facilitation of intelligence integration were important to COLMIL's successful execution of its campaign plan. The warfighting skills and competencies transferred to not just COL SOF but also to other COLMIL units led to a more disciplined and professional COLMIL force, one which loomed large as its operations increasingly had strategic effect. It is hard to disagree that COL SOF is a more professional force, better trained and inter-operable with US SOF, as a result of US SOF's persistent engagement. LTC Will Griego, who served as US Special Operations Advisor to COL SOF while assigned to the US Military Group, summarized the effects US SOF engagement upon COL SOF:

COL SOF is as good as US SOF at the tactical level. They carry the same equipment and have the same training and even have much of the same operational equipment. We [US SOF] beat them in resources and technology, but COL SOF is even better than many 'first world' SOF. COL SOF is one of maybe 15 SOF organizations in the world that is as good as they [the Colombians] are. We have no problem operating alongside them [such forces] in places like Afghanistan or elsewhere in the world, because they are totally professional and compatible.[59]

Planning assistance and training teams (PATT)

The US PATT mission (i.e. US advisory mission) began in early 2000 as battalions of the CD BDE commenced interdiction operations against FARC base and HCl labs in the Putumayo-Caquetá area. During that time, US SOF PATT provided the CD BDE staff operational planning advice and assisted in intelligence integration and execution of air mobile operations. They also assisted US SOF trainers in the planning and coordination of training of the BDE's subordinate units. With SOUTHCOM's ability to support the COLMIL campaign plan as a result of expanded authorities granted by the US Congress, COLMIL Commanding General Mora – after discussions with the SOUTHCOM CDR, General James T. Hill, when both staffs met in Cartagena in July of 2003 – agreed to station US military advisors (PATTs) with selected COLMIL units directly engaged in Plan Patriota. The purpose was to facilitate the coordination and synchronization of operational plans executed by COLMIL tactical units.

The PATT program was organized using the Battlefield Operating Systems (BOS) of operations, logistics, fire support, engineer, and intelligence; that is, individuals were assigned to support those particular areas within unit headquarters (e.g. mobile brigades).[60] PATT also provided feedback to the Commander of US Military Group-Colombia on the progress of COLMIL tactical operations, as well as on capacity gaps or capability breakdown, which in turn enabled timely US response as dictated by circumstances. In this area of filling capacity and capability gaps, the PATT program proved useful as it helped facilitate intelligence integration, conducted training for small unit leaders, and provided advice to security assistance officers in the US Military Group-Bogota on how to enhance the COLMIL institutional training and education in order to sustain or improve a capability.

As the COLMIL campaign progressed, the PATT program evolved from providing operational planning advice to also providing small unit training. PATT personnel were located at the COLMIL Joint Staff, COLAR division and brigade levels, and in elements of JTF-Omega. Beginning in 2007, the PATT Chief, LTC Chris 'Luke' Lukasevish, developed with his team the concept of Rural Combat and Combat Lifesaving MTTs. The focus of the Rural Combat MTT was to train two platoons in each brigade to conduct small unit operations against FARC mid-level and high-level targets.[61] This training gave the COLMIL brigade commander an enhanced capability to kill or capture FARC leaders, which was one of the main operational objectives of the campaign plan.[62] The effects of the

Rural Combat MTT could certainly be measured in the number of FARC leaders killed or captured by those platoons trained, but there was a different kind of effect which was the positive impact upon COLMIL morale of being linked to their American counterparts in a unified effort. This point was best described by LTC Lukasevish: 'For the COLMIL soldier, the US is all-knowing. He believes he is getting the best training in the world. When you think you are being trained by the best, when you engage the enemy, you will have more confidence, because you have been trained by the best...professionalism, discipline.'[63]

At the same time, a Combat Lifesaving (CLS) MTT was created to enable rapid treatment and stabilization of wounded soldiers in the battlefield as well as to enable rapid evacuation. This CLS MTT trained close to 600 soldiers in casualty evaluation, pre-hospital trauma care, triage, in-flight emergency, and evacuation of sick and wounded.[64] According to LTC Lukasevish, there is anecdotal evidence that the skills taught in the CLS instruction were used to save lives in the battlefield.

Without a doubt, the PATT program fulfilled the mission it was intended to do, to provide operational planning and tactical training assistance to enhance the COLMIL warfighting capabilities in support of the campaign plan. The ability of the PATTs to train small units of COLMIL, facilitate intelligence integration, advise operational planning, and share experiences with their counterparts enhanced the common effort. The PATT program ended in May of 2010.

Conclusions

In the context of other theaters where the US has waged or continues to wage war against terrorism, the Colombian case and the military assistance provided by the United States has been a resounding success. By the end of the Uribe administration in 2010, the conflict had moved to a new phase, which now has been concluded with a peace agreement. Why was the US military able to legitimately claim success in its assistance to COLMIL? Key was the will within the Colombian leadership, especially as demonstrated by President Uribe and his senior military team – COLMIL leaders such as Generals Fernando Tapias, Enrique Mora Rangel, Carlos Ospina Ovalle ,and Freddy Padilla de Leon. Provided with political and strategic direction by elected authority, the military leadership laid the foundation for the transformation of their armed forces in conjunction with the efforts of an increasingly talented pool of subordinate leaders. In focusing upon the task of warfighting while strengthening the institutional warfighting capabilities of the armed forces, they created the capacity to absorb whatever input their American partners were willing and able to provide. The result, as is well known, was an insurgent threat decimated and ultimately willing to shift gears to a new form of struggle, one still opposed to the existing order but fought within it. This, of course, will require a different sort of response, but the ultimate capacities and capabilities for the defense of democratic order are in place and tested.

Indeed, from an initial position of looming strategic disaster, the Colombian polity has emerged much strengthened, as has its military. The successful partnership forged by the US armed forces and COLMIL was enabled by alignment of politico-military objectives by both countries, the operational support provided by the US to the COLMIL military campaign, and the US military assistance to the COLMIL as an institution. While COLMIL conducted its military campaign, the US military helped fill gaps in capacity and then to hone capabilities, notably in the areas of intelligence fusion, special operations training, logistics, medical, communications, information operations, civil affairs, air mobility, and maritime and riverine interdiction. The US military effort also focused on institutional building through its security cooperation programs (focused on training and education). This model worked because the COLMIL leadership had a sound military campaign backed by clear political objectives and a plan to modernize its force. It also had the capacity and capability to absorb assistance. Very few countries around the world have the ingredients found in this model of success.

Two challenges for the DOD thus emerge. Looking at the case at hand, the US must determine what form its partnership with the COLMIL should take in the next decades in order to ensure that Colombian forces remain a professional warfighting force capable of projecting power inside the country against still-existing threats, even as that same force moves to participate in a coalition of countries to defeat the enemies that threaten democracy and its way of life. In order to do so, US military assistance must continue in the foreseeable future in order to maintain interoperability, critical warfighting skills, and trust and confidence between senior leaders.

Looking beyond this case, the US – or any external democratic power seeking to aid another – must examine the points made above with respect to host nation capacities and capabilities. As any INGO can venture, absorption capability is one of the defining parameters of successful assistance. This, ironically, is not merely a matter of tangible assets but also of the premier intangible demonstrated by the Colombia case, will. Colombia's democracy, however imperfect, allowed the rallying of legitimacy to the side of democratic order and thus the growing of a response which now is held up as a model. Matters do not always work out so well, and the reasons why are as important as exploration of successes.

Notes

1. *Politica de Defensa y Seguridad Democratica*, Republica de Colombia, 2003, 13; available at: https://www.oas.org/csh/spanish/documentos/Colombia.pdf (accessed 1 March 2017).
2. For details in this journal, see Marks, "COLMIL Support for 'Democratic Security,'"197–220.
3. Notes taken by Major Carlos Berrios, USA, Deputy Army Section Chief, US Military Group-Bogota during discussions between General Ospina and senior US military leaders, August 2003.

4. Ibid.
5. Ibid.
6. See source in n.2 above.
7. Historically, the best comparison of conditions might be those experienced in the Burma theater by long-range penetration units such as the British *Chindits* or American *Merrill's Marauders*. Disease vulnerability alone was a daunting challenge, with development of advanced treatment protocols an integral part of sustaining the force.
8. Interview by author of COL James Collins, USA, former SOUTHCOM J2, Colombia Team Leader and one of the architects of the Intelligence Integration Program, 16 December 2010.
9. Ibid.
10. Ibid.
11. Ibid.
12. Ibid.
13. Ibid.
14. Interview by Dr Dave Spencer with Mr Pedro Nunez, US Embassy-Bogotá, Intelligence Fusion Center Liaison Officer, 18 November 2010.
15. Interview by author with COL James Collins USA.
16. Ibid.
17. Ibid.
18. Information provided by Mr Juan Soto, communications advisor to the COLMIL and CNP since 2001, 18 December, 2010.
19. Ibid.
20. Ibid.
21. Ibid.
22. Ibid.
23. Ibid.
24. 'Development of the Colombian Signal Branch,' draft authored by Mr Juan Soto, communications advisor to the COLMIL and CNP after 2001, and CPT Sigfredo Matos Rodriguez, who served as the J6 for the US Military Group in Colombia for 1.5 years; date unknown.
25. Interview by author with Major (R) Tony Santiago, former SOUTHCOM IO LNO to US MILGP, Colombia from 2002 to 2007, 22 December, 2010.
26. Ibid.
27. Ibid.
28. Ibid.
29. Ibid.
30. Ibid.
31. Ibid.
32. Ibid.
33. Information provided by LTC (R) David Diaz, US Military Group Civil Affairs LNO from 2002 to 2009, 17 December 2010.
34. Ibid.
35. Ibid. Acronym as per Spanish.
36. Ibid.
37. Ibid.
38. Ibid.
39. Ibid.
40. Ibid.
41. Ibid.

42. COLMIL had long sought to follow security efforts with a robust and unified civilian response on its own without success. It was not until the government organized itself under the auspices of the CCAI that a long-term state presence in areas long held by the FARC became achievable.
43. Ibid.
44. Information provided by LTC (R) David Diaz.
45. Interview by author with USN CAPT Mark Morris, former US Naval Section Chief, US Military Group-Bogota from 2005 to 2010, 21 December 2010.
46. Ibid.
47. Ibid.
48. Ibid.
49. Ibid.
50. Ibid.
51. Interview conducted by Dr David Spencer with COL (R) Kevin Higgins, CNP *Junglas* advisor after 2001 and former US Military Group Commander, 1999–2001, 9 November 2010.
52. Ibid.
53. Ibid.
54. Ibid.
55. Ibid.
56. Former SOUTHCOM CDR, Gen Charles Wilhelm presented General (R) Tapias, COLMIL CDR at the time, with a proposal at the Defense Ministerial in 1998 to create a CD Battalion along the US Army TO&E. The intent was for this battalion to have sufficient firepower to confront FARC. At that time, SOUTHCOM understood clearly that FARC was heavily involved in the all facets of the drug trade and that it had grown substantially in terms of combat power, hence the offer of building the CD battalion using the TO&E of a US Army battalion.
57. Interview conducted by Dr David Spencer with COL (R) Kevin Higgins.
58. CCOPE and CCOES essentially mean the same thing, Joint Special Operations Command. One takes two letters from *OPeraciones*, and the other takes two letters from *ESpeciales*. CCOES, as noted in the text, was made more robust and given greater stature, but missions remained unchanged.
59. Interview conducted by Dr David Spencer with LTC Will Griego, US SOF Advisor to COL SOF, US Military Group, 15 November 2010.
60. The idea of having US military personnel serving as PATT with COLMIL tactical units was initially presented to the COLMIL leadership in 2002, but it received a lukewarm reception. At the time COLMIL agreed to create joint mobile training teams to provide training to COLMIL leaders at the tactical unit level in order to enhance their critical warfighting tasks. When General Mora did agree to the idea in response to an offer from SOUTHCOM commander, General Hill, the PATT initiative was received with mixed reaction by some tactical unit leaders. However, the PATT program continued to evolve and proved its benefits to some COLMIL commanders, who valued the operational advice as well as the initiative exercised by some of the PATT to facilitate intelligence information and training.
61. Interview by author with LTC (P) Chris 'Luke' Lukasevish, former PATT Chief, US Military Group, Colombia from 2007 to 2008 and later Pol-Mil Planner for Colombia, Joint Staff, J5, Western Hemisphere, 16 December, 2010.
62. Ibid.
63. Ibid.
64. Ibid.

Disclosure statement

The views and opinions expressed in this article are those of the author and do not necessarily reflect the official policy or position of any agency of the U.S. government.

Bibliography

Berrios, Carlos. Interviews with:

Collins, James. Former SOUTHCOM J2, Colombia Team Leader and one of the architects of the Intelligence Integration Program, December 16, 2010.

Diaz, David. U.S. Military Group Civil Affairs LNO from 2002 to 2009, December 17, 2010.

Lukasevish, Chris. "Luke." Former PATT Chief, US Military Group, Colombia from 2007 to 2008 and later Pol-Mil Planner for Colombia, Joint Staff, J5, Western Hemisphere, December16, 2010.

Morris, Mark. Former U.S. Naval Section Chief, U.S. Military Group-Bogota from 2005 to 2010, December 21, 2010.

Santiago, Tony. Former SOUTHCOM IO LNO to U.S. MILGP Colombia from 2002 to 2007, December 22, 2010.

Soto, Juan. Communications advisor to the COLMIL and CNP since 2001, December 18, 2010.

Berrios, Carlos. Notes taken as Deputy Army Section Chief, U.S. Military Group-Bogota during discussions between General Ospina and senior US military leaders, August 2003.

Marks, Thomas A. "Colombian Military Support for 'Democratic Security'." *Small Wars and Insurgencies* 17, no. 2 (2006): 197–220.

Politica de Defensa y Seguridad Democratica, Republica de Colombia, 2003. Accessed March 1, 2017. https://www.oas.org/csh/spanish/documentos/Colombia.pdf

Soto, Juan, and Sigfredo Matos Rodriguez. "Development of the Colombian Signal Branch." draft; date unknown (used with permission).

Spencer, Dave. Interviews with:

Griego, Will. U.S. SOF Advisor to COL SOF, U.S. Military Group, November 15, 2010.

Higgins, Kevin. CNP *Junglas* advisor after 2001 and former U.S. Military Group Commander, 1999-2001, November 9, 2010.

Nunez, Pedro. US Embassy-Bogota, Intelligence Fusion Center Liaison Officer, November 18, 2010.

A double-edged sword: the people's uprising in Ghazni, Afghanistan

Matthew P. Dearing

ABSTRACT
In the recent era of state formation in Afghanistan, hundreds of small popular movements rebelled against the Taliban throughout the country. One in particular stands out – the Andar Uprising in the spring of 2012 gave a compelling case of local vigilantism in an area ripe with historic grievances and narratives of community defense dating back to the anti-Soviet jihad. This case is compelling as it shows one faction of the movement engaging in protective paramilitary behavior over the civilian population, while the other faction engages in predatory behavior. Controlling processes, incentives structures, and narratives were all factors correlating to the rise of a popular anti-Taliban resistance in Andar District that battled the Taliban and perceived oppression in their district. When patrons and the community engaged in complementary governance over the paramilitary group, in this case through the Afghan Local Police (ALP), paramilitary behavior was protective of the civilian population. However, when patrons and communities failed to provide complementary governance, as the case of the remaining Uprising force after ALP institutionalization, the paramilitaries engaged in predation on the local population.

Introduction

These Uprisers, they are like roundworms in your stomach, they are eating everything.

Khial Mohammad Hussaini

States in crisis, either in periods of formation or collapse, are often faced with the rise of popular movements that present themselves as double-edged swords – one element in support of, another against the status quo. Out of these movements arises competition for control over ever-greater opportunities in the market of protection.[1] Cornering the protection market brings opportunity to profit from a number of political and economic industries, such as access to lootable resources, taxation and land rights, or licit and illicit smuggling industries (to name just a few). Popular movements thus have to reconcile their ideological motives for rising up against the apparent need and opportunity for gaining material resources.[2] How a movement and its patrons respond to this challenge can give us better insight into a critical question in the field of armed non-state actors: *why some paramilitaries are protective of the civilian population, while others are predatory?*

In the recent era of state formation in Afghanistan (2001-present), hundreds of small popular movements rebelled against the Taliban throughout the country. Some were spontaneous grassroots movements based on grievances brewing over many years; others were inspired in part by external support from US Special Operations or other international actors, but many were a result of outside political entrepreneurs mobilizing and resourcing the rebellions. After an 'uprising' force was raised and if successful, the local notable in charge attracted attention in the media, declared either affiliation with the government or plans to reclaim local governance while ousting Taliban oppression. The mere raising of a militia opened a world of opportunities for armed groups and their commanders in the market of protection. Once armed and patrolling, disarming and demobilizing required incentives and oversight – usually employment or leadership positions in a new Afghan Local Police (ALP) detachment affiliated with government legitimacy and resourcing.

As such, the ALP program served as an entry point into the market of protection. If one thing was constant about the variety of uprisings – they were spread out and disjointed, rarely able to garner the robustness of a national uprising movement similar in scope to the Anbar Awakening in Iraq in 2006.[3] The spring of 2012, in Afghanistan, brought the first opportunity of a national awakening and real encouragement of truly protective paramilitary groups. After nearly a decade of foreign Taliban abuse and occupation, residents of Andar District, Ghazni Province fought back.

From the onset, the Uprising targeted retribution against foreign Taliban and their sympathizers. However, like most movements in Afghanistan's history, the success and spread of the Uprising was limited. The resistance did not take on the character of religious movements, nor did it have a strong intellectual base leading it, but it did have strong roots within the political–military (*tanzim*) networks that influenced the anti-Soviet resistance, namely Hezbi Islami. Like the Mujahedin parties during the anti-Soviet jihad and the civil war, the Uprising was plagued with corruption, infighting, and competition over authority and resources. It splintered and faded into obscurity, soon overshadowed by the growing professionalization of the ALP in the district. 'Uprisers' who remained outside the control of the Ministry of Interior (MoI) would serve under tacit guidance from the National Directorate of Security (NDS) and US Special Forces. As US troops departed Ghazni, oversight and resourcing of Uprising fighters was left to an Afghan government which Special Inspector General Afghanistan Reconstruction (SIGAR) (2015) noted had little capability to oversee national police or local police, let alone tacitly aligned militias. As a result, the Uprising engaged in the market of protection, preying on the population for resources and survival.

For over 18 months, the Uprising gave a compelling case of local vigilantism in an area ripe with historic grievances and narratives of community defense dating back to the anti-Soviet jihad. That the Uprising movement was embedded within a collective memory of historical grievance and resistance ideology is critically important both to the evolution of the Uprising and its changing character as legitimacy waned. Situated within a landscape abundant with lootable resource opportunities, the Uprising remained relatively protective in nature and abstained from gross levels of violence or predation targeted at civilians *until* patron and community buy-in declined.[4] Why did Uprising fighters first avoid the temptation of predatory behavior so often attributed to paramilitary groups but then later embrace it?

The Uprising was more than just a spontaneous revolt of angry residents – it was a calculated but clumsy strategy of misaligned state patrons mobilizing old mujahedin networks against the Taliban – a counterinsurgent strategy and a final gasp before US forces left the province to its own devices. At the Uprising's zenith, it seemed to encapsulate the passions of young and old in Afghanistan – even for a brief moment – as an indigenous movement, long neglected, took back its sovereign rights. But the passionate lost their way, factions emerged, conspiracies spread, and the process of state formation took over. Much like movements of the past, months after emerging, the Uprising split: part of it was captured by the nascent but well regulated ALP program, but the other remained an active franchise in the market of protection – outside the control of patrons or communities. Patrons in the US Special Forces and the Afghan intelligence services continued to use the Uprising franchise as a counterinsurgent force, but the community had limited control over their actions or interest in the members of the Uprising. While patrons offered strong incentives to join ALP, they also continued to incentivize free-market protection by maintaining alliances, weapons and resource provisions, and conducting joint operations.

As a result, one element of the Uprising continued to defend the population, while the other – free to operate with impunity – preyed on it. In short, the necessity for a local, informal security response led to continued state support to predatory paramilitaries in Ghazni.[5] Community controls were limited after the excitement of the Uprising declined. Among community members, it is apparent that social support toward the Uprising was much in line with tensions in the area for decades – some support toward Hezbi Islami fighters, some support toward Taliban, and some just wishing both could put down their arms. This case study supports a more general hypothesis: *When both patron and community controls are weak, it is more likely the paramilitary will engage in predatory behavior while seeking to monopolize the market of protection.*

This qualitative case study uses a partial process-tracing method to outline the factors that determine how paramilitaries develop over time in addition to congruence procedures to explore within case variation. George and Bennett suggest that process tracing can develop the 'causal mechanism' or the inanimate processes which connect cause and effect (2005, 137). Bates et al. argue that narrative description can highlight actors' 'preferences, their perceptions, their evaluation of alternatives, the information they possess, the expectations they form, the strategies they adopt, and the constraints that limit their action' (1998, 11). As such I rely on (1) primary source documents such as the Andar Uprising Manifesto and supportive locally produced publications, artifacts, and multimedia records; (2) interviews with US and Afghan subject matter experts and Uprising participants; and (3) field research in Ghazni from 2012 to 2013. The following study begins with a brief examination of the key variables leading to the rise and split of the Uprising. I then follow with a review of conflict dynamics leading to state collapse and state formation in Ghazni, followed by an in-depth examination of the three key variables, summarized below: (1) controlling processes; (2) incentive structures; and (3) narratives.

Controlling processes

Ghazni was a province ripe for external intervention. Decades of state neglect left local communities to rely upon personal connections and local power brokers, and a significant trust deficit emerged between state and society. The absence of real development and security for Pashtun districts east of Highway One gave greater influence to old mujahedeen networks, namely Hezbi Islami and Harakat members now affiliated with Taliban. Not only was this a recipe for an anti-Taliban resistance but also for the rise of ambitious power brokers seeking opportunity in an expanding security dilemma. The introduction of outside oversight, resources, and the institutionalization of the movement led to a formalized local police outfit. This magnified internal divisions within the movement, leading to greater professionalization of one paramilitary group and greater autonomy of another. The latter movement found freedom to operate in illicit and predatory behavior, while continuing to serve a counterinsurgency function for the state.

Incentive structure

Ghazni represents a region with significant but unrealized potential in the market of protection. Patrons at the provincial level found the state formation process could lead to significant profit and influence over the future business environment in Ghazni Province. Their support for paramilitary groups sought not only to expand security in the province but to facilitate their own business and political interests. However, these resources did not seem to draw paramilitaries to engage in predation of the scale represented in other areas such as northern Afghanistan; nor was there an ambitious criminal network tied to the Uprising fighters. Two important resources characterize the incentive structure: (1) access to state financing and (2) the resource-rich environment, namely access to profitable economic zones in Ghazni. The resource architecture in Ghazni favored the Andar Uprising in that it received initial support from state patrons, which did not seem to necessitate preconditions but likely served as a controlling process over the behavior and character of the paramilitary group. Lootable resources such as chromite, artisanal minerals, and valuable land were available to the paramilitaries, though they did not appear driven by these opportunities. The rudimentary development of the mining industry in Ghazni likely prevented interest from developing among paramilitaries. Finally, the extent of resource support from within the community was not entirely clear in this case. While the Uprising received some support from Hezbi networks, the majority appears to have been provided by state patrons and US forces through institutions, such as the ALP and NDS. State support, though, was not consistent, and as it waned for the Uprising fighters, the militias began preying on the local population to sustain their opportunities in the protection market.

Narratives

The Uprising relied upon support of residents, family, friends, outside networks, and patrons. Embedded within this support network were resistance narratives based upon collective norms of community defense. There were a number of factors that served to disadvantage the Taliban and aided in the development of anti-Taliban paramilitaries in Ghazni. Many of these factors, embedded within social narratives and networks, were based off the realities of localized grievances and actualized violence in the province over the last thirty years. In addition, these narratives were felt and transferred via established networks and facilities such as mosques, communities, media platforms, and other safe spaces that nurtured resistance ideology. This section finds that patrons, clients, and the community shared in a collective norm emphasizing resistance, protection, and defense of the community. While norms served as an important factor influencing behavior, this did not prevent some Uprising fighters from extending the concept of community defense to what many in the community perceived as predatory behavior.

Controlling processes, incentives structures, and narratives were all factors correlating to the rise of a popular anti-Taliban resistance in Andar District. As a result, the Uprising produced a paramilitary force to battle the Taliban and perceived oppression in their district. When patrons and the community engaged in complementary governance over the paramilitary group, in this case through the ALP, paramilitary behavior was protective of the civilian population. However, when patrons and communities failed to provide complementary governance, as the case of the remaining Uprising force after ALP institutionalization, the paramilitaries engaged in predation on the local population.

Rise of the state and resistance in Ghazni

With an estimated population of more than one million and situated 140 km south of Kabul, Ghazni province is divided into 19 districts and over 3100 villages. The province consists of an ethnic mix of Pashtuns (53%), Hazara (42%), and Tajik (4%) residents, with most of the latter residing within the capital, Ghazni city. The eastern and southern portions of the province reside along the Pashtun tribal belt, while the west resides within the confines of the Hazarajat region. Nearly 90% of residents live in rural districts, while 10% reside in urban areas. Ghazni city is a key strategic and economic hub for professionals engaged in legal and illicit markets, serving as a half-way point between Kabul and Kandahar cities. Certainly any armed faction seeking a monopoly over violence in the region is sure to gain monopolies over political and economic power as well.

Ghazni's influence spreads beyond just its landlocked location. It has been a focal point of religious personalities and networks since the nineteenth century, influencing power and politics in rural and urban settings, most notably as a zone of expansion for the Taliban. In the 1930s, the Nur ul Mudaris *madrasa* was built and served as one of the most important private religious schools in Afghanistan. Out of the *madrasa* network and among the Ghilzai tribes developed the *Harakati Enqelab Islami* (Islamic Revolution or referred here as Harakat), a moderate clerical party based on traditional Sunni Islam. In the early years of the jihad, it was one of the major mujahedeen parties that influenced anti-communist rebellions in the east. Hezbi Islami (Hezbi)[6] also developed a strong network in Ghazni province among young Pashtun intellectuals, where tribal structures were broken down or intermixed.[7] Here we see a divide between Islamist networks: modernists such as Hezbi – a more educated, urban, and modernized class; and traditionalists – the conservative, rural and pious class distinguished by Harakat. As the state collapsed, the non-aligned fronts within Harakat, loyal to mosque before state, were absorbed into the rising fundamentalism of the Taliban. During the Soviet occupation, the Andar population suffered particularly given the damage caused by Soviet offensives and factional fighting between Hezbi and Harakat.

The post-Taliban regime left a power void in Ghazni that its opponents sought to exploit. Hezbi and other parties captured key positions in district and provincial offices. Expectations for progress were high among Ghazni residents pleased to see the Taliban government dissolved. However, there were two key issues power brokers failed to address that led to growing mistrust between local communities and state patrons: civilian casualties and state neglect. The widespread predation of bandits and militias that the Taliban partially rooted out in the late 1990s was once again set free to prey on the population in the early days of the interim transition government. As the new market of protection expanded in 2003, Human Rights Watch reported a number of abuses the civilian population endured in Ghazni from private militia commanders, former mujahedeen, and Taliban. Accusations of thievery, rape, murder, and other forms of predation were prevalent in urban and rural areas with limited state reach. Moreover, the perception of US as liberators was far from clear to Pashtuns in Ghazni. In December 2003, two airstrikes intended to target suspected insurgent commanders instead killed 16 civilians, 14 of whom were Afghan children. One Kabul shopkeeper noted cryptically: 'This will have very bad consequences for the Americans in the future ... People will grow to hate them, day by day.'[8]

It did not help that Western promises of development, humanitarian delivery, and security fell short of expectations. Not only were development projects limited, they were misdirected. For example, from 2003 to 2006, there were only 28 Ministry for Rural Rehabilitation and Development projects in Andar district (a Pashtun population of over 88,000 residents), while in neighboring Jaghatu district (a Hazara population of under 24,000 residents) there were over 180 National Solidarity Program (NSP) projects.[9] Hazaras had an advantageous position over NGO projects, education facilities, and humanitarian programs given the vast difference in security between Hazara and Pashtun districts divided by Highway One, and the immediate securitization of Pashtuns by US and NATO forces in the early years of insurgency.

Decades of conflict had also broken down local authority structures in Ghazni, empowering rural religious networks with deep ties to Harakat and the Taliban. With an eroded tribal structure and new emerging power dynamics in urban areas, the clergy served as the foremost link between rural people and the Taliban. Their historic ties and capability to easily access the mosque allowed Taliban to engage in recruitment and resistance mobilization. The absence of government support in Ghazni, as well as other rural neighboring provinces such as Paktika and Zabul, which fighters often maneuvered through and used as safe havens, allowed the Taliban to fully infiltrate and control the population in southern and eastern Ghazni. In 2005, a journalist interviewed 22 Taliban in Ghazni, finding that only two were from the old Taliban hierarchy with the rest comprised of a younger, more charismatic group of fighters. In addition, the fledgling Afghan government could not meet its own administrative and security responsibilities. In March 2006, 40 highway policemen defected because of a delay in the payment of their salaries. Not only were social dynamics in flux at the village level, but authority structures from the district up to provincial administration were changing, as older authority figures were increasingly marginalized by rising political elites.

At every stage in the evolution of insurgency, it seemed the state was playing catch-up. By the spring of 2006, 28 Andar officials were assassinated in just six months.[10] In response to the violence, the government imposed a ban on motorcycles in the district (a common means of insurgent transport). In response, the Taliban imposed a ban on all cars and began placing anti-tank mines along the main roads leading to the district center. Journalists described empty streets in Andar where residents complained of a complete absence of police or security forces. One resident noted: 'It looks like 100 years ago. Everyone travels by bicycle or donkey. They do not dare to bring their vehicles on roads.' Within a few weeks, the government lifted the ban on motorbikes. Around the same time, the US military reported that nearly half of Ghazni's districts were under Taliban control. This was illustrated by a number of Afghan officials surrendering to the Taliban, notably Andar district chief Lahoor Khan, who after realizing he would be sacked by provincial officials, switched sides to the Taliban.[11]

Insurgent violence grew more brutal, and their rule over the population was increasingly draconian: preventing passage on roadways, shutting down district resources, destroying or cutting off cell phone service, and threatening anyone taking part in government aid programs. In July 2007, 23 South Korean missionaries were taken hostage by insurgents in Qarabagh district. In the summer, four Afghan judges were abducted and killed in Andar and eighteen Afghan mine clearance personnel were captured and later released. Tenuous relations between Taliban and Hezbi ruptured when a prominent Hezbi district judge, Qazi Abdul Rahman, was killed by Taliban, while other Hezbi notables involved in development and education activities also suffered Taliban attacks. In 2008, 46% of polled residents stated they had never seen the Afghan National Police, assassinations removed the Qarabagh and Andar district police chiefs, and a sustained assault on a US combat outpost in southern Nawa district led to the withdrawal of around 150 US troops. The Taliban effectively controlled a majority of the rural areas, with the state holding only nominal control over territory outside cities.[12]

From 2008 to 2013, civilian casualty rates increased by over 100% (rising from 431 to 878), as UN-funded aid projects were limited due to insecurity. In an ISAF Joint Command report on Andar dated April 2010, the assessment is scathing, with Afghan governance described as 'dysfunctional,' development in the district as 'minimal growth,' and security as 'the most dangerous and unsecure area in Ghazni province.' Even with an American battalion patrolling through Andar and neighboring Deh Yak district in 2011, the Taliban had a firm hold over daily life, administering over 28 schools, adjudicating property and water disputes through religious courts, levying taxes, and implementing strict order throughout the district. From early 2010 to early 2011, the US Army's Third Brigade Combat Team operating in Andar and Deh Yah had compiled 1,600 patrols, 7 air assaults, 100 insurgents killed or captured, and over 30 weapons caches seized. Yet by the end of their tour, US analysts estimated that Taliban fighters could amass the strength of over 400 fighters within Andar and Deh Yak districts, with a support network of nearly 4000 local auxiliaries providing food, aid, and intelligence. Along Highway One, the Polish Task Force White Eagle was given the role of securing north and south of Ghazni city; but they largely 'hunkered down' with control of white space limited to less than 1-km east and west of the highway.[13]

Rise of anti-Taliban resistance

The roots of the anti-Taliban Uprising actually begin from within the Taliban itself. In 2003, as the Taliban regrouped, a new generation of *madrassa* students took up arms. With battlefield losses high, their ranks depleted, the Taliban were willing to accept more outsiders, such as former mujahedeen rivals in Hezbi. Two prominent Hezbi brothers emerged in Andar, Rahmatullah and Abdul Malik. The two fought in a small Taliban cadre led by Maulawi Noorullah, an educated Talib respected for his commitment to education and a mediator between the Taliban and Afghan government. Noorullah was killed by coalition forces, while some within the group, including Rahmatullah and his brother, were detained by US forces in Bagram in late 2007 or early 2008. Their family had close relations with Hezbi notables in Peshawar, and Rahmatullah was released from Bagram prison in 2009, in part due to his connections to Abdul Jabbar Shilgari, a former parliamentarian and Hezbi affiliate in Kabul. After his release, Rahmatullah reportedly met with Hekmatyar's son-in-law Ghairat Bahir to discuss revival of a Hezbi front in Andar district.[14]

In May 2011, the government reinstated its ban on motorbikes in Deh Yak district to further complicate insurgent movements. The Taliban responded by closing a number of schools in the district, and soon thereafter the government relented on its vehicular ban. However, nearly a year later, both Andar and Deh Yak governments reinstated the ban on motorcycles for a third time. The Taliban responded again with collective punishment – closing over 100 schools, seizing government bankcards from teachers and other government employees, and closing routes to Ghazni City, the main economic hub for people of Andar. The influx of 'foreign Taliban' from outside Andar displayed exceedingly harsh forms of authority: locals were prevented from traveling on the main highway, the district center Miri was shut off from resident traffic, mobile phone towers were switched off from dusk till dawn, and aid deliveries were halted or torched in the street. Likely the most deplorable act of foreign Taliban in Andar was a decree to deny Islamic funeral rights for slain soldiers, police, and government employees labeled as spies. Such a ban meant treating Andar residents as non-Muslims, many of whom were former Hezbi affiliates with Rahmatullah. This behavior exceeded anything Rahmatullah and his colleagues believed in. His brother, Abdul Malik, dispatched a deputy to Quetta with the list of local complaints, foremost to have the ban on schools lifted. The Quetta leadership reportedly agreed to lift the ban, but instead sent nearly a dozen Taliban to arrest Abdul Malik for insurrection.[15]

The closing of schools had a real impact upon Andar residents. Rahmatullah embraced education and more progressive values common among Hezbi cadres. When he returned to the battlefield, his more open-minded disposition frustrated conservative Taliban leadership, who removed him from command for 'jihadi misconduct'. To nurture his devotion to the furtherance of Islamic knowledge, Rahmatullah was appointed to Andar's shadow education department. At some point between 2009 and late 2011, during the period of increased Taliban brutality, Rahmatullah underwent a crisis of conscience wherein he began to question his own devotion and the Taliban's legitimacy in Andar.[16]

Months prior to Malik's untimely arrest, Rahmatullah began to build a cadre of former Hezbi Islami loyalists intent on openly defying Taliban authority in the district.[17] Recruiting loyalists from Wardak province, Rashidan district and Tajiks from Ghazni city, Rahmatullah and his gang started to attract attention from Taliban. As the snows melted, young and old stood watch on the streets of Andar, distributed propaganda, encouraged residents to resist the foreigners, and bellowed out expletives at enraged Taliban returning from their winter slumber. Rahmatullah's gang set up a base of operations at a Hezbi safehouse in Payendi. The influx of both outside Taliban and outside Hezbi support rose the threat of a security dilemma in Andar and increased pressure on already weakened local authority structures.[18]

The morning after Abdul Malik's arrest in Ghander, residents protested the Taliban assault on their village. The same day, 20 Taliban enforcers rolled into the village on motorbikes, firing weapons into the air. In the mayhem, a 'white beard' elder named Abdul Samad was shot dead after he slapped a young, arrogant Talib. The crowd grew around the young Talib as he tried to explain his error as a mistake, but the new vigilantes cast his fate. Later, an elder decried: 'Their rule is over. They sleep in our houses and eat our food in the name of Islam, but then do nothing to solve our problems. We are fed up with them riding roughshod over the population.'[19]

Rahmatullah then organized 250 residents at a local school and gave a passionate speech outlining Taliban atrocities. In his speech, he committed himself to liberating the people of Andar against Taliban repression. He implored the people to either support or banish him if they did not agree with the resistance. The elders listened and agreed to discuss the matter from Taliban leadership. Taliban response was straightforward. Rahmatullah was running an illegal militia and must either join the infidels, join Taliban, or defend his cause. They gave him 30 minutes to decide. Rahmatullah rejected Taliban and began targeting insurgents blocking development projects and schools. His actions drew immediate support from the Andar tribe and discord from Taliban. A week after the uprising started, the Taliban launched a barrage of rockets on Ghazni city, ending a fragile agreement with the provincial governor that limited Taliban rocket attacks, which also bordered the Polish and American forward operating base.[20]

On 11 May, Uprising fighters were completing two days of training in Payendi village, when Taliban launched an assault. The immaturity of the Uprising militia became clear. These were untrained young fighters handicapped with old weapons, limited ammunition; they could barely make it through a firefight (seven of their weapons broke during the defense). Rahmatullah suffered a wound to his arm and was rushed to a Kabul hospital. While Taliban lost seven in the battle, it was said they put up a fierce offensive that clearly had an impact on Rahmatullah and his future involvement with the movement. He evacuated his family and never returned to Andar. Still, his low level mobilization served as the spark to set ablaze the passions of young and old Hezbi fighters and encourage non-Hezbi residents to join as well, such as Mahaz-i Milli commander, Wali Muhammad. Moreover, it attracted attention from outsiders and patrons in Kabul. Within weeks, hundreds of Afghans rallied to the call of the people's defense in Andar, standing up community defense forces in Qadamkhel, Kunsaf, Saheb Khan, Abdur Rahim, and Gandaher, villages known as Hezbi strongholds during the 1980s and 1990s that would become known as the 'salient' zone for the Uprising. In a moment, Andar looked much like it did during the days Harakat and Hezbi fought turf battles in the intra-mujahedin war, engaging in street battles and jockeying for small gains.[21]

The first clear sign of the Andar Uprising's commitment toward community defense came just two weeks after the Taliban assault on Payendi. A group of 17 foreign (Waziri descended) Taliban were ambushed by Uprising fighters in Qadamkhel and immediately turned over to provincial government officials.[22] This is a simple but important distinction that likely laid the foundation for the protective character of the Uprising in the short term. Instead of using extrajudicial violence against foreign insurgents, the group wielded patience and existing government institutions, indicating the group's desire for government cooperation and assistance. However, their political stance was not that simple. While the movement was anti-Taliban focused, it was not necessarily pro-government. Andar residents were embattled between abusive insurgents and a neglectful government. A rising movement leader, Lotfullah Kamrani, stated confidently that his followers 'have problems with the Afghan government as well,' notably regarding abuse of power and inefficiency. He also noted his commitment was not toward the Afghan government, but Andar residents.[23]

The Andar Uprising amassed over 400 volunteers as the holy month of Ramadan began in August, and Hezbi cadres began asserting themselves in leadership roles within the movement.[24] Social networks affiliated with Hezbi from as far back as the mujahedin era emerged to take advantage of the political openings. In statements released by Hekmatyar's media outlet after the first Uprising battles in Ghazni, he first claimed support for 'Hezbi Islami mujahedin battling their enemy in Andar' but later clarified his response saying, 'local tension had nothing to do with Hezbi Islami and Taliban.' Some argued the Taliban preferred the movement appear less like a popular uprising of the people and more like Hezbi commanders hijacking the event for political advantage. The reality was a combination of popular grievances and political entrepreneurs exploiting the opportunity at hand. Among Hezbi supporters within the government were former Ghazni Provincial Governor Faizanullah Faizan, who lent his home as a redoubt and operations center for Uprising fighters; in addition Abdul Jabar Shelgar, a former Ghazni parliamentarian and Amanullah Kamrani, provincial council member and brother to an emerging leader in the movement, Lotfullah Kamrani. Also known as 'the Engineer,' Kamrani was just 24 years old when he took charge of military operations in the movement. A graduate in computer science, he excelled in leadership and would inspire US Special Forces with his charisma as they would later appoint him as district ALP Commander in October 2012, and by 2014 the Ministry of Interior would appoint him district Chief of Police.[25]

By June, the movement attracted enough attention from Kabul that Afghan and US forces began running joint operations with Uprising fighters to push Taliban out of villages. The Uprising took up a defensive posture around at least five separate villages, but its capacity to clear insurgent-held territory and create new 'white space' on its own was limited.[26] In early July, a dozen Taliban were killed by Uprising fighters near Shahin village, but in mid-August, toward the end of Ramadan, some movement fighters planned to reach out and capture Alijan village but faced furious Taliban resistance and were forced to retreat. Within a week, the Uprising faced more tests as Taliban advanced its direct targeting against leadership elements. On 24 August, the now self-proclaimed leader Faizanullah Faizan suffered a leg wound in an attempted suicide operation on the outskirts of Ghazni city. On the night of 30 August, a Taliban informant infiltrated the Saheb Khan village Uprising post and allegedly poisoned the Uprising fighters and allowed Taliban access to the compound. When inside, they captured the fighters and torched the building. It was clear the movement had internal security issues that Taliban could exploit.[27]

It was not long before factions emerged over leadership, territory, and control. The loss of Faizan, who subsequently left Ghazni for medical treatment, offered an opportunity to answer a growing question, who really leads the movement? In the early stages after Rahmatullah fled, it was unclear who legitimately spoke for the fighters. Factions emerged and widened between elder Hezbi leaders and non-politicized youth. Some villages flew Hezbi flags; others flew the flag of Afghanistan.[28] Cases of internecine fighting began tearing the movement apart. Moreover, the role of government officials from the beginning had an influential role in directing and distilling the motivations of anti-Taliban fighters. Faizon, a former Provincial Governor himself, also served as an early mobilizer of Hezbi support.[29] Some argue Faizon was recruited by then-Minister of Border and Tribal Affairs and former Provincial Governor Asadullah Khaled to start the

Uprising by encouraging Rahmatullah and mobilizing more Hezbi support from outside the province. Khaled, who subsequently became Director of NDS, the Afghan intelligence arm, also flew to Andar in late June to meet the Uprising in Kunsaf, a rather remarkable journey for any member of national government given the deficit of security in the area. A former Harakat notable, confidant of Qari Baba, and member of Ghazni Parliament, Khial Muhammad Hussaini lobbied President Karzai to send a larger security force to Andar in order to save the Uprising from collapse, even though Hussaini was originally a critic of the Uprising, calling it an 'American project' run by 'blood-thirsty and dollar-hungry Hezbi Islami circles.'[30] All parties and personalities of influence in Ghazni could read the writing on the wall, that the Uprising was a critical turning point in Ghazni's future and an opportunity to settle old scores.

One of the most important patron influencers on the Uprising was NDS chief Asadullah Khaled, not only for his deep connections to paramilitary intelligence circles but for his roots in Ghazni Province. Born in Nawa district, southern Ghazni in 1969, to the Taraki Pashtun tribe, he had a father who was a parliamentarian during the reign of King Zahir Shah. During the *jihad*, Khaled's family was associated with Ittihadi Islami, alongside which Khaled fought in the 1990s against the Taliban. He was also affiliated with the Pashtun military faction of *Shura-e Nazar* within Jamiat Islami. His affiliation with Abdul Rasul Sayyaf brought him close to Kabul elites, namely Hamid Karzai, who saw him as a trusted insider and advisor. Khaled also worked alongside US intelligence services in early 2002 on the Stinger missile retrieval program as well as assisting with the establishment of the Kandahar Strike Force, an irregular paramilitary outfit in southern Afghanistan, conducting counter-terror missions with US Special Forces and CIA. Khaled was appointed governor of Ghazni in 2002 and served there until 2005.[31] His close personal relationship and loyalty to the United States was best exemplified when President Barack Obama visited the gravely wounded Khaled at Walter Reed Medical Center during his recovery from a 2012 Taliban assassination attempt.

Khaled's history, like many powerful figures in Afghanistan, comes with notoriety. In 2009, a diplomat testified to the Canadian parliamentary commission regarding Khaled's crimes and human rights abuses, noting his role in narcotics trafficking, gang operations, and running private prisons and torture chambers in Ghazni and Kandahar. Human Rights Watch and Canadian investigations found Khaled ran additional prisons in Kandahar during his tenure there as governor. Khalid's paramilitary force in Kandahar, Brigade 888, was particularly adept at garnering intelligence from captives. Dressed in US-style military uniforms or civilian clothes, the 60 or so men from Ghazni used brutal methods to extract intelligence (such as hanging prisoners from the ceiling 'trussed like a chicken'), which they shared with Canadian counterparts. Every few weeks, the palace guards hired a cleaner to paint over blood-stained walls to conceal the brutality from their patrons.[32]

Khaled's use of torture did not necessarily fall outside the range of acceptable behavior within the US patron-client chain. The 2014 Senate Intelligence Committee report on CIA interrogations examines in part a secret detention facility in Afghanistan known as COBALT or 'the Salt Pit,' where detainees were subjected to 'rough takedown' – beaten and dragged from their cells, clothing ripped off and bodies wrapped with Mylar tape, then hooded and pummeled by personnel. Given the CIA's willingness to engage in brutal treatment of detainees, Khaled's close association with the agency gave tacit endorsement to predatory behavior on his part and among his subordinate clients. Moreover, as a higher-level institution in the patron-client chain, the CIA inadvertently encouraged systematic violence and torture via its own policies and practices.[33]

Brutality placed aside, Khaled's leadership fidelity and genesis in Ghazni inspired many to join the uprising. He was said to have organized student groups from Ghazni at Kabul University to join. At one point Khalid noted: 'I am leading this in part because I am a son of Ghazni, and because I am a minister of tribal affairs and there are tribes living in Ghazni (…) Ghazni and the south of Afghanistan are burning in the same fire – you cannot talk with the Taliban, you have to be their slave or fight with them.'[34]

However, the involvement of government officials and former mujahedin like Khaled and Faizan also disillusioned many Ghazni residents, who saw the identity of the movement corrupted. One movement commander from Omarzai village praised the autonomy of the movement and noted his fear of government interference: 'We don't want anyone here, just leave us the way we are and let us fight for our people ourselves. Now they are trying to change this into a national uprising and into a business and these corrupt officials are trying to make money from it, not to help the people.'[35]

Also, the original mobilizer of the Uprising, Rahmatullah, expressed his displeasure with government interference and withdrew his support to the movement. The defections and outsider interference made even Western observers skeptical of the Uprising. One diplomat admitted: 'Now it's a bit of a mess. It started as an anti-Taliban type thing, then Hezb-i-Islami moved in, then the government and the N.D.S. got involved and there are lots of different players, and that makes the people who started the whole thing suspicious.'[36]

Despite the loss of credibility in the community, it was also seen as a quid pro quo opportunity for both sides. The state could provide resources, and the Uprising could wage a war on a major front in eastern Afghanistan. The leadership began positioning the movement on a broader, national scale, calling it a 'national uprising,' with hopes of replicating the Anbar Awakening in Iraq.

Formalizing the uprising

The strong links between a Hezbi core and government support in Andar seems to give support to what Amanullah Kamrani claimed was a deliberate plan to use Hezbi as the spark to what the government would term a 'popular' uprising at the national level.[37] At the district and provincial levels, political activists such as Khalil Hotak organized tribal elders to support the effort and its transition to a more formal institution. Both efforts sought to legitimize and control the Uprising. Hotak was Deputy Head of the Provincial Peace Council and a noted patron to police officials and the ALP. Before the Uprising, Hotak organized the *Nejat* (Salvation) Community Council, which claimed to have developed a plan for an uprising movement a full year before it actually took place:

> We had been in touch for more than a year with local elders, the very elders who are now leading the uprising in the field, to mobilize them for simultaneous public uprisings in all districts. An untimely confrontation happened, and the uprising started prematurely in Andar only. Asadullah Khaled and Faizan jumped to get the credit for the uprising. They have actually manipulated it and the prospect for a real popular uprising is now seriously facing failure.[38]

The function of the Nejat council was initially to raise an anti-Taliban resistance movement, but then once the movement occurred precipitously, Nejat reacted to what was needed at the time, training and recruitment of resistance fighters into the ALP. It also monitored local sentiments and made recommendations to the provincial governor as well as distributing humanitarian aid to local citizens. According to US officials in the area, Hotak and the council were closely allied with US Special Forces providing recommendations, including full lists of ALP recruits.

While the initial ideological drive of the movement began to diminish after Rahmatullah's departure, the injection of leadership and resources from Kabul, Hezbi networks, and now the link between US Special Forces, Hotak and the Nejat Council helped transition the informal Uprising militias into ALP. The Nejat Council vetting process gave a good impression of local, institutional buy-in, but questions remained regarding the loyalty of ALP to their assigned villages. Would ALP be loyal to the villages, Khalil Hotak, another sub-patron, or to the Ministry of Interior?

Inspired by the 'spontaneous movement' in Andar and committed to establishing a local police presence along Highway One, US Special Forces utilized the Uprising's motivation and need for resources to build an ALP detachment in October 2012. ODA team 1326, deployed to Andar, recruited, vetted, and trained the first group of 39 Local Police with Engineer Kamrani as its commander. To differentiate between Uprising members, who had dwindled from 250 to 150 by November, the team referred to the new groups as 'legitimate' ALP, continuing to work alongside with the Uprising militias. Robinson (2013) notes the Special Forces tried to work around Hezbi influence within the movement, which was proving to be tactically inefficient and susceptible to 'collapse' under a growing Taliban resurgence in the province. To help the movement and ALP guardians along, three Afghan Special Forces teams were deployed to reinforce the now three US Special Forces teams in the province. These teams would serve as subject matter experts in local political dynamics, conflict resolution, and facilitate training and mentoring of new recruits.

US Special Forces had a complex mission ahead of them. Diverging interests within the movement and within Kabul regarding how much support and oversight it should receive, many members within the movement still saw the government as much an enemy as the Taliban, and the popularity of the movement at the national level led Taliban to focus their efforts on disrupting it. Moreover, conventional US forces, comprised of only three companies in the province, were preparing to draw down from Ghazni. The US ODA teams had limited intelligence on the demographics and needs of the rural population, let alone the Uprising itself. Fortunately, they had political entrepreneurs who were cooperative and proactive in the provincial and district government in Andar, who all seemed to support the recruitment and validation of additional ALP in the district. The district governor, Mohammaed Kasim Disiwal, embraced the Uprising and even participated in some of the initial street battles. The district police chief, Ramazon, was strict and focused on preventing corruption among his policemen. These leaders would prove valuable in ensuring the ALP remained disciplined and motivated, but who would control the Uprising? As ALP expanded, Special Forces focus was more on controlling ALP, while the Uprising remained in the hands of NDS patrons who focused more on intelligence collection and countering foreign Taliban influence than on the particular behavior of its client in Ghazni.[39]

Long after ALP were established in Andar, institutional patrons continued to use Uprising militias for joint operations with mixed results. Uprising fighters brought unique intelligence capabilities primarily since they resided outside the chain of command. While they still had tacit connections to NDS that resourced the fighters, there was little control over them, absent incentives provided by NDS or US Special Forces patrons, discussed further below. Deputy Provincial Governor Ahmadi noted that US Special Forces 'have given them money and from time to time provide them with supplies. They do this to achieve their own military objectives.' Still, many Uprising fighters preferred their separation from the official chain of command, with one commander noting: 'The *patsoonian* (Uprising) don't belong at all to the government.'

The Alizai case in June 2014 exemplifies the limited oversight and bravado of Uprising militias. In a joint US–Afghan operation with US Special Forces, Afghan NDS, Commandos, Local Police, and Uprising militia under their commander Abdullah, a clearing operation was orchestrated near Alizai in Khadokhel village. Villagers claimed at least a dozen US soldiers were partnered with around 30 Afghan soldiers residing in Alizai while Uprising fighters engaged in an operation which killed 11 Taliban.[40] When Abdullah and his men returned to Alizai, they rounded up three men previously detained by ALP as suspected Taliban and escorted them out of sight from the safehouse, where they executed the men. A shopkeeper claimed to witness the shooting from a distance, 'They fired an uncountable number of times, more than 100.' Later, Matthieu Aikens interviewed Abdullah by phone, who acknowledged killing the men, claiming, 'Those three were Taliban,' adding, 'If anyone is saying that these three were civilians, that person is pro-Taliban, a Talib himself or is spreading Pakistani propaganda.'[41]

While, the ALP program included basic introductory lectures on ethics, rule of law, and human rights as part of the three-week training program, it hardly ensured compliance and did not guarantee that groups affiliated with ALP would receive training or even abide by it.[42] Uprising militias were occasionally subject to lectures by Special Forces regarding the laws of war and human rights, but Abdullah freely admits, and even boasts of, desecrating enemy bodies: 'Yes, dead bodies are left on the ground. We drag their dead bodies with a car.'[43]

Incentive structure

While rich natural resources were not easily exploitable before or during the anti-Taliban uprising, the knowledge of Ghazni's resource architecture has been evident since Soviet mining explorations in the 1970s.[44] Lootable resource opportunities were available in the vicinity of anti-Taliban areas of operation, yet predation directed at acquisition of these resources was not evident among clients. Still, patrons directing client actions had much to lose if valuable territory was ceded to the Taliban. Paramilitaries were another means of Hezbi networks and state representatives to advance political and business interests in Ghazni Province and profit from the state formation process. Controlling the market of protection in Ghazni also meant controlling other rich markets once the use of force was monopolized.

While industrial scale exploitation of minerals in Ghazni was years from breaking ground, land itself around Andar, Ghazni city, and Highway One was considered high value, in part due to access to future resource extraction capabilities and sites, but also current agriculture and development potential and links to important regional and export markets. Nearby, the Bande-Sardeh Reservoir along the Andar and Paktika border is situated on a 478-Km^2 area of speculative mineral deposits, including mercury, tungsten, gold, and lead. Two large agricultural canal systems, Andar right and left canals, divert water from the Jilga River downstream from the Sardeh Dam, serving as a substantial water supplier for much of eastern Ghazni Province, about 15,280 hectares downstream.[45] From 2004 to 2012, government officials, businessmen, and former mujahedin stole approximately 150,000 acres of land in Ghazni, and the success of the Andar Uprising may have been influenced by land mafia seeking to capture more land.[46] While it appears the Uprising fighters were disinterested in exploiting the natural resource potential in Andar, it is likely the movement opened a new market of opportunity for patrons already engaged in land capture.

All the makings of an extractive market of protection were evident, particularly with the most powerful figures in the security sector, Khalil Hotak and Musa

Khan Arkbarzada, also noted as the most connected figures to the land mafia. Hotak was accused of seizing 2000 *jeribs* of government land and building a residential township on it in Sultan Mahmmud-e Ghaznawi area. Musa Khan Arkbarzada, governor of Ghazni province, has held business partnerships with notorious figures such as Abdul Qadir Wahidi, a gang leader involved in the land mafia, forcible dispossession of people's land, and a spokesman for the Islamic State's faction in Afghanistan. Long before the Uprising, American and Afghan officials cited a laundry list of corruption within Ghazni government offices: police stealing truckloads of gasoline; judges and prosecutors accepting bribes; politicians and administrators engaged in illicit hashish and chromite smuggling rings; and command positions sold to the highest bidder, reaching as high as USD 50,000.[47]

If the resource architecture of Ghazni motivated outside patrons supporting the Uprising, the injection of cash served to shatter the *raison d'etre* within. State resources were supplied at a critical time when the Uprising movement was losing momentum and required intervention. According to Sher Khan, the district governor of Andar until the summer of 2012, commanders received up to 4,000 Pakistani rupees (USD 42) to join the movement. There were also rumors of a USD 200,000 payment that came from Asadullah Khalid to a select few in the movement, including Faizon, to recruit and supply the Uprising. The injection of cash served to upset the internal momentum of the movement by dividing it, as factions arose, and locals described two separate groups: one as *arbakai*, a loose term for state-financed militias, and the other as 'uprising,' the more grassroots faction of the movement. But the latter seemed to increasingly fall by the wayside as Uprising fighters joined the market of protection.[48]

It was evident that US forces were not quite clear on how best to respond to these paramilitary groups and feared close support might upset the perception of legitimacy. As noted, some called the Uprising in Andar a 'deception,' organized and planned in the corridors of the Kabul palace and the US embassy. Yet some US proponents, including ISAF General John Allen, seemed to view the Andar Uprising in the shadow of Iraq's Anbar Awakening.[49] Allen described the movement in one sense as spontaneous, in another as supported by the state: '...part of this is a genuine effort, a genuine desire on behalf of the Afghans to truly make this an Afghan spontaneous uprising, but an Afghan-supported effort, too. Which I think is great.'

Allen claimed the US had no role in mobilizing or supporting anti-Taliban movements in Afghanistan. 'Each one,' in his words, was 'an organic movement.' This statement was clearly an effort to distance the US as outsiders from local movements, which the US hoped would spread elsewhere. He did offer, in the same breath, to support each individual movement with arms, education, and development aid through partnership with GIRoA. As early as August, the Afghan government and US forces were reportedly providing wheat and other foodstuffs to the Uprising. In 2013, one Uprising commander, Abdullah, acknowledged that all of his resourcing came from US forces. 'Everything is provided by the foreigners, including the weapons, salaries and other equipment.' And the deputy Provincial Governor of Ghazni acknowledged that the US provided resources to the movement to further US objectives in the province.[50]

The Uprising manifesto contended the Uprising was only the first phase of a broader movement, with subsequent phases serving to bolster security and development within the area through the full resources of the Afghan Government to include civil society projects, job creation, and youth engagement through sports. Kamrani noted while touring an abandoned medical facility in Andar that his movement's job was to clear the areas of Taliban and free the population; now that they are liberated, the government 'should pay attention to them.' In doing so, the state sought to tame the violence wielding elements of the movement into the ALP.[51]

While the injection of cash split the movement, without military presence and resource distribution, it is clear the movement would have fallen into disarray much sooner and been forgotten much like the hundreds of small local uprisings that have occurred in Afghanistan's state formation era. By September 2012, growth and territorial spread within the Uprising came to a standstill. Kamrani stated in an interview that he had about 25 groups of 15 to 20 members each, spread throughout Andar, conducting ambushes and offensive operations daily. Questions rose as to how unified the diverse groups were, albeit controlling only a cluster of villages to west and south of the district center Miri. NDS and Afghan National Army deployed additional forces to the area to make it one of the 'most heavily militarized zones in Ghazni.'

In October 2012, only six villages were under the movement's full control with a dozen villages serving as buffer zones between Taliban held areas and Uprising-controlled areas. The flood of ANSF and resources kept the paramilitaries active, with many of Kamrani's fighters bearing ANSF camouflage uniforms and weapons. The founding ideology that mobilized and brought new recruits did not seem to have the same resonance to the 375 Andar villages outside the liberated zones. It seemed that the factions were beginning to look for a way out. The Hezbi faction began negotiating with Taliban, passing letters regarding disarmament and reintegration with the Taliban. This group was also most inclined to remain autonomous from the government, while the NDS controlled faction was split between remaining under the tutelage of NDS or converting into ALP. The latter program was quickly outpacing the rest as it held a monopoly on resources and support from US forces.[52]

The first ALP class was commissioned in Andar on 21 October 2012 at Miri district center with an initial recruitment limit of 200.[53] While most of the ALP were direct transitions from Uprising fighters, a large contingent of Uprising fighters remained, particularly the strongly allied Hezbi faction led by Abdullah that had no intention to officially join the government. Uprising fighters continued to participate in joint operations alongside ALP, Afghan national security forces, and US Special Forces. By the end of 2014, the Uprising operated in Gelan, Muqur, and Andar districts, and a number of allegations of abuse followed their path. Multiple reports to government and non-government organizations complained of 'systematic extortion of money, food, firewood and clothes' as recorded by UNAMA. One Gelan resident noted, 'Whenever they saw a nice turban or jacket or a good-looking pair of shoes, they would take it for themselves.' Uprising members targeted residents as Taliban based on the length of their beards. In June 2014, during a joint operation in Andar, the Hezbi faction commander Abdullah executed three detainees while they were in custody of Afghan security forces. In January 2014, an ALP unit beat a shopkeeper to death in Gelan district after accusing him of selling food to Taliban. In January 2015, a 19-year old Andar resident was summarily executed by an Uprising militia, and a collective punishment event was orchestrated by Uprising fighters involving forcible detention and beating with metal chains of 40 civilians. The Uprising had obviously decided to use harsher tactics and threats to coerce popular support.[54]

The surge in armed groups, government security forces, and Taliban had caused 102 civilian deaths in Andar by November 2012. In another estimate, April 2012–13, the Andar Uprising lost at least 60 fighters to Taliban attacks. While casualty figures are difficult to determine, it is clear the presence of vigilante groups led to an increase in Taliban reprisals, particularly in the form of targeted killings. UNAMA documented five incidents from April to December 2012 in which Taliban killed community members for their alleged involvement with the Andar Uprising. However, there is no evidence to suggest these Taliban reprisals led to overly violent anti-Taliban acts, let alone indiscriminate vigilante violence against civilians in Andar during the same period. There was at least one public case of ALP extrajudicial violence. In October 2013, a religious leader in Andar issued a public decree declaring war on all residents who supported the ALP. The *mullah* was reportedly killed by ALP forces soon after the decree was issued. Some believed the Taliban responded to this killing by sending a remote-detonated IED to a wedding party at Sahib Khan village that killed 18 people, mostly women. Villagers and reportedly ALP responded with vengeance by finding the 'suspected' Taliban assassin and executing him on the spot.[55]

While the Uprising turned predatory, the ALP could be considered a relatively protective organization in comparison for three reasons. First, the impetus of the movement itself created conditions highly amenable for an ALP insertion in Andar, which brought a package of US security forces, international aid projects, and government attention. The security architecture was ripe for anti-Taliban sentiment, and the support and coordination between Afghan National Security Forces and ALP guardians was consistent. Kamrani was the natural selection for the new position of Andar ALP Commander, although he admitted his men 'were compelled' to join 'because we were between a rock and a hard place.' By the time of ALP validation in October 2012, support for the Uprising had quickly diminished. Abdul Qayuum Sajjadi, a minister representing Ghazni province, said the government had planned to support the Uprising, but over time the plan became less popular. Sajjadi explains, the international community expressed concerns '…as to whether such a movement has a clear future path. As to whether they can or can't be controlled.' Evidence collected by UNAMA suggests the Uprising was losing support and engaging in coercion in response.[56]

Second, the resource agenda suddenly shifted from support to the Uprising toward ALP. New ALP were paid 6000 afghanis (USD 120) a month, but even under a new banner and payroll, the group continued to use 'Uprising' language and bravado as motivation, denoting the ALP as a 'synonym' for the uprising. In one instance in May 2013, two young adults met with a strategic communications advisor (SCA) who worked for the Andar District Governor. The men wished to join the Uprising, but the SCA advised them to join the ALP instead due to associated benefits and privileges of working for the government as opposed to an autonomous organization. The men then followed up with a visit to the District Governor, bringing other ALP candidates along. The men listened to the Governor's message about joining the ALP.[57] This type of support from mentors (the SCA) and the District Governor was a positive sign of local institutional development. The ALP seemed to take on the identity of the Uprising, while those still engaged in the original Uprising group began taking on the identity of militias run amok.

Third, the resources ALP brought toward development in Andar were important for expanding state-society relations. An UNAMA report from December 2012 shows that the NSP launched numerous development projects in 40 villages of Andar, including bridges, canal projects, and enhanced drinking water supply, a vast improvement from the less than thirty projects implemented from 2003 to 2006. One of the largest projects was the 22-km canal construction of the Sarda Dam, providing hundreds of jobs to residents. These projects were a response to the residents' cry for development and education. The Uprising, and now the ALP, opened roads, protected cell phone towers, safeguarded the district center, reopened schools, and activated development projects, like the rehabilitation of the Bande Sardeh irrigation canal system in Andar.

The ALP solution was not a perfect one. While still active, it remained a short-term program with an uncertain future. It had limited resources, and many ALP posts were left far outside the reach of police or army backup. This reality necessitated a proactive relationship with Uprising fighters. The program was also unable to bring in all of the Uprising fighters either due to questionable backgrounds, limited registration numbers, or members who still saw the Afghan government as an enemy. The Andar ALP had many setbacks as well, to include insider threats and infiltration from Taliban. Hasty recruitment practices to fill the ranks may have led to the death of 17 ALP in Andar in early 2013 according to Faizon: 'We have repeatedly warned the ALP recruiters and trainers to conduct proper and accurate vetting processes for people who want to join the ALP ranks. We have told them not to enroll unknown people or people who are not vouched by tribal elders, but they don't listen. They are trying to meet the recruiting deadline and get credit for it.'[58]

Within the Uprising, the inability to equitably distribute resources left many disappointed. Some groups with patronage connections received more than those without, including food, weapons, and ammunition. In addition, there was an overriding feeling of neglect from movement participants and their resident supporters regarding the Afghan government. This starkly presented a Catch-22 for the government and the movement's success. Government support to movement fighters was seen as corrupting the original intent and fundamental purpose of the movement, self-defense and autonomy against oppression. However, given resource scarcity, namely food, supplies, and weapons, lack of government support was perceived as neglect and disinterest in the movement. Finally, when the government did respond, it was haphazard and biased based on established patronage networks. The movement manifesto described the uprising youth as 'thrown away from the scene by greedy and unintuitive elders.' It called for representative councils to address the people's needs and grievances. In addition, it argued for investment in institutions over individuals – a call to end the patronage system of government in place.

Narratives

One of the most important normative foundations that patrons and clients shared in Ghazni was oppression from outsiders. This concept helped direct the passion and direction of client violence in the initial stages of the Uprising. Generally, it served as a directional aid for Uprising fighters to distinguish enemy from ally, foreign vs. local. However, when patron oversight over Uprising fighters diminished, they began targeting anyone who appeared to fit the scope of a 'foreign fighter.' Anyone who 'fit the profile' of a Taliban – length of beard, darkened turban, unfamiliar complexion – was subject to predatory treatment. This had the unintended consequence of unjust targeting of Pashtuns or those with a pious complexion.

Foreign occupation was a powerful grievance mechanism for both Taliban and Uprising fighters in which each side embodied the concept of occupied. There were two types of occupiers in Ghazni: international coalition forces (primarily US and Polish forces), which supported the state, and anti-state 'foreign fighters' or outsiders who migrated into Ghazni, many from Pakistan, but other fighters from Central Asia, Caucasus, and the Middle East. Felbab-Brown discusses how the 'insider-outsider' dynamic in a homogenous community like Andar can spark resistance to outsiders pressuring a community to change. While Westerners embodied a large contingent of foreign forces occupying Ghazni, they were more often restricted to forward operating bases. By the end of 2012, US and Polish forces rarely ventured outside bases, leaving the average Afghan with little more than the occasional military convoy passing by as a reminder of Western occupation. Kamrani expressed the length of depravation people in Andar faced 'over the last ten years,' while at the same time, people felt neglected by the state as Taliban committed 'atrocities against the people.' NATO forces would only come for 'an hour or two' and then leave, while the Taliban returned upon their departure.

Still, Western forces offered significant development and resource opportunities blocked by harsh foreign Taliban. This second form of foreign occupation increased over the last decade of conflict and caused locals, including local Taliban representatives, to grow more indignant toward these outsiders with draconian rules and impertinent behavior. In one Uprising tract, an author describes how the *Jihad* against the Americans was not one created by Afghans, rather 'externally supported' by militants from Pakistan, alluding to a growing perception that the real problem was foreign Taliban not Afghan Taliban.[59] A number of statements by local Afghans in media and through government or NGO interviews described the enemy as 'foreign,' 'Punjabi,' or 'Pakistani.' The Uprising leader, Kamrani, suggests an outsider role in Ghazni when describing the foreign fighters the Uprising captured: 'This war is someone else's war. It's not the Taliban's war.'[60]

In the beginning of the Uprising, the state was also perceived as an outsider. Western forces and the Afghan state were synonymous entities to Andar residents who rarely saw benefits of Western development or the centralization of governance in Ghazni until the Uprising compelled those forces to engage in the district. Even state patrons who sponsored the movement realized the inefficiencies and inequities within the government and that only by bridging resident grievances with the capabilities the state offered could the movement succeed. The Uprising was a mechanism for Andar residents to liberate themselves from outsider oppression and to end the era of state neglect. At the same time, Uprising leaders such as Kamrani expressed the ambiguity between competing outsiders in Andar, as if they were two sides of the same coin: 'As for the government I say that we accept the system. It is a legitimate system. But those in charge are not real men.' He then goes on to characterize the Taliban as 'a mutual project of Americans (…) I don't see them as different from the Americans. I cannot see them as our friends. I don't know whether to call them a friend or an enemy.'[61]

Hence, consistent and strong support from the US was a necessary ingredient to draw the lines in the sand between the Americans and Taliban, and to ensure a positive outcome from the anti-Taliban resistance. Given the strong commitment of US and Afghan patrons to see Andar succeed, relationships between Kamrani and his American counterparts flourished. He was eventually appointed district chief of police and served as a link between original Uprising members and the state. Before that, as Uprising commander, he understood the importance of strategic communications. For over a decade, the Taliban monopolized the narrative by utilizing traditional religious networks and places of worship. The insurgency long dominated the resistance narrative in rural mosques, particularly in Ghazni, and capitalized on the effects of state collapse by empowering religious leaders who continued to serve as de facto authorities in rural areas.

Patrons of the Uprising knew that strategic communications would play a key part in the success of the movement. By June, the movement took on the name of *Da Milli Pastun Ghorzang* (the National Uprising Movement), a title carefully selected to identify concepts, such as nationhood and collective resistance. The Provincial Governor frequently spoke at rallies celebrating the valor of the Uprising and calling upon the silent majority to join them: 'I call upon all Afghans to stand up and be counted. This is the best way of salvation and prosperity for the countrymen.'[62]

In the fall of 2012, magazines were published in Kabul and distributed throughout the eastern and southern provinces of Afghanistan romanticizing the Uprising and depicting the tribulations of Andar residents under oppressive foreign Taliban rule. One story recounts Mullah Abdul Salam, a scholar and commander in the Uprising whose home is terrorized by Taliban. The story is an emotional appeal addressing family safety and intended to evoke a passionate response. Two dozen foreign insurgents of Punjabi, Arab, and Waziri descent ride roughshod through the village, terrorizing the residents as a gang of criminals. Some of the insurgents get off their motorbikes and begin to beat the residents with the butt stock of their weapons. 'Kids crying were heard in the village at night, women were shouting and militants were terrifying them with knives.'[63] The gang breaks into Mullah Salam's home, beats his sister, and then subjects her to fire. The insurgents pillage the home and find 60 copies of the 'Holy Quran,' which they throw into a pile of garbage, douse with fuel, and torch. They conclude their havoc by burning Salam's home to the ground.

Stories like these were spread throughout the province by word of mouth and through journals like *Patsoon*. The growing social media sphere in Afghanistan also captured the stories and posted the journals on a Facebook page devoted to the Uprising. Messaging also depicted religious legitimacy for the movement. One journal entry discussed a verdict by an Andaran religious leader: 'In Islam, it is compulsory for each Muslim to defend himself and his belongings; so, you are authorized to fight against [trespassers], including armed Taliban, and all of those armed rebels that attack your Qurans, homes, women and children.'[64]

This theme sought to give religious legitimacy to the Uprising and undermine the Taliban's greatest source of influence within rural areas. It also emphasized the defense of the most hallowed elements in life, faith, family, and shelter. Other leaders, such as Faizon, talked about the Uprising as a 'counter jihad' against the Taliban: 'My jihadi struggle which started to drive out the Soviets still continues to counter what these ignorant Taliban have brought upon the people in the name of jihad.'[65]

One called the Uprising a 'holy obligation' that each Afghan and 'pain-filled Pashtun' should support, lest all Pashtun communities be 'put captive in the

Punjabi chains.' Here, the author seeks to link Taliban oppression with slavery by a foreign ethnic identity often described as a significant demographic in Paskistan's security establishment. Another writes of how the Taliban delivered communities into a 'sacred' government but then 'lost its objective.' Another asserts that jihad cannot come from 'external substance' but must come from within. The author speaks directly to 'Talib Jana,' an expression of endearment, and recites how Pakistan had indoctrinated naïve Afghans to fight on their behalf. The author then questions the legitimacy of the Taliban jihad, declaring it is not an Islamic regime, rather an autocratic regime under the control of Pakistan: 'Can you protect the Afghan and Muslims without Pakistan's permission? Hey Talib! You protect your soil from Americans and you hand it back over to Paksitani invaders in the name of Islam? Put your head down and be ashamed.'[66]

Another prominent theme was an attempt to elicit an emotional connection to one's honor from past descendants to future generations. One author summons people to 'stand up and prove your old history's glory,' claiming citizens have a 'responsibility' established by their people and history. A number of photographs and artwork depicting heroic Pashtuns could be found circulating on cellphones among young Pashtuns in Ghazni.

Of note, some of the journal articles were clearly unsupportive of American and the international community's efforts in Ghazni. One author self-describes as a Talib and calls Europeans, Canadians, and Americans 'alcoholics' residing in Kabul. He also condemns the US as working alongside Pakistan in labeling Taliban and Pashtuns as 'one entity.' And the author rebukes the Taliban for aiming rockets at Afghan civilians rather than Americans or the ANSF.[67]

Government patrons maintained in public that the Uprising was an autonomous 'people's movement' in hopes that the Taliban would have difficulty refuting it or labeling it a state or Western conspiracy. Reporting from journalists suggests Asadullah Khaled controlled media access to the Andar Uprising fighters and the overall narrative to ensure a sanitized version of events reached the media circuit. The movement's survival depended much on the perception of it as a genuine people's resistance rather than as a continuation of the Hezbi–Harakat feud or as a government sponsored militia. Even the authors of the Uprising's manifesto acknowledged the role strategic communications played in crafting the image of events in Andar: 'The success of this uprising was mostly due to good propaganda, which in this war was needed more than fighting.'

Some argue that the Uprising journals written mainly by young urban men in Kabul represented a broader intellectual trend within the Andar Movement that displayed an 'anti-mullah' bias. This would fit with common Hezbi attitudes concerning traditional religious figures that comprised their adversaries in Harakat and Taliban. Habib (2013) argues this bias was reflected among movement fighters against the general population as they gained control over villages and began appearing more like 'mischief-makers' than community defenders.

The Uprising was unable to craft favorable views by all. The manipulation by state and US patrons deflated Rahmatullah's interest in the movement and led to his refusal to rejoin it after his injury in Payendi and evacuation to Kabul. He chastised the Uprising as a sham, run by 'Mafiosi' who had 'nothing to do with the uprising and its main aims.' One resident cursed the Uprising for its predation: 'For God's sake, take these people away from us! We cannot stand their brutality.' When brazen leaders like Commander Abdullah bragged of dragging bodies in the streets, executing suspected Taliban in public, and proclaiming his gang's autonomy – 'The *patsoonian* don't belong at all to the government' – it was clear the current of the movement had changed. Abdullah's behavior was never publicly endorsed by patrons in Kabul, but behind the scenes his method of extending the writ of the state followed a similar pattern: while brutal, these forces served the interest of short-term counterinsurgency goals, a view patrons and clients both shared.[68]

While the geographic spread of the Andar Uprising was limited, the psychological impact it had on residents (supporters and opponents) was profound. The main impetus, reopen the schools, was overwhelmingly successful, as quality and access to education were significantly improved. Even in areas the Taliban claimed or regained control over, they relaxed their strict rules concerning education.[69]

Conclusions

The anti-Talban Uprising in Andar is best characterized as a hybrid organization: one element of the Uprising exhibited protective behavior; the other went beyond protection, taking the rule of law into its own hands and preying upon the population. The first group was reliant upon state patrons, mostly representative of the community, received state resources, and shared in a collective narrative of community defense. Patrons relied upon the community through representative groups such as the Nejat Council, ensured disciplinary structures were in place, and provided development programs to the community to win over support. The second group represented contentious and narrow Hezbi politics within the community that did not have broad acceptance throughout the district. They operated outside the rule of law and with impunity against even suspected criminals, drawing scorn from their social base. Moreover, patrons continued to support the Uprising as a covert counterinsurgency force, giving the group greater latitude to operate with impunity.

Certainly, the security architecture played a part in mobilizing the Uprising – over a decade of foreign insurgent brutality against the local population coupled by systematic state neglect and failure of international forces to serve as productive change agents in the province. However, it is also clear that historical animosities between Hezbi and Harakat social networks played a role in setting off the Uprising and in preventing significant unity within and among local communities. The most protective elements of the Uprising saw substantial material and social incentives from US and Ministry of Interior patrons via the ALP, allowing those patrons to have institutional control over a large faction of the Uprising.

However, a small faction of the Uprising remained detached from institutional oversight. Even as it received incentives from NDS patrons, the Uprising found an opening in the market of protection. Across both ALP and the Uprising, the patrons and clients shared in cooperative and prudent normative values, represented in Uprising literature and patron statements. Both sides saw value in taking back the sovereignty of Ghazni from an oppressive insurgent force. As state formation ensued, both patrons and clients endorsed the state as a necessary component of their movement and extending security throughout Ghazni. An irony of state formation in Andar is best represented through Engineer Kamrani, an original movement figure who was fairly rigid in his position against the state in the beginning, yet put this aside when he accepted his commission as Andar's Chief of Police.

Notes

1. The market of protection is a term I borrow from Lane, 'Economic Consequences of Organized Violence'. It represents the industry in the use of force. In periods of state formation, consumers of protection (citizens) seek an efficient price/service ratio in the market, while producers of the service seek to monopolize and maximize profit. Legitimate governments are in the business of providing efficient (cost-effective) markets of protection, while challengers such as bandits, mafia, and private security contractors seek to provide less efficient markets that maximize profits.
2. This follows along the classical greed versus grievance literature regarding nonstate armed actors. See Collier and Hoeffler, "Greed and Grievance in Civil War"; and Berdal and Malone, *Greed and Grievance*.
3. Long, "The Anbar Awakening."
4. During its climb to prominence, from April to December 2012, UNAMA documented only 45 civilian casualties in Ghazni, the majority of which were directly or indirectly related to the presence of the Andar Uprising. UNAMA noted the Andar Uprising did not target civilians, However, the increased presence of Afghan Army counterinsurgency activities, Taliban attacks, and community militia presence contributed to civilian casualties. See UNAMA, *Afghanistan Annual Report*, 48.
5. Paramilitary groups are auxiliary forces sponsored either overtly or tacitly by a state to defend against rebel organizations and forward institutional interests. Paramilitaries are both a product and strategy of local rule and state formation, and a product and strategy of state collapse. See Tilly, "War Making and State Making"; Kalyvas, *The Logic of Violence in Civil War*; Klare, "The Deadly Connection", 117; and Bates, *When Things Fell Apart*, 147–48. Predation is viewed as corruption, rent seeking, and perpetuating violence against society, similar to the behavior of criminal organizations that derive benefits from the nonbureaucratic political economy of violence. See Reno, "Persistent Insurgencies and Warlords," 54.

6. More commonly referenced as Gulbuddin Hekmatyar's Hezbi Islami, or HIG. There is also a moderate political wing of Hezbi Islami in Afghanistan (HIA) with political representatives throughout ministries, provinces, and parliament. I refer to those associated with the historical *tanzim* or political/military front, however there are often ambiguities between HIA, HIG, and many associate factions; locals tend to refer to them all as Hezbi Islami or Hezbi, the latter which I refer to.
7. Roy, *Islam and Resistance in Afghanistan*, 111.
8. Constable, "Afghan militias cling to power."
9. Naval Postgraduate School 2007.
10. Giustozzi, *Koran, Kalashnikov and Laptop*.
11. Younus, "Taleban Call the Shots"; and Reuter and Younus, "The Return of the Taliban."
12. DOD, *Report on Progress Toward Security*, 59; and Bergh et al., *Conflict Analysis: Jaghori and Malistan*, 8–10.
13. Broadwell and Loeb, *All in*, 165; and Robinson, *One Hundred Victories*, 203.
14. *People of Ghazni Manifesto*; Habib, "Who Fights for Whom"; and Moreau, "How the Taliban Drove Afghan Villagers."
15. Pajhwok, "Taliban Shut Schools After Government"; Sieff, "Taliban Closes Dozens of Afghan Schools"; Habib, "Who Fights for Whom"; *People of Ghazni Manifesto*; and Alizada, "Afghan Local Militias."
16. Interviews with Afghan officials; Habib, "Who Fights for Whom"; and *People of Ghazni Manifesto*.
17. Engineer Lotfullah Kamrani, to be discussed later, claimed in an interview that he was also part of this cadre. See Quraishi, *People & Power*.
18. Habib, "Who Fights for Whom."
19. Moreau, "How the Taliban Drove Afghan Villagers."
20. Interviews with Afghan officials; *People of Ghazni Manifesto*; and Foschini, "The Battle for Schools."
21. Interviews with US and Afghan officials; and Habib, "Who Fights for Whom."
22. *People of Ghazni Manifesto*; Habib, "Who Fights for Whom"; Ron Moreau claims the foreign Taliban were held by one of the uprising commanders, Wali Muhammad, and were either swapped with Taliban for Abdul Malik's release or freed when Muhammad's house was torched by a Taliban reprisal gang.
23. Interviews with US officials; Foschini, "The Battle for Schools"; and Quraishi, *People & Power*. See Felbab-Brown, *Aspirations and Ambivalence*, 150. She contends that Kamrani told his people they would fight the US after taking care of the Pakistani Taliban.
24. Peter, "Locals Turn Against Taliban." By end of June, Kamrani alleged they had over 500 armed fighters, controlling 31 villages and extended as far as Giro district in the south. See Foschini, "The Battle for Schools."
25. Interviews with US officials; Habib, "Who Fights for Whom."
26. Felbab-Brown (149) numbers Uprising fighters at 250, controlling 50 villages and 4000 residents. It is likely the Uprising had strong control in a few select villages, and limited control in others.
27. Interviews with US and Afghan officials; Habib, "AAN Reportage (2)."
28. Engineer Kamrani traveled in an SUV that flew the flag of Afghanistan; see Quraishi, *People and Power*.
29. Habib, "AAN Reportage (2)"; and Khaama, "Former Governor for Ghazni." Faizon was an Andar Pashtun commander affiliated with Hezbi. He was a minor commander during the jihad but broke with Hekmatyar after 2001, still maintaining close ties to the Hezbi network. He was director of the Sarda dam project in Andar

and became governor of Andar district in 2007, but was forced to resign under charges of corruption.
30. Habib, "Who Fights for Whom"; and Habib, "The Morphing of the Andar Uprising." Hussaini is an important member of the Andar tribe who served as a senior official in the Taliban government, but joined the Karzai government in 2004 as governor of Zabul.
31. Clark, "What Exactly is the CIA Doing in Afghanistan?"; and Human Rights Watch, *Today We Shall All Die*.
32. Military Police Complaints Commission, *Final Report*; Parliament of Canada, *Special Committee on the Canadian Mission*; Human Rights Watch, *Today We Shall All Die*; and Smith, "House of Pain."
33. Senate, *Committee Study of the Central Intelligence Agency's*. While the report redacts the country, media reports confirm COBALT, also known as the Salt Pit, was in Afghanistan. See Windrem and Reynolds, "How the CIA Tried"; Rosenberg and Landay, "Prosecutors Probing Deaths"; and Daily Beast, "Inside the CIA's Sadistic Dungeon."
34. Rubin and Rosenberg, "Ragtag Revolts in Parts."
35. Ibid.
36. Ibid.
37. Habib, "Who Fights for Whom."
38. Ibid.
39. See Robison, *One Hundred Victories*, 206–8.
40. Aikens, "Exclusive: A US-backed Militia." UN reports listed 11 Taliban killed and ISAF reported three ANSF casualties and one ISAF casualty.
41. Ibid. An ISAF inquiry 'found no information that substantiates the allegations' of this event. While, the UN conducted its own investigation of the executions in Andar and 'verified the allegations of extrajudicial killings of three men by a pro-government militia.'
42. DOD, *Report on Progress Toward Security*, 69.
43. Goldstein, "Afghan Militia Leaders."
44. Dearing and Braden, "Robber Barons Rising"; and USGS, *Summary of the Katawas Gold*.
45. USGS, *Summary of the Katawas Gold*, 650–53.
46. Ghaznavi, "Ghazni's Mafia State"; Maftoon, "Warlords Grab 75,000 Acres"; Pajhwok, "10,000 Acres of State Land"; Pajhwok, "200 ALP Members Deployed"; and Killid Group, "Powerful Plunder Public Land."
47. Oppel, "Corruption Undercuts Hopes"; Masoud, "Ghazni in the Grip"; and Ibrahimkhail, "Advisor to Ghazni's Acting Governor."
48. Farmer, "Armed Uprising Against Taliban"; UNAMA, *Afghanistan Annual Report 2012*; Rosenberg and Rubin, "Ragtag Revolts in Parts"; *People of Ghazni Manifesto*; Habib, 'Who Fights for Whom"; Felbab-Brown, *Aspirations and Ambivalence*; and Peter, "Locals Turn Against Taliban."
49. Habib, "Who Fights for Whom"; Trofimov, "Once Touted Afghan Force"; and Farmer, "Armed Uprising Against Taliban."
50. Lubold, "Are We Winning in Afghanistan?"; and Aikens, "Exclusive: A US-backed Militia."
51. Andar, "How Taliban Lost Their Objectives?"; and Quraishi, *People & Power*.
52. Interviews with US and Afghan officials; Quraishi, *People & Power*; and Habib, "The Andar Uprising."
53. Within a few months, the district limit would increase to 300, according to Trofimov, "Once Touted Afghan Force."

54. Pajhwok, "200 ALP Members Deployed"; CJSOTFA, "Newest Afghan Local Police"; UNAMA, *Afghanistan Annual Report 2012*, 87; UNAMA, *Afghanistan: Midyear Report 2014*, 42–7; and UNAMA, *Afghanistan Annual Report 2014*, 88.
55. Habib, "Who Fights for Whom"; Habib, "The Andar Uprising"; Habib, "AAN Reportage (2)"; Trofimov, "Once Touted Afghan Force"; UNAMA, *Afghanistan Annual Report on Protection,* 2014; and Pajhwok, "Women among 18 Killed."
56. Trofimov, "Once Touted Afghan Force"; and Quraishi, *People & Power*.
57. Sayara Strategies, "Atmospherics Reports."
58. Nordland, "20 Afghan Police Officers."
59. Quraishi, *People & Power*; and Andar, "How Taliban Lost their Objectives."
60. Quraishi, *People & Power*.
61. Ibid.
62. Musa Khan quoted in Pajhwok, "Uprising Against Taliban Spreads."
63. Anonymous, "People and Authorities."
64. Ibid.
65. Habib, "Who Fights for Whom."
66. Jamal, "If We Lose Andar's Battle"; and Khuzai, "Ghazni People's Uprising."
67. Jamal, "If We Lose Andar's Battle."
68. Habib, "Killing Mullahs and Wedding Guests"; Goldstein, "Afghan Militia Leaders"; and Aikens, "Exclusive: A US-backed Militia."
69. Sayara Strategies, "Atmospherics Reports."

Disclosure statement

The views and opinions expressed in this article are those of the author and do not necessarily reflect the official policy or position of any agency of the U.S. government.

Bibliography

Aikens, Matthieu. 2014. "Exclusive: A US-backed Militia Runs Amok in Afghanistan." *Al Jazeera*, July 23.

Alizada, Sayed Rahmatullah. 2013. "Afghan Local Militias Demand Support." *IWPR*, August 5.

Andar, Mohammad Anwar. "How Taliban Lost Their Objectives?" *Patsoon* 1, no. 1 (2013): 2–4.

Anonymous. "People and Authorities." *Patsoon* 1, no. 1 (2013): 1–2.

Bates, Robert. *When Things Fell Apart: State Failure in Late-century Africa*. New York: Cambridge University Press, 2008.

Berdal, Mats, and David M. Malone, eds. *Greed and Grievance: Economic Agendas in Civil Wars*. Boulder: Lynne Rienner, 2000.

Bergh, Gina with Christian Dennys and Idrees Zaman. *Conflict Analysis: Jaghori and Malistan Districts, Ghazni Province*. Kabul: Cooperation for Peace and Unity, 2009.

Broadwell, Paula with Vernon Loeb. *All in: The Education of General David Petraeus*. London: Penguin Press HC, 2012.

CJSOTFA. 2012. "Newest Afghan Local Police Confirmed during Ceremony." *Defense Video and Imagery Distribution System*, October 21.

Clark, Kate. 2013. "What Exactly is the CIA Doing in Afghanistan? Proxy Militias and Two Airstrikes in Kunar." *Afghanistan Analyst Network*, April 28.

Collier, Paul, and Anke Hoeffler. "Greed and Grievance in Civil War." *Oxford Economic Papers* 56 (2004): 563–595.

Constable, Pamela. 2003. "Afghan Militias Cling to Power in North: Officials Fear Reforms' Effects Are Limited." *Washington Post*, October 28.

Daily Beast. 2014. "Inside the CIA's Sadistic Dungeon." December 9.

Dearing, Matthew P., and Cynthia Braden. 2014. "Robber Barons Rising: The Potential for Resource Conflict in Ghazni, Afghanistan." *Stability: International Journal of Security & Development* 3, no. 1 (2014): 1–14.

DOD (Department of Defense). *Report on Progress toward Security and Stability in Afghanistan*. Washington, DC: U.S. Department of Defense, June 2009.

Farmer, Ben. 2012. "Armed Uprising against Taliban Forces Insurgents from 50 Afghan Villages." *Telegraph*, August 14.

Felbab-Brown, Vanda. *Aspirations and Ambivalence: Strategies and Realities of Counterinsurgency and State Building in Afghanistan*. Washington, DC: Brookings Institution Press, 2013.

Foschini, Fabrizio. 2012. "The Battle for Schools in Ghazni – Or, Schools as a Battlefield." *Afghanistan Analyst Network*. July 3.

Ghaznavi, Humayoon. 2012. "Ghazni's Mafia State within a State." *IWPR*, August. http://www.iwpr.org.af/ghaznis-mafia-state-within-a-state.

Giustozzi, Antonio. *Koran, Kalashnikov and Laptop: The Rise of the Neo-Taliban Insurgency in Afghanistan*. London: C. Hurst & Co., 2008.

Goldstein, Joseph. 2015. "Afghan Militia Leaders, Empowered by U.S. to Fight Taliban, Inspire Fear in Villages." *New York Times*, March 17.

Habib, Emal. 2012. "Who Fights for Whom in the Andar Uprising?" *Afghanistan Analysts Network*. August 10.

Habib, Emal. 2012. "AAN Reportage (2): the Andar Uprising – Has the Tide Already Turned?" *Afghanistan Analysts Network*. September 3.

Habib, Emal. 2012. "The Andar Uprising – Co-opted, Divided and Stuck in a Dilemma." *Afghanistan Analysts Network*. October 30.

Habib, Emal. 2013. "The Morphing of the Andar Uprising: Transition to Afghan Local Police." *Afghanistan Analysts Network*. April 2.

Habib, Emal. 2013. "Killing Mullahs and Wedding Guests, Banning Last Rites: The Worsening Andar Conflict." *Afghanistan Analysts Network*. November 6.

Human Rights Watch. *"Today We Shall All Die" Afghanistan's Strongmen and the Legacy of Impunity*. New York: Human Rights Watch, 2015.

Ibrahimkhail, Shakeela. 2015. "Advisor to Ghazni's Acting Governor Found as Daesh Spokesman." *Tolo*, February 13.

Jamal, Jaseem. "If We Lose Andar's Battle, Afghans Are Failed!" *Patsoon* 1, no. 1 (2013): 6–9.

Kalyvas, Stathis. *The Logic of Violence in Civil War*. Cambridge: Cambridge University Press, 2006.

Khaama Press. 2012. "Former Governor for Ghazni Province Injured in Militant Attack." August 24.

Khuzai, Talib Jan Zra. "Ghazni People's Uprising; Taliban Are Not a National Opposition." *Patsoon* 1, no. 1 (2013): 4–6.

Killid Group. 2012. "Powerful Plunder Public Land." September 17.

Klare, Michael T. "The Deadly Connection: Paramilitary Bands, Small Arms Diffusion, and State Failure." In *When States Fail: Causes and Consequences*, edited by Robert I. Rotberg, 116–134. Princeton: Princeton University Press, 2004.

Lane, Frederic C. "Economic Consequences of Organized Violence." *The Journal of Economic History* 18, no. 4 (1958): 401–417.

Long, Austin. "The Anbar Awakening." *Survival* 50, no. 2 (2008): 67–94.

Lubold, Gordon. 2012. "Are We Winning in Afghanistan?" *Foreign Policy*, September 5.

Maftoon, Saifullah. 2012. "Warlords Grab 75,000 Acres of Ghazni Land." *RAWA News*, May 28.
Masoud, Ahmad. 2014. "Ghazni in the Grip of Mafia, Corruption and Insurgency." *Khaama*, December 28.
Military Police Complaints Commission. *Final Report. following a Public Interest Hearing*. Ottawa: Government of Canada, 2012.
Moreau, Ron. 2012. "How the Taliban Drove Afghan Villagers to Rise up against Them." *Newsweek*, June 25.
Nordland, Rod. 2013. "20 Afghan Police Officers Killed in 2 Attacks, including a Mass Poisoning." *New York Times*, February 27.
Oppel, Richard A. 2009. "Corruption Undercuts Hopes for Afghan Police." *New York Times*, April 8.
Pajhwok. 2012. "Taliban Shut Schools after Government Ban Bikes." April 19.
Pajhwok. 2012. "10,000 Acres of State Land Grabbed in Ghazni." April 10.
Pajhwok. 2012. "200 ALP Members Deployed to Andar District." October 21.
Pajhwok. 2012. "Uprising against Taliban Spreads." June 3.
Pajhwok. 2013. "Women among 18 Killed in Ghazni Bombing." October 27.
Parliament of Canada. *Special Committee on the Canadian Mission in Afghanistan*. Number 015, 2nd Session, 40th Parliament. Ottawa: Parliament of Canada, 18 November 2009.
People of Ghazni Manifesto. 2012, November. Ghazni. Obtained via email from Uprising member.
Peter, Tom A. 2012. "Locals Turn against Taliban in Eastern Afghanistan." *Christian Science Monitor*, June 4.
Quraishi, Najibullah. 2013. *People & Power – Afghanistan: My Enemy's Enemy*. Al Jazeera Documentary 25 min. January 17.
Reno, William. "Persistent Insurgencies and Warlords: Who is Nasty, Who is Nice, and Why?" In *Ungoverned Spaces: Alternatives to State Authority in an Era of Softened Sovereignty*, edited by Anne L. Clunan and Harold A. Trinkunas, 57–76. Stanford, CA: Stanford University Press, 2010.
Reuter, Christoph, and Borhan Younus. "The Return of the Taliban in Andar District: Ghazni." In *Decoding the New Taliban*, edited by Antonio Giustozzi, 101–118. New York: Columbia University Press, 2009.
Robinson, Linda. *One Hundred Victories: Special Ops and the Future of American Warfare*. New York: Public Affairs, 2013.
Rosenberg, Carol, and Jonathan Landay. 2011. "Prosecutors Probing Deaths of Two CIA Captives." *Miami Herald*, June 30.
Rosenberg, Matthew, and Alissa J. Rubin. 2012. "Ragtag Revolts in Parts of Afghanistan Repel Taliban." *New York Times*, August 26.
Roy, Olivier. *Islam and Resistance in Afghanistan*. 2nd ed. Cambridge: Cambridge University Press, 1990.
Sayara Strategies. 2013. "Atmospherics Reports 1–2 of the South Ghazni Communications for Stabilization Campaign." 1–31 May.
Senate. *Committee Study of the Central Intelligence Agency's Detention and Interrogation Program*. Senate Select Committee on Intelligence. Declassified December 3.
Sieff, Kevin. 2012. "Taliban Closes Dozens of Afghan Schools." *Washington Post*, April 26.
Smith, Graeme. 2010. "House of Pain: Canada's Connection with Kandahar's Ruthless Palace Guard." *Globe and Mail*, April 10.
Special Inspector General Afghanistan Reconstruction (SIGAR). *Afghan National Police Personnel and Payroll Data*. SIGAR 15–26 Audit Report. January. Washington, DC: U.S. Government Printing Office, 2015.

Tilly, Charles. "War Making and State Making as Organized Crime." In *Bringing the State Back in*, edited by Peter Evans, Dietrich Rueschemeyer, and Theda Skocpol, 169–187. Cambridge: Cambridge University Press, 1985.

Trofimov, Yaroslav. 2013. "Once Touted Afghan Force Falls on Hard times." *Wall Street Journal*, March 27.

United Nations Assistance Mission Afghanistan. *Afghanistan Annual Report 2012 on Protection of Civilians in Armed Conflict*. Kabul: UNAMA, 2013.

United Nations Assistance Mission Afghanistan. *Afghanistan Annual Report on Protection of Civilians in Armed Conflict: 2013*. Kabul: UNAMA, 2014.

United Nations Assistance Mission Afghanistan. *Afghanistan: Midyear Report 2014 Protection of Civilians in Armed Conflict*, July. Kabul: Kabul, 2014.

United Nations Assistance Mission Afghanistan. *Afghanistan Annual Report 2014 on Protection of Civilians in Armed Conflict*. 18 February. Kabul: Kabul, 2015.

U.S. Geologic Survey. *Summary of the Katawas Gold Area of Interest*. Washington, DC: USGS, 2011.

Windrem, Robert, and Talesha Reynolds. 2014. "How the CIA Tried to 'Break' Prisoners in 'the Salt Pit.'" *NBC News*, December 16.

Younus, Borhan. 2006. "Taleban Call the Shots in Ghazni." *Institute for War & Peace Reporting*, May 5.

The North Caucasus: from mass mobilization to international terrorism

Elena Pokalova[‡]

ABSTRACT

Insurgencies have proven to be highly adaptive movements that exploit their environments and change and mutate in order to survive. States and international actors have long grappled with ways to thwart such adaptations. In this respect, disengagement initiatives that offer insurgents opportunities for alternative livelihood seem to present a viable mechanism for weakening insurgencies. Analyzing the case of the North Caucasus insurgency, this article examines the interrelation between such variables as insurgent crises, government disengagement programs, and foreign attempts to co-opt the insurgency. It is argued that disengagement programs implemented during the second Chechen conflict prevented the insurgent command from pledging allegiance to Al-Qaeda because insurgents had to preserve their local orientation to compete for their bases of support. In 2014, however, the North Caucasus insurgents pledged allegiance to the Islamic State of Iraq and Syria as no viable disengagement opportunities existed at the time and their only route for survival was to join a global insurgency.

Throughout history, insurgencies have shared expertise, training, and weapons. For instance, members of PIRA traveled to Colombia to train FARC. LTTE maintained close contact with the South African ANC. The Afghan Arab foreign fighters transferred their expertise to numerous conflicts worldwide. Insurgents have adopted successful strategies from each other that have allowed them to adapt and survive.

Likewise, insurgencies with local limited agendas have transformed to broader movements with a global reach. For example, Nigeria's Boko Haram,

---

[‡]The views expressed in this article are those of the author and do not reflect the official policy or position of the National Defense University, the Department of Defense, or the U.S. Government.

which came into existence as an opposition movement to the Nigerian government, has transitioned into an ally of Islamic State of Iraq and Syria (ISIS), pledging allegiance to Abu Bakr al-Baghdadi in March 2015. One faction of Somalia's Al Shabaab, which started as a group opposing the country's Western-style government, pledged allegiance to Al-Qaeda in February 2012. In China, the Uyghur militants started as a local ethno-nationalist separatist uprising. Yet over the years they have been pushed out of China and have embraced a more global insurgent orientation.

Partnerships with global insurgent actors offer many advantages to local insurgencies going through crises. They offer a brand name that makes them seem stronger.[1] Cooperation can help groups survive.[2] As has been demonstrated with competition between Al-Qaeda and ISIS, global actors even compete for allegiances. Still, while exchanging fighters, weapons, and expertise, insurgencies do not always align with each other. Thus, Boko Haram pledged allegiance to ISIS but did not proclaim such allegiance to Al-Qaeda.[3] In Russia's North Caucasus, the insurgents also pledged allegiance to ISIS but did not pledge allegiance to Al-Qaeda.

This article analyzes under what conditions local insurgencies transition towards global ones and embrace broader, more global goals. Based on the case of Russia's North Caucasus insurgency, I analyze how an insurgency that started as a mass mobilization ethno-nationalist separatist movement with strong local roots transitioned into a terrorist outlet that pledged allegiance to ISIS. The North Caucasus case is important as it represents three distinct phases of an insurgency: insurgent victory in the first Chechen conflict; transitioning of the insurgency in the second Chechen conflict without a pledge of allegiance to Al-Qaeda; and further transitioning of the insurgency with a pledge of allegiance to ISIS. Each of these will be examined.

The first phase is the first 1994–1996 Chechen conflict. In this phase, the separatist insurgents came out victorious, and government disengagement initiatives as well as foreign influences on the insurgency produced little impact. In the second phase, the 1999–2009 counterterrorist operation in Chechnya, the insurgents suffered military defeat and had to adapt to survive. In this period, insurgents survived by adopting some global jihadi narratives. However, the insurgent command had to compete for their supporters who had the option of exiting the insurgency through amnesties backed up by employment opportunities in Akhmad Kadyrov's Chechnya. As a result, the insurgent command retained the local orientation of the insurgency and did not pledge allegiance to Al-Qaeda. In the third phase, from 2009 to the present time, the North Caucasus insurgency was significantly weakened. Facing the threat of complete annihilation, the insurgents had to adapt further. This time, no alternative disengagement options were left open. Hence, the insurgents faced less pressure in terms of sustaining their constituencies. In 2014, the Caucasus Emirate factions started pledging allegiance to ISIS.

The discussion proceeds with a review of relevant theoretical considerations on insurgent adaptation, the role of disengagement initiatives, and the significance of co-optation efforts on the part of foreign entities. I then turn to the analysis of the interaction of the variables of insurgent crises, disengagement programs, and the presence of foreign co-optation efforts in the three phases of the North Caucasus insurgencies. The article concludes with policy implications aimed at weakening insurgencies and preventing their transformation into global threats.

Insurgent adaptations

In the asymmetry of warfare, insurgencies fall on the weak side. Yet insurgencies seem to have enormous advantages in their adaptive capabilities. To survive, insurgent networks have to come up with creative mobilization mechanisms that keep fighters motivated to challenge the legitimacy of the state. Only in certain conflicts do they reach a stage where they rely on regular forces such as those at the disposal of government institutions. At the same time, they are not restricted by considerations of legitimacy governments have to satisfy when changing their approaches. As a result, insurgents historically have developed creative strategies to attract militants and to keep them engaged.

As Anthony Vinci points out, for insurgencies 'continuing survival means finding solutions that can last, adapt and evolve'.[4] Adaptation for insurgents is the key to survival. For instance, Al-Qaeda has survived the post-9/11 invasion in Afghanistan by decentralizing its command structure.[5] Stephen Biddle demonstrates how the Taliban was able to survive due to their ability to learn how to thwart American surveillance.[6] In Iraq, the insurgency was able to routinely implement organizational changes and innovations that granted it significant advantages.[7] In China, the Uyghur insurgents survived by fleeing to Pakistan where they developed ties with Al-Qaeda. In Chechnya, facing a military defeat, Dudayev's insurgent forces adapted by switching to guerilla warfare and adopted terrorist tactics.

The success of insurgent adaptation is dependent on the availability of alternatives.[8] On the one hand, insurgencies might lose individuals due to involuntary disengagement as a result of military annihilation, arrests, or deportation. In moments of crisis, when facing defeat, insurgencies have to adjust for fear of losing people. As Bjorgo and Horgan find, 'Terrorist groups and individuals are more likely to look for an exit when they feel they are losing than when they believe they can win'.[9] The loss of flexibility and failure to adapt in such cases can lead to insurgent defeat. For instance, Mehta argues that LTTE lost to Sri Lankan forces due to its increased resistance to change.[10]

On the other hand, alternatives might be present in the form of amnesties or rehabilitation programs that constitute venues for voluntary disengagement. Such initiatives are also referred to as pull factors, or forces that 'attract an individual to a more promising alternative'.[11] Such disengagement initiatives might be attractive to insurgents who are tired of violence and are looking for ways to disengage. Further, such programs become instrumental in weakening insurgencies when they are facing crises and their members are looking for viable ways to put violence behind them. Thus, when facing defeat, insurgencies not only have to adapt, but they also have to compete for constituencies in case amnesties or rehabilitation programs are available to pull individuals away. For instance, FARC lost many insurgents when Colombia implemented relocation programs for former fighters helping them reintegrate into civilian life.[12]

At the same time, when insurgencies adapt, they often interact with foreign entities seeking expertise, training, or financial support. Transnational insurgents might help weak insurgencies by importing expertise, funding, or weapons.[13] Following the Soviet–Afghan war, Afghan Arabs have been especially instrumental in sharing their experiences from Afghanistan in such civil wars as in Tajikistan, Bosnia, or Algeria. Often, in such cases, in sending support, foreign entities have ulterior motives of co-opting local insurgencies. For instance, Bakke discusses how foreign actors attempt to co-opt local struggles in which they participate.[14] In some cases, local insurgencies retain their local orientation and resist co-optation, as is the case with the civil war in Tajikistan. In other cases, local insurgencies shift and pledge allegiance to a global entity, as Al Shabaab did to Al-Qaeda in 2012.

While much research has focused on insurgent adaptations, disengagement initiatives, and foreign co-optation efforts separately, little has investigated the interaction of these factors. Further, few studies exist analyzing the conditions under which locally oriented insurgencies turn global and embrace broader aspirations. In this regard, the North Caucasus case is especially valuable since it allows for controlling for both insurgent successes and failures. Further, it allows for controlling for the absence and presence of a pledge of allegiance to an international insurgent entity.

Crisis, disengagement, and co-optation in the first Chechen conflict

The first Chechen conflict unfolded as an ethno-nationalist separatist struggle for independent Chechnya. The conflict was waged by General Dzhokhar Dudayev, who was elected in October 1991 by 90.1% of the Chechen voters in an election with a 72% voter turnout.[15] Following his election, Dudayev declared Chechnya independent from Russia and prepared to defend the separatist Ichkeria with all means possible. In the years preceding the first Chechen conflict, Dudayev faced significant internal opposition. It was Russia's handling of the conflict that prompted the consolidation of Dudayev's forces as well as the mobilization of the Chechen population to support the separatist cause.

In November 1994, the Russian government attempted to overthrow Dudayev with the help of his opposition forces in Chechnya by providing them with clandestine support, but an attempted storming of Grozny failed. At the same time, the Kremlin's intervention was perceived as a direct attack on Chechnya. President Yeltsin's subsequent ultimatum to lay down weapons provoked the official response from Grozny calling the ultimatum 'the declaration of war against the Chechen state'.[16] Dudayev was able to impose martial law, declare mobilization, and call for a holy war against Russia. Thousands of people started arriving in Grozny to show their support for Dudayev. Demonstrations in support of the separatists broke out in front of Dudayev's presidential palace.[17] The young, the unarmed, and those ready to become suicide fighters demonstrated their determination to fight for independent Chechnya.[18] Dudayev was able to achieve mobilization of a large share of the Chechen population. Dudayev's force at the beginning of the first Chechen conflict was estimated to be around 20,000 people.[19]

The first Chechen conflict started favorably for the Chechen insurgents.[20] The Russian federal forces undertook an assault against Grozny on 31 December 1994, but it failed. The mobile separatist combat units were able to successfully block the Russian troops that were not well trained in urban combat. The Russian military suffered a defeat at the hands of the insurgents, despite the massive bombardments of the city. Subsequently, the Russian command reorganized its forces into more mobile groupings and adapted its tactics to better suit the urban environment. By March 1995, the federal forces were able to secure control of Grozny. By June 1995, they controlled 85% of the Chechen territory.[21]

As the separatists were pushed into the mountains, defeat seemed imminent. Adapting, the insurgent forces were able to reverse the situation. They switched to guerilla tactics. Dudayev announced that the war was going to move to Russian territory: 'Our quick, manoeuvrable groups will quietly move in [to Russian cities]'.[22] Shamil Basayev declared that the separatists would rely on guerilla warfare and subversive operations to counter the Russian forces.[23] Subsequently, the separatists implemented the tactic of terrorism and staged such hostage terrorist attacks as the raid on Budennovsk in June 1995 and the attack on Kizlyar/Pervomaiskoe in January 1996.

In April 1996, the separatists suffered one of the most significant setbacks of the first Chechen campaign when Dzhokhar Dudayev was killed. Despite losing their leader, they were able not only to recover but to advance in Argun, Gudermes, and Shali. In August 1996, they regained control of Grozny. Following the military defeat, the Russian government acceded to negotiations and signed the Khasavyurt peace agreement with separatist leader Aslan Maskhadov on 31 August 1996.

Thus, despite the setbacks of the first Chechen campaign, the separatist command altered its strategy and was able to reverse the course of the conflict. Due to the separatist successes, Russia's disengagement efforts during the first

Chechen conflict produced minimal results. Moscow attempted to implement an amnesty just two days after the beginning of the operation to restore constitutional order, on 13 December 1994. Around 500 individuals took advantage of the initiative,[24] or 2.5% of the estimated 20,000 insurgent force. Further, about 100 fighters laid down weapons in response to President Yeltsin's 1995 amnesty, and in 1996 an amnesty was used to exchange 11 insurgents for 12 police officers taken hostage during the raid on Pervomaiskoe.[25] The amnesty that did produce impressive results followed the Khasavyurt agreement and was thus not a disengagement initiative. Rather, it was a measure to prevent the clogging of the justice system after the end of the conflict. Around 5000 individuals were amnestied as a result of the March 1997 amnesty,[26] constituting 25% of the initial insurgent force of 20,000.

Further, due to the successes of the insurgents, foreign influences on the first Chechen conflict were minimal. At the very outset of the first Chechen conflict, Dzhokhar Dudayev appealed to foreign powers for support. For instance, Chechen Foreign Minister Yusef turned to the leaders of the Muslim world asking for moral and financial support against the Russian aggression.[27] According to the Minister, in response to his appeal, fighters who had gone through the war in Afghanistan headed to Chechnya from Algeria, Yemen, Sudan, and other Muslim countries.[28] The media reported the presence of foreign fighters in Grozny as early as December 1994. Fighters who arrived to support the Chechen separatists included individuals from the Baltic republics and Ukraine, as well as volunteers who had gained combat experience in the conflicts in Afghanistan, Abkhazia, and Nagorno-Karabakh.[29] According to the Russian government, by 1996, 600 foreigners were fighting along with the Chechen separatists.[30]

Among foreign fighters who came to support separatist Chechnya was Sheikh Fathi, who appeared in the region in the early 1990s. A Jordanian of Chechen descent, Sheikh Fathi was instrumental in attracting veterans of the Soviet–Afghan war to the struggle.[31] Among these veterans was Khattab, who in the Chechen context became the figurehead most associated with foreign fighters due to his alleged links to Al-Qaeda. Khattab headed an Islamic Battalion that incorporated most of the foreign fighters.[32] With him, Khattab also brought foreign funds to Chechnya that flowed through such charities as Al Haramein.[33] To train insurgents in unconventional tactics, Khattab, with Basayev's help, built a training camp Kavkaz in the village of Serzhen-Yurt.

The presence of Afghan Arab foreign fighters and financial assistance from foreign sources notwithstanding, the role of outside entities in the first Chechen conflict was limited. Khattab himself was cautious in efforts to influence the nature of the Chechen insurgency. As he explained in his memoir, Khattab was apprehensive of Chechen Sufis and initially did not attempt to influence the religious beliefs of his students.[34] Chechnya only appeared in Osama bin Laden's statements in 1996, after the Chechen insurgents emerged victorious. In his declaration of war against the US, bin Laden praised the Chechen separatists for their success: 'The sons of the land of the two Holy Places had come out to fight against the Russian in Afghanistan, the Serb in Bosnia-Herzegovina and today they are fighting in Chechenia and – by the Permission of Allah – they have been made victorious over your [U.S.] partner, the Russians'.[35] Thus, while the Chechen separatists received outside support during the first conflict, their military successes did not create a need to transform the insurgency by adopting a foreign ideology.

The first Chechen conflict enjoyed a rather large base of support. Dudayev was able to mobilize a significant number of followers who remained loyal to the cause until the end of the conflict. Even though the separatists suffered a number of setbacks, adaptation allowed them to regain the initiative and to recapture Grozny, which signified military victory for them. Due to insurgent successes, government disengagement initiatives failed to attract a large number of insurgents. Further, the strength of the insurgent forces precluded the need to embrace a foreign ideology, and foreign fighters who participated in the first Chechen conflict did not incite significant splits among the insurgent leadership. The insurgency remained a local project against the Russian government.

The North Caucasus insurgency vs. Al-Qaeda

The second Chechen conflict started much more favorably for the federal forces. According to the official estimates, insurgent forces at the beginning of the second Chechen conflict consisted of 15–20,000 fighters.[36] Fighting that started in Dagestan in August 1999 quickly moved to Chechnya. The federal forces were much better prepared this time. Following bombardments of Grozny, the ground troops entered Chechnya on 30 September 1999. By the spring of 2000, the Russian troops had successfully taken control of the majority of Chechen territory. The phase of positional fighting was over. Until the official end of the counterterrorist operation in April 2009, the conflict continued as a low intensity guerilla war with numerous terrorist attacks and counterterrorist operations.

Even judging by the official estimates of 15–20,000 insurgents, the second conflict did not have as wide a support base as the first. In fact, conflicts among insurgents were reported from the very beginning of the 1999 counterterrorist operation. De facto independent Chechnya separatist leader Aslan Maskhadov, elected president in 1997, faced opposition from Shamil Basayev, who was pushing for a more radical agenda.[37] The lack of unity among the Chechen forces was complicated by the presence of foreign fighters, who by 1999 were attempting to co-opt the Chechen struggle for global jihad.

To prevent the repeat of the first conflict, Aslan Maskhadov was seeking Western support for a negotiated settlement with Russia.[38] Western diplomacy, however, did not produce many outcomes. At the same time, as the insurgents were further pushed by Russian forces, they started looking for alternative sources of support. The radical wing turned to the Taliban for recognition. On an official visit to Afghanistan in January 2000, Zelimkhan Yandarbiyev met with Mullah Omar, after which the Taliban issued an official recognition of Chechnya's independence.[39]

Foreign ideologies started affecting the insurgency. By the 2000s, Salafi Islam gained a significant following in the North Caucasus. Afghan Arab foreign fighters, including such figures as Abu al-Walid, Abu Omar al-Saif, and Abu Jaffar, attempted to exploit this fact and swing the insurgency in support of global jihadi goals. The Russian Government claimed around 2500–3000 foreign fighters to be operating in Chechnya in 2000.[40] While providing support, expertise, and funding, these fighters introduced radical Islamist frames and narratives into the Chechen insurgency.[41]

Al-Qaeda portrayed the struggle in the North Caucasus as its own battlefield. Back in 1996, Al-Qaeda's Ayman al Zawahiri attempted to cross the Russian border to Chechnya. While this attempt failed, Zawahiri articulated his own vision for the North Caucasus as a bridge to the Muslim lands:

> If the Chechens and other Caucasian mujahidin reach the shores of the oil-rich Caspian Sea, the only thing that will separate them from Afghanistan will be the neutral state of Turkmenistan. This will form a mujahid Islamic belt to the south of Russia that will be connected in the east to Pakistan, which is brimming with mujahidin movements in Kashmir. The belt will be linked to the south with Iran and Turkey that are sympathetic to the Muslims of Central Asia.[42]

In its narratives, Al-Qaeda routinely referred to Chechnya as one of its global fronts. In the statements of Osama bin Laden and Ayman al Zawahiri, Chechnya figures as an Islamic nation fighting against the enemies of Islam in the name of the restoration of the global Islamic Caliphate.[43]

Despite Al-Qaeda's statements and the efforts of Afghan Arab foreign fighters to co-opt the insurgency, the Chechen command did not pledge allegiance to Al-Qaeda. In fact, insurgent forces split in their opinion towards the foreign influences. Afghan Arabs were associated with Salafism that in the North Caucasus was often perceived as foreign. Religious conflicts between Sufis and Salafis accompanied the spread of Salafi Islam.[44] Among the insurgents, Salafi influences did not enjoy unanimous recognition. As one separatist insurgent put it: 'It was all those Arabs and Arabized Chechens who had brought turmoil, split, and chaos to the Chechens [...] Having forgotten their roots ... they wanted us to forget about our Chechenness [nokhchalla], our tradition, roots ... They were a huge threat'.[45]

At this time, to maintain strength, insurgent forces had to appeal both to their secular ethno-nationalist separatist supporters and more radical ones who supported the Salafi jihadi views. By the 2000s, though, it became increasingly unlikely the insurgents would regain momentum as they had in 1996. Witnessing military defeat and ideological splits within the insurgent forces, many fighters expressed interest in disengagement. As one fighter explained,

'Taking into consideration the realities of the day, it was absolutely indispensable for us to pull out of the war, get back to normal life'.[46]

In this context of the failing insurgency and the presence of foreign actors attempting to co-opt it, the Russian government once again turned to disengagement initiatives. On 13 December 1999, the Russian State Duma announced an amnesty for individuals willing to voluntarily lay down weapons. The amnesty turned out to be one of the more successful disengagement efforts, as reportedly around 2500 individuals took advantage of it and 750 of these were pardoned.[47] If indeed 15–20,000 people constituted the insurgent force at the beginning of the second Chechen conflict, then those who applied for the amnesty accounted for 13–17% of the force.

On 6 June 2003, the Russian government implemented another amnesty tied to the new constitution and presidential elections in Chechnya. The new constitution, affirmed in the March 2003 referendum, solidified the status of Chechnya as a subject of the Russian Federation, thus contradicting the very spirit of the separatist insurgency. This amnesty turned out to be less successful, with only 171 insurgents disengaging.[48] According to Chechen officials, in 2003 there remained around 3000 insurgents operating in the republic.[49] Based on this estimate, around 6% of the fighters took advantage of the amnesty.

One of the most successful disengagement initiatives of the second Chechen conflict was the September 2006 amnesty that followed the death of Shamil Basayev. Shamil Basayev was one of the most charismatic insurgent leaders, who had staged multiple terrorist attacks in Russia. He was also one of the leaders most associated with the radicalization of the insurgency and embracing some Islamist narratives. The elimination of Basayev was perceived as a great success achieved by the security services. For instance, commenting on his death, Ramzan Kadyrov declared: 'I consider this day as a date of the logical conclusion of the extremely hard struggle with the illegal armed formations that the special services, federal forces and law enforcement agencies have been engaged in'.[50]

Indeed, Basayev's death seemed to have significantly impacted the insurgency. Subsequently, the separatists went through leadership, structural, and ideological adjustments. The number of terrorist acts in the North Caucasus dropped drastically around 2006, and insurgents minimized their activity.[51] Following Basayev's death, the insurgency further transitioned to embrace Islamist ideas, and the next leader, Doku Umarov, founded the Caucasus Emirate in 2007 – a move that was disapproved of by many Chechen nationalists. In 2006, the number of insurgent forces was estimated around 1000 fighters.[52] According to the government sources, between 450 and 603 fighters disengaged in response to the 2006 amnesty.[53] Based on these numbers, insurgents lost between 45 and 60% of their force. While these numbers might be on the higher end, it seems that the death of Shamil Basayev prompted insurgents who did not want to fight for the establishment of an Islamic state in the Caucasus to disengage.

While the numbers of individuals who disengaged during the second Chechen conflict are high, insurgent crises and foreign influence alone are not sufficient in explaining the success of the amnesties. What also impacted the success of the disengagement initiatives was the alternative employment scheme created by the Russian government. At the outset of the second Chechen conflict, Vladimir Putin started implementing a policy that came to be known as Chechenization, or the transferring of the responsibility over the Chechen conflict from the federal center back to Chechnya.[54] In 2000, Putin introduced direct presidential rule in Chechnya and appointed Akhmad Kadyrov as head of his administration. To support the Kadyrov administration, Moscow sent significant amounts of funds to Chechnya. Between 2002 and 2006, Grozny received 30.6 billion rubles (equivalent to USD 1.25 billion).[55]

In the first Chechen conflict, Akhmad Kadyrov fought as a separatist. Kadyrov served as a mufti of independent Chechnya and staunchly opposed the spread of Salafism and the influences brought about by Afghan Arabs.[56] Due to his role in the separatist movement and appointment as a religious leader in separatist Chechnya, Kadyrov enjoyed popularity among some insurgents and the Chechen population. As a result, when Akhmad Kadyrov officially disassociated himself from the insurgency and switched to the Russian side in September 1999, he was able to bring with him other insurgents.[57] Kadyrov made use of the government amnesties and worked through liaisons with fighters who wanted to disengage.[58] Individuals who disengaged from the insurgency received protection from Kadyrov and were offered employment in Kadyrov's institutions.

Amnestied individuals found employment in Kadyrov's administration, law enforcement agencies, and security services. By 2003, around 50–60% of the employees of internal ministry divisions in Grozny were former fighters, while similar agencies outside the capital consisted of 80% former fighters.[59] In 2006, Akhmad Kadyrov's son Ramzan reported that 99% of the Kadyrov Battalion were former insurgent fighters and 90% of the Yug and Sever Battalions consisted of amnestied individuals.[60] Altogether, around 7000 former fighters found employment in Kadyrovs' security services,[61] though these numbers include individuals who did not qualify for the official amnesties and were unofficially pardoned.[62]

The disengagement initiatives of the second Chechen conflict provided a viable alternative to the separatist fighters who wanted to leave the insurgency. An insurgent victory seemed unlikely, and the insurgent command had to adapt. The insurgency came to rely more on foreign sources of funding and expertise. In return, the insurgent command had to embrace some of the foreign ideological narratives even though they did not have universal support among the insurgents. Consequent splits were exploited by the government introduction of amnesties that were backed up by an opportunity to gain employment in the forces of Akhmad and Ramzan Kadyrov. Facing the pressure of losing more fighters who had a viable opportunity to disengage, the insurgent command retained the local orientation of the insurgency against Russia and did not pledge allegiance to Al-Qaeda.

The North Caucasus insurgency vs. the Islamic state

Despite the completion of the Russian counterterrorist operation in Chechnya in 2009, insurgency in the North Caucasus did not end. Insurgent activities spread across the Republics of the North Caucasus, and counterterrorist operations as a government response to them became routine. The number of terrorist attacks in the North Caucasus reached a peak in 2010, especially affecting Dagestan, Ingushetia, and Kabardino-Balkaria.[63] Since 2010, however, insurgent activities in the North Caucasus have been on the decline. According to the human rights group Memorial, in 2013 insurgent activities were 1.5 times lower than in 2012; in 2014 such activities were half the level of 2013; and in 2015 insurgent activities were 3.5 times lower than in 2014.[64] The number of casualties of insurgent activities and terrorist attacks has significantly declined.[65]

Since 2009, the insurgent forces in the North Caucasus have been much weaker than in the first or second Chechen conflicts. In 2011, the number of insurgents was estimated to be between 500 and 800 people.[66] The base of insurgent supporters has also significantly changed. On the one hand, since the 1990s, Salafism has gained a significant religious following in the North Caucasus. However, Salafi communities have been routinely subjected to harassment, detentions, searches, and abuse by the Russian authorities.[67] Discriminatory actions against Salafi communities have spurred radicalization, creating pools of potential Salafi recruits. On the other hand, with the insurgent support a number of radical Salafi groups known as *jamaats* came into existence across the North Caucasus by the mid-2000s.[68] Further, such insurgent ideologues as Anzor Astemirov, Yasin Rasulov, and Said Buryatsky promoted Salafi jihadi narratives among the insurgents.[69] This way, radical Salafis became part of the insurgency.

Despite the growing popularity of Salafi jihadi ideology, conflicts persisted between the insurgent factions that wanted to continue their fight against Russia and those who wanted to join global jihad. While Doku Umarov embraced some Salafi jihadi rhetoric and even declared war on all enemies of Islam,[70] he retained the orientation of the insurgency against Russia. Umarov still had to appease his nationalist insurgent constituency. In 2010, conflicts between Umarov and nationalists such as the Gakayev brothers, Tarkhan Gaziev, and Aslambek Vadalov forced him to temporarily resign.[71] Umarov himself explained this *fitna*, or split, as a result of subversive activities by foreign fighters led by Mukhannad, who was allegedly an Al-Qaeda representative in the North Caucasus.[72]

While the Caucasus Emirate insurgency was undergoing crises occasioned by factions competing for constituencies supporting different ideologies, the Russian government implemented a different counterterrorism approach.

During the presidency of Dmitry Medvedev, the Kremlin adopted a soft approach to the North Caucasus issue. Medvedev's 2009 'Concept on Countering Terrorism in the Russian Federation' acknowledged the social roots influencing the problem of terrorism. As a result, Medvedev's administration turned to such issues as economic development and modernization, dialog initiatives among religious groups, and rehabilitation programs for former fighters.[73]

Similar to the use of amnesties previously, the Russian government resorted to Committees on Reintegration of former fighters as a mechanism to disengage insurgents. As Aleksandr Bortnikov, head of the FSB, explained, Committees on Reintegration were meant to become a key element of prevention of terrorism efforts.[74] Indeed, the Committees were rather successful in disengaging insurgents and rehabilitating former fighters.

The first Committee on Reintegration was created in Dagestan in November 2010. In its first two years of existence, the Committee processed 46 petitions.[75] The most successful Committee on Reintegration was established in Ingushetia. Since its inception in September 2011, the Committee has rehabilitated 70 individuals.[76] Similar Committees opened in Kabardino-Balkaria and Karachay-Cherkessia. In Kabardino-Balkaria, a Committee on Reintegration came into existence in January 2012. The Committee remained practically inactive until 2016, when it processed 18 cases.[77] In Karachay-Cherkessia, a Committee on Reintegration opened in March 2012, but not much has been reported about its work.

Considering that in the 2010s insurgent forces only counted hundreds of individuals, the results from the Committees were quite significant. However, unlike the amnesties of 1999, 2003, or 2006, the work of the Committees was not supplemented by an alternative employment scheme such as that of the Kadyrov agencies. For instance, out of the total of 70 individuals who went through the Ingushetia Committee, only 13 people received assistance with employment.[78] Further, the work of the Committees was soon halted with the return of hard-line measures against terrorism. Thus, in Dagestan, the Committee was effectively terminated in 2013. The only Committee that continued functioning was that of Ingushetia.

Despite the promise of the soft approach to terrorism and the successes of the Committees on Reintegration, the Russian government reverted to hard-line measures as it prepared for the 2014 Sochi Olympics. Dialogs once again gave way to counterterrorist operations and sweeps.[79] The Russian security services were able to successfully eliminate the insurgent leaders, including Doku Umarov, as well as his successors Aliaskhab Kebekov and Magomed Suleimanov. Salafi communities once again were subject to raids, disappearances, executions, and torture. The authorities expanded the practice of placing individuals suspected of ties to radicalism on watch lists, or preventive registration of extremists.[80] In 2013, the Russian government amended the 2006 law on counterterrorism to include a compensation mechanism for terrorist attacks.

The law established that terrorists, their relatives, and close people would pay for damages. Subsequently, the practice of collective responsibility became common.

Russia's renewed onslaught in the North Caucasus crushed the Caucasus Emirate insurgency. At the same time, Russia's counterterrorist measures produced the following outcomes. First, the actions of the security services before the Sochi Olympics pushed many insurgents as well as radicalized Salafis to leave for Syria and Iraq. As one Salafi activist explained, the security services 'turned the green light on and opened the road' to the Middle East.[81] A member of the security services explained further: 'We opened borders, helped them [radicals] all out and closed the border behind them by criminalizing this type of fighting'.[82] By 2014, the outflow of individuals significantly declined, as participation in foreign illegal armed formations contrary to the interests of the Russian Federation became criminalized in the Criminal Code.[83] By then, many individuals had left to fight for ISIS in Syria and Iraq. At the time, no alternative mechanisms were in place along the lines of amnesties of the second Chechen conflict, and the Committees on Reintegration effectively halted their work. Insurgents who did not agree with the Caucasus Emirate command had no other options but to leave.

Second, the security services decapitated the insurgency by eliminating Doku Umarov, Aliaskhab Kebekov, and Magomed Suleimanov. However, the decapitation eradicated the less radicalized leadership who supported the locally oriented insurgency. Thus, Umarov tried to prevent the outflow of his forces to Syria and Iraq. In a statement on jihad in Syria, he called jihad in the Caucasus a superior one and encouraged his fighters to continue fighting in the Caucasus.[84] Kebekov, in turn, staunchly opposed ISIS. When the Caucasus Emirate factions started pledging allegiance to ISIS, Kebekov accused them of inciting chaos and suggested they leave the Caucasus.[85] In place of these leaders, the younger generations of fighters arrived who were more radicalized and more ready to be part of the global jihad.

In the meantime, similar to Al-Qaeda's efforts to co-opt the North Caucasus insurgency, ISIS has implemented a concerted recruitment strategy targeting the North Caucasus. Initially, the Russian language propaganda efforts were spearheaded by Omar al-Shishani, a Georgian from the Pankisi Gorge. In 2013, al-Shishani launched a FiSyria website posting news about militants from the Caucasus involved in battles in Syria. As al-Shishani swore allegiance to ISIS, he, along with a Karachai Abu Jihad, set out to target propaganda to co-opt the North Caucasus insurgency. In a 2015 video address, Abu Jihad called on the North Caucasus fighters to pledge allegiance to al-Baghdadi.[86] In May 2015, ISIS started printing a Russian language magazine, *Istok*, and has used its radio and social media accounts to spread its propaganda in Russia. As one Salafi activist in the North Caucasus stated, 'IS tried to create a feeling that the cream of the nation was with them.'[87]

Further, ISIS came into direct confrontation with Russia. While involved in its efforts to co-opt the North Caucasus insurgency, Al-Qaeda did not directly strike against Russia, despite having previously insinuated that Moscow was an enemy.[88] ISIS, on the other hand, directly proclaimed war against Russia. On 1 July 2014, al-Baghdadi issued a message that listed Russia as one of the ISIS enemies. Following Russia's intervention in Syria on 30 September 2015, ISIS spokesman Abu Mohammed al-Adnani declared jihad on Russia in October 2015. Since then, an ISIS-related group has claimed responsibility for downing the Russian airplane over the Sinai Peninsula, and ISIS has claimed responsibility for terrorist attacks in Moscow and Dagestan.

Given the crisis state of the Caucasus Emirate insurgency, the lack of disengagement routes for insurgents, the pressure from the Russian security services, and the onslaught of ISIS propaganda, in order to survive, the North Caucasus insurgents had to adjust. This time around, the insurgent command did not have to compete with disengagement programs for the commitment of insurgents. The insurgent leadership supportive of the Caucasus Emirate was effectively eliminated. Pledging allegiance to ISIS seemed the only viable alternative for maintaining the insurgent momentum.

A Dagestaini insurgent faction of the Caucasus Emirate under the leadership of Suleiman Zailanabidov was among the first to pledge allegiance to ISIS on 21 November 2014. Dagestani groups headed by Rustam Asilderov followed suit on 19 December 2014. Subsequently, on 21 June 2015, the joint command of insurgent factions operating in Dagestan, Ingushetia, Chechnya, Kabardino-Balkaria, and Karachay-Cherkessia pledged allegiance to ISIS. This constituted the majority of the Caucasus Emirate groups. ISIS has accepted the pledge and announced the establishment of its Vilayat Kavkaz in Russia's North Caucasus. Hundreds of individuals have left the North Caucasus to fight for ISIS.[89]

Conclusions

Similar to other insurgent groups, the North Caucasus insurgents have adopted numerous changes in their strategy in order to adapt and survive. Many of the insurgent adaptations brought successes to the insurgent command. Thus, the switch to guerilla warfare and adoption of terrorist tactics helped the insurgents achieve successes in the first Chechen conflict. Successful operations against the federal forces bolstered the position of the separatists. Insurgents were less pressured to disengage, and, therefore, few fighters applied for government amnesties. Insurgent spirit was strong, and foreigners who participated in the first Chechen conflict produced little impact on the insurgency.

The second Chechen conflict brought more challenges to the insurgents. Military failures pressured insurgents to diversify their sources of support: the insurgent command actively sought foreign funding. To secure outside support, insurgents had to adapt their ideology embracing some foreign Salafi jihadi narratives. In turn, Al-Qaeda was trying to portray the fighting in the North Caucasus as one of its battlefields. In this environment the Russian government implemented disengagement initiatives supported by employment opportunities in Chechnya. The offer of amnesties created viable incentives for fighters to disengage. As a result, insurgents had to compete for the loyalty of their fighters by preserving the core local orientation of the insurgency. No pledge of allegiance to Al-Qaeda followed.

Since 2009, the North Caucasus insurgency has been further weakened. In attempts to survive, the insurgent command adapted more extremely and embraced foreign narratives. This time around, the government's rehabilitation initiatives were terminated as security services clamped down on the insurgency in preparation for the Sochi Olympics. Thus, alternative venues to disengage were cut short. In the absence of the need to compete for the loyalty of the fighters, the North Caucasus insurgents risked complete annihilation at the hands of the security services. In this context, ISIS propaganda and efforts to co-opt the insurgency became more successful than such previous efforts by Al-Qaeda. The North Caucasus insurgents pledged allegiance to ISIS.

The analysis demonstrates that insurgents are more likely to disengage when they are facing defeat. As the Russian experiences with amnesties and Committees on Rehabilitation illustrate, disengagement initiatives can create alternatives for insurgents who might not agree with the outcomes of insurgent adaptation. While undoubtedly the Russian initiatives were not without flaws (many fighters who applied for amnesties were imprisoned and many were pressured into laying down weapons), they weakened the insurgent ability to radicalize for fear of losing more supporters. In this sense, disengagement initiatives backed up by alternative employment opportunities might be a policy instrument that could help governments not only weaken insurgencies but also curtail potential radicalization of insurgent movements.

Furthermore, the Russian case demonstrates how disengagement initiatives can be an effective instrument to prevent the transformation of a locally oriented insurgency to a global one if outside actors are trying to co-opt the movement. Amnesties or rehabilitation programs create competition for insurgents. This pressures the insurgent command to proceed cautiously while considering adapting foreign narratives. In the absence of such pressure, insurgents might radicalize further and replace local aspirations with global ones that are much more difficult to combat.

Notes

1. See Mendelsohn, *The Al Qaeda Franchise*.
2. Phillips, "Terrorist Group Cooperation."
3. Joscelyn, "Osama Bin Laden's Files."
4. Vinci, "Immortal Insurgencies."
5. Gunaratna, "The Post-Madrid Face of Al Qaeda."

6. Biddle, "Afghanistan and the Future of Warfare."
7. Serena, *It Takes More than a Network*.
8. Horgan, *Walking away from Terrorism*.
9. Bjorgo and Horgan, *Leaving Terrorism Behind*, 4.
10. Mehta, *Lost Victory*.
11. Noricks, "Disengagement and Deradicalization," 302.
12. Fink and Hearne, *Beyond Terrorism*.
13. Checkel, *Transnational Dynamics of Civil War*.
14. Bakke, "Help Wanted?"
15. Orlov and Cherkasov, *Rossiia – Chechnya*.
16. "Chechenskii uzel."
17. Ibid.
18. "Grozny sobiraet vse."
19. Sokirko, "Prizraki voiny."
20. For more on the Chechen insurgencies see Orlov and Cherkasov, *Rossiia – Chechnya*; Cohen, *Russia's Counterinsurgency in North Caucasus*; Schaefer, *The Insurgency in Chechnya*; and Kramer, "The Perils of Counterinsurgency."
21. "Pervaiia chechenskaiia."
22. "Guerillas to target Russia."
23. "Chechens plan to force Russian troops."
24. "Vse chechenskie amnistii."
25. Ibid.
26. "Amnistiia boevikov zakonchilas.'"
27. See note 16 above.
28. "Srok ul'timatuma istek."
29. "Voiskam meshaiut boeviki."
30. "Kommentarii voennykh spetsialistov."
31. Vidino, "The Arab Foreign Fighters."
32. Kudriavtsev, "Arabskie 'afgantsy.'"
33. Williams, "The 'Chechen Arabs.'"
34. Al-Suwailem, *The Experience of the Arab Ansar*.
35. Bin Laden, "Declaration of War."
36. "Itogi kontrterroristicheskoi operatsii."
37. Akhmadov and Lanskoy, *The Chechen Struggle*.
38. Akhmadov and Daniloff, *Chechnya's Secret Wartime Diplomacy*.
39. "The Taliban formally recognizes Chechnya."
40. Borisov, "Maskhadov pochti ne slyshen."
41. See Bakke, 'Help Wanted?'; and Pokalova, *Chechnya's Terrorist Network*.
42. Al-Zawahiri, "Al-Sharq Al-Awsat Publishes."
43. Bin Laden, "Al-Sahab Media Releases"; and Al-Zawahiri, "Al-Sharq Al-Awsat Publishes."
44. Akaev, "Severnokavkazskii vakhkhabizm."
45. Format preserved from the original. Souleimanov and Aliyev, *The Individual Disengagement of Avengers*, 64.
46. Ibid., 62.
47. See note 24 above.
48. "Massovye kapituliatsii v Chechne."
49. "V Chechne istek srok amnistii."
50. Stepanov, "Kto i kak."
51. See Pokalova, *Chechnya's Terrorist Network*.
52. Stepanov and Sokolova, "Za 4 dnia sdalis.'"

53. See note 26 above.
54. See Ware, "Chechenization"; Russell, "Ramzan Kadyrov"; Sakwa, "The Revenge of the Caucasus"; and Souleimanov, "An Ethnography of Counterinsurgency."
55. Ware, "Chechenization," 159.
56. "Kadyrov Akhmad (Akhmat-khadzhi)."
57. See note 48 above.
58. See note 49 above.
59. Krechetnikov, "Chechenskie siloviki."
60. Allenova, "Ramzan Kadyrov zabral sebe sdachu."
61. See note 26 above.
62. "O proekte amnistii."
63. See Pokalova, *Chechnya's Terrorist Network*.
64. Kara-Murza, "Islamskoe podpol'e."
65. "Severnyi Kavkaz – statistika zhertv."
66. Bondarenko, "Na Severnom Kavkaze deistvuiut."
67. *Counter-Terrorism in the North Caucasus*.
68. Yemelianova, *Radical Islam*.
69. Sagramoso, "The Radicalization of Islamic."
70. "Ofitsial'nyi reliz zaiavleniia."
71. Bocharova, "Amiry otkololis.'"
72. Iaroshevskii, "Doku Umarov protiv."
73. See *The North Caucasus Insurgency and Syria*.
74. Charnyi, "Vozmozhnost' sozdaniia."
75. Isaev and Gadzhieva, "V Dagestane komissia."
76. Khrustaleva, "V Ingushetii 70 byvshikh."
77. "Komissiia po adaptatsii boevikov."
78. See note 76 above.
79. Starodubrovskaia and Kazenin, *Severnyi Kavkaz*.
80. See note 73 above.
81. Ibid., 16.
82. Ibid.
83. Federal Law 302.
84. "Obrashchenie Amira Imarata Kavkaz."
85. "'Imarat Kavkaz' vstupil v konfrontatsiiu."
86. Paraszczuk, "Umar Shishani's Right-Hand Man."
87. *The North Caucasus Insurgency and Syria*, 7.
88. National Consortium for the Study of Terrorism and Responses to Terrorism (START).
89. "North Caucasian Fighters in Syria and Iraq."

Disclosure statement

The views expressed in this article are those of the author and do not reflect the official policy or position of the National Defense University, the Department of Defense, or the U.S. Government.

Bibliography

Akaev, A. 2002. "'Severnokavkazskii vakhkhabizm' – raznovidnost' islamskogo radikalizma." *Kavkazskii Uzel*, February 7.

Akhmadov, Ilyas, and Miriam Lanskoy. *The Chechen Struggle: Independence Won and Lost.* New York: Palgrave Macmillan, 2010.

Akhmadov, Ilyas, and Nicholas Daniloff. *Chechnya's Secret Wartime Diplomacy: Aslan Maskhadov and the Quest for a Peaceful Resolution.* New York: Palgrave Macmillan, 2013.

Allenova, Olga. 2007. "Ramzan Kadyrov zabral sebe sdachu." *Memorial*, January 16. http://www.memo.ru/hr/hotpoints/caucas1/msg/2007/01/m80184.htm.

Al-Suwailem, Samir Saleh. *The Experience of the Arab Ansar in Chechnya, Afghanistan and Tajikistan. Memories of Amir Khattab.*

Al-Zawahiri, Ayman. 2001. *Al-Sharq Al-Awsat Publishes Extracts from Al-Jihad Leader Al-Zawahiri's New Book.* December 2. http://gtrp.haverford.edu/aqsi/aqsi-statement/705.

"Amnistiia boevikov zakonchilas', no ee prodlenie ne iskliuchaetsia." 2007. *Memorial*, January 16. http://www.memo.ru/hr/hotpoints/caucas1/msg/2007/01/m80222.htm.

Bakke, Krisin M. "Help Wanted? The Mixed Record of Foreign Fighters in Domestic Insurgencies." *International Security* 38, no. 4 (2014): 150–187.

Biddle, Stephen. "Afghanistan and the Future of Warfare." *Foreign Affairs* 82, no. 2 (2003): 31–46.

Bin Laden, Osama. 1996. "Declaration of War against the Americans Occupying the Land of the Two Holy Places." August 23.

Bin Laden, Osama. 2007. "Al-Sahab Media Releases Bin Ladin Statement, Says Al-Jazirah 'Counterfeiting' the Facts." October 23. http://gtrp.haverford.edu/aqsi/aqsi-statement/376.

Bjorgo, Tore, and John Horgan, eds. *Leaving Terrorism Behind: Individual and Collective Disengagement.* London: Routledge, 2009.

Bocharova, Svetlana. 2010. "Amiry otkololis' ot Umarova." *Gazeta.ru*, October 10.

Bondarenko, Maria. 2011. "Na Severnom Kavkaze deistvuiut ot 500 do 800 boevikov." *Nezavisimaia Gazeta*, January 14.

Borisov, Timofei. 2005. "Maskhadov pochti ne slyshen." *Rossiiskaia Gazeta*, January 19.

Charnyi, Semen. 2012. "Vozmozhnost' sozdaniia federal'noi komissii po adaptatsii eks-boevikov obsuzhdaetsia na zasedanii prezidentskogo Soveta po pravam cheloveka." *Kavkazskii Uzel*, July 10.

"Chechens Plan to Force Russian Troops Out by Guerilla War." 1995. *BBC Summary of World Broadcasts*, May 10.

"Chechenskii uzel." 1994. *Izvestiia*, December 1.

Checkel, Jeffrey T., ed. *Transnational Dynamics of Civil War.* New York: Cambridge University Press, 2013.

Cohen, Ariel. *Russia's Counterinsurgency in North Caucasus: Performance and Consequences.* Carlisle Barracks: U.S. Army War College Press, 2014.

Counter-Terrorism in the North Caucasus: A Human Rights Perspective. 2014 – First Half of 2016. Moscow: Memorial, 2016.

Federal Law 302 "On Amending Certain Legal Acts of the Russian Federation," November 2, 2013.

Fink, Naureen Chowdhury, and Ellie B. Hearne. *Beyond Terrorism: Deradicalization and Disengagement from Violent Extremism.* New York: International Peace Institute, 2008.

"Grozny sobiraet vse, chto mozhet streliat' i vzryvat'sia." 1994. *Izvestiia*, December 15.

"Guerillas to target Russia." 1995. *The Advertiser*, February 20.

Gunaratna, Rohan. "The Post-madrid Face of Al Qaeda." *The Washington Quarterly* 27, no. 3 (2004): 91–100.

Horgan, John. *Walking away from Terrorism: Accounts of Disengagement from Radical and Extremist Movements.* London: Routledge, 2009.

Iaroshevskii, Maksim. 2010. "Doku Umarov protiv 'Al'-Kaidy.'" *Radio Svoboda*, September 27.

"'Imarat Kavkaz' vstupil v konfrontatsiiu s 'Islamskim gosudarstvom.'" 2014. *Kavkazskii Uzel*, December 29.

Isaev, Timur, and Karina Gadzhieva. 2012. "V Dagestane komissia po adaptatsii boevikov za dva goda rassmotrela 46 zaiavlenii." *Kavkazskii Uzel*, November 2.

"Itogi kontrterroristicheskoi operatsii v Chechne." 2009. *Kommersant*, April 17.

Joscelyn, Thomas. 2016. "Osama Bin Laden's Files: Boko Haram's leader wanted to be 'under one banner.'" *FDD's Long War Journal*. March 4. http://www.longwarjournal.org/archives/2016/03/osama-bin-ladens-files-boko-haram-leader-wanted-to-be-under-one-banner.php.

"Kadyrov Akhmad (Akhmat-khadzhi)." 2001. *Kavkazskii Uzel*, May 28.

Kara-Murza, Vladimir. 2016. "Islamskoe podpol'e." *Radio Svoboda*, June 7.

Khrustaleva, Elena. 2016. "V Ingushetii 70 byvshikh chlenov NVF vozvrashcheny k mirnoi zhizni." *Kavpolit*, September 4.

"Komissiia po adaptatsii boevikov v KBR rassmotrela za god 18 zaiavlenii." 2016. *Kavpolit*, December 26.

"Kommentarii voennykh spetsialistov." 1996. *Rossiiskaia Gazeta*, August 7.

Kramer, Mark. "The Perils of Counterinsurgency: Russia's War in Chechnya." *International Security* 29, no. 3 (2005): 5–63.

Krechetnikov, Artem. 2015. "Chechenskie siloviki: opora ili ugroza?" *BBC*, March 11.

Kudriavtsev, A. 2003. "Arabskie 'afgantsy.'" *Aziia i Afrika Segodnia*, October 31, no. 10.

"Massovye kapituliatsii v Chechne." 2006. *Kommersant*, July 10.

Mehta, Raj. *Lost Victory: The Rise and Fall of LTTE Supremo, V. Prabhakaran*. New Delhi: Pentagon Press, 2010.

Mendelsohn, Barak. *The Al Qaeda Franchise: The Expansion of Al-Qaeda and its Consequences*. New York: Oxford University Press, 2016.

National Consortium for the Study of Terrorism and Responses to Terrorism (START). 2016. Global Terrorism Database. http://www.start.umd.edu/gtd/search/Results.aspx?expanded=no&casualties_type=&casualties_max=&success=yes&perpetrator=20029&ob=CountryText&od=asc&page=1&count=100#results-table.

Noricks, Darcy M. E. "Disengagement and Deradicalization: Processes and Programs." In *Social Science for Counterterrorism: Putting the Pieces Together*, edited by Paul K Davis and Kim Cragin. Santa Monica, CA: RAND, 2009.

"North Caucasian Fighters in Syria and Iraq and IS Propaganda in Russian Language." 2015. Europol: The Hague, November 10.

"Obrashchenie Amira Imarata Kavkaz Dokku Abu Usmana k Modzhakhedam Sirii." 2012. Kavkaz Center, November 13. http://www.kavkazcenter.com/russ/content/2012/11/13/94315/video-obraschenie-amira-imarata-kavkaz-dokku-abu-usmana-k-modzhakhedam-sirii-.shtml.

"Ofitsial'nyi reliz zaiavleniia amira Dokki Umarova o provozglashenii Kavkazskogo Emirata." 2007. Kavkaz Center, November 21. http://kavkazcenter.com/russ/content/2007/11/21/54480.shtml.

"O proekte amnistii v otnoshenii lits, sovershivshikh prestupleniia v period kontrterroristicheskikh operatsii na Severnom Kavkaze." 2006. *Memorial*, September 21. http://www.memo.ru/hr/hotpoints/caucas1/msg/2006/09/m58618.htm.

Orlov, Oleg, and Aleksandr Cherkasov. *Rossiia – Chechnya: Tsep' Oshibok i Prestuplenii*. Moscow: Zven'ia, 1998.

Paraszczuk, Joanna. 2015. "Umar Shishani's Right-hand Man Calls On North Caucasian Jihadis to Join IS In Dagestan and Chechnya." *Jihadology*, April 21. http://jihadology.net/2015/04/21/guest-post-umar-shishanis-right-hand-man-calls-on-north-caucasian-jihadis-to-join-is-in-dagestan-chechnya/.

"Pervaiia chechenskaiia kampaniia 1994–1996 godov." 2014. *RIA Novosti*, December 11.

Phillips, Brian J. "Terrorist Group Cooperation and Longevity." *International Studies Quarterly* 58, no. 2 (2014): 336–347.

Pokalova, Elena. *Chechnya's Terrorist Network: The Evolution of Terrorism in Russia's North Caucasus*. Santa Barbara, CA: Praeger, 2015.

Russell, John. "Ramzan Kadyrov: The Indigenous Key to Success in Putin's Chechenization Strategy?" *Nationalities Papers* 36, no. 4 (2008): 659–687.

Sagramoso, Domitilla. "The Radicalization of Islamic Salafi Jamaats in the North Caucasus: Moving Closer to the Global Jihadist Movement." *Europe-Asia Studies* 64, no. 3 (2012): 561–595.

Sakwa, Richard. "The Revenge of the Caucasus: Chechenization and the Dual State in Russia." *Nationalities Papers* 38, no. 5 (2010): 601–622.

Schaefer, Robert W. *The Insurgency in Chechnya and the North Caucasus*. Santa Barbara, CA: Praeger, 2010.

Serena, Chad C. *It Takes More than a Network: The Iraqi Insurgency and Organizational Adaptation*. Stanford, CA: Stanford University Press, 2014.

"Severnyi Kavkaz – statistika zhertv." 2017. *Kavkazskii Uzel*. http://www.kavkaz-uzel.eu/rubric/1103.

Sokirko, Viktor. 2000. "Prizraki voiny." *Moskovskii Komsomolets*, March 18.

Souleimanov, Emil, and Huseyn Aliyev. *The Individual Disengagement of Avengers, Nationalists, and Jihadists: Why Ex-militants Choose to Abandon Violence in the North Caucasus*. New York: Palgrave Macmillan, 2014.

Souleimanov, Emil. "An Ethnography of Counterinsurgency: *Kadyrovtsy* and Russia's Policy of Chechenization." *Post-Soviet Affairs* 31, no. 2 (2014): 91–114.

"Srok ul'timatuma istek. Chto dal'she?" 1994. *Izvestiia*, December 2.

Starodubrovskaia, Irina, and Konstantin Kazenin. *Severnyi Kavkaz i Sovremennaia Model' Demokraticheskogo Razvitiia*. Moscow: Komitet Grazhdanskikh Initsiativ, 2016.

Stepanov, Aleksandr, and Viktoriia Sokolova. 2006. "Za 4 dnia sdalis' 80 boevikov." *Izvestia*, August 4.

Stepanov, Aleksandr. 2006. "Kto i kak unichtozhil Shamilia Basaeva." *Izvestiia*, July 10.

The North Caucasus Insurgency and Syria: An Exported Jihad? 2016. International Crisis Group, Report 238, March 16.

"The Taliban Formally Recognizes Chechnya." 2000. *The Jamestown Foundation Monitor*, January 18.

"V Chechne istek srok amnistii dlia chechenskikh boevikov." 2003. *Memorial*, September 2. http://www.memo.ru/hr/hotpoints/caucas1/msg/2003/09/m6567.htm.

Vidino, Lorenzo. 2006. "The Arab Foreign Fighters and the Sacralization of the Chechen Conflict." *The Fletcher School Online Journal for Issues Related to Southwest Asia and Islamic Civilization*, Spring.1–11. http://fletcher.tufts.edu/~/media/Fletcher/Microsites/al%20Nakhlah/archives/2006/vidino.pdf.

Vinci, Anthony. 2011. "Immortal Insurgencies." *Small Wars Journal*, September 18.

"Voiskam meshaiut boeviki i plokhaia pogoda." 1994. *Izvestiia*, December 21.

"Vse chechenskie amnistii." 2006. *Kommersant*, July 19.

Ware, Robert Bruce. "Chechenization: Ironies and Intricacies." *Brown Journal of World Affairs* XV, no. II (2009): 157–169.

Williams, Brian Glyn. "The 'Chechen Arabs': An Introduction to the Real Al Qaeda Terrorists from Chechnya." *Terrorism Monitor* 2, no. 1 (2004).

Yemelianova, Galina, ed. *Radical Islam in the Former Soviet Union*. London: Routledge, 2010.

Bolivia, a new model insurgency for the 21st century: from Mao back to Lenin

David E. Spencer and Hugo Acha Melgar

ABSTRACT

In Bolivia, a brilliantly executed insurgency was carried out between 1995 and 2005, so much so that few perceived it as such. Its most important characteristic was its correct evaluation of the relative correlation of forces and application of the right combination of all forms of struggle. This was possible because of its pragmatism. Though not bound by ideological dogmatism, it nonetheless displayed a deep understanding of insurgency and revolutionary theory. This allowed adaptation and evolution in a changing context. The main form of struggle was not military violence, although it was not absent, but rather violent social protest funded by drug trafficking proceeds. The strategy thus neutralized traditional counterinsurgency models, because it made it difficult to apply coercive force as the enemy was not clearly identifiable. Its success in Bolivia means that the emergence of a new model of insurgency, one still built upon the popular mobilization of people's war but more attuned to new global realities, is a reality.

Just as the US and its allies have developed increasingly sophisticated models of counterinsurgency, so the enemies of the West have also developed adapted models of insurgency designed to frustrate and defeat these efforts. One such model was successfully executed by the Coca Growers (referred to hereafter as Cocaleros) in Bolivia between 1995 and 2003, which was consolidated with the election of Evo Morales at the end of 2005. It is important to understand this model, because it breaks with many of the methods we currently associate with insurgency, yet fully applies the tried and true principles long identified by revolutionary theorists such as Mao, but perhaps even more so, Lenin.

Ironically, the 2005 electoral triumph of Evo Morales and his Movement to Socialism (MAS) party would not on its face be considered as the product of an insurgency, but this article will attempt to show that it was indeed an insurgency

– a brilliantly conceived and executed uprising that applied the principles of insurgency to maximum advantage in the context of Turn of the Century Bolivia.[1] Elements of this model are now showing up in other countries in the region. The Cocaleros were undogmatic in their approach, although they were guided by principles they had learned from the miners' unions. They adapted their methods over time, keeping what worked and very rapidly discarding what didn't. This application of principles combined with pragmatism is significant, because much of the West's counterinsurgency apparatus is intended to implement certain predictable methodologies. These, though, are neutralized by this new model, because its components make government capabilities inappropriate or even irrelevant.

To summarize, the Bolivian insurgency model was based on the following five lines of effort:

(1) Violence was limited but not unimportant. It was employed judiciously in two principal ways: first, guerrilla warfare was employed to protect the Cocaleros' main source of income, coca production, and was strictly limited to the drug producing areas (i.e. the Chapare). Second, flying columns accompanied the social protests during key events to employ selective violence to produce incidents between the anti-riot forces and the crowds to up the ante, embolden the masses, and delegitimize the government. Every attempt was made to keep the use of violence 'invisible' in the sense that in the Chapare it was attributed to individuals and amorphous 'drug traffickers' reacting to counter-drug operations, and during the protests it was attributed to marchers reacting to government repression, rather than as a deliberate and systematic line of effort by the Cocalero organization and its allies. Cocaleros and their allies were portrayed as innocents exercising their constitutional rights. The limited and selective use of violence made it politically difficult, and even undesirable (because it seemed so extreme), for the government to declare the Cocaleros as insurgents. Yet this played into Cocalero hands, because by not doing so, successive administrations failed to expose the real danger of the Cocaleros and their intention to overthrow the Bolivian government.

(2) Money gathered from quotas on coca production and trafficking was used to finance the violence, the social protests, and eventually the creation, expansion, and activities of a political party. It was also used to buy off key opposition individuals or groups. The steady flow of money was potent and gave the Cocaleros cohesion, staying power, and the ability to manipulate their environment.

(3) Social protests were the main 'visible' effort of the insurgency. These were neither random nor spontaneous. Each sub-component of the unions known as a *Senda* (trail) was assigned a quota of marchers to

participate in the protests for a determined period of time (called being, *En comision*), usually 18 months. This maneuver force was led by a highly trained cadre of junior and intermediate leaders operating under a very efficient chain of command. During their 'commissions,' marchers were paid a salary by the Federations and their families were looked after. This professional core of Cocalero protesters allied itself with other social groups such as the labor unions, miners, and the indigenous organizations. This allowed them to mobilize rapidly around just about every anti-government cause and to carry out prolonged marches that kept the country in perpetual crisis.

(4) A legal political party was formed that participated in the normal political process. This political party offered itself as the solution to the social chaos *that in reality was its own creation* and served to legally consolidate the gains obtained via illegal and illegitimate means.

(5) An information campaign aided by some mostly European NGOs presented the unrest not as a struggle to perpetuate the narcotics trade but rather as a struggle for long-suppressed indigenous rights. Thus, confronting the Cocaleros became politically incorrect, synonymous with repressing impoverished, indigenous peoples.

Truong Chinh developed the concept that has been translated into English as the 'War of Interlocking.' In Latin America, this term has been translated as the 'Combination of All Forms of Struggle' (*combinación de todas las formas de lucha*). It posits that to take power, all lines of action or effort occur simultaneously. All forms include legal political struggle, illegal political struggle, and various modes of violent, economic, social, and informational (and other) action. Not only do all occur simultaneously but none are rejected. The level of effort of each, or the form or forms of struggle that predominate at any given moment, depends on the relative correlation of forces between the insurgents and the government in time and space. As this correlation of forces shifts, so must the predominant forms of struggle if the insurgency wishes to progress towards victory. Insurgencies that are inflexible in their approaches tend to lose, because they are unable to adapt to the shifting correlations of forces. Their enemies figure out their patterns and crush them.

In twentieth and early twenty-first century insurgency, various forms of violence have generally predominated, because, as the insurgents claim, legal forms of political competition have been exhausted and the only way forward to compete politically is through violence. Within violence, there are various methods of action which change as the correlation of force shifts. When the state is strong and the insurgents are weak, violence tends to be more irregular, and the organizations that perpetuate the violence are more dispersed. As the state weakens, and the insurgency is able to mobilize more resources, the methods of violence tend to become more regular and the form of organization more concentrated. Should the state fail to respond adequately, the insurgency can become a regular or nearly regular army and eventually march into the nation's capital to establish a new government. However, should the government recover its strength, to survive, the insurgency will drop back to more irregular action and dispersed forms of organization. In theory then, insurgencies occur in wave-like patterns as the correlation of forces waxes and wanes, rather than in strictly linear patterns as some have represented. This allows the insurgency to continually act but still conserve its core forces and avoid defeat.

These patterns of rising and falling intensities of violence are what most insurgency analysts focus on. This is because in the West, insurgency is largely seen as a type of warfare, and while insurgents would not dispute that they are carrying out a form of warfare, most insurgencies think of their struggle as a form of politics with warfare being but one of the ways to achieve their political ends. The ultimate goal is to replace the existing regime with a new one. Therefore, there is much more depth to insurgency than just the military or violence line of struggle, even if this is often the predominant line of effort.

In theory, insurgencies can maintain this wave-like pattern of military activity indefinitely if they have the proper depth in other forms of struggle. The Vietnamese called this concept *dau tranh*, which in English means 'struggle'.[2] The Vietnamese maintained that the military struggle could be continually regenerated as long as the political struggle was maintained at a sufficient level. To the Vietnamese, the political struggle was essentially all of the forms of struggle other than the military struggle combined: political legal, political illegal, social, economic, informational, diplomatic, and so forth.[3] Thus, for counterinsurgency, it is necessary but not sufficient to defeat military *dau tranh*. Sufficiency is only achieved when the counterinsurgency also defeats the political struggle. For even if temporarily militarily defeated, the intact political infrastructure will eventually regenerate the military effort.

Since insurgency and counterinsurgency have largely been a military concern in the West, dealing with the non-military side of insurgency is precisely where Western nations are weak. We have built very sophisticated military capabilities to defeat irregular military forces, but the same sophistication does not exist in the non-military arena. There is certainly theoretical understanding of the need for this non-military struggle, but implementation has been severely lacking perhaps due to the military's sub-optimal preparation for this mission and the civilian agencies' lack of consciousness and incentives to perform this task. Without completely discarding the military struggle, it is into this gap that new forms of insurgency are stepping.

Ironically, in focusing on the non-military struggle, they are returning to very old roots, specifically the ideas and theory developed by Lenin. For Lenin, the principal struggle was always political. The military struggle was auxiliary to the political struggle. It could reach very advanced levels of violence, even to regular war, but it was always auxiliary and secondary to the political effort.

Though Mao's synthesis, due to its symbiosis of the military and the political, is often interpreted as akin to guerrilla war on steroids (with good behavior thrown in), nothing could be further from the totality of the approach. This was not different from what we have previously discussed with respect to the Vietnamese.[4] It was the Cubans with *foco* theory who subordinated the political effort to the military vanguard.

Still, Mao in many ways was captive to his time and place. Military effort achieved primacy in the seizure of power. Lenin was theoretically more flexible and wrote:

> Under no circumstances does Marxism confine itself to the forms of struggle possible and in existence at the given moment only, recognizing as it does that new forms of struggle, unknown to the participants of the given period, *inevitably* arise as the given social situation, changes. In this respect Marxism *learns*, if we may so express it, from mass practice, and makes no claim whatever to *teach* the masses forms of struggle invented by 'systematizers' in the seclusion of their studies.[5]

In other words, Lenin advocated that revolutionaries should embrace what produced results, and that they adapt and evolve as the situation evolved. He also wrote:

> Marxism demands an absolutely *historical* examination of the question of the forms of struggle. To treat this question apart from the concrete historical situation betrays a failure to understand the rudiments of dialectical materialism. At different stages of economic evolution, depending on differences in political, national-cultural, living and other conditions, different forms of struggle come to the fore and become the principal forms of struggle; and in connection with this, the secondary, auxiliary forms of struggle undergo change in their turn. To attempt to answer yes or no to the question whether any particular means of struggle should be used, without making a detailed examination of the concrete situation of the given movement at the given stage of its development, means completely to abandon the Marxist position.[6]

The Bolivian Cocaleros did this often, consistently and brilliantly, which the following narrative demonstrates.

Evolution of the Bolivian model

In 1980, Roberto Suarez – the world's first king of cocaine, who was later eclipsed by Pablo Escobar – financed a military coup by General Luis Garcia Meza. For the next two years, the Bolivian government became known for its close relationship to drug trafficking, earning the nickname of the 'narco-state.' Under the narco-state, the government actively collaborated in the expansion of coca cultivation in the Chapare, a jungle area in the Department of Santa Cruz. At the same time, assisted by the Argentine military government, it conducted a heavy crack-down on militant leftists. Under international condemnation, unable to meet its economic goals and facing a miners' strike that took the country to the verge of civil war, the military accelerated the transition to democracy, allowing

Hernan Siles Suazo, originally elected in 1980, to assume the presidency. The military coup had been launched to prevent his inauguration as he was considered a Marxist by the coup leaders.

Siles Suazo inherited a poor economic situation, but the socialist economic policies he implemented only accelerated a more severe economic crisis. By 1984, the Bolivian mines – until then Bolivia's main source of revenue – were economically broken. This was due to a combination of exhaustion of the mines, reduction of the price of Bolivian minerals, and economically unsustainable labor costs.

The mining unions that were behind much of this lack of sustainable labor costs had been formed in the early twentieth century. By the 1930s, they were dominated by Marxist thought and organization, which gave them a class struggle world-view, strategic thinking, planning, organization, and discipline, as well as a tradition of semi-violent militant struggle. The latter was reinforced when veterans of the Chaco War returned to the mines after 1935, bringing their personal side-arms with them, and, more importantly, experience in a war that was considered by many to be the first modern war in Latin America. The armed miners combined with other groups carried out the 1952 revolution through the National Revolutionary Movement (MNR). The MNR briefly jailed, retired, or suspended the army officer corps and organized workers and peasants into militias,[7] distributing to them surplus weapons from the Chaco War. These weapons have remained in the hands of the workers and peasants ever since. This meant that social protests in Bolivia usually involved violence, particularly when the miners went on strike, because they carried the conviction that they could defeat the security forces. In addition to their firearms, they also carried sticks of dynamite, which they were fond of tossing at their foes.

When the mines broke – to avoid sustained violence – the government offered to each miner a severance check of approximately USD 2000.00. A large proportion of the ex-miners took their severance pay and migrated to the Chapare region, where they acquired plots of land and began growing coca. Coca production soon expanded to some 40,000 hectares.

Yet the new democratic governments were not as tolerant of cocaine trafficking as the previous military regime had been. In August 1983, the government signed an agreement to receive US counternarcotics assistance to reduce drug trafficking to the United States from the Chapare. The United States trained a 300-man police unit, the *Unidad Móvil Policial para Áreas Rurales* (UMOPAR), also known as the Leopards.[8] The UMOPAR along with 1500 Bolivian troops entered the Chapare in mid-1984 and began to conduct eradication operations. In response, the coca-growing peasants organized unions along the lines of the model they brought with them from the mines. Eventually, the unions would represent 35,000 families grouped into 6 Federations which actively resisted the eradication efforts of the troops. The military was unprepared for such a strong peasant response and soon withdrew its forces.[9]

Blast furnace

In July 1986, the United States launched Operation *Blast Furnace* in cooperation with the Bolivian government. This combined operation involved operational troops from the Bolivian police and army with logistical and transportation support from the US military, to include six Black Hawk helicopters and 160 pilots and maintenance personnel to provide air mobility to the Bolivian troops. The operation lasted four months and although the results were short-lived, they did cause the price of coca to drop below the cost of production for the duration of the operation.

This also consolidated the power of the coca growers' federation of unions, which in the best miner union tradition, organized violent mass protests against the counter-narcotics operations, one of which managed to expel 150 Bolivian and US troops from the town of Santa Ana de Yacuma in the Beni at the end of the operation.[10] They also discovered that the mass protests in the Chapare had an unintended strategic consequence. The two national highways between the breadbasket of eastern Bolivia and the capital, La Paz, ran through the Chapare. The protests on the roads caused scarcity of food and other items in La Paz, which then caused general dissatisfaction with the government. Government concessions followed to prevent greater uprisings in the capital. This would become a key component in the insurgent strategy.

In this way *Blast Furnace* both set the pattern of US-Bolivian government cooperation and the pattern of resistance to these operations by the Cocaleros. Each side absorbed lessons learned and prepared for the future. On the one hand, the relative success of *Blast Furnace* caused the United States to develop plans for more sustained and better resourced counter-narcotics operations; on the other, the Cocalero Federations began making plans to up the ante and more effectively resist the counter-narcotics operations.

Law 1008

The Bolivian government passed the 'Coca and Controlled Substances Regimen' or Law 1008 in July 1988. This law identified cocaine as an illegal substance. It identified and controlled all substances that could be employed as precursor chemicals for the production of cocaine. However, it differentiated between coca for traditional use, which remained legal, and coca grown for cocaine, deemed illegal.[11] It established an office to organize and manage counternarcotics operations, the National Council against Illicit Drug Trafficking, known by its Spanish acronym, CONALTID.[12]

It divided the coca growing regions of the country into three categories. Designated as a site of legitimate activity was a zone in the Yungas of approximately 12,000 hectares of coca where traditional, low-alkaloid, coca was grown. This was used for the traditional chewing leaves, teas, and other products that have long been sold openly in Bolivia. An excess transition zone, where coca was being grown for illegal purposes, but where crops were already being substituted for a variety of legal and legitimate crops, was exempted from coercive action. A third zone of illicit production, mostly in the Chapare, was designated for aggressive eradication and alternative development.[13]

Law 1008 became the bane of the Cocaleros' existence, and abrogating this law became their main political objective and the justification of their insurgency. Violence in the form of military action was always considered a viable option, and the Cocaleros prepared for the possibility of open warfare. They developed ties to regional and international terrorist organizations and began importing advisers to teach them methods of irregular warfare. In particular, they were interested in techniques for the manufacture and employment of explosive devices. To instruct them, they brought in advisers from *Sendero Luminoso* in Peru, FARC and ELN in Colombia, and the Basque ETA. However, they did not limit themselves to this method. To develop a pool of militarily trained personnel, they ordered their young men to fulfill their national military service obligation, the evasion of which was nearly a national sport in other sectors of society. Favored was volunteering for service in Bolivia's elite units, such as the Parachute regiment, the Ranger regiment, or the *Satinadores*.[14] After returning from service, these men were organized into a paramilitary organization known as the Reservation Guard (*Guardia de Reserva*), as part of the Chapare is supposedly a national forest. Later, this force was renamed the Syndicate Police. From then on, armed resistance to police and army counterdrug operations became increasingly violent and featured ambushes, the employment of snipers, assaults, and improvised explosive devices (IEDs). It was not difficult to obtain weapons as the Bolivian military suffered from notorious corruption. Officers and NCOs willingly sold weapons and ammunition, particularly to men returning home after military service. While most recruits had little money personally, their contacts invariably did.[15]

Another important discovery for the Cocaleros was the self-imposed ethical and philosophical restraints of US-supported operations. Americans were highly sensitive to the poor social conditions in Bolivia, hence their constant concern to offer social programs and alternative development initiatives along with the counter-narcotics operations. They also reacted strongly to the presence and suffering of women and children amongst protesters. Finally, US and European media, heavily influenced by their own NGOs, had a significant impact on the policy debate in their own countries and the international pressure brought to bear on the Bolivian government. Playing this card, as would also be done by the Zapatistas in Chiapas, became an important component in the overall anti-government effort.

Additionally, the Cocaleros quickly came to the conclusion that they needed to influence national policy through political participation. The first efforts involved offering money to existing political parties to represent them and allow them to place electoral candidates. The Cocaleros were not particularly concerned about the ideological orientation of the party, and they approached several disparate parties. They were universally rejected, except by the leftist Izquierda Unida Party (PIU). Joining with PIU allowed them to participate in legal electoral politics and obtain some success, as four Cocalero representatives, among them Evo Morales, were elected to Congress in 1989.

Meanwhile, as Bolivia went through a series of economic and social crises, coca cultivation began to expand. In 1986, coca crops were estimated at 40,613 hectares. By 1993, they had reached 59,817 hectares.[16] At this time, coca was grown in Bolivia and Peru and then flown to Colombia for processing in local cocaine labs. However, the Colombians subsequently discovered that certain variants of coca grew well in their soil and stopped importing the leaves from outside. Colombians also took the refining process to Bolivia and Peru, where the locals began to process the leaves in their own countries because it was much more efficient to transport coca base or cocaine powder than to transport leaves. Subsequently, the trafficking from Bolivia became more direct to the final markets, and profits increased for the Cocaleros. By 1997, Bolivia was exporting 250 metric tons of cocaine per year with a street value of USD 7.5 billion.[17]

Cocalero strategy

The Cocalero Federations made strategic decisions through conferences and plenums, following the Marxist doctrine for labor unions. Conferences are held to establish strategy, plenums are held to make course adjustments to the strategic plan. At a 1995 Conference, a faction of the leadership, to include the President of the Six Federations, Evo Morales, proposed that the Cocaleros launch classic guerrilla warfare to overthrow the Bolivian government in order to put a stop to US-supported counternarcotics operations. Their view was that in the end, this was the only way to ultimately defend coca.[18] The chief political adviser for the Cocaleros, a long-time veteran from the miners' movement, Filemon Escobar, acknowledged that the conditions for guerrilla warfare in the Chapare were far more favorable than Ñancahuasú had been for Che Guevara in 1967. However, he warned the Cocaleros that despite this, an all-out guerrilla war would only attract the wrath of the US, and the movement would eventually be crushed.[19] Instead, he advocated a more Leninist approach of continuing to emphasize mass protests to push the rest of the country to the brink of collapse, accompanied by the creation of a Cocalero-controlled party, which he called the 'political instrument,' to participate in legal electoral politics.

After debating the merits of different approaches, the Cocalero leadership largely accepted Escobar's proposal. It kept the hawks within the fold, though, by approving the use of organized violence to resist to the counter-narcotics operations in the Chapare. This pacified the hawks, who included Evo Morales, because they continued to develop their fighting force for the day when it would eventually be used. They were extremely skeptical about the possibility of the Federation ever making significant gains through the legal political system and wanted to be ready to implement open warfare when the other options had been exhausted.[20] In this way, the Cocaleros were always prepared to implement much greater violence.

Lenin's approach to strategy is clearly evident. In his 1906 essay, 'Lessons of the Moscow Uprising,' Lenin discusses the internal debates his party had over the merits of the armed struggle versus unarmed forms of political struggle. It is clear that Lenin's view of insurgency contemplated a progression starting with street protests that, because of state intransigence and repression, would inevitably progress to barricades and end in an armed uprising. While the main action might be protests, the communists could not reject the option of armed struggle, and in fact needed to be wholly prepared for it.[21] The question was not in accepting or rejecting the use of armed struggle, rather the art of how and when to apply it. Lenin called this moment, 'the fusion of terrorism and the mass movement,' but this fusion needed to take place as part of a process of 'sanely and coolly weighing the conditions under which they would become possible.'[22] Until that day, they needed to intensively prepare. Lenin advocated that this preparation not only involve training and gathering weapons but also 'separate armed actions, such as attacks by armed squads on the police and on troops during public meetings, or on prisons, government offices, etc.'[23] This is almost exactly what the Cocaleros did.

Plan dignity

The Cocalero approach was severely tested during the 1998–2001 government of Hugo Banzer who, supported by the United States, implemented *Plan Dignidad* (*Plan Dignity*), a comprehensive counter-narcotics plan with the slogan of 'Zero Cocaine.'[24] Much criticized in anti-government circles, the truth is that this plan nearly succeeded in defeating the Cocaleros and eradicating coca cultivation in the Chapare.

Upon taking office, President Banzer convened a National Dialogue with broad sectors of society. The consensus supported completely eradicating drug trafficking from Bolivia to comply with the 1988 United Nations Declaration on Combating Drug Trafficking, to alleviate the impact on consumer nations, and to clean the image of Bolivia abroad.[25] Restoring dignity to Bolivia's name is why Banzer's plan was so-named.

Bolivia worked closely with the United States government to develop the counter-narcotics plan. The plan was composed of four pillars: (1) Alternative Development, (2) Prevention, (3) Eradication, and (4) Interdiction.[26] The objective was to completely eradicate illegal coca-cocaine production and trafficking from Bolivia by the end of the Banzer government and to incorporate the approximately 38,000 illicit coca producing families into the legal economy.[27] The US provided generous assistance on multiple levels. To help the country recover economically, the United States granted credit for development or food assistance exchanges, which significantly reduced Bolivia's foreign debt. In addition, the US put significant effort into developing effective alternative development projects. This was combined with robust counter-narcotics aid. Overall, the plan cost USD 952 million, of which USD 108 million (11%) was for eradication, USD 129 million (14%) for interdiction, USD 15 million (2%) for prevention, and USD 700 million (73%) for alternative development.[28] In FY2000, the US gave Bolivia USD 25 million counter-narcotics assistance and USD 85 million in alternative development assistance. For FY 2002, it provided USD 48.5 million in counter-narcotics aid and USD 74.46 million in alternative development aid. In FY 2003, Bolivia received USD 50 million in counter-narcotics assistance and USD 82.6 million in economic and social programs.[29] This aid was designed to offset the economic losses incurred, as it was estimated that drug trafficking injected approximately USD 600 million per year into the economy, up to 8% of the Bolivian Gross Domestic Product.[30]

The task force that carried out *Plan Dignity* was composed of the Counter Narcotics Struggle Special Forces (FELCN), the UMOPAR, the Task Force (Blue Devils [Navy], Red Devils [Air Force] and Green Devils [Army]), the Intelligence and Special Operations Group, the Chemical Substances Investigation Group, the Financial Investigative Unit, and the Drug Detecting Canine Center. Between 1997 and 2001, they carried out over 15,000 operations.[31]

Initially, *Plan Dignity* was not popular, and many Bolivians empathized with the plight of the Cocaleros, focusing on the economic misery caused by the eradication of coca. However, public opinion changed when the true nature of illicit cocaine and the criminals who controlled it became public.[32]

Notwithstanding, *Plan Dignity* was fiercely resisted, and violence was constant. While the figures are incomplete, between 1997 and 2003, the Andean Information Network (Red Andina de Información) reported that according to the Villa Tunari Public Defender (Defensoria del Pueblo) 35 Cocaleros were killed, 587 were seriously wounded, and 700 were jailed. During the same period and according to the same records, the military and police lost approximately 27 killed and 135 wounded.[33] This was probably low. Bolivian law prohibited spraying so eradication had to be done by hand. As a result, security forces were exposed to Cocalero action. The Cocalero military wing harassed military units from the moment they entered the Chapare, attacking their patrol camps day and night with sharpshooters, only desisting when they left. They also carried out ambushes with IEDs. Often these were placed to prevent the removal of roadblocks, and automatic fire was sprayed after either the IEDs exploded or when the army sent forward men to deactivate the explosives.[34] In 2001, the anti-explosives unit of the Chapare Ecological Police recorded 109 harassment attacks, 39 ambushes, and the successful deactivation of 22 IEDs. It also recorded losses of seven killed and 50 wounded.[35] The International Campaign to Ban Landmines reported that the Ecological Police put their casualties in 2003 at 7 military killed and at least 91 wounded by all causes, mostly by IEDs.[36]

In addition to the ambushes, IEDs, and harassment attacks, the Cocaleros carried out simultaneous protests, blocking roads, and surrounding eradication camps to force the Army out. Occasionally, they would also attempt to overrun the camps both with violence and with protesting masses. However, Cocalero resistance was not only limited to the Chapare. In the year 2000, for example, they carried out a large march that blocked the National Highway between Cochabamba and Santa Cruz, causing estimated economic losses of more than USD 100 million.[37]

Evolution of the political instrument

In politics, the Cocaleros continued to evolve. While they had been incorporated into the Izquierda Unida Party (PIU), which happily accepted their money, they did not control it, and they discovered that outside of the Chapare, the cause of coca was rejected by the vast majority of the population. Building upon failed past experiences of miners' unions, they decided they needed to expand their movement to represent more than just the Cocaleros.[38] For example, the cause of greater indigenous rights was widely accepted, not only by the majority of the national polity but especially by sectors of the international community interested in Bolivia. Based on this analysis, the Cocaleros very pragmatically shifted resources and manpower to aggressively coopt the indigenous rights movement and its leaders. This was not an unnatural shift since many of the Cocaleros were of partial or full indigenous blood, particularly of Aymara ancestry, and many were also either part of indigenous organizations (e.g. CSUTCB) or had relatives in them.

Cocalero penetration of indigenous organizations was not always well-received, but those who resisted were gradually marginalized or eliminated, and eventually the Cocaleros were able to dominate the most important indigenous groups. This was done through a systematic process of 'divide and conquer,' manipulating the relative lax discipline of the non-Cocalero organizations and exploiting the Cocaleros' comparatively vast wealth to influence the plenums of these organizations, particularly in getting Cocalero or pro-Cocalero candidates voted into leadership positions from which they could then steer the organization into making common cause with the Cocaleros.[39] In this way, they were able to dominate the CSUTCB and the miners' unions.

This broad national coalition then created the need for a legal national political movement, not controlled by others but fully controlled by the Cocaleros, which could represent all of these groups with a single political platform. The Cocalero leadership decided that it was no longer efficient to 'buy' political space from others. Instead, it would be better (and cheaper) to have a political party of their own.

When this decision was made, it was too close to the 1997 elections to go through the bureaucracy of creating a new party to participate in the elections, so they looked for an existing registered political party that they could take over. They found what they were looking for in the Movement to Socialism or MAS.[40] MAS was led by David Añez Pedraza, who had broken away from the Bolivian Socialist Falange in 1987 and formed the Unzaguista-Movement to Socialism or (MAS-U). In 1995, the party was registered in Cochabamba as the Movement to Socialism, dropping Unzaguista. The party was taken over by the Cocaleros for the 1997 elections. They essentially bought the party and chose David Añez as their candidate, because Evo Morales still lacked faith in electoral politics, convinced that armed struggle was the only way that power could be achieved.[41] Although the alliance of Cocaleros, Indigenous groups, and miners under the umbrella of MAS was too weak at the time to prevent the relentless forward progress of *Plan Dignity*, the Cocalero-controlled political instrument would pay off in the end by lending a veneer of institutional legitimacy to the insurgency.

At the time, *Plan Dignity* by most measures was highly successful. Net reduction of coca cultivation was approximately 70% between 1996 and 2001. Illegal coca production in the Yungas was nearly eliminated, and coca production in the Chapare was significantly reduced. Coca cultivation in Bolivia dropped steadily from 48,600 hectares in 1995 to 14,600 hectares by 2000.[42] Of the 38,900 hectares of coca in the Chapare in 1997, by February 2001, only 6,000 hectares were left.[43] Cocaine exportation dropped to less than 70 metric tons, about 28% of its peak levels.[44]

The water war: a tipping point

At the Cocaleros' nadir, when the Banzer government was at the height of its success with *Plan Dignity*, an event occurred that began to resurrect the fortunes of the Cocalero movement. Cochabamba is a city with an abundant natural supply of water. However, for various reasons, it has an extremely inefficient water supply system. In the late 1990s, it was believed that the solution was privatization. A contract was signed in 1999 with International Waters Limited (IWL, a British subsidiary of the San Francisco-based Bechtel Company), which created a Bolivian company, *Aguas del Tunari*.[45] Part of the negotiations was an agreement that rates could increase as much as 35%. This was acceptable because of the capital investment that would be needed and the expectation that water services would be extended to most inhabitants and become much more efficient than before. However, when the rate hikes were implemented, rates went up by as much as 200–300%, figures which in many cases represented up to 25% of a resident's monthly income.[46] The resulting anger fed organization of protest.

The first protesters came from the informal water entrepreneurs who tapped natural wells and aquifers around Cochabamba. This group's livelihood was destroyed when the contract with IWL gave Aguas del Turani rights over all sources of water in the region. The entrepreneurs created the Departmental Federation of Cochabamba Irrigators or FEDECOR. FEDECOR carried out the first relatively small protests in November 1999. Later, they united with the disenchanted consumers to form the 'Water and Life Coordinator' (hereafter referred to as the Water Coordinator), which sought the assistance of the Cocaleros to develop their plan of action.

Although severely battered by *Plan Dignity*, the Cocaleros still had money, organization, and experience. They had strong ties to Cochabamba through family and class, as many of the miners displaced in the 1980s who had not settled in the nearby Chapare had gone to Cochabamba city or its suburbs. Many Cocalero children and youth from the Chapare studied in Cochabamba's schools and universities, so it was not hard to convince the Cocaleros to send cadre to participate in the protests. By January 2000, the Water Coordinator consisted of FEDECOR, the rural and urban teachers unions, the Cochabamba factory workers, university students, the Chapare Cocaleros, and the Federation of Interdepartmental Transporters.[47]

This coalition carried out its initial protests during 11–13 January 2000, paralyzing the city. The protests ebbed and flowed through March, with cycles of protest, police repression, negotiation, and lulls. At the end of March, the government negotiating position began to weaken, and the Water Coordinator, sensing it was close to a tipping point, pulled out of negotiations and began what it called the 'popular consultation.' After getting 50,000 people to express in favor of rescinding the contract with Aguas del Tunari, the Water Coordinator called for a 'Final Battle.'[48] As in subsequent events, the Cocalero objective was no longer to gain improved water services for a reasonable price; it was about defeating the government and increasing national political leverage.

Not all of the coalition supported this 'final battle.' Many noted that the government was willing to negotiate a modification of the water contract that addressed the protesters' demands. The Civic Committee, Federation of Private Businesses, and Public Transportation Workers dropped their support for the Water Coordinator and accused the entity of now representing different interests. Indeed, they were correct. The Water Coordinator, by this time almost completely controlled by the Cocaleros, announced that it was no longer interested in negotiations, that it would only lift the protests if the Aguas del Tunari contract was completely rescinded.[49] Indefinite road blocks by Cocaleros and peasants in large numbers were implemented, and squads of young men violently invaded the offices of Aguas del Tunari, destroying and vandalizing the building and its offices.

The government reacted by sending military and police to break up the marches. They arrested the Water Coordinator leaders and used tear gas and rubber bullets to disperse the crowds. The Cocalero reaction was to intensify the protests. This coincided with a strike by the Police Special Group, the anti-riot police, demanding a 50% salary increase. One crowd tried to take over the headquarters of the Army 7th Division. To prevent this, some of the soldiers fired into the crowd, wounding several people, and a captain killed a 17-year-old youth. The image of the latter was repeatedly broadcast on TV until the government cut off the broadcasts, but the damage had already been done. The public was outraged, and the incident was used as a symbol to strengthen the mobilization even as military officers were reporting skilled tactics and maneuvering by 'small squads of men' who led the crowd and harassed the army and police. These reports were largely ignored outside the security forces. Another 30 persons were injured in the struggle, and then the Banzer government, seeing that it was facing politically unacceptable levels of violence, backed down and rescinded the Aguas del Tunari contract.[50]

The importance of the 'Water War' was that it was first time the Cocaleros participated in a social protest that was greater than their parochial concerns – and it had resulted in victory, not only against the Bolivian government, but against, in Cocalero minds, a 'neoliberal' international corporation, a perceived tool of 'Yankee Imperialism,' a foe similar in essence to the counter-narcotics policy. This was extremely important, because the victory signaled to them that 'the US' could be defeated. This experience taught the Cocaleros the strategic importance of making common cause with other social organizations and began a pattern of the Cocaleros seeking social conflict opportunities into which they could insert themselves. The objective, as in Mao's formulation of contradictions, was to rapidly escalate relatively minor controversies into major national social protests. For this very purpose, the different organizations banded together and formed the Mobilization Central Coordinator (Coordinadora de Movilizaciones Única Nacional) or COMUNAL to organize and coordinate national level protests whenever the opportunity arose.

Finally, it was the first time that the Cocaleros protested in a major city, and this taught them that the urban space, not the countryside, was the location for decisive battles. Demonstrating their trademark tactical flexibility, the Cocaleros quickly assimilated urban tactics into their essential toolbox. Still, though they noted the power and impact that protesting and operating in a major city had, they also realized that battle in a regional city was not decisive. For such a result, they had to conduct urban operations in the center of political power. Thus they concluded they had to take the battle to the capital, La Paz.

End of *plan dignity*

Cocalero ability to join and take over protests led by other organizations soon manifested itself. The Teachers' Federation declared an indefinite national strike in support of instructors from Oruro, who began a March from Oruro to La Paz and organized protesters and hunger strikes in all of the major cities. COMUNAL joined the teachers and organized road blocks along all of the country's major highways, particularly the east-west highways between Santa Cruz, Cochabamba, and La Paz. It also mobilized the CSUTCB and the COB to protest in the Altiplano, especially in and around Achacachi. What had started out as a teachers' protest was essentially taken over by Evo Morales and the Cocaleros in the Chapare and by Felipe Quispe in Achacachi.[51] The roads remained blocked for over a month in the Chapare, requiring military force to open them and disperse the protesters. Reportedly, even businessmen protested against the government, because the road blocks were seriously affecting their enterprises.[52]

The government attempted to break the movement by negotiating separately with each of the groups, and it achieved what would be the last success of a democratic government in dealing with the Cocalero movement. On August 23, the CSUTCB signed a document of 70 points with the government and suspended the roadblocks in La Paz. Felipe Quispe, CSTUCB chief executive and the most influential indigenous leader of the day, declared that he was not against the national counternarcotics policy. Little did Quispe understand that he had just signed the end of his political career.

Outraged, Morales believed he could precipitate open rebellion and ordered the Cocalero columns to try to take the military Base Verde III located 190 km from Cochabamba and the eradication outposts of Loma Alta, Urkupina, Bolivar A, Bolivar B, and Isinuta. The military reported 'many but undetermined' casualties among the assaulting Cocaleros during the August 13–September 26 assaults. However, the Cocaleros only admitted the death of a single woman. On 27 September, the Cocalero movement took a number of journalists to Loma Alta, where they witnessed the 'protests,' a force of approximately 800 Cocaleros assaulting the military outpost. Right in front of their eyes, a Cocalero was hit by rifle fire and died.

Try as they might, the Cocaleros could not overrun the bases, and the military would not withdraw. Instead, Banzer ordered a huge mobilization of troops to force open all the highways in the country. Internal Cocalero documents about these events heavily criticized Morales, and some Cocaleros even demanded that he be removed from his position. A recommendation was made to shift focus from the counter-eradication effort to broader political action.

Yet the Cocaleros were closer to success than they believed. Resolve of the government was fading as a political transition took place. Banzer, due to illness (lung cancer), withdrew from public life, and power was increasingly passed to his vice president, who became president on 7 August 2001. This would be decisive for the Cocalero movement and for the country. Although Quiroga declared that he would continue *Plan Dignity*, he was not as strong-willed as Banzer. From the very beginning, he tried a softer approach towards the Cocaleros, which had immediate consequences.

In November, the Cocaleros upped the ante by declaring road blocks between Santa Cruz and Cochabamba. The government declared that it would not allow the roads to be blocked and sent in 2000 police and Army reinforcements to secure natural chokepoints. Evo Morales declared a total blockade at Eterazama and concentrated a huge crowd of Cocaleros. This led to days of confrontation that reached a peak on 15 November, when clashes led to the deaths of three Cocaleros. Violence continued through 22 November, after which the government sought a way out by accepting the mediation of the Catholic Church, the Public Defender, and the Permanent Assembly on Human Rights from 26 to 28 November. The Cocaleros got exactly what they wanted. In exchange for lifting the roadblocks, the government agreed to suspend coca eradication in the Chapare.[53] Quiroga had lost his nerve in the face of increasingly large and violent political protests.

Quiroga's softer approach had immediate and palpable consequences. Coca crops quickly rose to 19,900 hectares by 1 June 2001. A GAO report noted that US and Bolivian officials attributed the rise to the Quiroga government's faltering commitment to crop elimination and a weakened governing coalition. They also indicated that they thought members of the government coalition might be making deals with the well-organized Cocaleros political party. In addition, critics, and even some who had supported *Plan Dignity*, claimed that while eradication has been successful in dramatically reducing coca cultivation, it had hurt the overall economy.[54]

The faltering of Quiroga's commitment to *Plan Dignity* and the weakening of the government coalition became the tipping point to include increasingly violent action against the government. Lenin's fusion of terrorism with the mass movement began to take place. After the Water War, armed squads that carried out violent action began to accompany virtually every protest.

Black February

The successes obtained from the Water War and the Highway Blockades encouraged others to carry out protests of their own, which in turn were magnified by the Cocaleros and their allies to support and strengthen their own position as a national power broker. This further weakened the government. In 2001 and 2002, violent social protests were daily occurrences, wearing down government will and ability to govern.[55] Increasing government incapacity in turn generated broader support for the 'political instrument' or Cocalero political party. The percentages of the vote in support of the MAS began to rise. President Gonzalo Sanchez de Lozada, or 'Goni', won a very close election in 2002, but perhaps as important, MAS achieved a very close second place. No party achieved a majority, so Goni became president of Bolivia with the support of less than a third of the population.

On 9 February 2003, the president announced a bill to freeze salaries and raise taxes by 12.5% for the top 20% of taxpayers.[56] This decision was made because of serious budget deficits and the desire to avoid the alternative of raising fuel prices, which would have a greater impact on the poor. The Cocaleros saw it as a measure that could be exploited given the relative weakness of Sanchez de Lozada's government. On 11 February, the Special Security Group Police in close proximity to the National Palace in La Paz went on strike to demand salary raises. On 12 February, the COB ceased negotiations with the government and declared a 24-h period of civil disobedience. The CSUTCB also announced a 'rising' against the government. Finally, the Cocaleros, through the 'People's High Command,' declared a strike in the city of Cochabamba.[57]

That same day, students from the Colegio Ayacucho, mobilized by the teachers' union, marched to Murillo Plaza and were confronted by soldiers of the Colorados Presidential Guard in riot gear, who attempted to stop them. The soldiers were forced to retreat into the Palace when rebel police fired tear gas at them, an eventuality for which they were unprepared, having no gas masks.[58] This left the outside of the building unprotected, and the students threw rocks, which they were carrying in their backpacks, at the government palace, breaking some of the windows.[59] The presidential guard then tossed tear gas grenades from inside the building down on the students and began launching gas grenades at the police on the other side of Murillo Plaza. The police launched tear gas grenades back at the army.

Attempts were made to mediate negotiations between the Army and Police, but these broke down. Eventually, the tear gas escalated to bullets, which according to the OAS were fired first by the police.[60] The Palace Guard was reinforced by elements of the Military Police, and additional police reinforced the strikers. Snipers on roofs, almost certainly from the Police Immediate Action Group or GAI, began shooting into the palace.[61] This, combined with the possibility of a mob invasion of the palace, forced the President and his Ministers to evacuate via armored car.[62]

By late afternoon and evening, there were no police patrolling the city. Organized mobs, some of which showed the same skills and tactical proficiency reported during the Water War and some led by police, set fire to the Vice Presidency, the Congressional Library and Archive, Ministry of Work and Sustainable Development, the Military Court, and the headquarters of the three political parties of the governing coalition.[63] Though students from the UMSA saved the Congressional Library and Archive from burning, preventing the loss of national historic documents, mobs with similar intent were mobilized in Oruro, Cochabamba, and Santa Cruz. Clearly, an attempt was being made to destabilize the entire country.

On 13 February, clashes broke out between the military, deploying in various directions to restore order in La Paz and El Alto, and the mobs, resulting in approximately 11 killed and 50 wounded. Many claimed that the military reaction was excessive, and several officers were investigated and put on trial, although human rights groups claimed that the judicial process was slow and inefficient.[64] At the request of the Bolivian government, a multinational team from the OAS came to Bolivia to investigate and found that the army had acted legitimately and proportionately, although it questioned some of the rules of engagement and decisions made by specific officers. In general, the OAS laid responsibility for the violence squarely on the police.[65] Ominously, the reports of organized groups operating during the events again went largely unexamined.

Gas War (Black October)

Black February showed the Cocaleros that their thesis of action against the political center was correct. In addition, the relative weakness of the national government made it so that a relatively small political conflict could be escalated through mass protests, and peripheral violence into a major national crisis that could push the government to the edge of collapse. The Cocaleros were certain that if they pushed just a little harder, the 'next time' would drive the government across the point of no return. It was now merely a matter of time before the next major event which they determined would be the culminating event.

The Cocaleros began to prepare by organizing several groups: the CSUTCB, which controlled the Aymara-dominated high plain around La Paz; the *Central Obrera Regional* or COR, which controlled the gateway to La Paz, El Alto; and the *Unión Revolucionaria de Maestros* (URMA), which controlled La Paz itself. Each received money and various other forms of support, and agreements were made to mobilize forces, when the time was right. Felipe Quispe, leader of the CSUTCB, later revealed that a plan was developed to take place in three phases, with Venezuela and various NGOs providing funding.[66] The phases, at least for CSUTCB, were: *Phase Flea*, provoke the enemy and bite him; *Phase Fire Ant (Sikititi)*, swarm the enemy with protests; and *Phase Taraxchi*, the final assault on the establishments and homes of the powerful and oligarchy.[67] These phases correspond quite well to Lenin's concepts of escalation from protest to armed uprising. While this concept may have been unique to the CSUTCB, the overall plan was similar to that animating all of the major opponents of the state. The opportunity to implement the plan presented itself in September and October of that same year, a series of events that is commonly called 'The Gas War' or 'Black October.'

The government was experiencing serious trouble with the national budget. The solution seemed to be natural gas. To earn additional revenue, the Bolivian government was exploring deals to sell part of its huge reserves to American and Mexican firms. The Sanchez de Lozada government estimated that sales to Mexico alone were projected to produce government revenues of USD 400 million per year over a period of 20 years. The opposition claimed that this deal only benefited the multi-national companies involved.

Still, it was the decision to build a pipeline from Bolivia to export the gas north via the port of Mejillones, Chile that led to explosion. The plan was for the gas to be sent via pipeline to Chile, where it would be liquefied and then exported. In Bolivia, wounded national pride over the loss of its coast to Chile in the War of the Pacific, 1879–1883, had left sensitivity to any such dealings with Chile. Popular opinion favored instead a pipeline to the Port of Ilo, Peru. This meant a pipeline that was 260 km longer than the proposed pipeline to Mejillones, thus much more expensive, making it economically less attractive. However, the Peruvians tried to make the option attractive by offering very generous terms to the Bolivians. The opposition also wanted to keep more of the money in the country by doing the liquefaction processing in Bolivia. President Quiroga had declined to make a decision and left it to Sanchez de Losada when he became president in 2002. Sanchez de Losada, who was a pragmatist, expressed a preference for the Chile route. The Cocaleros and their allies took full advantage of this preference.

CSUTCB made the opening move to implement *Phase Flea*. The first clash took place at Warisata, a major Aymara center on the road to Lake Titicaca, where the locals blocked the highways during the night to protest – not the sale of gas via Chile – rather the government's failure to comply with an agreement signed earlier by government ministers. The blockades trapped many international tourists. The military was sent on 20 September to rescue the tourists and to sort out the situation. As they began making arrests and breaking up the crowds, the protesters called CSUTCB head Felipe Quispe concerning the arrests of three protest leaders and claimed that the army was going to kill them. Quispe ordered those of his followers who were members of the EGTK,[68] or who had been trained in guerrilla warfare, to dig up the weapons and ambush the security forces.[69] The ambush killed one policeman and wounded several others.[70] The objective of the ambush was to attract response and assassinate Minister of Defense Carlos Sánchez Berzaín, but he left Warisata in a helicopter, which CSUTCB had not anticipated.[71] The army reported they were attacked with modern, high caliber weapons. The protesters claimed that they were only using old Chaco War weapons that had been distributed to the popular militias in the 1950s.[72] In the subsequent firefight, four locals were killed, including an 8-year old girl, and the military was able to break the blockade.

Phase Flea was a total success. The death of the girl helped distract the nation from the reality that CSUTCB had initiated the violence; it stirred emotions and served as an initial rallying cry for a much larger protest against the government. The successful mobilization of mass protests put into motion *Phase Fire Ant*. As Felipe Quispe admitted years later, cadre were sent to whip up the masses.[73] On 25 September, the COB (essentially, the miners' federation) declared it was joining the protests; on 26 September, Evo Morales' MAS joined; and on 27 September, CSUTCB joined. On 29 September, an 'indefinite' strike was declared. Members of the three organizations began converging on La Paz on 3 October.

The Cocaleros anticipated that this next phase would see the definitive merger of 'terrorism with the mass movement,' in other words, that it would get very violent, that the government might lash out aggressively out of desperation and target their leaders. To ensure the survival of their leaders and make sure that the Cocaleros would be in a position to pick up the pieces after it was over, Evo Morales was sent out of the country. He travelled to Libya, Geneva, and Caracas and only returned when the danger had passed and the outcome of the uprising was relatively assured.[74]

The key to the protest was the city of El Alto, the gateway to the city of La Paz. La Paz is built in a bowl-like valley surrounded on all sides by steep slopes. At the top is the Altiplano or high plains. La Paz is connected to eastern Bolivia by a highway that winds up the steep slopes and comes out on this high plain. Most commodities (food, fuel, and other items) that supply La Paz pass along this road from eastern Bolivia. Over the years, mostly poor people occupied the area in the Altiplano along the road on the edge of the slopes leading down into La Paz. This area was incorporated into a city known as El Alto.[75] The international airport is also nearby, so whoever controls El Alto controls land and air access to La Paz. Knowing this, the insurgents gathered their forces here on October 8 and blocked the roads. They especially focused on cutting off fuel supplies into the city.

Between 9 and 12 October, there were serious clashes between armed and semi-armed marchers, particularly miners from Oruro, and government security forces. While most of the marchers were unarmed, accompanying the marches were groups of young men with weapons and explosives. Among them were members of EGTK, but it was later reported that documents from the Raul Reyes computers captured in Ecuador revealed that among the armed squads were up to 60 members of the Colombian FARC.[76] In this way, the marches were accompanied by selective acts of violence and sabotage. Among the most notable acts: on 10 October, a natural gas pipeline into La Paz was dynamited near the 'Boliviana' Beer plant; on 13 October, three overhead crosswalks were dynamited along the road to Rio Seco; and on 15 October, a train on the El Alto to La Paz track was derailed in such a manner as to block the highway between El Alto and La Paz. In addition, numerous commercial locales were looted and burned, some by the armed squads and some by the unarmed masses.

The clashes grew in violence. On the 9th, two people were killed and 26 wounded in the clashes. Stopped tanker trucks began to pile up behind government lines. On 10 October, the government flew in reinforcements from other parts of the country. On the 11th, three more people were killed and dozens wounded in an attempt to break the blockade and send two tanker trucks into La Paz. This effort was not successful, and attempts to mediate failed because the leaders of the protests were not interested in negotiating. Their objective was to overthrow President Sanchez de Lozada.

The most violent day was 12 October, when the military was ordered to force the blockades with 12 tanker trucks, six for civilian consumption and six for the military. Resistance was fierce, and the opposition claimed that 26 people were killed and more than 100 wounded in the clashes.[77] The violence did not consist of the army and police firing indiscriminately at unarmed civilians as has often been portrayed. There was give and take, with the armed squads among the protesters producing losses among the security forces, and the security forces firing back. On 14 October, the Association of Parents reported that approximately 17 soldiers had been killed in the clashes. These losses were not reported by the government.[78] This was clear evidence that the violence was not one way.

On 13 October, several additional organizations joined the marchers: The National Confederation of Transporters, the Confederation of Rural Teachers, the Confederation of Urban Education Workers of Bolivia, the Departmental Federation of Urban Workers of La Paz, and the Confederation of Health Workers. In addition, Cocaleros in the Chapare set up road-blocks to support the road-blocks in El Alto. Realizing they could no longer hold out against this mob unless they wanted to commit a massacre, the army abandoned El Alto and withdrew into La Paz proper during the night.

On 14 and 15 October, there was a lull, which both sides used to reorganize and gather forces. The only violence was a clash between the army and a column of miners from Oruro making their way down into to La Paz. Three died. Meanwhile, the three parties of the government coalition met and came up with a compromise proposal on natural gas. This went nowhere, as that had never been the actual issue in play. The real objective had always been the overthrow of the government. Claiming that they couldn't compromise because now there was blood on the government's hands, Evo Morales and Felipe Quispe ordered a full advance into La Paz.

Insurgent victory

On 16 October, 100,000 marchers descended into La Paz and surrounded the government buildings. They threatened to employ 'total violence' if the government did not resign. The Cocaleros were willing to take the confrontation to the next level, open civil war. The government and establishment politicians were not. They still thought they could make deals. As a result, on 17 October, Gonzalo Sanchez de Lozada and his cabinet resigned as the government administration of Bolivia, a capitulation that led the Cocaleros to order as unnecessary the third phase, *Taraxchi*.

Though some, such as Felipe Quispe, one of the more radical leaders, wanted to implement Phase 3 and bring the revolution to a quick and bloody end, the Cocaleros were more pragmatic. To them, Phase 3 was only to be implemented in case there was no other alternative. Otherwise, it was not a good optic vis-à-vis the international community. If the whole government resigned, it would be obvious that the constitutional order had been broken and that power had been seized through insurrection. MAS wanted power, but it wanted the appearance of winning through at least a modicum of institutional legitimacy. It knew that this was important to the outside world and understood the power of perception.

The Cocalero trump card was Vice President Carlos Mesa. Before becoming the Vice President, he had been a journalist and was perceived by Sanchez de Lozada's advisors to be the right complement to enable Sanchez to win the 2002 elections, because his popularity and influence on public opinion were seen as a boost to the business-like, blunt personality of Goni. The problem was that Mesa was not ideologically tied to Sanchez de Lozada or his party. To convince him to accept the nomination to Vice President, he was bribed. This fact did not escape the Cocaleros' intelligence, which was very efficient in gathering this type of data on all kinds of political personalities across the spectrum of Bolivian politics. During the February 2003 crisis, Mesa had threatened resignation and only desisted when he asked for and received another substantial sum to retain his loyalty. The Cocaleros knew this and therefore saw him as someone who could be manipulated for the right price.

Evo Morales, who had purposefully avoided most of the action, now suddenly appeared, swiftly approaching Vice-President Carlos Mesa to offer him both power and money to stay in place and create the illusion that, although there had been a popular uprising, the constitutional order had been maintained. The only thing that had happened had been the resignation of a 'criminal' and unpopular president. Mesa agreed and withdrew his initial resignation. He would serve as president for the nearly two following years.[79]

It was a Cocalero master-stroke. Mesa was asked for and delivered an executive order that in its essence characterized the insurgents as innocent protesters and therefore not legally responsible for any of the violence, while at the same time putting all of the responsibility on the overthrown president, his cabinet (except for Mesa), and the military high command. They were to all be captured and tried for their 'crimes.'

Morales' verbal agreement with Mesa also stipulated that the latter would only serve as a caretaker president and focus on preparing for new elections and a new government, which if they occurred soon, while the Cocaleros still had the initiative, would be handily won by Evo Morales. At first Mesa stuck to his deal and began to take steps to prepare the way for the next government. He called for a referendum on the gas industry as well as for a convention to write a new constitution. These measures were approved. This was legally convenient to justify the MAS plan to radically alter Bolivian government and society. Also, in this way, rather than provoking opposition by coming up with the measures themselves, they would be able to claim that they were merely fulfilling the mandate of the previous government. This again follows Lenin's strategy closely. He called for the creation of a provisional government, amnesty for all the 'fighters,' and a constituent assembly to consolidate the legitimacy of the victory won by the mass uprising.[80]

Mesa pushed for nationalization of Bolivia's gas industry. A law was passed to increase taxes from 27 to 50% on exported gas. On the international front, he pushed for sovereign access through Chile of a Pacific Ocean port. His government also modified the existing constitution to allow for the convening of a constituent assembly. The assembly was approved but did not take place under Carlos Mesa, instead during Evo Morales' first term. In this way, it was portrayed as merely the continuation of the constitutional mandate.

In general, the political climate was calmer during the first 18 months of the Mesa government, because Mesa kept most of his promises to Morales. This allowed Bolivia to increase its exports and implement an austerity plan that greatly reduced the debt. However, Mesa's success caused him to develop ambitions of staying in power until 2007, the end of Sanchez de Lozada's constitutional term. Mesa's mistake was to believe that the Cocaleros would allow him to fulfill the constitutional mandate. Their reason for refusing to go along with this move was simple: If Mesa continued to enjoy success and stayed in place until 2007, there was nothing that guaranteed that the Cocalero coalition with the other social movement organizations would be able to maintain cohesion and win the subsequent elections. For the moment, they had cohesion and the initiative, and wanted to take advantage of it.

The Cocaleros were not going to allow Mesa to break the verbal agreement with Morales. To make matters worse for Mesa, since he did not belong to a political party, he began to face resistance from the traditional parties as well, who had ambitions of their own. None had ever regarded him as anything but a temporary caretaker. The latter undermined him in Congress, for example, approving a hydrocarbons law that did not call for total nationalization. Since the Gas War rallying banner had been gas nationalization, the Cocaleros used the new hydrocarbons law as a pretext to force Mesa out of power as they had Goni. They began new marches, again blocking the roads and highways across the country in Cochabamba, La Paz, Sucre, Santa Cruz, Montero, Potosí, and Oruro.

Caught between these marches and opposition in Congress, Mesa continuing in power became impossible. After several months of the chaos, he submitted his resignation on March 6, 2005. Congress did not accept it, but the act marked the end of any cooperation between Mesa and Congress, which began to resist all of his initiatives, forcing him to rule by decree. Facing mounting opposition from both the right and the left, he successfully resigned on June 6, 2005.[81]

Congress's plan was to make the President of the Senate, Hormando Vaca Diez (MIR), the new President of Bolivia, or if he wouldn't or couldn't, to turn to the President of Congress, Mario Cossío (MNR), to finish Goni's constitutional presidential term. The Cocaleros and their allies were filling La Paz with protesters to prevent this from happening. Thinking they could out-maneuver the Cocaleros by moving the meeting, it was decided to hold the legislative session in Sucre, Bolivia's historical capital. This was a mistake because Sucre is only accessible by two roads, which are easily blocked, and an airport with a precarious schedule due to weather conditions. Upon learning that the Legislature was moving to Sucre, the Cocalero-led opposition immediately began assembling marchers to besiege that city. They moved much quicker than the Legislature had anticipated, demonstrating their capacity to organize and coordinate their masses. The legislators moved by air, and the military put on a display of force to keep the protesters out of the urban area; but it was Bolivia's winter, and weather prevented all of the legislators from arriving quickly. This meant that they could not do a quick vote and present the country with a fait accompli. Armed elements accompanied the marchers and were in place before the Legislature could act. They sent a warning to the Legislature that if Hormando Vaca Diez or Mario Cossío were made president, there would be civil war.[82]

Although their main tactic was not military action, they were prepared to use it on a massive scale. The Cocaleros demanded that the President of the Supreme Court, Eduardo Rodríguez Veltzé, become president with the sole mandate to prepare new presidential elections.[83] Besieged and threatened in Sucre, and unwilling to go to war, the Legislature caved in to the Cocaleros' demands. The elections were held in December 2005 and resulted in a clear victory for Evo Morales and MAS. The insurgency was now consolidated and the uprising legitimized through internationally recognized elections.

Conclusions

Reflecting on the success of the Bolivian insurgency, it is evident that the Cocaleros won because they applied the correct combination of all forms of struggle. Leading the forms of struggle were semi-violent protests versus open military conflict. This is remarkable given the almost exclusive tradition in Latin America of insurgency via mostly armed conflict, but is not unlike what has recently been attempted elsewhere.[84] The Cocaleros correctly assessed the relative correlation of forces and applied that combination of forms of struggle which carried them to victory. The most important characteristic that led the Cocaleros to this correct combination was their eminent pragmatism, over ideological dogmatism, yet profound understanding of insurgency and revolutionary theory. The outcome was a brilliant strategic victory, so much so that the victory was not really perceived by the international public as an insurgency.

What is clear is that the strategy was not necessarily brilliant from its conception but rather became so as it adapted and evolved. First in importance was its evolution in its understanding of *power*. Initially, it was merely the power to stop eradication at the local level. This did not work, so the Cocaleros sought to influence policy through a co-opted political party. This did not work very well, either, so they sought to create their own political party to share political power; and while this gave them significant influence, it did not give them control. Thus, they decided to take power to institute a new order to their liking and design.

The political instrument (as they called their party) was vital, because it allowed them to consolidate power and suborn like-minded fellow travelers even as the real battle for power was fought in the streets. There were two approaches. The first, drawn from great experience in the mines, was that of the experienced union leaders and organizers who were familiar with the power that had been achieved by the miners through their mass protests since the 1952 revolution. The second was drawn from the *ferreros* or the believers in guns, who understood that as necessary power would not be obtained without major violence if not civil war.

Fortunately for the Cocaleros, the former dominated, because there was a tradition of mass protests and a history of limited successes obtained. The state may have surrendered but averted major tragedy. Nevertheless, the second approach was a significant element, employed to protect the Cocaleros' income and mass actions, as well as being held in reserve in case the Cocaleros really ran into a brick wall and needed extraordinary violence to blast open the way. Perhaps Bolivia would have turned into a typical guerrilla warfare insurgency had President Banzer lived to complete his second term and *Plan Dignity* been seen through to the end. However, this did not happen, and the Qurioga government did not have the stomach to confront the Cocaleros at the level to which they were willing to take matters.

Due to this, the second brilliant aspect of the Cocalero insurgent strategy was their limited, targeted application of violence, with the Leninist understanding that it had to be subordinate to the political struggle and only selectively employed. First, it was used to protect drug trafficking, the source of Cocalero money. In this, the insurgency was able to avoid detection by attributing the violence to faceless 'drug traffickers.' Additionally, at critical moments, the Cocaleros did resort to violence that produced significant casualties and brought the country to the brink of open war. This demonstrated that they had the will and the means to go to the next level. The government always blinked at these moments, which slowly but systematically tipped the balance of power in the Cocaleros' favor. This tipping process became increasingly visible after 2000. The big moments were the Water War, the November 2001 marches in the Chapare, Black February, the Gas War, the marches to overthrow Mesa, and the siege of Sucre. The scale of violence or willingness to employ violence escalated with each event but never reached open warfare, even though the situation often went right to the brink of open warfare. Each time, the government shied from the fight. Thus each incident of brinkmanship squeezed a significant political concession from the state and paved the way for an eventual Morales political victory. The Cocaleros applied violence just enough to make systematic progress towards their ultimate objective, to take power, but not enough violence to reveal the insurgency and/or provoke a strong reaction, either from the government or its international backers.

This clearly demonstrates a return to a more Leninist approach to insurgency in Latin America from the recently dominant Maoist trend of using violence as the principle form of struggle. Such emphasis, practitioners in other struggles might note (e.g. Nepal or the Philippines), could not only be assessed as doctrinally flawed (ignoring e.g. the prescription by Mao that the united front was the decisive element) but in many ways as culturally specific to the region. Not in question, though, is that changing Latin American conditions have caused a reconsideration of insurgent strategy, most particularly, in the Bolivia case. The reality was that a weak, poor democracy suffering significant levels of corruption simply lacked the ability to muster sufficient legitimacy and hence coercive power.

The high political cost of the use of military force – due to alleged and real human rights abuses during the Cold War – and significantly reduced military budgets after 1990, with corresponding reductions of military capabilities, left a vacuum in both self-defense and coercive capacities much less capabilities. The police had neither the will nor the ability to fill the resulting vacuum. This was exacerbated by the perception that in democracy, societies needed less policing, leading to the design of deliberately weaker forces that were unequal to the security challenge. Subsequent experience showed that for the democratic age, perhaps greater, more capable policing was required to provide adequate security in post-Cold War Latin America.

Perhaps as importantly, post-Cold War judicial systems have remained weak and politicized in Latin America, and levels of impunity are relatively high. In this sense, in the post-Cold War era, far more avenues for struggle are open to radical opposition political groups, making it unnecessary to rely so heavily on violence, even as the very weakness of the state compels the use of some level of violence as both an attractive and effective option.

Finally, the Cocaleros understood that the motor of the insurgency was money. Money was more important than guns. Money sustained the organization, gave it coherence and power. Money paid for the armed organization that defended the Coca. Money paid for the marchers and sustained them over prolonged periods of time, helping them to outlast the patience of the government. Money paid for the political instrument and helped it grow quickly into the second force of the country. Money bought non-Cocalero social organizations and bent them to the Cocaleros' will. Money corrupted government officials and prevented the efficient application of counter-narcotics and security strategies. Money was available in previously undreamed of quantities through illicit markets. This is perhaps one of the most significant differences between Cold War and Post-Cold War insurgencies in Latin America and around the globe.

As we look to the near future, we can expect that similar insurgent strategies will be applied against governments where similar conditions exist. Colombia, for example, is a country to watch. Is FARC really negotiating the demobilization of its forces and the reincorporation of its members into Colombian society as M-19 did or the FMLN did in El Salvador? Or, is it using the peace process to transform its struggle to look something like Bolivia?[85]

FARC is in a much different situation than were FMLN or M-19. It has a great deal of money compared to previous insurgencies. Why would it suddenly give it up to become an unpopular, weak political party? Most of the governments of the countries in the region are currently sympathetic to FARC's political cause, and FARC has been increasingly mobilizing large country-wide marches to express opposition to the government. Ten years ago, these marches hardly existed. Now, they are a regular feature of the Colombian political landscape, mobilizing 10,000, 30,000, or even 60,000 marchers. Colombia appears to be a much stronger democracy than Bolivia ever was, but it still has many of the same problems that Bolivia did. There is considerable drug trafficking in Colombia. Certain regions of Colombia still lack substantial security, and corruption is still a significant problem, even if much reduced from thirty years ago. Thus it remains to be seen what is at hand. Regardless, the emergence of a new model of insurgency, one still built upon the popular mobilization of people's war but more attuned to new global realities, is a reality.

Notes

1. Transition between the twentieth and the twenty-first century.
2. The seminal source on this subject remains Pike, *PAVN*.
3. This is not unlike the Chinese concept of 'political warfare'; see Marks, *Counterrevolution in China*.
4. See Marks, *Maoist People's War in Post-Vietnam Asia*.
5. Lenin, *Guerrilla Warfare*.
6. Ibid.
7. Composed mostly of Chaco War veterans, therefore combat hardened compared to the regular army conscripts.
8. Mendel, "Counterdrug Strategy – Illusive Victory," 74–87.
9. Ibid.
10. Ibid.
11. The variant of coca for the production of cocaine has been bred for this purpose and has a much higher alkaloid content. It cannot be chewed or used to make traditional teas. Thus, the Cocalero argument that it was being grown for traditional reasons, often repeated in the international press, was spurious.
12. *Consejo Nacional contra el Tráfico Ilícito de Drogas*.
13. CICAD, *Evaluación de los Compromisos plasmados en el Plan Dignidad*.
14. An archaic Spanish term meaning trail blazer or pathfinder.
15. Interview with anonymous source who did his military service in the Ranger Regiment from 1990 to 1992, 23 September 2014.
16. CICAD, *Evaluación*, 6.
17. Government of the Republic of Bolivia, *Memoria*, 380.
18. Rodríguez, "Evitar la Confrontación."
19. Ibid.

20. Ibid.
21. Lenin, *Lessons of the Moscow Uprising*.
22. Lenin, *A Militant Agreement for the Uprising*.
23. Lenin, "The Third Congress of the R.S.D.L.P."
24. Cocalero sympathizers have often portrayed this slogan as 'Zero Coca,' but traditional coca crops and coca uses were protected by Law 1008. Only coca for illicit uses was made illegal.
25. Government of the Republic of Bolivia, *Memoria*, 375.
26. Ibid.
27. Ibíd., 378.
28. Defensor del Pueblo, *Estudio de Violencia Intrafamiliar en Contextos de Violencia Generalizada*, 17.
29. Storrs, *Andean Regional Initiative (ARI)*, 15.
30. Government of the Republic of Bolivia, op. cit., 378–9.
31. Ibid., 381.
32. Ibid., 380.
33. Navia Gabriel and Pinto Cascán, "Mutilados y olvidados de Chapare."
34. Ibid.
35. Guísela, "Hay 100 desactivadores de cazabobos."
36. International Campaign to Ban Landmines, *Landmine Monitoring Report 2004*.
37. Government of the Republic of Bolivia, op. cit., 379.
38. Rodríguez, "Evitar la Confrontración."
39. http://www.bolpress.com/art.php?Cod=2014070403.
40. Movimiento al Socialismo.
41. See note 38 above.
42. Storrs, *Andean Regional Initiative (ARI)*.
43. See note 17 above.
44. See note 31 above.
45. Shultz and Draper, *Desafiando la Globalización*.
46. Barrero Cordero, "La Guerra del Agua en Cochabamba," 94.
47. Daroca Oller, "Protesta y Acción Social en Cochabamba," 7; also Humberto, "Bolivia," 48.
48. Daroca Oller, Ibid, 8.
49. Ibid.
50. Ibid., 10–1.
51. Vargas, op. cit., 48–9.
52. Ledebur, *Coca y Conflicto en el Chapare*, 6; Vargas, op. cit., 49.
53. Ledebur, Ibid, 7.
54. The General Accounting Office, *Efforts to Develop Alternatives to Cultivating Illicit Crops in Colombia Have Made Little Progress and Face Serious Obstacles*, 21.
55. Camacho Balderrama, *La 'Rebelión' de Febrero*.
56. At this time, only 5% of Bolivians paid taxes.
57. Camacho Balderrama, *La 'Rebelión' de Febrero*.
58. Informe De La Organización De Los Estados Americanos (OEA) Sobre Los Hechos De Febrero Del 2003 En Bolivia.
59. http://boliviaprensa.com/index.php/noticias-bpa/745-bolivia-recuerda-los-hechos-de-febrero-negro.
60. Ibid.
61. Ibíd.
62. Ibid.
63. OAS.

64. Amnesty International, *Bolivia, Crisis y Justicia*.
65. OAS.
66. Ibid.
67. http://eju.tv/2013/08/el-mallku-revela-que-fall-una-emboscada-para-matar-a-snchez-berzan/.
68. Ejército Guerrillero Tupak Katari, a relatively obscure guerrilla group.
69. "Yo Ordene la Emboscada de Warisata."
70. "Fuego cruzado en Warisata deja 5 muertos y heridos."
71. http://eju.tv/2013/08/el-mallku-revela-que-fall-una-emboscada-para-matar-a-snchez-berzan/.
72. Guísela, "Warisata."
73. http://eju.tv/2013/08/el-mallku-revela-que-fall-una-emboscada-para-matar-a-snchez-berzan/.
74. http://www.fmbolivia.com.bo/noticia40042-evo-morales-escapo-a-libia-en-hechos-de-octubre-de-2003.html.
75. 'The Heights' in English.
76. http://eju.tv/2008/10/un-abogado-dice-que-las-farc-actuaron-el-2003/.
77. http://www.rebelion.org/homeroteca/bolivia/031018po.htm.
78. http://www.rebelion.org/homeroteca/bolivia/031018po.htm.
79. See http://eju.tv/2008/10/un-abogado-dice-que-las-farc-actuaron-el-2003/.
80. See note 22 above.
81. http://alainet.org/active/8383&lang=es.
82. http://alainet.org/active/8383&lang=es.
83. Ibid.
84. See e.g. Marks, "Terrorism as Method in Nepali Maoist Insurgency, 1996–2016," 81–118.
85. Refer to contributions by Ospina and Marks in this special issue.

Disclosure statement

The conclusions and opinions of the authors are their own and do not represent the views of the U.S. government or its policy.

Bibliography

Primary Sources
Official Documents
CICAD. *Evaluación del Plan Dignidad*. Washington, DC: Organización de Estados Americanos, n.d.
Defensor del Pueblo. *Estudio de Violencia Intrafamiliar en Contextos de Violencia Generalizada: Trópico Cochabambino*. n.p., 2006.
The General Accounting Office. *Efforts to Develop Alternatives to Cultivating Illicit Crops in Colombia Have Made Little Progress and Face Serious Obstacles*. GAO-02-291, February 2002, 21.
Government of the Republic of Bolivia. *Memoria: Gobierno Constitucional Hugo Banzer Suarez 1997–2001*. La Paz: Imprenta Oficial, 2002.
Organization of American States. *Informe De La Organización De Los Estados Americanos (OEA) Sobre Los Hechos De Febrero Del 2003 En Bolivia*. Accessed October 3, 2014. http://www.oas.org/OASpage/esp/Documentos/InfBO-051203.htm4

Storrs, Larry K. *Andean Regional Initiative (ARI): FY2002 Supplemental and FY2003 Assistance for Colombia and Neighbors*. Washington, DC: Congressional Research Service, June 12, 2002.

NGO Reports
Amnesty International. *Bolivia, Crisis y Justicia: Jornadas de violencia en febrero y octubre del 2003*. November 30, 2004.
International Campaign to Ban Landmines. *Landmine Monitoring Report 2004*. Accessed November 10, 2014. http://www.the-monitor.org/index.php/publications/display?url=lm/2004/bolivia.html#Heading4353
Ledebur, Kathryn. *Coca y Conflicto en el Chapare*. Washington, DC: Washington Office on Latin America (WOLA), July 2002.

Documents
Lenin, Vladimir I. "The Third Congress of the R.S.D.L.P. April 25–May 10, 1905." *Draft Resolution of the Armed Uprising*. Accessed December 12, 2014. https://www.marxists.org/archive/lenin/works/1905/3rdcong/4.htm#v08fl62-369
Lenin, Vladimir I. *Guerrilla Warfare*. 1906. Accessed December 12, 2014. https://www.marxists.org/archive/lenin/works/1906/gw/i.htm
Lenin, Vladimir I. *Lessons of the Moscow Uprising*. 1906. Accessed December 12, 2014. https://www.marxists.org/archive/lenin/works/1906/aug/29.htm
Lenin, Vladimir I. *A Militant Agreement for the Uprising*. 1905. Accessed December 12, 2014. https://www.marxists.org/archive/lenin/works/1905/feb/21.htm

Interview
Anonymous. "Bolivian Ranger Regiment private from 1990–1992." September 23, 2014.

Secondary Sources
Books
Pike, Douglas. *PAVN: People's Army of Vietnam*. Novato, CA: Presidio Press, 1986.
Marks, Thomas A. *Counterrevolution in China: Wang Sheng and the Kuomingtang*. London: Frank Cass, 1998.
Marks, Thomas A. *Maoist People's War in Post-Vietnam Asia*. Bangkok: White Lotus, 2007.
Shultz, Jim, and Melissa Crane Draper, eds. *Desafiando la Globalización: Historias de la Experiencia Boliviana*. La Paz: Plural Editores, 2008.

Journal Articles
Barrero Cordero, Juan. "La Guerra del Agua en Cochabamba: un Caso de Palabras que Hablan mal." *Investigación Ambiental Ciencia y Política Pública* 1, no. 1 (2009): 91–100.
Camacho Balderrama, Natalia. "La 'Rebelión' de Febrero: una Historia que no se Puede Reeditar." (2003). Accessed November 21, 2014. http://biblioteca.clacso.edu.ar/ar/libros/osal/camacho.doc
Daroca Oller, Santiago. "Protesta y Acción Social en Cochabamba." *Los Cuadernos de Trabajo*, Programa de Naciones Unidas para el Desarrollo, (n.d.).
Humberto, Vargas R. "Bolivia: un País de Re-configuraciones por una Cultura de Pactos Políticos y de Conflictos." In *Movimientos Sociales y Conflicto en América Latina*, edited by Jose Seoane, 85–102. Buenos Aires: CLACSO, 2003.
Marks, Thomas A. "Terrorism as Method in Nepali Maoist Insurgency, 1996–2016." *Small Wars and Insurgencies* 28, no. 1 (2017): 81–118.
Mendell, William W. "Counterdrug Strategy – Illusive Victory: From Blast Furnace to Green Sweep." *Military Review* (December, 1992): 74–87.

Rodriguez, Alberto K. "Evitar la Confrontación: Entrevista con Filemón Escobar." *Encuentro* no. 44 (July 20, 2007).

News Articles

Contreras Baspineiro, Alex. "¡Qué se vayan todos! Renunció el presidente Mesa, los problemas suman y siguen." June 7, 2005. Accessed November 17, 2014. http://alainet.org/active/8383&lang=es

Guísela, López R. "Hay 100 desactivadores de cazabobos." *El Deber*, March 15, 2004.

Guísela, López R. "Warisata: la masacre de hace un año todavía duele." *El Deber*, September 20, 2004.

Navia Gabriel, Roberto, and Pinto Cascán, Darwin. "Mutilados y olvidados de Chapare." *El Deber*, August 5, 2007.

Quispe Huanca, Felipe. "CSUTCB, máxima instancia superior de las rebeliones." bolpress.com, July 4, 2014. Accessed November 21, 2014. http://www.bolpress.com/art.php?Cod=2014070403

Quispe Huanca, Felipe. "Bolivia Recuerda los Hechos de Febrero Negro." February 2013. Accessed October 3, 2014. http://boliviaprensa.com/index.php/noticias-bpa/745-bolivia-recuerda-los-hechos-de-febrero-negro

Quispe Huanca, Felipe. "El Mallku revela que falló una emboscada para matar a Sánchez Berzaín." August 4, 2013. Eju.tv. Accessed November 21, 2014. http://eju.tv/2013/08/el-mallku-revela-que-fall-una-emboscada-para-matar-a-snchez-berzan/

Quispe Huanca, Felipe. "Evo Morales escapó a Libia en hechos de octubre de 2003." November 10, 2010. Accessed November 21, 2014. http://www.fmbolivia.com.bo/noticia40042-evo-morales-escapo-a-libia-en-hechos-de-octubre-de-2003.html

Quispe Huanca, Felipe. "Fuego cruzado en Warisata deja 5 muertos y heridos." September 21, 2003. Accessed November 12, 2014. http://www.bolivia.com/noticias/AutoNoticias/DetalleNoticia16029.asp

Quispe Huanca, Felipe. "Un abogado dice que las FARC actuaron el 2003." Eju.tv. October 17, 2008. Accessed November 19, 2014. http://eju.tv/2008/10/un-abogado-dice-que-las-farc-actuaron-el-2003/

Quispe Huanca, Felipe. "Yo Ordene la Emboscada de Warisata." May 28, 2006. Accessed November 12, 2014. http://www.comocayogoni.com/noticias.php?opc=ampnot&sec=2&pk=53

Index

Note: Page numbers in *italics* refer to figures
Page numbers in **bold** refer to tables
Page numbers with 'n' refer to notes

Abdullah (Uprising commander) 185–7
'absolute nomadism' phase 63
Abu Jihad 213
ACCU (*Autodefensas Campesinas de Córdoba y Urabá*) 104–5n16
Acheverria, Jose Antonio 68
al-Adnani, Abu Mohammed 214
al-Baghdadi, Abu Bakr 202, 213; Russia as ISIS enemies 214
'adventurist' guerrilla campaigns 58
Afghan Arabs 204; associated with Salafism 208; foreign fighters 206
Afghan Local Police (ALP) 169, 184, 188
Afghanistan: Andar district 175; anti-Taliban movements 185; Deh Yah district, Afghanistan 175; detention facilities in 181; insurgency in 71; people's uprising in 168–97; religious schools 173; state formation in 169; *see also* Ghazni, Afghanistan
Aguas del Tunari 233–5
Aikens, Matthieu 184
Alea, Tomas Gutierrez 55
Alijan village, Iran 179
Alizai case 183
Allen, John 185
Allende, Salvador 67, 69
Alliance for Progress 23
Al Qaeda 71, 202, 203, 215; North Caucasus insurgency vs. 207–11
Althusser, Louis 62
'American Dream' 46
'American imperialism' 58
American Popular Revolutionary Alliance (APRA) 46–7, 50
American strategy 44, 120

Anbar Awakening, Iraq 169
Andar district, Afghanistan 175
Andar Uprising Manifesto 169–72
Andean Information Network 231
Anderson, Jon Lee 73n8
Anderson, Perry 76n98
annihilation 117, 118, 123, 126
anti-Soviet jihad 169–70
anti-Taliban resistance 176–81, 190
anti-urban leanings 58
APRA *see* American Popular Revolutionary Alliance (APRA)
Area de Distensión see demilitarized zone
Argentina 22, 23
Arkbarzada, Musa Khan 184–5
The Art of Guerrilla Warfare (Gubbins) 11
Asilderov, Rustam 214
Astemirov, Anzor 211
AUC (*Autodefensas Unidas de Colombia*) 101, 105n16, 140
Autodefensas Campesinas de Córdoba y Urabá see ACCU (*Autodefensas Campesinas de Córdoba y Urabá*)
autodefensas see self-defense groups (*autodefensas*)
Autodefensas Unidas de Colombia see AUC (*Autodefensas Unidas de Colombia*)
autogolpe (self-coup) 31
Automated Logistics System (SLOG) 150
Ayacucho, Peru 20–1, 24, 26
Ayers, Bill 72n6

Back on the Road (Guevara) 45
Bahir, Ghairat 176
Bakke, Krisin M. 204
'banana republics' 49

INDEX

Bande-Sardeh Reservoir 184
Banzer, Hugo 230, 236
Basayev, Shamil 205, 206; elimination of 209
Batista, Fulgencio 44, 49, 51–3, 55–8, 66–8
Battlefield Operating Systems (BOS) 162
Bay of Pigs 67
Bayo, Alberto 51
Belaúnde Terry, Fernando 30
Bell, J. Bowyer 57, 74n54
Berrios, Carlos 4, 138
Betancur administration 89, *91*
Biddle, Stephen 203
bin Laden, Osama: praise for Chechen separatists 206–7; *see also* Al Qaeda
Bjorgo, Tore 203
Black February 237–9
Blanqui, Auguste 53
Blast Furnace operation 227
'blitzkrieg' strategy 11
Bloques 86, 122–3, 131
Boko Haram 201–2
Bolivarian Movement for a New Colombia 83, 100
Bolivarian Revolution 85
Bolivia 4, 11–12, 44, 61–4, 70, 120, 133n15; fiasco in 1966–1967 54; mines 226
Bolivian insurgency model 222–3; Black February 237–9; *Blast Furnace* operation 227; coca production 222, 233; Cocalero strategy 229–30; counter-narcotics plan 230–1; counterinsurgency 224; evolution of 225–6; gas war 239–42; guerrilla warfare 222; information campaign 223; insurgent victory 242–5; Law 1008 227–9; legal political party 223; plan dignity 230–2, 236–7, 246; political instrument evolution 232–3, 246; social protests 222–3; water war 233–5
Boot, Max 51, 74n35
Bortnikov, Aleksandr 212
BRIM *see* mobile brigades
British East India Company 49
Burbank, Jane 76n91
Buryatsky, Said 211

Cano, Alfonso 131
capitalism 3, 47, 65
Castaneda, Jorge 46, 73n11; assessment of Guevara 60
Castaño Gil, Carlos 101, 104n16

Castro, Fidel 23, 49, 50, 52, 71, 119, 131; brand of revolution 55, 58; guerrillas 53; movement 51; in prison, Mexico (1956) 50; regime 66
Caucasus Emirate insurgency 211, 213, 214
Center for Coordination of Integrated Action (CCAI) 154–5
center of gravity, concept of 121
Central Obrera Regional (COR) 239
Chaco War 226
Chanan, Michael 74n51
Chang, Jung 9
Chechen conflict *see* first Chechen conflict; second Chechen conflict
Chechenization 210
Chechnya 203; counterterrorist operation in 202; Kremlin's intervention 205
Chiang Kai-shek 64
Childs, Matt D. 75n56
China 26; communist revolutions in 6, 7, 29; Cultural Revolution in 28; Uyghur militants 202, 203
China of Mulele 60
Chinese Communist Party (CCP) 2, 13
Chinese Cultural Revolution (1960) 43
Chinese People's Liberation Army (PLA) 10
Chinh, Truong 10, 84
Chou En-lai 6
CIA interrogations 181
civil affairs 153–5
Civil Defense Committees (CDC) 33
civilian population 119, 128; mobilization of 124
Clandestine Colombian Communist Party (PCCC) 83, 100
Clausewitz 2; Clausewitzian approach 117, 121
COBALT 181
'Coca and Controlled Substances Regimen' 227
coca growers *see* Cocaleros
coca production 222, 233, 248n11
cocaine trade 85
Cocalero Federations 229
Cocaleros 221–2; Cocalero strategy 229–30; Escobar's proposal 229; forms of struggle 245; guerrilla warfare 229; indigenous rights movement 232; insurgent strategy 246; as insurgents 222; Law 1008 and 228; leadership 232–3; military wing 231; money in insurgency 247; penetration of indigenous organizations 232; in social protest 235; water war 233–5

INDEX

Cochabamba 233, 234
Cohen-Sodal, Annie 75n76
Cold War 18; role of 22–4
COLMIL (Colombian military) 121, 124, 126, 132, 139–42; campaign 142–5, *144*; CCAI implementation 154–5; centers of excellence 148; CENTRIXS system 148; civil affairs 153–5; closing capability gaps 146–63; communications 149–51; data networks 150; information and psychological operations 151–3; Integrated Communications Network (RIC) 149–50; intelligence center (CIME) 148; operational support to 146; planning assistance and training teams (PATT) 162–3; riverine operations and maritime interdiction 155–7; strategic communications network 149–51; US intelligence support to 148–9; US Special Operations Forces (SOF) 157–62
Colombia 4–5, 14, 23, 81, *82*, 98, 104n4; cocaine labs 229; drug trafficking in 248; intelligence 136n50; riverine operations and maritime interdiction in 155–7; Tolima 83; Toribio 128; Vietnamese people's war variant in 122–5; *see also* Bolivarian Movement for a New Colombia; *specific organizations/political parties*
Colombia, US aid to counterinsurgency in 138–66; closing COLMIL capability gaps 146–63; COLMIL (Colombian military) *see* COLMIL (Colombian military); Colombian Army (COLAR) 142–3; counterdrug focus (1999–2002) 140–2, **141**; counterinsurgency strategy 142–6; FARC and 139; illegal drug production 138–9; Joint Task Force Omega (JTF-O) 145, 151–2, 160; Plan Colombia strategy 140; Plan Patriota military campaign *139*, 142–5
Colombian Army (COLAR) 93, 101, 142–3
Colombian Army Counterdrug Brigade (CD BDE) 140, 142, 158
Colombian Army Special Operations Command (COESE) 143
Colombian Imagery Library Archive (CILA) 150
Colombian Marine Corps (COLMAR) 155–7
Colombian National Police (CNP) 139, 142, 150, 153, 154, 157
colonialism 45
Comando Conjunto de Operaciones Especiales (CCOPE) 161

Comando de Operaciones Especiales del Ejercito (COESE) 160
Combat Lifesaving (CLS) MTT 163
'Combination of All Forms of Struggle' 223
Combined Enterprise Information Exchange System (CENTRIXS) 148–50
'Commander Segundo' 58
Commando Battalion 159
Committee on Reintegration 212
Communist Party of Colombia (PCC) 83, 122
Communist Party of Peru (PCP) 20–1, 24, 26
Communist Party of Peru – Shining Path (PCP-SL) *see* Shining Path (*Sendero Luminoso*) (PCP-SL)
Communist Party of the Philippines (CPP) 100
community defense 170, 172, 178
COMUNAL (Coordinadora de Movilizaciones Única Nacional) 235
CONALTID (National Council against Illicit Drug Trafficking) 227
'Concept on Countering Terrorism in the Russian Federation' 212
controlling processes 171
Cooper, Frederick 76n91
Cooperating Nations Information Exchange System (CNIES) 150
counter-narcotics (CN) 101; plan 230–1
counter-revolution: pattern of 66; strategy 66
Counterdrug (CD) Battalion 158
counterdrug focus: US assistance (1999–2002) 140–2, **141**, 157–8
counterinsurgency 4, 5, 14, 32, 101, 138, 142–6, 170, 193, 224
counterterrorism, legal framework for 32
CPP *see* Communist Party of the Philippines (CPP)
criminality, as insurgent foundation 81–97; FARC (1982–2002) 80–111
CSUTCB 232, 236, 238, 239
Cuba 23; Castroite revolution 55, 56; guerrilla war in 44; 'Sierra Maestra model' in 52; *see also* Castro, Fidel; Guevara, Ché; Havana, peace agreement discussions in
Cuban Revolution 4, 13, 23, 44, 45, 47, 49, 54, 55, 58, 66, 67
Cultural Revolution 9, 24, 26, 35, 55

Da Milli Pastun Ghorzang movement 191
Dagestan: Committee on Reintegration 212
The Dancer Upstairs (film) 16n24

INDEX

data networks 150
dau tranh concept 224
de la Cadena, Marisol 73n15
de Leon, Freddy Padilla 163
De Palma, Anthony 74n42
Dearing, M. 4–5, 168
Debray, Regis 4, 13, 44, 47, 51, 54, 61–4, 71, 74n34
December 1987 Plenum 122
'decisive battle' 117
'decisive victory' 117–19
Defense Attaché Offices (DAOs) 149
Defense Information Systems Agency (DISA) 149–50
Deh Yah district, Afghanistan 175
del Pino, Rafael 51
demilitarized zone 98, *99*, 143
demobilizations 153
Democratic Security strategy 4, 102, 126, 142–6, 154
Deng Xiaoping 8, 24
Department of Defense (DOD) Counternarcotics (CN) funding 140, 145
Department of State, International Narcotics and Law Enforcement (DOS-INL) Bureau 140, **141**, 157
detention facilities, in Afghanistan 181
dictatorial regimes, brutal 66
Diez, Hormando Vaca 244
Directorio Revolucionario as a *grupo terrorista* (Acheverria) 68
disengagement initiatives 203–4, 215
Disiwal, Mohammaed Kasim 183
Dominican Republic 66
drug trade 5, 85, 94, 106n33, 139, 158
Dudayev, Dzhokhar 204; facing internal opposition 204; foreign powers for support 206; impose martial law 205

Echavarria, Antulio 134n19
Eisenhower administration 49, 52
Ejército de Liberación Nacional see National Liberation Army (ELN)
El Alto 241
El Salvador 6, 84, 97
electronic intelligence 136n50
empowerment 5
Escobar, Filemon 229
Escobar, Pablo 85, 93, 225

Faizan, Faizanullah 179
Faizon 179, 185, 195n29
Fanon, Frantz 57

FARC (Revolutionary Armed Forces of Colombia) 4, 5, 23, 117, 122, 125, 129–30, 204, 241, 248; approach 126; base areas and mobility corridors *88–9*; Bloque primary objectives *87*; center of gravity 124–5; criminal foundation for insurgent defeat (1982–2002) 80–111; criminality, as insurgent foundation 81–97; defeating 148; demilitarized zone 98, *99*; initial reformulation of strategy 131; JTF-O and 145; leadership 130; major base areas *88*; as national security threat 140; organizational structures *86*; Pastrana administration and 140, 142–3; revenues for 93, 139; self-examination 124; strategic plan 121; as threat to state 97–102
Farhi, Farideh 14
Fathi, Sheikh 206
FEDECOR 234
first Chechen conflict (1994–1996) 202, 214; amnesty 206; foreign influences on 206–7; guerilla warfare 205; struggle for independent Chechnya 204–5
FMLN (*Farabundo Martí National Liberation Front*) 84, 97, 134n27
focismo 44, 52, 68–71; emergence of 54–65
focistas 51, 59
foco theory 4, 12, 36, 52, 57, 60, 100, 119, 120, 125, 225; 'Marxianisation' of 61
focoist, 'coherent strategy' of 71
Foreign Military Financing (FMF) 140
Frank, Andre Gunder 64, 65, 75n85
Freedman, Lawrence 10
'Freedom for Palestine' 70
French Revolution 66
'Fronts of War' (*Cuadrilla*) 85–8, 122
Fuerzas Armadas Revolucionarias de Colombia see FARC (Revolutionary Armed Forces of Colombia)
Fujimori, Alberto 31, 32
Fulbright program 25

Gadea, Hilda 45, 47, 50, 51
Galula, David 7
gas war 239, 242; clashes 241–2; phase Fire Ant 240–1; phase Flea 240; phase Taraxchi 242
Gaviria administration 89, *92*
Ghazni, Afghanistan: people's uprising in 168–97; rise of anti-Taliban resistance 176–81; rise of state and resistance in 173–6

INDEX

Giap, Vo Nguyen 10, 11
Gill, Lesley 76n97
Girling, J.L.S. 74n49
GIRoA 185
global insurgency 202
global mythology 68
global revolutionary strategy 64
globalization 5
Gonzalez, Mike 73n22
Gott, Richard 49, 73n23
Grandin, Greg 75n87
Granma 44, 45, 51, 52
'gravitational forces' 121
Griego, Will 161
Grozny: foreign fighters in 206; recapture of 205, 207; Russia's attack on 205
guajiros (hillbillies) 53
Guatemala coup 66
Gubbins, Colin 11
Guerra, Lillian 67, 74n41, 76n95
guerre revolutionnaire 7
guerrillas: ex-M-19 126; *focos* 63, 72
'guerrilla theorists' of Twentieth Century 43, 44
guerrilla warfare 2, 14, 18, 43, 44, 49, 52, 54, 58, 81, 122; in first Chechen conflict (1994-1996) 205; in Sierra Maestra 50, 51; urban warfare 14
Guevara, Ché 4, 8-9, 11-13, 23, 36, 71, 75n55,n57-8,n60,n69, 76n88-9, 100, 229; anti-urban leanings 58; approach 55; career 44; Castaneda's assessment of 60; as icon for 'Palestina Libre' 70; legacy 43; memorabilia 44; political radicalism 47; in prison, Mexico (1956) 50; relationship to the continent 48; revolutionary myth 44; revolutionary thought, evolution of 44-54; six months in Guatemala 49; speeches and writings, drift of 64; themes 44; theory of insurgency 68-72
'Guevarist line' 57
Guzmán Reynoso, Abimael 13, 20-1, 24, 26-9, 35, 37n24

Habib, E. 192
Harakati Enqelab Islami (Islamic Revolution) 173
Hargrove, Tom 107n36
Havana, peace agreement discussions in 116, 135n37
Hazaras 173, 174
Heuser, Beatrice 72n2
Hezbi Islami 169, 170, 173, 178, 195n6

High Value Target (HVT) program 146
higher education: in Latin American countries 22
Hill, James T. 162
Hinojosa, Ivan 76n101
Historias de la revolucion (film) 55, 56
Ho Chi Minh 2, 10-11, 133n16
Holliday, Jon 9
Horgan, John 203
Horowitz, David 76n96
Hotak, Khalil 182, 184-5
hyperinflation 31

Illia, Arturo Umberto 59
Image Product Library (IPL) 150
imperialism 3; American 47-8, 58; Yankee 57
improvised explosive devices (IEDs) 228, 231-2
incentive structure 171-2, 184-9
'indigenismo' 46
Information Operations (IO) integration 151-3
Infrastructure Security Strategy (ISS) 158, 160
Ingushetia Committee 212
insurgency 5, 14-15, 19, 81, 89, 101, 138, 170, 175; adaptation 203-4; criminality as foundation for 81-97; non-military side of 224; violence and 223-4
Integrated Communications Network (RIC) 149-50
Intelligence Integration Program 148, 149, 151
intelligence support, to Colombia 148-9
internal dynamism 64
'internal war' 55
international americano 65
International Campaign to Ban Landmines 232
International Military Education and Training (IMET) 139
International Waters Limited (IWL) 233-4
'internationalisation' of the *foco* 61
Iran: Alijan village 179
Iraq 71, 72, 213; Anbar Awakening 169, 181, 185; insurgency 203
ISIS (Islamic State of Iraq and Syria) 71, 72, 202; direct confrontation with Russia 214; *Istok* 213; pledging allegiance to 214; al-Shishani allegiance to 213
Islamic Revolution *see Harakati Enqelab Islami*

INDEX

Islamic State: North Caucasus insurgency vs. 211–14
Islamic State of Iraq and Syria see ISIS (Islamic State of Iraq and Syria)
Istok 213
Izquierda Unida Party (PIU) 229, 232

Jabar Shelgar, Abdul 179
jamaats 211
Jiang Qing see Madame Mao
Jiangxi debacle 13
jihad: anti-Soviet 169–70; ideology 211; *focos* 72; in Syria 213
jihadis, modern 69
Joint Inter-Agency Task Force- South (JIATF-S) 150
Joint Task Force Omega (JTF-O) 145, 151–2, 160
Junglas, CNP 157

Kabardino-Balkaria: Committee on Reintegration 212
Kabila, L. 60
Kadyrov, Akhmad 202, 210
Kadyrov, Ramzan 210
Kamrani, Amanullah 179, 181–2, 186, 190
Kamrani, Lotfullah 179
Kandahar prison 180
Karachay-Cherkessia: Committee on Reintegration 212
Karel, K.S. 73n29
Kebekov, Aliaskhab 212, 213
Keen, Colonel Ken 159
Kennedy, John F. 23, 58
Kennedy, Paul 66
Kerttuenen, Mika 1
Khalid, Asadullah 179–80, 192
Khan, Lahoor 175
Khan, Sher 185
Khasavyurt peace agreement 205, 206
Khattab 206
Khial Mohammad Hussaini 168
Khruschev, Nikita 58
kidnapping 85, 93, 95–6, 100–1, 103, 106n33
Kiernan, V.G. 13
Kilcullen, David 14
Kremlin 205; North Caucasus issue 212

La batailla de Santa Clara 55
La Paz 236, 239, 241
La Violencia 83
Lacquer, Walter 51, 74n36, 74n44
Lanceros battalion 159–60
land rights 169

Latin America 118; culture 46; university traditions 21–2; see also 'Marxist Strategy in Latin America'; Organisation of Latin American Solidarity (OLAS)
'Latin America: The Long March' 62
Law 1008 227–9
Lawfare 102, 110–1n67
Lawrence, T. E. 48
leadership: Cocaleros 232–3; FARC 130; see also revolutionary leadership
legitimacy 103
Lenin 2, 224, 225; 'Lessons of the Moscow Uprising' 230
Leninist theory 65
Liberalism 22
Lifton, Robert Jay 72n3
Lin Biao 8
Little Red Book, Mao's 8, 12
llano groups 52, 53, 55, 56, 59, 74n30
Llosa, Mario Vargas 68
local insurgencies 204
local security 122
lootable resources 169, 172, 184
López, Mariscal Solano 118
LTTE 201, 203
Lukasevish, Chris 'Luke' 162
Lumumba 60

Mackinlay, J. 14–15
Madame Mao 24, 28
madrasa schools 173
Mahadevan, Prem 1
Malik, Abdul 176–7
Malkovich, John 16n24
Mao Tsetung see Mao Zedong
Mao Zedong 2–3, 6–13, 43, 46, 51, 52, 60, 64, 74n37, 118, 133n11, 225, 235, 247; *Little Red Book*, Mao's 8, 12
Maoism 7–13; foundations of 6–13; heretical 57; insurgency in Peru 70; model of 'peoples war' 55; peasant revolutionary model 51; see also post-Maoism, identifying phase of
Maoist approach 120
Marighella, Carlos 14
Marín Marín, Pedro Antonio see Marulanda Vélez, Manuel
market of protection 168–9, 194n1
Marks, T. A. 1, 4, 74n50, 80, 135n38
Marquetalia 83
Marquez, Gabriel Garcia 68
Marti, Jose 50, 52
Marulanda Vélez, Manuel 83, 84
'Marxianisation,' of the *foco* 61

Marxism 2, 62, 97; continental revolution 46; seminars on 23; theory, 'objective conditions' in 133n13
Marxist analysis 131
'Marxist Strategy in Latin America' 62
Marxist theory 48; objective conditions in 133n13
Masetti, Jorge Ricardo 58, 59
Maskhadov, Aslan 205; Western support for settlement with Russia 207
mass line 3, 8, 13, 15
mass mobilization 5–6; insurgency 18; political 55
Matthews, Herbert 53
Mayan language 49
Mayer, Arno 66, 76n94
mayorales 53
'mediology,' development of 61
Medvedev, Dmitry 212
Mehta, Raj 203
Melgar, Hugo Acha 5, 221
Memmi, Albert 48, 73n21
Mesa, Carlos 243–4
Meza, Luis Garcia 225
Midnight Express boats 157
military: assistance 138; destruction and demoralization of 123
Military Assistance Program (MAP) funds 140
Military Information Support Team (MIST) 151–2
military victory: concept of 117–20; reformulation of 125–8; of the state 128–32
mining industry 172
Miri district 186
Mitterand, François 61, 62
mobile brigades 98, 129, 135n42, 135n46, 136n46, 145, 160
Mobile Digital Network (MDN) 150
mobile radio stations 152
mobile training teams (MTTs) 153
mobility corridors 95
mobilization 2, 3; of civilian population 124; mass 5–6, 18
Mobilization Central Coordinator 235
Moncada barracks, attack on 50, 52
Mono Jojoy *see* Suárez Rojas, Víctor Julio
Montoneros (guerrilla group) 23
Moore, Harold G. 75n59
Mora (General) 155, 159, 162, 163, 166n60
Morales, Evo 221, 229, 236, 237, 243
Morley, Sylvanus Griswold 47
Moss, Robert 74n43

motorbikes, ban on 176
Motorcycle Diaries, The (Guevara) 45
Movement to Socialism (MAS) party 221, 233, 238, 243
Muhammad, Wali 178
Mulele, Pierre 60, 61
Murillo Plaza 238
Myth of the Guerrilla, The (Bell) 57

narcoterrorism *144*
narcotics trade 89; growth 85
narratives 172–3, 189–93
National Agency Against Terrorism (DINCOTE) 32
National Consolidation Plan 154
National Consolidation Strategy (*Plan de Consolidacion Nacional*) 153
National Council against Illicit Drug Trafficking (CONALTID) 227
National Geographic 48
National Geospatial-Intelligence Agency (NGA) 150
national interests 118
National Liberation Army (ELN) 84, 160
National Liberation Committee 60
National Revolutionary Movement (MNR) 226
National Solidarity Program (NSP) 174, 188
Navarro, Antonio 135n39
Naxalite 12
Nejat (Salvation) Community Council 182, 193
Nepal 1, 9, 12, 14, 15, 31
Neruda, Pablo 58, 75n61
New Democracy 29, 31
'new way of operating' 122
Nigeria: Boko Haram 201–2
Nixon Doctrine 66
Nixon, Richard 8, 11
NLF (Viet Cong) 57–8
non-military struggle 224
Noorullah, Maulawi 176
North Caucasus: terrorist attacks in 211
North Caucasus insurgency 201, 202; first Chechen conflict (1994–1996) 202, 204–7; forces 211; insurgent adaptations 203–4; Islamic State vs. 211–14; Al-Qaeda vs. 207–11
North Vietnamese Army (NVA) 58
NSPD-18 146
Nzongola-Ntalala, Georges 61, 75n73

Obama, Barack 180
'objective conditions,' in Marxist theory 133n13

INDEX

Odria, Manuel A. 47
Olympics, Sochi 213, 215
Omar, Mullah 208
One Hundred Days of Solitude (Marquez) 68–9
Operation *Blast Furnace* 227
'Operation Dragon Rouge' 60
Operation Jaque 130, 131
Operation Marquetalia 83
operational support concept 145
Organisation of Latin American Solidarity (OLAS) 57
Ospina Ovalle, Carlos 4, 96, 116, 143, 163

Padilla, Freddy 155
Paisa 55
'Palestina Libre' 70
Palmer, D. S. 4, 18
Palmyra 69
Pan Africanism 46
Pan Americanism 46
Pan Arabism 46
paramilitaries 170, 184, 194n5; and congruence procedures 171–3
Paret, Peter 72n1
Pasado y Presente 59
Pashtuns 173, 174
Pastrana administration 84–5, 89, 97, 98; and FARC 140, 142–3, 145
Pastrana Arango, Andrés 98, 102
patria grande 46
Patsoon 191
Payendi, Taliban assault on 178
Payne, Kenneth 71, 76n102
PCC *see* Communist Party of Colombia (PCC)
PCCC *see* Clandestine Colombian Communist Party (PCCC)
PCP *see* Communist Party of Peru (PCP)
PCP-SL *see* Shining Path (*Sendero Luminoso*) (PCP-SL)
Peace Corps 23, 26
Peasant Self-Defense Forces of Córdoba and Urabá (ACCU) 104n16
Pedraza, David Añez 233
Peoples Guerrilla Army 59
People's Republic of China (PRC) 28
people's war: in 21st century 1–16; launch in 1980 24; Maoist foundations 6–13; post-Maoism, identifying phase of 13–15; strategy and tactics for 28–30; as strategy for power 1–6; violence in 2–3
Pérez, Alan García 30

Peru *19*, 46, 139, 229, 240; Ayacucho 20–1, 24, 26; Maoist insurgency in 70; *see also* Communist Party of Peru (PCP); Shining Path (*Sendero Luminoso*) (PCP-SL)
Peruvian response, to insurgent challenge 31–4; refloating the economy 32; results and implications 34; revamping security 32–3; targeting resources at local level 33–4
Pfeffer, Richard M. 9
Phillips, David Atlee 45, 73n9
Pike, Douglas 11
PIU *see* Izquierda Unida Party (PIU)
Pizarro Leon Gomez, Eduardo 134n23
plains groups 74n30
Plan Colombia strategy 140–1
Plan Dignity (Plan Dignidad) 232, 246; counter-narcotics plan 230–1; end of 236–7; Quiroga's commitment to 237; success of 233; task force 231
Plan Meteoro 129
Plan Patriota 126–31; COLAR scheme of maneuver in *144*; military campaign *139*, 142–5
planning assistance and training teams (PATT) program 162–3, 166n60
Pokalova, Elena 5, 201
Pol Pot 9
police stations 124
Polish Task Force White Eagle 176
political violence 31, 35
political warfare 3
'popular consultation' 234
Porch, D. 10, 15n11
post-Maoism, identifying phase of 13–15
poverty 33
Prabhakaran 135n38
precaristas 53
Prensa Latina 58
Presidential Decision Directive 73 (PDD-73) 140
Problems of Strategy in Guerrilla War Against Japan (Mao) 51, 52
process-tracing method 171–3
professionalism 118
'proof-of-life' 95
Proof of Life (film) 107n37
protection market 168–9, 194n1
'protracted people's war' 119
protracted war 8, 10
psychological operations, IO and 151–3
Putin, Vladimir 210

Qazi Abdul Rahman 175
quajiros 53

INDEX

quasi-colonial upper-class 46
'quasi syndicalist' 53
Quetta 176–7
Quispe, Felipe 236, 239, 240, 242

radical populism 69
radicalisation, pattern of 68
Rahmatullah 176–81
ransoms 96–7, 101
Rasulov, Yasin 211
rebel 'Simbas' 60
Red Star Over China (book) 10
Regional Maritime Training Center 156–7
Reid-Henry, Simon 50, 73n27
Reminiscences of the Cuban Revolutionary War (Guevara) 56, 57
Renacer 131
Reservation Guard (*Guardia de Reserva*) 228
resource-rich environment 172
Restrepo, Orlando 134n30
'revisionist' line 57
Revolution in the Revolution (Debray) 54, 62–3
Revolutionary Armed Forces of Colombia *see* FARC (Revolutionary Armed Forces of Colombia)
'revolutionary immortality' 43
revolutionary leadership: initial government response 30–1; origins of insurgent movement 20–5; in people's war 18–39; Peruvian systemic response to insurgent challenge 31–4; strategy and tactics for people's war 28–30; university radicalization and Shining Path 25–8
Revolutionary Military Government (GRM) 27
revolutionary process 120
Revolutionary Student Federation (FER) 26
Reyes, Raul 96, 131
RIC (*Red Integral de Comunicaciones*) *see* Integrated Communications Network
Rich, P. B. 1, 43
Rich, Paul 4
RISO graphic printer 152
Rittinger, Eric R. 76n92
Robinson, Linda 182
Rossellini, Roberto 55
Rouge, Khmer 9
'roving rebel' 52
Rural Combat MTT 162–3

rural-urban alliance 71
Russia: alternative employment scheme 210; Committees on Reintegration 212; counterterrorism measures 212–13; federal forces' control of Grozny 205; security services 213

Saheb Khan village 179
Sajjadi, Abdul Qayuum 187–8
Salafism 208, 210, 211
Salam, Mullah Abdul 191
Salt Pit *see* COBALT
Salvatore, Ricardo D. 47, 73n17
Samper administration 94, 98
San Cristóbal of Huamanga University 24–5, 27
Sanchez Ceren, Salvador 127
Sanchez de Lozada, Gonzalo 237–8, 239–40, 242
Sartre, Jean-Paul 62
Sayyaf, Abdul Rasul 180
Schram, Stuart 75n86
Scott, James C. 7
second Chechen conflict 207, 214–15; alternative employment scheme 210; amnesties 209, 210, 212; disengagement initiatives of 210–11; Duma's amnesty 209; foreign ideologies 208; Taliban's recognition 207–8
Second Moscow International Film Festival 56
Security Cooperation Offices (SCOs) 149
self-defense groups (*autodefensas*) 83, 101
Semana 128
Senate Intelligence Committee: report on CIA interrogations 181
Sendero Luminoso see Shining Path (*Sendero Luminoso*) (PCP-SL)
settler colonialism 45
Al Shabaab 202, 204
Shah of Iran 66
Shahin village 179
Shakespeare, Nicholas 16n24
Shilgari, Abdul Jabbar 176
Shining Path (*Sendero Luminoso*) (PCP-SL) 4, 13, 18–39, 71; initial government response 30–1; Latin American university traditions 21–2; origins of insurgent movement 20–5; Peruvian systemic response to insurgent challenge 31–4; refloating the economy 32; results and implications 34; revamping security

INDEX

32–3; role of cold war 22–4; strategy and tactics for people's war 28–30; targeting resources at local level 33–4; University of San Cristóbal de Huamanga 24–5; university radicalization and 25–8
al-Shishani, Omar 213
Sierra Maestra 51, 53, 54, 56, 58, 59, 72, 119; in Cuba 52; guerrilla war in 50
'Sierraisation', phase of 61
Siles Suazo, Hernan 226
'Simbas' 60
Sino-Soviet split 8, 21, 23, 58
SIPERNET 150
Sitta, Abdullah Abu 69
Sitta, Salman Abbu 76n100
smuggling industries 169
Snow, Edgar 10
Snyder, Jack 66, 76n93
Sochi Olympics 213, 215
social conservatism 83
social networks 178
Somalia: Al Shabaab 202
South America: military regimes 70
Soviet Union 22
Special Inspector General Afghanistan Reconstruction (SIGAR) 170
Special Intelligence Group (GEIN) 32
Special Operations Command Forward (SOC FWD) 161
Spencer, David E. 5, 221
state financing 172
state formation: in Afghanistan 169
state legitimacy 129
strategic communications advisor (SCA) 188
Strategic Plan 4, 81, 85, 93
strategy: American 44, 120; 'blitzkrieg' 11; Cocalero 229–30; Colombian counterinsurgency 142–6; counter-revolutionary 66; Democratic Security 4, 102, 126, 142–6, 154; 'coherent strategy,' of *focoist* 71; global revolutionary 64; Plan Colombia 140; for seizing power 1–6; and tactics, for people's war 28–30; *see also* Infrastructure Security Strategy (ISS); National Consolidation Strategy (*Plan de Consolidacion Nacional*); *Problems of Strategy in Guerrilla War Against Japan* (Mao)
Suarez, Roberto 225
Suárez Rojas, Víctor Julio 96, 97, 131
subject matter experts (SMEs) 151
'subjective conditions' 133n13
Suleimanov, Magomed 212, 213

Sumaliot, Gaston 60
Summers, Harry 133n18
Sun Tzu 3
Symbionese Liberation Army (SLA) 107n35
Syria: ISIS in 72, 202; jihad in 213

table of organization and equipment (TOE) model 155, 158
Tajik 173
Taliban 169–93, 203, 207; assault on Payendi 178; recognition of Chechnya's independence 207–8; resistance against 176–81, 190
Tapias, Fernando 163
taxation 82, 85, 106n33, 129, 169, 238
Teachers' Federation 236
'terror-crime nexus' 122
terrorism 81, 100; attacks in North Caucasus 211
Test Ban Treaty 58
Tet Offensive 11, 123
Third World 8, 44, 55, 69, 118
Thomas, Hugh 74n39
Thornton, Thomas Perry 74n48
Tirofijo 131
Tolima, Colombia 83
Toribio, Colombia 128
tourism 45
transnational insurgents 204
Trinquier, Roger 7
Trotskyism 63
Truong Chinh 84, 223
Tupamaros 23
Turbay administration 89, *90*
26th July Movement 50, 53

Umarov, Doku 209, 211, 212, 213
UNAMA 187–8, 194n4
Unidad Móvil Policial para Áreas Rurales (UMOPAR) 226
Unión Revolucionaria de Maestros (URMA) 239
'united front' tactics 55
United Fruit Company 49
United Left (IU, political party) 27
United Nations Declaration on Combating Drug Trafficking 230
United Self-Defense Groups of Colombia (AUC) 101, 105n16
United States: 'American Dream' 46; 'American imperialism' 58; American strategy 44, 120; *Blast Furnace* operation 227; Cold War and 22–3; counter-revolution and military intervention

INDEX

64–8; Cuba and 23; informal imperialism 47–8; policy 65, 66; *see also* US aid to counterinsurgency, in Colombia; *specific organizations*
University of San Cristóbal de Huamanga 24–5, 27
universities: Latin American traditions in 21–2; radicalization, and Shining Path 25–8
Unzaguista-Movement to Socialism or (MAS-U) 233
Uprising, formalizing 181–4
urban guerrilla warfare 14
Uribe administration 125, 126, 131
Uribe, Alvaro 102–3, 142, 148
Uruguay 23
US aid to counterinsurgency, in Colombia 138–66; civil affairs 153–5; communications 149–51; counterdrug focus (1999–2002) 140–2, **141**; counterinsurgency strategy 142–6; enhanced support to Colombia **147**; expanded authorities (2003–2010) 145–6; information and psychological operations 151–3; intelligence support 148–9; planning assistance and training teams (PATT) 162–3; riverine operations and maritime interdiction 155–7; strategic context 138–40; US Special Operations Forces (SOF) 157–62
US Caribbean School in Panama 67
US Coast Guard (USCG) 156
US Marine Corps (USMC) 156
US Military Civil Affairs (CA) community 153
US Navy (USN) Riverine Training Facility 156
US Southern Command (US SOUTHCOM) 145, 146, 148–53, 156, 161, 166n56; SOUTHCOM IO LNO 152; SOUTHCOM J2 148–9
US Special Forces 183
US Special Operations Command South (SOCSOUTH) 161

US Special Operations Forces (SOF) 157–62
Uyghur militants 202, 203

vehicular bans 176
Velasco Alvarado, Juan 70
Veltzé, Eduardo Rodríguez 245
Venezuela 6, 96
Viet Cong *see* NLF (Viet Cong)
Viet Minh, in Indochina 7, 10, 11
Vietnam War 64
Vietnamese people's war: variant in Colombia 122–5
Villa Tunari Public Defender (Defensoria del Pueblo) 231
Vinci, Anthony 203
violence 18; in people's war 2–3
voluntarism 1–2; approach of *focismo* 63
Von der Goltz, Baron Colmar 135n42

Wahidi, Abdul Qadir 185
Wallerstein, Immanuel 76n90
war: interpretation 121; *see also specific types/wars*
'War of Interlocking' 223
Warhol, Andy 9
'Water and Life Coordinator' 234
Water Coordinator 234–5
water war 233–5
Weber, Max 2
Weiviorka, Michel 134n32
Westerners 189
Westmoreland, William 133n17
White, Harold 47, 49
Wolf, Antonio Navarro 126
Wolf, Eric 7, 74n38

Yandarbiyev, Zelimkhan 208
Ye Jiangying 10
Yeltsin administration 205
Yon Sosa: Trotskyite MR-13 movement 63
Yusef (Chechen Foreign Minister) 206

Zailanabidov, Suleiman 214
Zawahiri, Ayman al 208
Zona de Despeje see demilitarized zone